BECOMING A MIDDLE LEVEL TEACHER:

Student-Focused Teaching of Early Adolescents

Cathy Vatterott

University of Missouri-St. Louis

Boston   Burr Ridge, IL   Dubuque, IA   Madison, WI   New York   San Francisco   St. Louis
Bangkok   Bogotá   Caracas   Kuala Lumpur   Lisbon   London   Madrid   Mexico City
Milan   Montreal   New Delhi   Santiago   Seoul   Singapore   Sydney   Taipei   Toronto

The McGraw·Hill Companies

Mc Graw Hill **Higher Education**

Published by McGraw-Hill, an imprint of The McGraw-Hill Companies, Inc., 1221 Avenue of the Americas, New York, NY 10020. Copyright © 2007. All rights reserved. No part of this publication may be reproduced or distributed in any form or by any means, or stored in a database or retrieval system, without the prior written consent of The McGraw-Hill Companies, Inc., including, but not limited to, in any network or other electronic storage or transmission, or broadcast for distance learning.

This book is printed on acid-free paper.

1 2 3 4 5 6 7 8 9 0 DOC/DOC 0 9 8 7 6

ISBN-13:   978-0-07-236172-8
ISBN-10:   0-07-236172-7

Editor in Chief: *Emily Barrosse*
Publisher: *Beth Mejia*
Sponsoring Editor: *Allison McNamara*
Marketing Manager: *Sarah Martin*
Editorial Coordinator: *Emily Pecora*
Production Editor: *Chanda Feldman*
Design Manager: *Violeta Diaz*
Photo Research Coordinator: *Natalia Peschiera*
Photo Researcher: *PoYee Oster*
Production Supervisor: *Rich DeVitto*
Composition: *10/12 Times by ElectraGraphics*
Printing: *45# New Era Matte, R.R. Donnelley & Sons*

Cover: © Creatas/PunchStock

Credits: The credits section for this book begins on page 418 and is considered an extension of the copyright page.

Library of Congress Cataloging-in-Publication Data

Vatterott, Cathy.
    Becoming a middle level teacher / Cathy Vatterott,--1st ed.
        p. cm.
    Includes bibliographical references and index.
    ISBN: 978-0-07-236172-8 (alk. paper)
    1. Education—United States. I. Title.
B235.G88B76 2007
110—dc21   2006063317

The Internet addresses listed in the text were accurate at the time of publication. The inclusion of a Web site does not indicate an endorsement by the authors or McGraw-Hill, and McGraw-Hill does not guarantee the accuracy of the information presented at these sites.

www.mhhe.com

PREFACE

Early adolescents are a remarkable group, fascinating in their complexity. At their best, they are full of promise, idealism, energy, joy, passion, and compassion. At their worst, they may be plagued by self-doubt, anxiety, insecurity, restlessness, social ineptitude, and confusion. They are poised at a critical crossroad in their lives, eager to make decisions and to realize their dreams, yet unsure of how to do so.

As students, early adolescents are developmentally ready to be given more responsibility and control over their own learning. Sadly, they are not often granted that opportunity. Traditional teacher focused methods of organizing instruction, delivering curriculum, and assessing learning limit access to learning for some students and may in fact interfere with their academic success. Traditional methods can be oppressive to early adolescents, stifling the natural curiosity and desire for knowledge that thrives in them. That natural curiosity and drive to make sense of the world is the teacher's greatest resource in engaging learners, and can be productively channeled into meaningful learning through student focused instruction.

Teaching style at the middle level profoundly affects student performance. Some teachers struggle to motivate early adolescents with traditional teacher focused methods, while other teachers ignite students' enthusiasm with student focused methods. Some teachers struggle to control middle school students with traditional discipline, while other teachers invest time in personal relationships that render traditional discipline measures almost unnecessary. Consistently, the same student exhibits two different types of behavior—unmotivated and obstinate with some teachers, enthusiastic and compliant with others.

Becoming a Middle Level Teacher outlines an approach to student focused instruction that can provide greater academic success for the maximum number of students and at the same time assist early adolescents in navigating the difficult transition of puberty. The goals for this book are to:

- Provide the reader with an accurate picture of the early adolescent learner
- Convince the reader that student focused instruction is the most effective method of teaching early adolescents
- Illustrate to the reader that it is possible to teach in a student focused manner without sacrificing rigor or content learning
- Persuade the reader that student focused instruction is a pleasurable and rewarding way to teach and learn

Themes

Throughout the book, you will notice four recurring themes:

A critical link exists between developmental needs and learning. For early adolescents, the developmental needs associated with puberty are the driving forces behind the design of learning activities.

Relationships are key to motivation, which is key to learning. The teacher-student relationship, relationships between students, and the personal relationship of the student with the content, are the milieu within which all meaningful learning occurs.

Middle school students are entitled to be involved in decisions that affect their learning. Middle school students should be full participants in the learning process, having input about the design of learning activities, choices of activities and rubrics used for evaluation.

Implementing student focused instruction is both challenging and rewarding for teachers. Student focused instruction represents a fundamental shift in teacher time and energy from traditional teaching. It requires teachers to invest time in the planning design of activities and rubrics, freeing them to monitor students during activity-based learning.

Organization of the book

The book is divided into two parts–*Part I: The School and the Learner* and *Part II: The Strategies.*

Part I: The School and the Learner covers the foundations of the middle school learner. The history of the middle school, adolescent development; the physical, social, and emotional needs of middle school students; and goals of a student focused curriculum at the middle level are covered in depth.

Part II: The Strategies provides the tools one needs to develop teaching skills and to become an effective middle school teacher. It examines the curriculum, demonstrates the steps in long range curriculum planning, provides examples of specific teaching strategies and, ultimately, encourages the reader to reflect on the role of his/her own beliefs and attitudes in successful student focused teaching. Several features will assist the reader in understanding the concepts in this book:

Reflective questions allow the reader opportunities to reflect on information or to personalize concepts.

Application activities at the end of the chapters prompt the reader to process, analyze, or apply concepts through specific tasks.

Classroom activities (in Part II)—actual learning activities created by actual teachers—serve as concrete examples of learning tasks. When available, examples of student work are also shown.

Teacher voices, from personal conversations with the teachers features in this book, present concepts in plain language. In my interviews, teachers said many things I wished to say, but that seemed so much more authentic coming from them. I wanted you to hear them speak from their hearts as they did to me. As much as the teachers and my editor would allow, the teacher's words are as they spoke them in our conversations in their classrooms.

Student voice, from personal interviews with the students of the teachers featured in the book, provide another point of view. The student voices have been left in tact, with fractured grammar, run-on sentences, and slang. I thought it was important to hear from them too. After all, the book is for them.

The teachers featured in this book

Over the years, my experiences as a middle school principal, my conversations with my own early adolescent son, and my continued contact with middle level schools, served to validate the importance of student focused instruction in engaging early adolescents. I knew that many middle school teachers were teaching in the student focused way that I believed was best. It was not hard to find them. I began by going to several middle schools I knew by reputation to be excellent schools. Principals referred me to a few teachers in each building that they identified as *student focused*. They gave me many more names than I could use. I chose 20 teachers to visit and interview, and used their student activities to illustrate my ideas. Those teachers are:

Tony Ambrose	Parkway Central Middle School
Greg Bergner	Parkway Central Middle School
Kathy Bhat	North Kirkwood Middle School
Kerry Brown	Pattonville Heights Middle School
Debbie Bruce	Parkway Central Middle School
Shannon Burger	Parkway Central Middle School
Mike Burgio	Pattonville Heights Middle School
Mike Hirsch	Wentzville Middle School
Josette Hochman	Parkway Central Middle School
Mike Holdinghaus	North Kirkwood Middle School
Jason Holmes	Parkway Central Middle School
Pat Johnson	Pattonville Heights Middle School
Ed Kastner	Wydown Middle School
Janet Peabody	North Kirkwood Middle School
Gloria Sadler	Wydown Middle School
Nicole Schoenwiess	LeMasters Elementary School
Diane Schumacher	Parkway Central Middle School
Jan Von Harz	Pattonville Heights Middle School
Stephanie Walton	Pattonville Heights Middle School

One school, Pattonville Heights Middle School, is particularly close to my heart—I served as an assistant principal there in the late 1980's and learned much from the experience. I visit "The Heights" often and have fond memories of my time there. Another school, Parkway Central Middle School, has served as a PDS for my university for years and has been a wonderful laboratory for me and my preservice students.

Acknowledgments

This book would not have been possible without the talent and creativity of the 20 middle school teachers whose activities and voices are featured here. Their insights were invaluable in refining and clarifying my original ideas. They taught me how student focused instruction works in real classrooms on a day-to-day basis. The classroom activities they so unselfishly shared provided tangible illustrations of student focused instruction. They are responsible for bringing the theory to life.

During the time I spent with the teachers, usually during their planning time, they were never too busy to talk to a student or a colleague. I was most impressed by how respectful they were of their students' intelligence, integrity, and natural desire to learn. I cannot say enough about these exceptional teachers. I remain in awe of what they do every day—their energy, their caring, and their commitment. I hope their examples and their words inspire you the reader, entice you to create student focused learning activities, and empower you to empower students.

THE SCHOOL AND THE LEARNER

Middle school students are a unique breed with unique needs. In Part One of this book you will learn about the basics of middle school education. You will learn what distinguishes a middle school from a junior high school, and why middle schools hold great potential for meeting the needs of early adolescents. You will learn that early adolescents' needs form the foundation for middle school philosophy, which is the rationale for the organizational structures unique to middle schools. You will connect middle school philosophy with the positive beliefs that support a unique type of learning—student focused instruction.

In this section, you will also learn about the developmental characteristics of early adolescents—the physical, intellectual, emotional, and social characteristics that evolve as a result of the changes of puberty. I hope you will come to appreciate the implications those characteristics have for middle school instruction. You will explore the diversity of today's early adolescents and learn that they are diverse not only in their stage of puberty but in their ethnicity, social class, and learning needs. And finally, you will examine how teachers prioritize relationships to create a positive classroom climate that sets the stage for and supports effective learning.

The knowledge you gain in Part One of this book will form the foundation for Part Two. In Part Two you will learn to develop appropriate curriculum, to implement both student-focused and teacher-focused instructional strategies, and to assess early adolescents' learning.

CHAPTER 1

UNDERSTANDING THE NEED FOR STUDENT-FOCUSED INSTRUCTION

❯ INTRODUCTION

Today's early adolescents are exposed to more negative influences, are offered more choices, have more freedom with less supervision, and are making more decisions that will affect the rest of their lives than any similar group before them. Schools and teachers have never played a more pivotal role in the life of early adolescents than they do today. The teacher's influence over students has never been stronger and the stakes have never been higher (Johnston, 1999).

Middle school teachers today face many challenges. They need specific knowledge, skills, and attitudes that will enable them to work effectively with early adolescents. Successful middle school teachers strive to reach five goals:

- To understand and accept the behavior of early adolescents as normal
- To respect early adolescents as adults, but to remember that they are still children
- To engage and challenge early adolescents' curious minds
- To teach early adolescents to be tolerant and accepting of differences
- To prepare early adolescents to be productive adults

Early adolescents are a unique breed. In transition from childhood to adulthood, they are experiencing many physical and emotional changes and seeing the world in new ways. The key to reaching and teaching them is to empower them with the tools to control their own learning through student-focused instructional methods (Vatterott, 1999). The goal of this book is to show the reader how to teach early adolescents most effectively, in a manner that will not only promote academic success but will also support their emotional and social development. **The purposes of this chapter are to help you**

- understand the relationship between middle school practices and the needs of early adolescents.
- become familiar with middle school philosophy.
- become aware of the beliefs that underlie student-focused instruction.
- understand the concepts of *power over* and *power with* and their role in classroom dynamics.
- understand the necessity of student empowerment for maximizing student success.
- appreciate the value of student-focused instruction in promoting student success at the middle level.
- analyze the relationship of school practices to student success and failure.

Essential Questions

After reading and completing the activities in this chapter, you should be able to answer the following questions:

1. How do middle school practices help meet the specialized needs of early adolescents?
2. What beliefs about learners are the basis for the middle school philosophy?
3. What beliefs about learners are the basis for the philosophy of student-focused instruction?
4. How do the attitudes of teachers about power in the classroom affect their ability to implement student-focused instruction?
5. How do school practices such as ability grouping influence student success and failure at the middle level?
6. What are the fundamental differences between student-focused instruction and teacher-focused instruction?

✦ THE MIDDLE SCHOOL LEARNER

Who is the middle school learner? Middle school learners are best described as children in transition—from childhood to adulthood, from dependent to independent, who are struggling to understand their changing bodies and minds, their personal relationships and the world around them. The changes of puberty are without a doubt their preoccupation—they are faced with startling and rapid physical changes, developing sexuality, unpredictable emotions, and the formidable task of shaping their new adult identity. Intellectually they are honing their abilities to think and reason abstractly, but they may not be able to apply those skills consistently and in all areas of their lives (George & Alexander, 2003; McDaniel, Necochea, Rios, Stowell, & Keitzer, 2001).

The diversity of middle school learners is incredible. The pace and timing of the changes of puberty vary greatly among individuals (Manning, 1993). No group of school-age children is more diverse physically, emotionally, socially, and intellectually than middle school learners. In addition, these students are increasingly diverse in their socioeconomic status, ethnic and religious backgrounds, language, family structure, and family values (Brown, 2002; Kellough & Kellough, 1999; Landson-Billings, 2001). (The changes and diversity of puberty will be discussed in Chapters 2 and 3.)

As a result of the changes of puberty, middle school learners have a great many needs. They have physical needs for activity, rest, and proper nutrition; emotional and social needs for affirmation and acceptance; and intellectual needs for competence and challenge (Manning, 1993; Manning & Bucher, 2001). This combination of physical, intellectual, social, and emotional needs is the basis for determining appropriate middle school practices (George & Alexander, 2003; Lounsbury & Vars, 2003). Dorman (1984) summarized the needs of early adolescents through seven broad needs shown in Figure 1.1.

Middle Schools and Junior High Schools

In the early 1900s educators began to recognize and accept the unique needs of early adolescents. The first effort to meet those unique needs was the creation of junior high schools (Beane, 2001; Lounsbury & Vars, 2003; Van Til, Vars, & Lounsbury, 1967). Although junior high schools were originally designed to provide a transition for early adolescents, organizationally and philosophically they more often resembled the content-centered high school than the child-centered elementary school (Lounsbury & Vars, 2003). In the 1960s, middle schools emerged as the second effort to meet early adolescent needs, with different organizational structures from

FIGURE 1.1

Seven Needs of Young Adolescents.

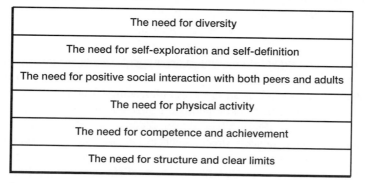

| The need for diversity |
| The need for self-exploration and self-definition |
| The need for positive social interaction with both peers and adults |
| The need for physical activity |
| The need for competence and achievement |
| The need for structure and clear limits |

Source: Dorman, 1984; NMSA, 2001C.

THE FAR SIDE® BY GARY LARSON

**Although it lasted only 2 million years, the
Awkward Age was considered a hazardous
time for most species.**

those of the junior high school and a more child-centered philosophy (Anfara &
Waks, 2002; Eichhorn, 1966; Pate & Muth, 2003).

The organizational differences between the junior high school and middle
school are shown in Table 1.1. A typical junior high school includes grades 7 and 8
or 7, 8, and 9 and is organized by subject departments (math, science, etc.). Students
attend six to eight different classes of equal length and take a limited number of
nonacademic classes (such as art or music) for a semester or year. A typical middle
school includes grades 6, 7, and 8 and is organized around interdisciplinary teams
(Kellough & Kellough, 1999). A typical team is comprised of one teacher from each
of the core academic subjects (math, science, language arts, and social studies).
These teachers share a team of around 100 to 150 students in the same grade. The
students spend much of their day with their team of teachers and the 100 to 150 students on their team. Their schedule may be blocked so that they spend large blocks

of time in their team as opposed to changing classes every hour. Nonacademic classes may be scheduled quarterly to allow shorter exposures to more subjects (George & Alexander, 2003). (Teaming and organizational structures will be explained in greater detail in Chapter 5.)

TABLE 1.1	
Comparison of Traditional Junior High School and Typical Middle School	
Traditional Junior High School	**Typical Middle School**
Grades 7 and 8 or 7, 8, and 9	Grades 6, 7, and 8
Teachers work in subject departments	Teachers work in interdisciplinary teams
Students change teachers and rooms every hour	Students are assigned to teams and spend most of the day with a small team of teachers
Students choose a few elective courses (art, family and consumer science) and take those courses for a semester each	Students take all electives for 6 to 10 weeks each (sometimes called an exploratory wheel)
School counselors are available for advising on an as needed basis	Advisory program—Scheduled nonacademic time with teacher for academic and behavioral monitoring

Today, few middle schools and junior high schools look like the traditional junior high school or the true middle school described above. Many middle level schools are hybrids; that is, they have some characteristics of both types of programs (Anfara & Stacki, 2002). Individual schools often implement middle school programs gradually, depending on budget, space limitations, staff commitment, and community involvement (Dickinson, 2001). Unfortunately, some junior high schools have simply changed the name to middle school, added the sixth grade, and continued to operate as a traditional junior high school (Anfara & Stacki, 2002; McEwin, Dickinson, & Jenkins, 2003). On the other hand, some junior high schools have completely revamped their programs to reflect middle school practices, even though they do not include the sixth grade. These junior high schools are actually more progressive than the 6–7–8 middle schools organized and managed like traditional junior high schools. The name of the school may or may not align with the list of typical organizational practices.

Turning Points

By the early 1990s the number of middle schools in this country outnumbered junior high schools (Miles & Valentine, 2001). Today, middle schools outnumber junior high schools about three to one because middle school programs, such as teaming, exploratory courses, and advisement, do a better job of meeting the special needs of children going through puberty. In 1989, an important study entitled *Turning Points* (Jackson & Davis, 2000) reinforced that idea. The study concluded that young adolescents were at a critical stage of their development and that school practices were often mismatched with their developmental needs. The study made the following recommendations:

- Create small communities for learning.
- Teach a core curriculum of common knowledge.
- Ensure success for all students.
- Empower teachers and administrators.
- Staff schools with experts in teaching young adolescents.
- Improve academic performance through fostering better health and fitness.
- Re-engage families in the education of young adolescents.
- Connect schools with communities. (Carnegie Council on Adolescent Development, 1989, 1996)

The specific recommendations of *Turning Points* validated years of work by middle level educators as well as the philosophy and organizational structures of the middle school. It brought national attention to the needs of middle school students and accelerated the pace of change in junior high schools and middle schools around the country (Lounsbury & Vars, 2003). *Turning Points* became an important resource for educators and was often presented to school boards as a rationale for change at the middle school level.

In the early 1990s, an important research study concluded that when the *Turning Points* recommendations were implemented "comprehensively and with fidelity" in middle level schools, students showed significant increases in reading and math achievement compared to students in schools with no implementation (Anfara & Lipka, 2003; Felner, Kasak, Mulhall, & Flowers, 1997). This study further validated the efforts of middle schools to provide the best education for early adolescents. The National Middle School Association (NMSA, 2003a) later published additional research supporting middle schools.

Middle School Philosophy

Whether a school is organized as a middle school or a junior high school, what is most important is that the philosophy of the school reflect a concern for the needs of early adolescents (Williamson & Johnston, 1999). The predominant philosophy of middle school has been well articulated in publications by the National Middle School Association, the only educational organization dedicated specifically to the improvement of education for early adolescents. It has articulated the predominant philosophy of the middle school well. NMSA advocates middle level schools that are developmentally responsive to the needs of early adolescents and characterized by the following:

- Educators committed to young adolescents
- A shared vision
- High expectations for all
- An adult advocate for every student
- Family and community partnership
- A positive climate
- Curriculum that is challenging, integrative, and exploratory
- Varied teaching and learning approaches
- Assessment and evaluation that promote learning
- Flexible organizational structures
- Programs and policies that foster health, wellness, and safety
- Comprehensive guidance and support services (Erb, 2001; NMSA, 2001b, 2003a, 2003b)

Middle school philosophy can best be summarized as a series of beliefs about the most appropriate practices for early adolescents (see Figure 1.2):

- The middle school should be *child-centered* and *needs-based*. The physical, intellectual, emotional, and social needs of early adolescents should drive the decisions we make about students. (Arnold, 1993; Patterson, 2003)
- The goal of the middle school is to promote *academic success* for all students, to master learning skills, remediate deficiencies that may impede future academic success and develop positive attitudes about learning. (George, 2002)
- Instructional *strategies should be adapted* to fit the needs of middle schools students, both as a group and individually. (ASCD, 1975; NMSA, 2003a; 2003b; Tomlinson, 2003)
- Teachers should have respect and empathy for the experience of puberty.
- Middle school students should be treated with the same *respect and empathy* with which we would treat adults. (Erb, 2001; Manning, 2000)

Middle School Philosophy.

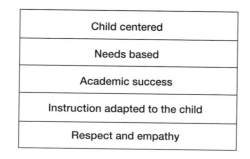

| Child centered |
| Needs based |
| Academic success |
| Instruction adapted to the child |
| Respect and empathy |

Relationship between Early Adolescent Needs and Middle School Practices.

Developmental Needs of Early Adolescents		Middle School Practices
Physical Needs		Organization
Emotional Needs	combined needs	Curriculum
Social Needs	serve as the ——→ rationale for	Teaching Strategies
Intellectual Needs		Support Services

Developmentally responsive middle schools make the needs of early adolescents a priority (ASCD, 1927; NAASP, 1985; NMSA, 2001b). Those needs drive the philosophy, which drives school practices, and provide the rationale for middle school structures and programs (NMSA, 2003b; Smith, 2002) (see Figure 1.3).

Although it is possible for a traditional junior high school to be needs based, the structures and programs of the middle school make it easier to meet the needs of early adolescents (Lucas & Valentine, 2001; McEwin et al., 2003; Pitton, 2001). An effective middle school eases the burden of the transition from the nurturing self-contained classroom of elementary school to the independent, impersonal world of many high schools. More specifically, the physical, intellectual, emotional, and social needs of developing early adolescents drive the following adaptations at the middle level:

- *Organizational adaptations* such as interdisciplinary teaming, flexible block scheduling, skills grouping, and remedial programs (Dickinson, 2001; NMSA, 2003a; 2003b; Patterson, 2003; Wunderlich, Robertson, & Valentine, 2002)
- *Curricular adaptations* such as integrated units, exploratory curriculum, and wellness curriculum (Beane, 1997; Caskey, 2002; Lounsbury & Vars, 1978; O'Steen, Cuper, Spires, Beal, & Pope, 2002; Waks, 2002)
- *Teaching strategies* such as student-focused instruction, cooperative learning, and interdisciplinary units (Flowers, Mertens, & Mulhall, 2003; NMSA 2003a, 2003b)
- *Support services* such as advisor/advisee programs, guidance services, and community outreach (Allen, Splittgerber, & Manning, 1993; ASCD, 1975; NMSA, 2003a; 2003b; Smith 2002)

Although the adaptations of the middle school are designed to serve the needs of the early adolescent, they do not guarantee academic success for all students (Anfara & Lipka, 2003; Smith, 2002). A more specific philosophy and set of practices is necessary to reach that goal. Positive beliefs about learners and a willingness to empower students form the foundation for the more specific student-focused philosophy and practices discussed in this book.

→ THE PHILOSOPHY OF STUDENT-FOCUSED INSTRUCTION

Student-focused instruction is activity-based instruction that is adapted to students' specific learning needs and that empowers students to make decisions about their learning. Student-focused instruction is an excellent model for implementing middle school philosophy because it is inherently child centered and needs based (Vatterott, 1999). At the core of the philosophy of student-focused instruction are two sets of beliefs—beliefs about learners and beliefs about power. These are consistent with the beliefs of middle school philosophy (*shown in parentheses below*) (Vatterott, 1999).

Beliefs about Learners

Beliefs about learners reflect a confidence in the desire and ability of children to learn.

1. The ability to learn is more influenced by personal factors than by innate ability. School climate, interpersonal relationships, social and emotional needs, internal and external messages that students receive affect learning much more profoundly than innate ability (NMSA, 2001c; Stevenson, 2002) *(needs based, child centered)*.
2. Children are inherently good, industrious, curious, and eager to learn. Teacher optimism breeds success (George, Stevenson, Thomason, & Beane, 1992) *(child centered, respect and empathy)*.
3. Learning is a naturally pleasant and intrinsically rewarding activity. It can, however, be made distasteful by boring methods, lack of relevance, punitive grading systems, and lack of student input (Kohn, 1993) *(adapting instruction)*.
4. Students learn by constructing meaning and through active experience (Cawelti, 2003) *(child centered)*.
5. All students can be successful learners but may require different paces or different paths (NMSA, 2001c; Slavin, 1997) *(academic success, adapting instruction)*.
6. All progress in learning is valuable and motivating. Lack of progress is demotivating (Vatterott, 1999) *(academic success)*.
7. Student input is valuable and has worth. Students are entitled to be in control of their learning, yet still need the guidance of adults (Alexander, 1995) *(respect and empathy)*.
8. Students need and desire power over their own learning and are motivated by the prospect of choice and the opportunity for personal expression (Powell, 2001) *(needs based, child centered)*.
9. The unique nature of the individual is valuable. Students' *personal signatures* bring rich and wonderful diversity to classrooms (Brown, 2002) *(respect and empathy)*.

10. The acting out of these beliefs by teachers and principals will improve learning and provide more success for more students than the traditional system (Vatterott, 1999) *(academic success)*.

╭ REFLECTIVE QUESTION

R eview the beliefs above. Which do you agree with? Which do you disagree with? Which beliefs are you unsure about?

Beliefs about Power

The mismatch between early adolescent needs and traditional power structures can interfere with learning. Traditional approaches that do not allow students control over their learning are deficient in meeting early adolescent needs (NMSA, 2001c). As a child-centered, needs-based philosophy, student-focused instruction requires a nontraditional view of power (Vatterott, 1999).

Student-focused beliefs about power reflect an acceptance of early adolescents' need for power and a trust in their ability to use power responsibly (Alexander, 1995). As with student-focused beliefs about learners, these beliefs about power are

Students should be empowered to make decisions about their learning and their school.

also consistent with the beliefs of middle school philosophy (Vatterott, 1999) *(shown in parentheses below)*.

1. Students are entitled to the power to make decisions about their learning (Alexander, 1995; Lounsbury & Vars, 2003) *(child centered, respect and empathy)*.
2. Power is a strong developmental need of early adolescents (Powell, 2001) *(child centered, needs based)*.
3. Students can be trusted with decision-making powers (Alexander, 1995; DeVries & Zan, 2003) *(respect and empathy)*.
4. Student empowerment is necessary to fully engage early adolescent learners (Lounsbury & Vars, 2003; Powell, 2001) *(academic success, adapting instruction)*.

These beliefs mirror the changing power relationships among other groups. The evolution of democracy, in this country and around the world, has profoundly affected traditional power relationships. Many previously disempowered groups have gained power. In the United States, children, once viewed as powerless, are gaining legal rights and protections once reserved only for adults. Reflecting the society at large, schools have reformed their own antiquated power structures with building-based management and shared decision making. Teachers, administrators, and parents are working together in a collaborative fashion to improve schools (Vatterott, 1999).

> Gone are the vestiges of "Scientific Management" popularized early in this century by Frederick Winslow Taylor, whose watchwords were compliance, control, and command. The foundations for this system were fear, intimidation, and an adversarial approach to problem solving. Today it is in our best interest to encourage everyone's potential by dedicating ourselves to the continual improvement of our own abilities and those of the people with whom we work and live. (Bonstingl, 1992, p. 6)

Even in progressive middle schools, students are routinely excluded from participating in decisions or solving school problems that affect them. Skeptics would say that middle school students cannot be trusted to make decisions about their learning and are not mature enough or knowledgeable enough to be involved in decisions about school programs. As children gain more rights in the society at large, it seems logical they should also gain power in school (Vatterott, 1999). "In a democratic school it is true that all of those directly involved in the school, including young people, have the right to participate in the process of decision making" (Apple & Beane, 1995, p. 9). Middle level students, at a social and moral crossroad, are uniquely poised to benefit from empowerment (Arnold, 1993; Vatterott, 1999).

The difficulty in any discussion about student empowerment today lies in the discrepancy between empowerment as commonly conceived in educational circles and the broader concept of power in our culture (Vatterott, 1999). Kreisberg (1992) defined **empowerment** as "a process through which people and/or communities increase their control or mastery of their own lives and the decisions that affect their lives" (p. 19). This definition reflects the commonly held view of teacher empowerment (Barth, 1990). **Student empowerment** could be defined similarly as a process by which students increase their control or mastery of their own learning and decisions that affect their classroom and school (Vatterott, 1999). This concept of empowerment appears inconsistent with how most people view power:

> Predominant theories of power define power in terms of the ability to control others, to impose one's will on others. Power is viewed in terms of relationships of domination. This is the conception of power as *power over*. (Kreisberg, 1992, p. 21)

In autocratic cultures, power has traditionally been thought of simplistically as *power over*. In this context, power exists in a limited quantity and people are either powerful or powerless. It is suggested that a *balance of power* exists, as on two sides of a scale, implying that as one person or group gains power another loses it (Kreisberg, 1992; Vatterott, 1999). Conceptualized in this fashion, power relinquished is power lost, advantage lost. Any form of student empowerment would automatically result in teacher disempowerment. "Empowerment is a theory in search of a compatible conception of power" (Kreisberg, 1992, p. 22). Kreisberg suggests that the evolution of democracy in governments and social structures has created the need for a new concept of power:

> The definition of power as domination and control is limited; it is incomplete. There is another dimension, or form, or experience of power that is distinctly different from pervasive conceptions. The ignored dimension is characterized by collaboration, sharing, and mutuality. We can call this alternative concept *power with* to distinguish it from *power over*. (1992, p. 61)

Many schools today reflect a view of power as *power with*. For instance, if teachers and administrators work together to jointly make decisions about curriculum, administrators are not exercising power over the teachers (in that decision) but are sharing *power with* them (Vatterott, 1999). Current strategies of quality circles and total quality management have employed the *power with* concept in the business world with positive results of increased productivity and improved morale. The empowerment of teachers has shown similar advantages (Barth, 1990). Just as teacher empowerment can lead to improved motivation and productivity, student empowerment in middle level schools can produce equally valuable results (Alexander, 1995; Lounsbury & Vars, 2003; Vatterott, 1999). Student empowerment is an essential component of student-focused instruction.

REFLECTIVE QUESTION

What do you remember about the power relationships between teachers and students when you were in middle school?

Promoting Academic Success:
Have Schools Institutionalized Failure?

The goal of student-focused instruction is to empower all students to be academically successful. Traditional practices have empowered some students and guaranteed failure for others (Vatterott, 1999). To understand why student-focused instruction is preferable, it may be helpful to revisit some traditional practices.

An elite group of middle level students is already empowered in our present *star system* (Van Hoose, Strahan, & L'Esperance, 2001). Armed academically with literate parents, safe and comfortable homes, and few if any learning problems, these are students who have developed the skills and attitudes that enable them to be successful in school. With those skills and attitudes they have amassed a history of school success and learning related self-esteem.

On the other hand, unsuccessful students in the middle school are at the bottom of the power hierarchy. They are disempowered and somehow not part of the group. Politically speaking, they are oppressed. Faced with these conditions as well as a lack of control over the myriad changes of puberty, many of them react with apathy, withdrawal, hostility, or rebellion and earn the label of at-risk students (Vatterott, 1999).

Brain-based research has shown us that attitude is critical in the motivation to learn. Emotion drives attention, which drives learning and memory (Sylwester, 1995), and the perception of emotional threat causes learners to "downshift" and withdraw from the learning experience (Pitton, 2001; Pool, 1997). A major factor contributing to a lack of motivation in students at risk is the disempowering nature of the school experience itself:

> Ability groups, grade retention . . . working alone, denial of strengths and focus on weaknesses, learning that is information-rich and experience-poor, and an irrelevant curriculum that students must endure and frequently ignore. All of this suggests to me that we educators are a major part of the problem rather than merely the helpless victims of cultural circumstances. (Barth, 1990, p. 126)

The traditional system is disempowering first because there is a clear expectation that a certain number of students will fail (Levine, 2003). Assured that some will fail, schools establish programs of detention, in-school suspension, retention, and special programs that reinforce students as failures and further disenfranchise them from the system (Raebeck, 1992). Reinforcing the belief that some students cannot learn, such practices perpetuate *a system that not only allows but also actually expects failure.* Learner self-esteem and a sense of belonging influence motivation far more than was ever believed in the past. If educators are to reduce the amount of student failure, they must be prepared to investigate how the system itself contributes to the problem (Patterson, 2003; Vatterott, 1999). Practices that cause students who are poor, minority, learning disabled, or language impaired to be unsuccessful should be examined closely. Before the goal of academic success for all can be realized, many well-established practices must be examined and systemic obstacles must be dealt with (see Figure 1.4).

F I G U R E   1 . 4

Traditional Practices That Institutionalize Failure.

Sorting and ranking of learners
Ability grouping
Retention
One-shot learning and grading
The star system and at-risk practices
Punitive discipline
Pull-outs/traditional special education

Sorting and Ranking Learners

The most formidable obstacle to student success is the pervasive practice of sorting and ranking learners (Canady & Hotchkiss, 1989). In far too many schools, the bell-shaped curve is the icon that dictates programs and labels the teacher or the curriculum "too easy" when enough students do not fail.

> The bell-shaped curve, still considered the ideal outcome of aggregate assessment in many schools, is ultimately destructive of learning environments and the spirit of mutual improvement. The bell curve (and some other grading systems) has the effect, perhaps unintended, of setting up unnecessary and counterproductive scarcities of student success in competitive, win-lose environments. (Bonstingl, 1992, p. 7)

The practice of sorting and ranking students is embedded in the traditional system. In the sorting and ranking system, when failure does occur, it is seen as the fault of the student and the blame is placed squarely there (Atkins & Ellsesser, 2003). There is something wrong with the students; they need to be fixed (Glasser, 1969). Special programs are created for at-risk students to separate them from successful students. The most common of these programs is **ability grouping**, the practice of grouping students into high, average, and low ability tracks for academic benefit. Ability grouping is used as remedy under the misguided perception that it will benefit students (Vatterott, 1999).

Recent research indicates that the impact of ability grouping on student success is largely negative (George, 1993; George & Alexander, 2003; Oakes, 1985, 1998; Slavin, 1990). This is possible, not because ability grouping *couldn't* work but because *teacher expectations adversely impact students' beliefs about themselves as learners,* which impacts the brain's ability and motivation to learn (Atkins & Ellsesser, 2003). The threat of not being successful in learning shuts down the ability of the brain to learn (Jensen, 1998).

> It doesn't take long for children to find out where they fit in the five pigeonholes of the bell curve, and the student's narrow academic self-image becomes, all

too often, intertwined in self-fulfilling prophecies played out throughout life. (Bonstingl, 1992, p. 7)

The cumulative impact of years of ability grouping on measures of student intelligence appears to be significant (for a good synthesis of research, see George & Alexander, 2003; *Educational Leadership*, October 1992; and *Curriculum Update*, June 1993).

Ability grouping for middle level students is especially damaging as students form identities in relation to peers and adults:

> Cut off from alternative routes to competence and self-esteem and preoccupied with developing an acceptable identity, middle grades students who must repeat a grade or who are tracked into lower ability groups learn to define themselves as losers. (Wheelock & Dorman, 1988, p. 30)

Failure orientation in these students is often exacerbated by traditional practices once believed to help failing students (Vatterott, 1999). Granted, at the extremes of the bell-shaped curve lie a small number of students with exceptional needs. For the severely handicapped and the truly gifted, some separation may be necessary to optimize their success. But research on learning styles and preferences has shown that many students who don't learn the same way or at the same pace as others aren't necessarily handicapped (Oakes, 1985; Slavin, 1997). Ability grouping is inconsistent with student-focused instruction because it handicaps learners by labeling them failures. (Grouping alternatives will be discussed in Chapter 5.)

REFLECTIVE QUESTION

Do you remember being ability grouped in school? What effect did it have on your attitudes about school?

The problems of sorting and ranking are not limited to ability grouping. They occur in grading as well. Practices such as **one-shot grading** (allowing only one try/one test for a task) and penalties for nonacademic factors (such as neatness or lateness) tend to sort learners into winners and losers (Vatterott, 1999). When the bell-shaped curve is applied to grading, students are forced to compete for a limited number of good grades. Competitive grading interferes with performance as well as personal relationships and a sense of community (Kohn, 1993). Assessment, which sorts and ranks learners with grades, quickly causes students to self-group into the "good students" and the "bad students." One-shot grading is not student focused because it limits academic success for students (Canady & Hotchkiss, 1989; Guskey, 2003).

Grades and tracks not only label and separate students, but they also deny some students membership in the pro-school group. When students are unsuccessful academically, they feel disconnected and drop out, either physically or symbolically by creating their own antischool groups (Cusick, 1989). They find other ways to meet their needs for acceptance and membership, sometimes in dangerous or antisocial ways (Glasser, 1992). Only through academic success do students gain true acceptance and membership in the pro-school group. Unwittingly, many traditional practices in the classroom and the school at large inhibit success because they impede membership or send the wrong messages to specific groups of students (Glasser, 1992). Any practice that ranks or labels students has the potential to create members and nonmembers of the community (Kohn, 1996). A number of school practices, discussed below, discourage membership for some students.

The "Star System"

Ability grouping and one-shot grading both perpetuate a "star system" (Van Hoose, Strahan, & L'Esperance, 2001). Ability grouping creates stars from the high track group who get labeled as the smart ones and often make the honor roll, further advertising their star status. One-shot grading punishes many students who, given more time or additional feedback, could improve their performance and grades (Guskey, 2003). Honor rolls give star status to students with the highest grades. This star status is further exacerbated by communities who reward honor roll students with discounts, free baseball tickets, and those ubiquitous bumper stickers: "My son's an honor roll student at XYZ Middle School." Star systems are not student focused because they define success too narrowly (Van Hoose et al., 2001; Vatterott, 1999).

Any program in which only a small number of students are chosen to get star billing can discourage membership. Competitive sports teams where only the best athletes can play or competitive tryouts for cheerleading squad send a message to students that they are not part of that group (Van Hoose et al., 2001).

Punitive Discipline

Discipline that causes something unpleasant to happen to a student or that seeks to embarrass or humiliate students in front of their peers is counterproductive to membership (Glasser, 1992). Punishment spoils the rapport between teacher and student, provokes resistance and resentment that may be taken out on peers, and has a negative impact on learning (Kohn, 1993). It often causes a desire for revenge on the group and distances the offender from other students (DeVries & Zan, 2003). Discipline that consistently removes students from the classroom or the school (such as in-school suspension) further alienates students from the group and gives them less opportunities to bond with the group (Vatterott, 1999). Punitive discipline is not student focused because it does not treat students with respect and empathy and does not empower students to improve (Kohn, 1996). (Alternatives to punitive discipline will be discussed in Chapter 4.)

Pull-out Programs

Pull-out programs for special education that consistently remove students from the learning community cause students to feel less like they are members of that community (Patterson, 2003). Such programs often give students a disjointed view of the curriculum and interfere with the development of a student-content relationship. In

Teacher and student share responsibility for learning.

addition, when students return to the classroom, they have missed sharing in other experiences the group has had. Practices such as these make a certain segment of the student population feel disconnected, as if they don't belong (Vatterott, 1999). Pull-out programs are not student focused because they stigmatize students and interfere with students' social needs.

✦ STUDENT-FOCUSED INSTRUCTION— MORE SUCCESS FOR MORE STUDENTS

In this era of accountability and academic standards we need all students to succeed (Eisner, 2004). Student focused instruction is an approach to teaching and learning that is consistent with beliefs and practices shown by research to maximize student success (Blum, 2005; Glasser, 1992). Student-focused instruction capitalizes on what educators know about learning (Vatterott, 1999). It utilizes knowledge about developmental needs of early adolescents, brain-based research, motivation, learning styles, failure orientation, ability grouping, control theory, and just plain human nature (McDaniel et al., 2001). It applies what has been learned about teacher empowerment to the task of empowering students. If middle level schools are to provide academic success for more students, it seems obvious that the locus of change should reside in students and should be based on their developmental needs (Alexander, 1995; Keefe & Jenkins, 2002; Vatterott, 1999).

TEACHERS' VOICES

About Student-Focused Instruction

"It puts the ownership in the hands of the learner—especially the student who hasn't had the opportunity to be successful."

Gloria Sadler, eighth grade social studies
Wydown Middle School

"I usually pick the topic and from there try to come up with projects or ideas that will allow them to accomplish my goals, kind of on their terms."

Mike Burgio, seventh grade science
Pattonville Heights Middle School

"They like having choice, me not telling them, 'It's got to look like this, it's got to be my way. . . . It gives them a chance to be creative."

Stephanie Walton, seventh grade math
Pattonville Heights Middle School

Student-focused instruction is based on trust: trust in the energy, commitment, and potential of students. It is a trust in the students' capacity to develop (Alexander, 1995; Rogers, 1969). It is a trust in people to do the right thing, a trust that is modeled daily by all adults within the school—secretaries, janitors, counselors, bus drivers, and teachers. In student-focused instruction, teachers and students share responsibility for student success and failure (DeVries & Zan, 2003; Driekurs, Grunwald & Pepper, 1982; Vatterott, 1999). Students have input into classroom decisions, are held accountable for their actions, and allowed to solve their own problems (Strahan, Smith, McElrath, & Toole, 2001). Students are allowed to control, to some extent, the how, when, and why of tasks and assignments (Alexander, 1995).

Traditional Instruction versus Student-Focused Instruction

Kohn (1996) characterizes a learner-centered classroom as one where teachers *work with* students rather than *doing to* students. To further understand what student-focused instruction is, it may be helpful to examine what it is *not*. To understand how student-focused instruction differs from traditional teacher-focused instruction, let us compare the two types of instruction.

Traditional **teacher-focused instruction** most closely resembles the didactic instruction many of us experienced in elementary and high school (Vatterott, 1999). All content is chosen by the teacher and most often delivered in direct instruction such as lecturing or asking questions of students. Teacher talk predominates with little student talk. Curriculum is typically organized part-to-whole. Activities rely heavily on textbooks and workbooks (Daniels & Zemelman, 2004), and assessment is viewed as separate from learning.

Teacher-focused instruction is a helpful tool for some types of learning, but it is not appropriate as the predominant method of learning for early adolescents (Vatterott, 1999). Chapter 8 will discuss how and when teacher-focused instruction is appropriate and will offer suggestions as to how those methods can be adapted to be more student focused.

Student-focused instruction is best typified by student input into curriculum themes or curriculum planned around student questions (Beane, 1993, 1997, 2001; Vatterott, 1999). Curriculum is organized around broad concepts, principles, or ideas. Instruction is planned around active, relevant learning activities that allow for student choices. Students often work in groups and the learning activity is often also the assessment (Cetron & Cetron, 2004; Eisner, 2004; Gross, 2002).

Student-focused instruction shares many qualities with constructivism. **Constructivism** is the belief that learning occurs as the child constructs meaning by connecting new concepts to existing structures of knowledge (Brooks & Brooks, 1993; DeVries & Zan, 1995, 2003). Constructivist theory developed out of research in cognitive psychology and provides a way of explaining how learning happens (Cawelti, 2003). It was first applied in the field of early childhood education, but the developmental and child-centered nature of constructivism makes it applicable to adolescents as well (Vatterott, 1999).

Philosophically, constructivism draws heavily from the work of Piaget (Cawelti, 2003). Piaget (1954, 1970) believed that learning occurs through the child's interaction with the environment. According to constructivist theory, cognitive development in young children is a result of the learner's individual constructions of meaning (Brooks & Brooks, 1993; DeVries & Kohlberg, 1987). Children do not acquire knowledge through the mimetic approaches of committing information to short-term memory and mimicking an understanding of it on a test. Instead, they gain understanding by making connections of new concepts to existing structures of knowledge, thus constructing their own meaning (Alpert, 2004; Cetron & Cetron, 2004; DeVries & Zan, 2003; Eisner, 2004). The child's interests and prior experiences become the "fuel" of the constructive process (DeVries & Zan, 1995; Piaget, 1970).

Abbott and Ryan note that "as scientists study learning they are realizing that a constructivist model reflects their best understanding of the brain's natural way of making sense of the world" (Abbott & Ryan, 1999, p. 67). Brain-based research confirms that the desire to make meaning is innate and that emotion, relevance, and the creation of organizing patterns contribute to meaning making (Alpert, 2004; Jensen, 1998). The belief that the nature of learning is an internal construction of knowledge leads to what Brooks and Brooks (1993) call "honoring the learning process." If teachers respect the worth of a child's existing knowledge and experience, they will utilize it as they plan learning activities (Alexander, 1995; Alpert, 2004; Vatterott, 1999). Table 1.2 summarizes the differences between traditional teacher-focused instruction and student-focused instruction.

TABLE 1.2

Traditional Teacher-Focused Instruction versus Student-Focused Instruction

	Traditional Teacher-Focused Instruction	Student-Focused Instruction
Beliefs	Some can learn	All can learn
	Teaching is telling	Teaching is monitoring
	Failure is punished	Failure is learning
Roles	Teacher as worker	Teacher as leader
	Student as product	Student as worker
Practices	Learning as listening	Learning as doing
	Content curriculum	Process curriculum
	Paper and pencil tests	Performance assessment
	ABCDF grading	Descriptive feedback
	One-chance learning	Mastery learning
	Ability grouping	Mixed ability grouping
	Pull-out programs	Class within a class
	Retention	Intensive remediation
	Punitive discipline	Behavioral support

Source: Vatterott, 1999.

STUDENTS' VOICES

About Student-Focused Instruction

"We're learning and having fun at the same time. Sometimes you don't even know you're learning."

Maria, seventh grade

"You need some freedom and space to, like, do what you want to do."

Nick, seventh grade

"It's nice when they give you more choices—you can always find an outlet for the best way you learn."

Ashley, eighth grade

Implementing Student-Focused Instruction

The implementation of student-focused instruction requires a different view of curriculum and instruction, different roles for teachers and students, and different learning tasks from those of traditional teacher-focused instruction (Pitton, 2001; Smith, 2003). Student-focused instruction is advantageous for students of all ages, but is especially appropriate for middle school students, given their unique developmental needs (Vatterott, 1999).

One difficulty in implementing student-focused instruction lies in the issue of student empowerment (McDaniel et al., 2001). Existing power structures in school systems and existing models of power within schools and classrooms must be reexamined and new models created. Creating conditions for student-focused instruction does not require a decision between *power with* or *power over*. It is not an either/or decision. Because teachers are entrusted by parents with the safety and well-being of a large number of children, it will always be necessary for teachers to maintain some power over their students (Vatterott, 1999). Realistically, the current climate of teacher accountability necessitates some autocratic decisions by the teacher (Dreikurs et al., 1982).

The role of the teacher in student-focused instruction is to mediate the student and the curriculum, acting as coach, facilitator, and monitor (Flowers et al., 2003; Keefe & Jenkins, 2002; O'Steen et al., 2002). Teachers determine basic outcomes of instruction, custom design instruction for different types of learners, and function as taskmasters, priority setters, and standard-bearers for student work (Pitton, 2001). Most important, teachers must create the optimum work environment for productivity and assure that some students are not allowed to interfere with the productivity of the group (Kreisberg, 1992). This requires the development of a sense of community within the classroom and the school, where students work together to reach group and individual goals (Strahan et al., 2001). Teachers must blend together the two concepts of power and create a hybrid power, which maximizes students' control over their own learning while balancing the needs of students, the teacher, and the system (Anfara & Stacki, 2002; Smith, 2003).

In a student-focused classroom, there is a trust in the student to do well, develop good habits, and master learning (Alexander, 1995). All children can learn, but some will learn more easily and more quickly than others. Children learn in different ways and so require a variety of methods and paths to reach the same destination (NMSA, 2001c; Slavin, 1997). In a student-focused classroom, failure in learning or behavior is viewed as an opportunity to learn, not to be punished.

Successful implementation of student-focused instruction in middle schools requires teachers to

- relate the scope and intensity of the changes of puberty to early adolescent needs (discussed in Chapters 2 and 3).
- know how to adapt instruction to meet the special needs of early adolescents (discussed in Chapters 2 and 3).
- understand the basic tools of student empowerment such as class meetings, personal relationships, and student choice (discussed in Chapter 4).

- become familiar with the structure and role of the middle school curriculum and co-curriculum in meeting the needs of students (discussed in Chapter 5).
- be able to use curriculum guidelines to plan standards-based instruction (discussed in Chapter 6).
- be able to create student-focused learning activities (discussed in Chapter 7).
- be able to differentiate instruction using a variety of student-focused and teacher-focused methods (Chapters 8 and 9).
- be able to use performance assessments to promote student motivation and learning (discussed in Chapter 10).
- reflect on their personal beliefs about learners and how those beliefs impact learning (Chapter 11).

Summary

Middle schools were created in an effort to meet the unique needs of early adolescents (Beane, 2001; Lounsbury & Vars, 2003). The philosophy of the middle school is child centered and needs based, and places the highest priority on academic success for all students (NMSA, 2001b, 2001c, & 2003b). Traditional practices have limited the number of academically successful students. Student-focused instruction has the potential to provide more success for more students at the middle level than is possible with teacher-focused instruction. The student-focused classroom has the ability to address the needs of early adolescents through student empowerment, individualization, and student choices (Vatterott, 1999).

Key Terms

ability grouping
constructivism
empowerment
one-shot grading

student empowerment
student-focused instruction
teacher-focused instruction

Application Activities

1. Contact three middle schools or junior high schools in your area. Using the descriptions from Table 1.1, determine how closely each school resembles a traditional junior high school or a true middle school. In what ways are each of the schools hybrids of both junior high schools and middle schools?

2. Reflect on your total school experience to date. List at least three examples of *power over* or *power with* that you have experienced as a student.

3. Visit the National Middle School Association's website at www.nmsa.org. What resources are available to help middle school teachers? Read one research summary to learn more about a specific middle school topic.

CHAPTER 2

UNDERSTANDING MIDDLE LEVEL LEARNERS—PHYSICAL AND INTELLECTUAL DEVELOPMENT

❖ **Patterns of Physical Development during Puberty**

What Are the Characteristics of Physical Development during Puberty?

What Are the Implications of Physical Development for Instruction?

❖ **Patterns of Intellectual Development during Puberty**

What Are the Characteristics of Intellectual Development in Early Adolescents?

What Are the Implications of Intellectual Development for Instruction?

❖ **Patterns of Diversity in Early Adolescent Learning Preferences**

Differences in Learning Style

Students with Special Needs

The Question of Attention Deficit Disorder among Middle School Students

What Are the Implications of Individual Styles for Instruction?

➜ INTRODUCTION

Teaching early adolescents requires an understanding of the unique characteristics of children aged 10 to 14 who are going through the process of puberty, the transition from being a child to being an adult. The scope of physical, psychological, and cognitive changes experienced during puberty is unmatched throughout a child's lifetime, with the possible exception of the period from birth to three years of age (George & Alexander, 2003; Manning, 1993). The legacy of those changes and the experience of puberty will continue to influence children into their adult years (Carnegie Council on Adolescent Development, 1989; Stevenson, 2002). When we understand middle level learners, we become aware of the intensity of their physical, emotional, and social needs and appreciate the powerfulness of those needs in creating meaningful learning opportunities (Vatterott, 1999).

Even though early adolescents share many similarities, as a group they are best defined by their variability (Manning & Bucher, 2001). As individuals, early adolescents are more different than alike (George & Alexander, 2003). Physically, the timing of the changes of puberty may create a developmental span of as much as five years between early and late developers of the same age (Manning, 1993). Diversity is equally evident in emotional, social, and intellectual development (Lounsbury & Vars, 2003). The single most defining characteristic of puberty is the diversity of the experience among early adolescents (Van Hoose, Strahan, & L'Esperance, 2001). This chapter will deal with the physical and intellectual development of early adolescence. Chapter 3 will deal with the emotional and social development of early adolescence. **The purposes of this chapter are to help you**

- appreciate the scope and diversity of the physical and intellectual changes of early adolescence.
- understand the relationship between early adolescent needs and early adolescent behavior.
- understand and appreciate the diversity of learning styles of early adolescents.
- appreciate the challenges that the changes of puberty bring to special needs students.
- understand the necessity of adapting instructional practices to the needs of early adolescents.
- become aware of the critical impact of culture on the process of early adolescent development.

Essential Questions

After reading and completing the activities in this chapter, you should be able to answer the following questions:

1. What changes do early adolescents experience in their physical development?
2. How do individuals differ in their physical development?
3. What changes do early adolescents experience in their intellectual development?
4. How do individuals differ in their intellectual development?
5. What typical behaviors result from the physical and intellectual changes of puberty?
6. What are the instructional implications of the physical and intellectual changes of puberty?
7. How do students differ in their approach to learning?

✦ PATTERNS OF PHYSICAL DEVELOPMENT DURING PUBERTY

Puberty is the natural, biological transition of a human body from that of a child to that of an adult capable of sexual reproduction (Reiter, 2001; Tanner, 1980). Along with the physical changes come emotional, social, and intellectual transitions as well. The first evidence of these changes is often the development of **secondary sex characteristics** (Herman-Giddens et al., 1997; Herman-Giddens, Wang & Koch,

2001). Secondary sex characteristics are physical changes such as breast development, genital development, and pubic hair growth that signal the beginning of the
process of puberty, but they may appear long before children are actually capable of
sexual reproduction (Manning & Bucher, 2001; Reiter, 2001). For girls, for instance,
the technical start of puberty is the first menstrual period, but secondary sex characteristics may appear years earlier (Herman-Giddens et al., 1997). Although all children go through a similar *sequence* of changes during puberty, the *timing* of those
changes varies greatly from one individual to the next (Havinghurst, 1976;
Stevenson, 2002). The age of the onset of puberty varies greatly among individual
children (Havinghurst, 1976; Reiter, 2001). Tables 2.1 and 2.2 show the prevalence
of specific changes by age and race for girls and boys.

TABLE 2.1

Percentage of Girls with Secondary Sex Characteristics by Age
and Race

Percentage of Girls with Breast Development

AGE	6 or under	7	8	9	10	11	12
White girls	2.9%	5.0%	10.5%	32.1%	61.5%	85.4%	96.0%
African American girls	6.4%	15.4%	37.8%	62.6%	80.2%	96.0%	98.9%

Percentage of Girls with Pubic Hair Development

AGE	6 or under	7	8	9	10	11	12
White girls	1.4%	2.8%	7.7%	20.0%	46.4%	74.3%	92.2%
African American girls	9.5%	17.7%	34.3%	62.6%	85.6%	95.2%	98.9%

Percentage of Girls with Menses (First Menstrual Period)

AGE	9 or under	10	11	12
White girls	0%	1.8%	13.4%	35.2%
African American girls	2.7%	6.3%	27.9%	62.1%

Source: Herman-Giddens, Slora, Waserman, Bourdony, Bhapkar, Koch, & Hasemeier, 1997

TABLE 2.2

Percentage of Boys with Secondary Sex Characteristics by Age and Race

Percentage of Boys with Genital Development

AGE	8	9	10	11	12	13	14	15 and over
White boys	29.3%	35.7%	48.1%	72.5%	90.7%	93.9%	100%	100%
African American boys	37.8%	58.2%	69.7%	78.1%	89.1%	98.1%	96.2%	100%
Mexican American boys	27.3%	31.6%	46.4%	72.1%	81.5%	94.0%	100%	100%

Percentage of Boys with Pubic Hair Growth

AGE	8	9	10	11	12	13	14	15 and over
White boys	0%	4.3%	10.3%	35.7%	71.5%	75.5%	96.8%	100%
African American boys	5.3%	21.0%	35.9%	53.0%	82.4%	89.3%	94.9%	100%
Mexican American boys	2.7%	3.3%	6.7%	31.0%	49.1%	74.8%	96.7%	100%

Source: Herman-Giddens, Wang, & Koch, 2001

There is no *normal* age for the onset of puberty. If a group of early adolescents of the same age were compared, a six-year span in development could be possible between early developing girls and late developing boys (Herman-Giddens et al., 1997; Herman-Giddens, Wong, & Koch, 2001; Van Hoose et al., 2001). That is, some children would still be two years away from the onset of puberty, others would be experiencing puberty, and others would have completed the transition. As a group, girls experience the onset of puberty about two years earlier than boys (George & Alexander, 2003; Milgram, 1992). Although there is a wide range of ages at which individuals enter puberty, the *average* age for girls is 12 while the *average* age for boys is 14. The *average* age at which children begin to develop secondary sex characteristics has decreased since the 1960s—about one and one-half years for boys and about six months to one year for white girls (comparative figures are not available for African American girls) (Herman-Giddens et al., 1997; Reiter, 2001; Tanner, 1980). However, the average age of the start of menstrual periods has remained stable for 45 years for white girls (at 12.88 years) and decreased only slightly in African American girls (from 12.52 years in the late 1960s to 12.16 years today) (Herman-Giddens et al., 1997). The decreased figure for African American girls is not necessarily significant. The 12.52 figure is based on limited studies from the 1960s and researchers believe that if the age has, in fact, decreased for African American girls, it is probably due to improved nutrition and health. On the average, however, African American girls do begin their menstrual periods about 8.5 months earlier than white girls (Herman-Giddens et al., 1997; Herman-Giddens et al., 2001). Table 2.3 shows the average ages for the onset of secondary sex characteristics for boys and girls.

TABLE 2.3

Average Ages of the Onset of Secondary Sex Characteristics

Females	White Girls	African American Girls	
Beginning of breast development	9.96 years	8.87 years	
Pubic hair development	10.51 years	8.78 years	
First menstrual period	12.88 years	12.16 years	
Males	**White Boys**	**African American Boys**	**Mexican American Boys**
Beginning of genital development	10.6 years	9.5 years	10.4 years
Pubic hair development	12.0 years	11.2 years	12.3 years

Source: Herman-Giddens et al., 1997; Herman Giddens et al., 2001.

The *rate* of the process of puberty also varies among individuals (George & Alexander, 2003; Havinghurst, 1976; Manning, 1993). Early developing girls may begin puberty at age 8.75 and complete the process by age 13 while late developing girls may *begin* puberty at age 13.25 and not complete the process until age 18. Early developing boys may begin puberty at the age of 9.5 and complete the process at 12.5 while late developing boys may begin puberty at age 14 and end at age 17 (Manning, 1993). Some early adolescents may complete the process in as little as 18 months while others may take as long as six years (George, Lawrence, & Bushnell, 1998; Havinghurst, 1976). There is no indication that the *rate* at which children experience the process of puberty has changed in recent years (Reiter, 2001).

What Are the Characteristics of Physical Development during Puberty?

- **Increased hormones during puberty cause children to develop secondary sex characteristics.**

In the transformation from child to adult, an increase in hormones causes the body to undergo many changes. In girls, these changes include breast development, the appearance of pubic hair, the widening of the hips, and the beginning of menstruation (Herman-Giddens et al., 1997). In boys, these changes include the enlargement of the testes, growth of the penis, the appearance of pubic hair, and an increase in body and facial hair (Herman-Giddens et al., 1997; Stevenson, 2002).

Some boys also experience fatty tissue development in the chest area, giving a breastlike appearance to the chest, much to their embarrassment. Other changes for both sexes due to greater hormone production include increased perspiration and body odor, and sometimes acne or other skin problems (Manning, 1993; Milgram, 1992).

The high level of hormones coupled with erratic surges of different hormones at different times of the day produce many inconsistencies in behavior (Kellough & Kellough, 1999). An early adolescent may be sitting peacefully in class and suddenly experience a jolt of adrenaline that makes him or her feel like jumping out of the seat. Mood swings are common at this age, a result of the emotional stress of adolescence as well as the physical result of hormonal fluctuations (George & Alexander, 2003; Manning & Bucher, 2001).

Early adolescent girls' moods may be aggravated by the emotional anxiety of not knowing when their first menstrual period will happen (some girls are eager, some dread it) and the physical unpredictability of periods during the first few years of menstruation (Milgram, 1992; Stevenson, 2002). The frequency of menstrual periods in pubescent girls can be wildly erratic from twice a month to twice a year with no discernible pattern for an individual girl. The need to use the restroom frequently is not hysteria but simple reassurance for most girls during this time.

For boys, the greatest influence on mood is the overabundance of testosterone. The increase in testosterone in adolescent boys causes the voice to deepen, causes hair to form on their bodies, and allows their muscles to enlarge (Manning, 1993; Stevenson, 2002). It also causes irritability, body odor, nocturnal emissions, and spontaneous erections (Milgram, 1992). In adolescents and adult men, high levels of testosterone correlate with higher levels of aggression, competitiveness, and increased sex drive (Herman-Giddens et al., 2001; Lacayo, 2000).

"The average man has 260 to 1000 nanograms of testosterone per deciliter of blood plasma. For women the range is 15 to 70. . . . Testosterone in the blood of teenage boys can jump to as high as 2,000 nanograms, which helps explain teenage boys" (Lacayo, 2000, pp. 61–62).

Early adolescents alternate between having lots of energy and feeling restless, to feeling tired and listless (Manning & Bucher, 2001; Kellough & Kellough, 1999). Due to the availability of large amounts of adrenaline, early adolescents can summon up unusual physical strength when confronted with an emotional crisis (just watch two early adolescents in a physical fight!). Overall, however, physical and mental endurance are very short during puberty and early adolescents tire easily (Kellough & Kellough, 1999; Manning, 1993). This is due partly to the amount of energy that is drained by the demanding process of growth (the comparison to a pregnant woman is appropriate) and is often aggravated by poor diet and sleeping habits (Kantrowitz & Springen, 2003).

- **Early adolescents experience growth spurts.**

Growth spurts, rapid periods of growth, occur in both boys and girls (Manning, 1993; Stevenson, 2002). Although the average gain in height for early adolescents is two to four inches a year, during a growth spurt, a child can grow as fast as five inches in three months. From ages 10 to 15, this averages to a gain of 10–20 inches in height and 40–50 pounds in weight (George et al., 1998; Van Hoose, Strahan, & L'Esperance, 2001). Because children of the same age may be five years apart in experiencing the onset of puberty, the following scenario is all too common: Two friends of the same age and the same size enter the sixth grade. By the end of the eighth grade one has grown very little while the other has grown 12 inches in height and 40 pounds in weight. To compound the differences, as girls on the average experience their growth spurt two years earlier than boys (Milgram, 1992), early developing girls and late developing boys can be quite noticeable in a crowd of middle school students (Havinghurst, 1976; Stevenson, 2002).

- **Body growth is disproportionate.**

Growth of bones and muscles can occur at different rates—that is, bones can grow faster than muscles, increasing the risk of muscle tears and often causing real *growing pains* (Havinghurst, 1976; Kellough & Kellough, 1999; Van Hoose et al., 2001). If bone growth is not yet complete, bones and ligaments have difficulty sustaining heavy pressure. Many contact sport injuries during this age result from the fragile nature of stressed bones and muscles. Also, during puberty the bones in the tailbone ossify, fusing into one bone (Van Hoose et al., 2001). This can make sitting in hard desks for long periods of time difficult.

Extremities (legs, arms, feet, hands, noses, and ears) grow faster than the rest of the body, often resulting in a gawky or unattractive appearance (Kellough & Kellough, 1999; Manning, 1993; Milgram, 1992). Have you ever seen a German

Early adolescent boys enjoy rough housing.

Shepherd or other large breed dog as a puppy? Their feet are much too large for their body and they often trip and fall over their feet. Early adolescents have much the same problem when feet and legs grow faster than the rest of the body. The dual effects of rapid growth and uneven growth of the extremities can also result in a lack of coordination, awkwardness, and clumsiness (George et al., 1998; Stevenson, 2002). In addition, rapid growth can also lead to a temporary lack of body awareness or spatial orientation. That is, early adolescents don't realize how big they are or how long their arms and legs have become (like a pregnant woman who thinks she can still fit through a small space). When moving through spaces, they don't quite know where their bodies are. This results in a lot of unintentional bumping into people, furniture, walls, and countertops (Milgram, 1992). Add this problem to the awkwardness of big feet, and the result is a lot of minor mishaps, bumps, bruises, falls, and other embarrassing situations.

REFLECTIVE QUESTION

What do you remember about the physical changes you experienced during this period of your adolescence? How did you feel about your physical development? How do you remember feeling different from other adolescents?

- **Early adolescents have special nutritional needs.**

The fast-paced growth of puberty can also produce enormous appetites and frequent hunger (George & Alexander, 2003; Van Hoose et al., 2001). It was once estimated that the average middle school student needs to eat every two hours. That may not be true for all middle school students, but hunger is a frequent source of frustration for students during the school day. On the other hand, their appetite can be quite capricious and they can become picky eaters (Kellough & Kellough, 1999). The growing body's demand for specific nutrients also triggers cravings or food jags that can last for days (Jensen, 1998, 2001). During specific periods of growth, early adolescents may crave such foods as red meat, dairy, nuts, or fruit in large quantities.

As most experienced middle school teachers know, those nutritional needs make eating breakfast an important habit for early adolescents.

> Children who eat breakfast have been shown to have improved attention in late-morning task performance; retrieve information more quickly and accurately; make fewer errors in problem-solving activities; concentrate better and perform more complex tasks. (Wolfe, Burkman, & Streng, 2000, p. 55)

Unfortunately, not all breakfasts are equal in assisting learning. A starchy sugary breakfast will sustain a child for only one or two hours. A breakfast of fat, protein, and complex carbohydrates can maintain blood sugar for several hours (Jensen, 1998, 2000).

- **Early adolescents become overly concerned about body image.**

With so many physical changes happening so fast, it is not surprising that early adolescents are often concerned about their appearance and have a need for privacy (Stevenson, 2002). The feelings of uncertainty about how fast changes are happening are lessened somehow by the constant checking in the mirror (Milgram, 1992). "Have I grown since yesterday? Is there a new pimple coming? Do I look the same as yesterday?" These are the kinds of questions that may haunt early adolescents. As they are so unsure of their identity, appearance becomes a critical factor in how they define themselves (George & Alexander, 2003; Havinghurst, 1976). The emphasis on physical beauty in the media and fashion magazines contributes to this concern. Aware that people are judged in many ways by their appearance, early adolescents spend a great deal of time orchestrating the physical image they present to the world (Kantrowitz & Wingert, 1999; Milgram, 1992). This is not the most attractive time in a child's life. Fully understanding the advantage of attractiveness in the adult world, early adolescents worry that they may look this way for the rest of their lives. They need reassurance that when they have finished growing, their appearance will improve.

In general, body image is less troubling to boys than to girls (George & Alexander, 2003). Boys tend to define themselves more by accomplishments and less by appearance. It is understandable then that boys feel more satisfied with their bodies than girls and are more likely to rate the different aspects of their appearance the same. Girls, who are more likely to base much of their self-esteem on appearance,

Early adolescent girls are often overconcerned about their appearance.

often *compartmentalize* their approval of their bodies by assigning different values to different parts of their bodies (resulting in more overall dissatisfaction). The changes of puberty are more likely to cause girls to be disappointed in their bodies, while boys seem to be more concerned with task mastery and achievement than with physical appearance (Kantrowitz & Wingert, 1999).

In one historical study of American girls, the researchers noticed a disturbing trend—body image becoming more prominent in the self-worth of girls. Fifty years ago, when girls discussed self-improvement, it often focused on service to others or improving school performance. Now the focus is primarily on appearance (Stevenson, 2002). "In adolescent girls' private diaries and journals, the body is a consistent preoccupation, second only to peer relationships" (Brumberg in Kantrowitz & Wingert, 1999, p. 69).

Early adolescents struggle with how they feel about their bodies, whether their bodies are acceptable (Havinghurst, 1976; Milgram, 1992). Concerns about body shape, size, and proportions cause much concern about weight. Weight seems to be more of a concern to girls, whose body fat often increases with puberty and who often view breasts and widening hips as fat (Sprenger, 2005; Stevenson, 2002). When girls view models in fashion magazines, they can become very negative about the changes in their weight and the shapes of their bodies (Kantrowitz & Wingert, 1999). After all, the emaciated models they see in fashion magazines resemble the prepubescent female body more than the body of an early adolescent girl developing into a woman. It is not surprising that eating disorders are becoming more prevalent among early adolescent girls (Price, 2005; Manning & Bucher, 2001).

> One recent study found that 39 percent of girls in grades five to eight said that they were on a diet; 13 percent of those girls said they had already binged and purged, symptoms of bulimia. (Kantrowitz & Wingert, 1999, p. 69)

Girls who have come to believe that a woman's worth is based solely on her physical appearance can become pathologically obsessed with body weight (Milgram, 1992). Eating disorders tend to occur in girls who are already battling low self-esteem, girls who are perfectionists in many areas of their lives, or girls who are preoccupied with body image as their *only* identity and receptacle of self-worth (Kantrowitz & Wingert, 1999).

The overconcern of early adolescents with body image leads to a concern that their physical appearance is judged acceptable or unacceptable in every social interaction (Sprenger, 2005). They want desperately to fit in and feel good about the way they look (Milgram, 1992; Stevenson, 2002). When it comes to early adolescent appearance, acceptance is most easily accomplished through clothes and hairstyles (Havinghurst, 1976; Manning, 1993). When asked by one researcher "what one thing would you change about yourself?" an overwhelming majority of middle school students replied they would change their hair (Van Hoose et al., 2001). Hair seems to be a focal point for all the other things that early adolescents find unacceptable about their appearance. Unlike gangly extremities and acne, hair is something that can be *fixed*, giving early adolescents some sense of control. Clothes fall into that category as well (Milgram, 1992). The right clothes can hide embarrassing physical characteristics, help the body to look more *normal*, and most important, signal that the adolescent is *in style* (Kantrowitz & Wingert, 1999). What early adolescents wear is an important reflection of the group to which they wish to belong and clothes are often their method of access to a specific peer group (Havinghurst, 1976). A change in style of dress is one of the first signs that early adolescents are changing their allegiance from one social group to another.

STUDENT'S VOICE

About the Changes of Puberty

"The hardest thing about being my age is dealing with everything changing so quickly."

Chad, seventh grade

REFLECTIVE QUESTION

Think of a time (as an adult or an adolescent) when you were in a social situation and when you were embarrassed about your appearance (bad haircut, wrong clothes, etc.). How did it make you feel about yourself? How did it influence the way you interacted with others?

What are the Implications of Physical Development for Instruction?

- **Teach about physical changes and what is normal.**

Early adolescents can benefit from learning about the physical changes of puberty and understanding the differences in the timing of changes among individuals (Havinghurst, 1976; Manning & Bucher, 2001). The middle school health, physical education, or science curriculum can address the same kind of information as is found in this chapter (Kellough & Kellough, 2002; Stevenson, 2000). Early adolescents have many questions like "Am I normal?" and "When will I start (or stop) growing?" Understanding the diversity of the experience of puberty is helpful in easing early adolescent concerns.

- **Teach about the impact of healthy habits on physical and mental health.**

Early adolescents need to be made aware of how delicate their growing bodies are and how easily they can be affected by their health habits (George &

Alexander, 2003; Havinghurst, 1976). Health programs should stress the importance of sound nutrition, proper exercise, and personal hygiene (Manning, 1993; Stevenson, 2002). Students must understand that a healthy diet, exercise, and sleep are all essential for learning (Sousa, 1998; Stevenson, 2002). Adequate sleep is often overlooked when students are having learning problems (Sprenger, 2005; Wolfe, 2005). Middle school students need a *minimum* of eight hours of sleep each night, and early adolescents who are experiencing growth spurts may need as much as *10 to 12* hours (Jensen, 1998; Kantrowitz & Springen, 2003).

- **Reinforce healthy habits in the classroom.**

It is important to focus on the value of nutrition as part of your classroom routine. Teachers should help students see the relationship between healthy habits and their ability to improve their school performance and to control their emotions (Jensen, 2000; Sprenger, 2005). Teachers and school administrators may want to discuss the possibility of scheduled snack breaks. Teachers should also consider keeping some emergency snacks like crackers or fruit in the room (Kellough & Kellough, 1999).

If students are having trouble staying on task, are lethargic, or are extremely irritable, teachers may ask students to consider whether their problem could be related to adequate sleep or a proper diet (Stevenson, 2002). Teachers may also want to talk with parents about the relationship of diet, sleep, or exercise to learning or behavior problems.

- **Provide for plenty of exercise, movement and activity.**

The most important implication for instruction is the early adolescent's need for exercise, movement, and activity (NMSA, 2001c). Studies of adolescents have shown that 50 percent of them need excessive mobility while learning. Another 25 percent need occasional mobility with only 25 percent needing minimal mobility (Jensen, 2000). The opportunity for physical movement should be part of the daily classroom routine (Bell, 2003; Kellough & Kellough, 1999; Sousa, 1998). When students are expected to sit for more than 20 minutes, frequent stand-and-stretch breaks are critical to sustained attention (Jensen, 2000). Teachers should allow students to move around the classroom and take stretch breaks when needed; they should build movement into classroom activities (George & Alexander, 2003; Sousa, 1998).

Middle schools should consider the benefit to learning of recess or other breaks that allow students to get physical exercise (Jensen, 2000; Kellough & Kellough, 1999). Many middle schools arrange their schedules so that the gymnasium is available during lunch, giving students the opportunity to run or play physical games during their lunchtime. Daily exercise, even short walks, should be a priority (George & Alexander, 2003; Jensen, 2000; Sousa, 1998). Chapter 4 will offer more specific recommendations for classroom practices that respect the physical needs of early adolescents.

TEACHER'S VOICE

About Physical Activity

"Kids that are more physically active get better grades and are less depressed."

Janet Peabody, physical education

North Kirkwood Middle School

- **Create comfortable working conditions for students.**

Middle school students often complain about how uncomfortable school desks are. Furniture that accommodates different sizes and shapes will increase student comfort and the ability to focus. Tables and chairs allow for more comfort and freedom of movement than traditional student desks. Many middle school teachers have a few soft chairs or pillows in their rooms and allow students to work in different positions. Allowing students to choose to work standing up, sitting on the floor, or sitting with feet up often results in more focused learning (Jensen, 2000; Sousa, 1998).

Wise middle school teachers create as much physical space as possible within their classrooms so students can move easily. They try to arrange furniture so that aisles are wide and they avoid leaving things that can be tripped over (George et al., 1998). Some newer middle schools are now being designed with hallways wider than normal to give middle school students extra space to move (George & Alexander, 2003). Many middle schools construct their schedules so that different teams or grade levels change classes at different times. That results in fewer students in the hall at any one time. Many middle schools also use a system of *staggered release*, in which individual teachers delay when they release their students by 30 seconds to one minute. This short amount of time eliminates traffic jams and overcrowding. The use of staggered release is especially helpful at lunchtime or at the end of the day when large numbers of students are dismissed at the same time.

Middle schools that are sensitive to differences in physical development avoid programs that cause students to compete physically, such as sports teams on which only the best athletes are allowed to play. Experts recommend that middle schools avoid intensive competitive interscholastic sports (Kellough & Kellough, 1999; Manning, 1993). Many middle schools choose instead to emphasize all-play sports or intramurals (NMSA, 2001f). (For more about developmentally appropriate sports programs, see Chapter 5.)

➔ PATTERNS OF INTELLECTUAL DEVELOPMENT DURING PUBERTY

Sometime between the ages of 11 and 14, early adolescents begin the intellectual transition between the concrete stage of thinking and the abstract stage of thinking (George et al., 1998; Gross, 2002). According to Piaget (1954, 1970), most children are in the concrete stage of cognitive development from age 7 to age 12. During this stage, children perceive the world and learn through concrete experiences—what they can see, touch, and manipulate. Between the ages of 11 and 14, as early adolescents transition into abstract thought—they develop the ability to conceive of things they cannot see, touch, or manipulate (George & Alexander, 2003; Piaget, 1970). This transition represents a huge leap in intellectual reasoning capacities. As with other changes occurring during puberty, the timing of this transition varies greatly among individual children. *Most* early adolescents are concrete thinkers in *most* subject areas during their time in middle school. Their transition into abstract thought is uneven and sporadic and is rarely complete until high school (Piaget, 1970). The early adolescent's application of abstract thought processes is evident in increasing abilities to hypothesize, analyze, experiment, and reflect (George & Alexander, 2003). As a result of more frequent abstract thinking, early adolescents are curious, questioning, critical, and idealistic (Kellough & Kellough, 1999). These qualities are apparent not only in their approach to academics and the world around them but also in their social lives and their inner personal lives (Milgram, 1992). This new intellectual development allows early adolescents to see the world through new eyes with new perspectives.

What Are the Characteristics of Intellectual Development in Early Adolescents?

- **Early adolescents are transitioning from concrete to abstract thinking but function mostly at the concrete stage.**

For all intents and purposes, middle school students are concrete thinkers. Concrete thinkers tend to view situations as either black or white, right or wrong. They have difficulty with issues that are not clear-cut and with situations that are contrary to fact (George & Alexander, 2003; Piaget, 1954, 1970). They have limited abilities in perspective, both in visually predicting what objects would look like from a different perspective and in seeing the other person's side of an issue (George & Alexander, 2003).

As early adolescents become abstract thinkers, they develop the ability to conceptualize, to create not only visual representations of objects in their minds but also to create new ideas and to think about relationships between ideas (Mandeville & Radcliffe, 2002; Manning & Bucher, 2001). It has been said that concrete thinkers can manipulate things, whereas abstract thinkers can manipulate ideas. Abstract thinkers begin to understand the process of logic and the ability to use logic to create a series of possible outcomes (Piaget, 1954, 1970). From this they learn to hypothesize, by thinking through all possible outcomes (Kellough & Kellough, 1999; Manning & Bucher, 2001). They begin to develop emotional and social perspectives, along with the ability to see the other side of an issue, or to take another's point of view (Manning, 1993; Van Hoose et al., 2001).

Only a small percentage of eighth graders are operating fully at the abstract level of thought (George, Lawrence, & Bushnell, 1998), yet the curriculum of the middle grades contains many abstract concepts that teachers struggle to teach to con-

Abstract Concepts Taught in Middle School.

Language Arts	Science
Main idea	Photosynthesis
Symbolism	Molecular structure
Metaphor	Respiration
Mathematics	**Social Studies**
Equations	Democracy
Ratio	Solar system
Order of operations	Forms of government

crete thinkers (see Figure 2.1). There is a correlation between the small number of eighth graders who are abstract thinkers and the ones who are ready for algebra, a relationship supported by research showing that most 13-year-olds may not be neurologically ready for algebra or geometry (Jensen, 2000). Does this mean that middle schools should not attempt to teach algebra or geometry? No. It just means that abstract concepts must be taught *concretely*. In the Chicago Math Project, algebra was successfully taught to sixth graders using math manipulatives and other concrete methods. Successful middle school teachers use *concrete* methods to teach abstract concepts to *concrete* learners (George et al., 1998).

As with other changes that occur in early adolescents, the development of abstract thought varies among individuals (Gross, 2002). Some 11-year-olds have reached the stage of abstract thinking (not necessarily the gifted students) while many high school students have still not attained this stage (not necessarily the remedial students). The development of abstract thought also varies within individuals from one subject area to the next (George & Alexander, 2003). For instance, a student may be able to understand the abstract concept of democracy in social studies but not be able to comprehend equations in math.

- **Early adolescents enjoy using their new mental abilities.**

Cognitive behavior of early adolescents is driven by the desire to practice with their new tools (Milgram, 1992). Early adolescents are eager to apply their new mental abilities, even though they are inexperienced with abstract thought processes (George & Alexander, 2003). Using these newly acquired tools is exciting and brings a feeling of adulthood (Milgram, 1992). Early adolescents enjoy predicting, hypothesizing, analyzing, and experimenting—in schoolwork and in their everyday lives (Inlay, 2005). They like to use their cognitive skills to solve real-life problems, making problem-based learning a wonderful strategy for this age (Storz & Nestor, 2003). They enjoy problem solving but sometimes suffer from what Elkind (1981) calls "pseudostupidity," a tendency to overcomplicate simple problems. For example, given their new abilities of analysis and perspective, students may reread and overanalyze test questions they think are too easy, only to give the wrong answer (Milgram, 1992). Early adolescents also enjoy making generalizations (sometimes in the extreme—as in "*everyone*'s doing it"). They enjoy developing their sense of humor by creating their own jokes (Kellough & Kellough, 1999). Their sense of humor is becoming increasingly more sophisticated, but they will still ask to have jokes explained that they do not understand. On the other hand, they often do not understand sarcasm and are likely to get their feelings hurt, making it wise for teachers to avoid the use of sarcasm.

- **Early adolescents are developing the capacity to be reflective.**

In practicing their new thinking abilities, early adolescents have a tendency to daydream and to imagine possibilities ("What would happen if . . . ?"). They are also capable of thinking about their own thinking (Kellough & Kellough, 1999). The ability to reflect on their own thinking has its advantages and disadvantages. Early adolescents are developing their abilities to evaluate and analyze their own behavior and to learn from it (Mandeville & Radcliffe, 2002; Stevenson, 2002). Opportunities for self-evaluation can help them to develop those abilities further. They can especially benefit from reflecting on how they learn best, what they need to do to stay focused, and what their preferred style of learning is. On the other hand, they are very aware when they don't understand a task or when a task is beyond their abilities (McDaniel, Necochea, Rios, Stowell, & Kritzer, 2001; Milgram, 1992). They tend to become very self-conscious, especially when they see that other students who are more advanced in their thinking are capable of the same task (Easton, 2002).

Early adolescents are generally not cognitive risk takers (Milgram, 1992). Although they enjoy challenging tasks, the risk of embarrassment must be low, and assistance must be readily available when frustration sets in (Storz & Nestor, 2003). If a learning task is viewed as too challenging or the potential for embarrassment is perceived to be high, students may refuse to attempt the task (Easton, 2002). Their defense is often that they are capable but just don't *choose* to do the task:

> When faced with tasks that appear to be difficult, many early adolescents say to themselves "I could figure that out if I really wanted to but I don't want to." Such a rationalization is much easier than admitting that the task is difficult and may be beyond their present level of reasoning. (Van Hoose & Strahan, 1988, p. 16)

To combat these tendencies, teachers need to model an attitude of persistence for students, offer multiple paths to understanding, and provide no-risk learning that allows students to tackle hard tasks without fear of failing grades (for more about grading see Chapter 10).

- **Early adolescents are opinionated and often critical.**

As they move into the stage of abstract thinking and their intellectual capacity increases, early adolescents are capable of higher level thinking skills (Havinghurst, 1976; Piaget, 1954, 1970). It's as if they've suddenly gained the capacity for evaluation (Bloom's highest level of cognitive thought) and they love making judgments

(Mandeville & Radcliffe, 2002). They enjoy practicing this skill in their develop-ment of personal attitudes and perspectives, from their preferences in food, music, and television shows to their opinions, however naïve, about such controversial adult topics as politics, religion, abortion, or gun control. They seem to have strong opinions about just about everything and are eager to share them. This tendency dis-plays itself through frequent argumentative behavior (Manning & Bucher, 2001; Milgram, 1992). Early adolescents *enjoy arguing* to convince others and to clarify their own thinking. They enjoy the intellectual process of defending their opinions and proving what they believe (Tomlinson & Doubet, 2005). A wise middle school teacher avoids arguing with students and provides opportunities for students to share their opinions and to debate curriculum-related issues.

- **Early adolescents question everything.**

  As their opinions develop, early adolescents question why the world is the way it is (Inlay, 2005). "Why do we have poor people?" "Why are there wars?" "Why do we have taxes?" "Why do we have to go to school?" "Why do we need laws?" They no longer blindly believe everything adults tell them and they often ask for proof. Their questioning reflects their ability to understand the larger world and their con-cerns about issues that they fear will affect them: "Will pollution get worse?" "Is my neighborhood safe from earthquake, tornadoes, floods?" "Will race relations ever get better?" Although early adolescents are intensely focused on their personal and fam-ily lives, they also worry a lot about social concerns (Milgram, 1992). When 12- to 15-year-olds were asked about their social concerns, the most frequently mentioned were AIDS, child abuse, prejudice, drug abuse, and violence (Kantrowitz & Wingert, 1999).

  Early adolescents are especially skeptical and questioning about authority and rules. This is an appropriate developmental task as they assert their independence and define themselves as adults (Havinghurst, 1976; Stevenson, 2002). Questions about authority and rules should be dealt with in a logical, information-giving fash-ion that explains the purpose and value of authority and rules. Experienced middle school teachers have learned not to take the questioning of *their* authority personally.

- **Early adolescents are very curious.**

  On the positive side, early adolescents also ask a lot of questions to better un-derstand the world around them. Their new level of understanding brings new ques-tions and a genuine curiosity also reminiscent of the characteristics of preschoolers (Kellough & Kellough, 1999). When addressed, the questions of early adolescents about the world around them can be a powerful tool in motivating these students and extending learning in the classroom (O'Steen et al., 2002; Storz & Nestor, 2003).

- **New cognitive development results in a new level of understanding about family, friendships, love, and authority.**

  Early adolescents come to understand the depth and complexity of personal re-lationships (Havinghurst, 1976; Kellough & Kellough, 1999). They realize how im-portant their families are to them. Their new cognitive abilities allow them to be reflective and self-evaluative about their relationships with people and also to have very intense feelings about those relationships. They are often curious about the details of their teachers' families and personal lives.

• **Early adolescents are idealistic.**

The onset of abstract thinking brings with it the ability to imagine possibilities for the future. Not only do early adolescents have strong opinions about the way the world ought to be, but their new cognitive abilities allow them to create a picture of the ideal in their mind (Kellough & Kellough, 1999). When they are critical of the way the school is run, the way a store operates, or the way a product is made, they are comparing it to the ideal they have created. This idealism is often in direct conflict with adult realism, but when confronted with logic, early adolescent idealism is often unswayed. Early adolescent idealism is evident in these students' criticism of adults for not being perfect, or at least not being the ideal adult they have conceptualized in their minds (the ideal adult they plan to become, of course) (Stevenson, 2002). Criticism is the early adolescent's way of formalizing his or her own ideals about the people and the world around them.

STUDENT'S VOICE

About Concrete Thinkers

"I wish teachers knew a little more about how we think. It would help them make assignments and help them understand us."

Juan, eighth grade

What Are the Implications of Intellectual Development for Instruction?

• **Use concrete hands-on methods whenever possible**.

Early adolescents learn best when they can see, touch, smell, or taste objects (Havinghurst, 1976; Storz & Nestor, 2003). Middle school teachers should illustrate concepts visually whenever possible, by outlining, webbing, or using pictures or other visual props (George & Alexander, 2003; Gross, 2002). (One teacher began a lesson on human body systems with a calf's brain on his desk.) Components or examples of concepts can be represented on cards that students can organize or use to play card games. Students can role-play relationships between concepts or steps in a process. For example, a health teacher explained the circulatory system by setting up stations around the classroom for each stop blood makes along its path. Students followed the path the blood would follow and exchanged colored Ping-Pong balls that represented oxygen and carbon dioxide molecules. A math teacher taught graphing by using masking tape on the floor for the horizontal and vertical axis and using students as points on the graph.

- **Use analogies—use the known to teach the unknown.**

Constructivist learning theory and recent brain research confirm that learning takes place when students connect new ideas to previous knowledge (Fuhler, 2003; Havinghurst, 1976). Analogies allow students to connect new concepts and relationships to concepts with which they are already familiar. Analogies use the known to explain the unknown. A language arts teacher might use song lyrics to illustrate the structures of poetry or an episode of a television show to explain elements of fiction. Conflicts between people can be used to illustrate conflicts between nations. A social studies teacher started class with a question on the board: "How do you clean a driveway?" He used the concept of spraying a driveway with a hose to discuss the topic of rivers and tributaries. Students can be also introduced to concepts and then be asked to come up with their own analogies.

- **Discuss and clarify abstract concepts.**

Even though early adolescents have difficulty understanding abstract concepts, they grow cognitively through discussions of them. Middle school teachers should begin by using what students already know and clarify concepts with familiar examples or analogies (Fuhler, 2003; George et al., 1998). It is helpful to build discussions around student questions about the concept, to capitalize on curiosity, and to use real-life simulations whenever possible (Storz & Nestor, 2003). Encouraging students to share their opinions can help teachers gauge the level of student understanding and help to clear up misconceptions.

- **Provide plenty of opportunities for success.**

To maximize success, it is helpful to give choices in assignments, to give ungraded feedback, and to encourage self-evaluation (Stevenson, 2002). It is also helpful to arrange class schedules so that extra time is available for students who need it (Bell, 2003). Many teachers use catch-up days, peer tutors, or after-school help sessions to assure that students do not fall too far behind.

- **Make it clear that nonparticipation is not an option.**

Success becomes possible when teachers *expect* participation. Teachers should clarify to students that they are expected to attempt all learning tasks but that help will be available if the task is too hard (Bell, 2003). Allowing students to refuse to work enables the defense mechanism of "I could do it if I wanted to" and enables academic failure (Vatterott, 1999). When teachers insist that everyone participate, it becomes harder for students to fail. Teachers should also be watchful for learner frustration and allow students to take a break when frustrated. That may mean switching activities temporarily, or even allowing a specific student to opt out of a specific subject for a day or two. This helps students understand how adults deal with frustrating learning experiences throughout their lives.

✦ PATTERNS OF DIVERSITY IN EARLY ADOLESCENT LEARNING PREFERENCES

Differences in Learning Style

In addition to diversity in the development of abstract thought, early adolescents differ widely in their approach to learning (George & Alexander, 2003; Manning & Bucher, 2001). There are many ways those differences can be described. **Learning style** is the predominant style or method by which a student learns best (Dunn & Dunn, 1978). Research on learning styles, multiple intelligences, field dependence/field independence, and brain research have shown that students have a profile for the way they learn best (Keefe & Jenkins, 2002). Dunn and Dunn's research (1978) on learning styles indicates that students differ in four key dimensions: environment, emotional support, sociological composition, and personal/physical elements. Components of the dimensions are listed in Table 2.4.

Environmental differences included preferences for soft or bright lighting, quiet or noise, and formal or informal seating. In the area of emotional support, students differ in their ability to be self-directed, with some students needing more support and structure than others (Johnston, 1994). Sociologically, some students prefer to learn alone, some prefer learning in groups, and others prefer learning from an adult (Sousa, 1998). Learning modality preferences may be auditory, visual, tactile, or kinesthetic (learning hands on or with bodily movement). Some students learn better in the morning and some in the afternoon; some students need to move more often than others (Jensen, 2000; Sousa, 1998). Numerous studies have found that student achievement increases when teaching methods match their learning styles (Armstrong, 1994; Dunn, Beaudry, & Klavas, 1989).

Gardner's (1983, 1999) **theory of multiple intelligences** indicates that people show an inclination to develop strengths in at least seven different "intelligences": Linguistic, logical-mathematical, spatial, bodily-kinesthetic, musical, interpersonal, intrapersonal. Gardner has recently added two more intelligences—naturalistic and existential—but currently they are not as widely accepted as the original seven. Students who have strong tendencies in specific intelligences, similar to learning styles, prefer specific kinds of learning tasks (Armstrong, 1994; Manning & Bucher, 2001; Stevenson, 2002). A summary of those preferences is shown in Table 2.5.

Students also differ in their tendency to be either field-dependent or field-independent learners. Field-dependent learners perceive whole patterns rather than parts, tend to be people-oriented, and to work well in groups. Field-independent learners are more analytical, perceive separate parts of a whole, are task-oriented, and enjoy working alone. Research shows that many at-risk students, as many as 85 percent in one study, learn in a field-dependent modality (Johnston, 1994). That style is mismatched to traditional instruction, which is often predominantly field-independent. See Table 2.6 for characteristics of field-dependent and field-independent learners.

TABLE 2.4

Dunn and Dunn's Learning Styles

Dimension	Elements
Environment	Sound Light Temperature Seating design
Emotional support	Motivational support Persistence Structure Individual responsibility
Sociological support	Individual Pairs or teams Adult Varied
Personal/physical	Modality (visual, auditory, tactile, or kinesthetic) Time Mobility

Source: Dunn & Dunn, 1978.

Students with Special Needs

An inattention to individual learning differences is especially evident in the experiences of students with special needs. How they differ in learning style from their academically successful peers may be what contributes most to their academic problems (Dunn et al., 1989; Johnston, 1994). Students with special needs are likely to have learning styles or preferences that are different from those of the more successful learners in your classroom. For instance, a study of K–12 modality preferences showed that only 19 percent of all K–12 learners learned best auditorily (an overused instructional strategy), 46 percent learned best visually (a strategy sometimes used), and 35 percent learned best kinesthetically—hands on or through bodily movement (an underused strategy) (Sousa, 1998). Research on *students with special needs* has estimated that from *40 percent to 70 percent* of students with special needs are *kinesthetic* learners (Sousa, 1998). When those preferences are added to tendencies of field dependence and other characteristics of certain learning styles and are clustered within an individual student, what emerges is a profile of a learner who is out of sync with the traditional classroom environment (Johnston, 1994):

> Students who were less motivated than their classmates and who preferred
> distracters (music, low illumination, informal or casual seating, peers rather than
> alone or with the teacher, tactile rather than auditory or visual instructional
> resources) scored right-hemisphere significantly more often than left-hemisphere.
> . . . Left-hemisphere youngsters in grades 5–12 preferred a conventional formal

TABLE 2.5

Summary of the "Seven Ways of Teaching"

Student Intelligence	Preferred Teaching Activity	Preferred Method of Learning
Linguistic	Lectures, discussions, Word games, storytelling, Choral reading Journal writing	Read about it Write about it Talk about it Listen to it
Logical-mathematical	Brain teasers Problem solving Science experiments	Quantify it Think critically about it Conceptualize it
Spatial	Visual presentations Art activities Imagination games Mind-mapping Metaphor Visualization	See it Draw it Visualize it Color it Mind-map it
Bodily-kinesthetic	Hands-on learning Drama Dance Sports that teach Tactile activities Relaxation Exercises	Build it Act it out Touch it Get a "gut feeling" Dance it
Musical	Superlearning Rapping Songs that teach	Sing it Rap it Listen to it
Interpersonal	Cooperative learning Peer tutoring Community involvement Social gatherings Simulations	Teach it Collaborate on it Interact with Respect to it

Intrapersonal	Individualized instruction
	Independent study
	Options in course of study
	Self-esteem building
		Connect it to your personal
		   life
		Make choices with regard
		   to it

Source: Armstrong, 2000.

classroom seating design, more structure, less intake, and visual rather than tactile or kinesthetic resources during learning significantly more often that their right-preferred classmates. (Dunn et al., 1989, p. 51)

Knowledge of differences in learning styles and multiple intelligences is not meant to be applied in an exact fashion—teachers should not necessarily design

TABLE 2.6

Field-Dependent and Field-Independent Learning Preferences

Learner Preference	Field Dependent	Field Independent
Setting	Cooperative, loose structure, informal	Formal, structured, individual
Focus	Concepts, general principles	Information Details
Social	Work together to benefit group	Work alone Everyone for himself or herself
Reward	For effort Group contribution Common good	For outcome Quality of completed product on predetermined standards
Success	Helping group Getting group approval	Meeting standard Getting approval of authority

Source: Johnston, 1994.

seven different projects, one for each intelligence, or try to accommodate every learner preference individually (Gardner, 1999). This information is meant to *sensitize* teachers to the vast range of differences in learner preferences and learner behavior (Stevenson, 2002). This information should discourage teachers from judging certain learners to be superior based on their preferred mode of learning (Armstrong, 1993). The freedom, flexibility, and choices inherent in student-focused instruction accommodate many differences in learners and therefore facilitate success for more learners (Levine, 2003).

The Question of Attention Deficit Disorder among Middle School Students

Distinctive as America's number one childhood psychiatric disorder, attention deficit/hyperactivity disorder (ADHD) supposedly affects from 3 percent to 5 percent of the school-age population (yet in some schools 10 percent to 15 percent of students are medicated for it) (Hancock, 1996; Reif, 1993). **ADHD** is a syndrome of behaviors such as inattention, hyperactivity, and impulsivity that interfere with classroom learning (Armstrong, 1997). When the syndrome occurs without hyperactivity, it is referred to **ADD** (Reif, 1993). Most sources use the two terms interchangeably. The number of children being medicated with the stimulant drug Ritalin for ADHD has more than tripled since 1981. The rate of Ritalin use in the United States is at least five times higher than in the rest of the world (Hancock, 1996).

Recent concerns by pediatricians that Ritalin is being overprescribed have led to a closer look at the problem of ADHD (Hancock, 1996). Diagnosis is a guess at best. There is no blood test or brain scan to prove that a child has ADHD. The diagnosis is made by looking at the *frequency and intensity* of behaviors such as inattention, hyperactivity, and impulsivity (Armstrong, 1997). (A typical ADHD checklist is shown in Table 2.7).

ADHD can be severe in some children, and medication may be necessary for those children to function in school. Many children diagnosed with ADHD are simply physically active, high-energy children (Armstrong, 1997; Reif, 1993). Given the checklist in Table 2.7, however, *many* middle school students could be diagnosed ADHD! According to most experts, ADHD usually emerges early in a child's life, with the child showing definite tendencies by the age of six. Children with no previous problems in school do not typically *develop* ADHD in middle school (Levine, 2003). If an early adolescent suddenly *seems* to have ADHD, it's probably a result of testosterone or other hormones and not necessarily a lifelong problem.

Some symptoms of ADHD that are evident in middle students can be exacerbated by the learning environment or the learning task. In *The Myth of the A.D.D. Child* (1997), Thomas Armstrong challenges the ease at which high-energy children are diagnosed and points to the mismatch of student and classroom practices:

> They appear to be indistinguishable from so-called normals when they are in classrooms or other learning environments where children can choose their learning activities and pace themselves through those experiences . . . perhaps most significantly, children labeled A.D.D. behave and attend quite normally

TABLE 2.7

American Psychiatric Association ADHD Checklist

Pays little attention to details; makes careless mistakes	Has short attention span
Does not listen when spoken to directly	Does not follow instructions; fails to finish tasks
Has difficulty organizing tasks	Avoids tasks that require sustained mental effort
Loses things	Is easily distracted
Is forgetful in daily activities	Fidgets; squirms in seat
Leaves seat in classroom when remaining in seat is expected	Runs about or climbs excessively at inappropriate times
Has difficulty playing quietly	Acts as if "driven by a motor"
Talks excessively	Blurts out answers before questions are completed

Source: Hancock, 1996.

when they are involved in activities that *interest* them, that are *novel* in some way, or that involve high levels of *stimulation*. (p. 16)

Teachers are *not* qualified to diagnose ADHD based solely on classroom experience. ADHD should be diagnosed by a qualified doctor, preferably a neurologist, and only after obtaining a detailed history of the child (Armstrong, 1997). The use of high-interest student-focused activities (addressed throughout this book) and classroom practices that respect the physical needs of active early adolescents (addressed earlier in this chapter) can significantly reduce attentional problems of many middle school students (Reif, 1993; Storz & Nestor, 2003).

What Are the Implications of Individual Learning Styles for Instruction?

The great diversity in learning styles and preferences among middle level students has additional implications for instruction beyond those for early adolescent cognitive development. In addition to the use of concrete teaching methods, teachers must also be mindful of the diversity of learning needs in their classroom (Bell, 2003; Manning & Bucher, 2001). Teachers need to *do more* so students can *learn more* (Jensen, 2000; Levine, 2003). When introducing new material, they need to provide learners with overviews as well as step-by-step instructions. They should show as much information visually as possible and should alternate between showing the big picture and showing the details (Bell, 2003). A diverse group of learners requires differentiation of instructional tasks, which provides for learner choices (Kellough & Kellough, 1999; Levine, 2003). For ADHD students and other students with special needs, the case for student-focused instructional methods becomes all the more compelling (Armstrong, 1997; Reif, 1993).

Summary

Given the dramatic changes of puberty the picture of today's early adolescent is a complex one. As a group, these students are incredibly diverse. Their physical development results in much restlessness and insecurity. Intellectually, they often struggle to think abstractly and to solve problems. They exhibit a variety of learning styles, some of which may be out of sync with traditional teacher-focused methods. This is especially common for students with special needs.

The process of puberty sets in motion a series of dramatic physical, social, emotional, and intellectual changes in early adolescents that result in unique physical, intellectual, emotional, and social needs. Those needs are so prominent that when teachers fail to address them, early adolescents are handicapped as learners. This chapter discussed the physical and intellectual changes and needs of early adolescents. Chapter 3 will discuss the emotional and social changes and needs of early adolescents.

KEY TERMS

attention deficit disorder (ADD)
attention deficit hyperactivity disorder
  (ADHD)

learning style
puberty
theory of multiple intelligences

APPLICATION ACTIVITIES

1. Visit a middle school during lunch or passing time where you can observe a large number of students. Do clothes indicate which students belong to which social group? Describe at least two different styles of clothes that reflect two different social groups.

2. Pick three of the abstract concepts shown in Figure 2.1. Brainstorm some ideas for how those concepts could be presented to learners in a hands-on manner. Think of some real-life analogies that could be useful to teach those concepts (such as a factory or a bakery for photosynthesis).

3. Look at the preferred methods of learning in Table 2.5. Which box best describes your preferred method of learning? Which methods of learning would you least prefer?

CHAPTER 3

UNDERSTANDING MIDDLE LEVEL LEARNERS—EMOTIONAL AND SOCIAL DEVELOPMENT

❖ **Patterns of Emotional and Social Development during Puberty**

Two Important Developmental Tasks

Emotional Characteristics of Early Adolescents

Social Characteristics of Early Adolescents

The Development of Sexuality

What Are the Implications of Social and Emotional Development for Instruction?

❖ **Impact of Culture on the Process of Early Adolescent Development**

Social Forces That Make Adolescence More Challenging Today Than in Previous Generations

Special Risks for Today's Early Adolescents

→ INTRODUCTION

Chapter 2 discussed the physical and intellectual changes of puberty. Teaching early adolescents also requires an understanding of the importance of the emotional and social changes that occur during puberty. How well early adolescents negotiate this sometimes stormy period of their life will influence who they will become, what they will become, and how they will contribute to the world (Carnegie Council on Adolescent Development, 1996; Havinghurst, 1976). When we understand middle level learners, we become aware of the intensity of their physical, emotional, and social needs and appreciate the powerfulness of those needs in creating meaningful learning opportunities (Jobe, 2003; Stevenson, 2002; Taylor & Lorimer, 2003). When we understand the fragility of early adolescents, we understand why student-focused instruction represents the most developmentally appropriate strategies for middle level learners (Vatterott, 1999).

As with their physical and intellectual changes, early adolescents exhibit a great deal of diversity in their emotional and social development (Manning, 1993). Some students are quite childlike in their leisure interests and interactions with others, yet other students seem quite precocious. Early adolescents' level of intellectual development influences their ability to process feelings and to solve social problems (Havinghurst, 1976; Milgram, 1992). **The purposes of this chapter are to help you**

- appreciate the scope and diversity of the emotional and social changes of early adolescence.
- appreciate the challenges that the changes of puberty bring to students with special needs.
- understand the relationship between early adolescent needs and early adolescent behavior.
- understand the necessity of adapting instructional practices to the needs of early adolescents.
- become aware of the critical impact of culture on the process of early adolescent development.

Essential Questions

After reading and completing the activities in this chapter, you should be able to answer the following questions:

1. What changes do early adolescents experience in their emotional and social development?
2. How do individuals differ in their emotional and social development?
3. What typical behaviors result from the emotional and social changes of puberty?
4. What are the instructional implications of the emotional and social changes of puberty?
5. What social forces in our culture hinder the process of early adolescent development?

✦ PATTERNS OF EMOTIONAL AND SOCIAL DEVELOPMENT DURING PUBERTY

Two Important Developmental Tasks

Emotionally and socially, early adolescents are faced with two developmental tasks: determining their identity and developing a sense of competence (Havinghurst, 1976). Erikson (1963) defined these struggles as **identity versus role confusion** (the need to define oneself and to develop appropriate roles) and **industry versus inferiority** (the need for competence and achievement) (Gross, 2002). These two issues and the strong desire to resolve them drive most of the social and emotional changes that early adolescents experience (Vatterott, 1999).

The Development of Competence

Early adolescents' need to develop a sense of competence and achievement is related to their search for identity and the development of a positive self-image (Erikson, 1963; Gross, 2002; Havinghurst, 1976). In the development of competence and achievement, early adolescents ask, "Am I a good person?" "What am I good at?" (Scales, 1991). To help them answer these questions, middle level students need opportunities to identify and solve problems, complete tasks, and set and reach goals (Sagor, 2002). They need to have knowledge about the world around them in order to make sense of it. This curiosity is evident in early adolescents' tendency to exhibit intense interest in new activities that often wanes quickly (Manning, 1993). Parents of early adolescents have learned not to invest too much money in new hobbies that may be all-consuming for a few months and then are never looked at again.

According to Scales (1991), early adolescents need to discover "what they are good at" and be recognized for it. That development of competence is strongly compromised when students are not academically successful. After all, school is their job at this stage in their life. The drive for competence is very strong in early adolescents ("I *will* be good at *something!*") (NMSA, 2001c). When early adolescents cannot find competence in academics, they *will* discover what they are good at (Sagor, 2002; Vatterott, 1999). If we are lucky, students who are not good at academics will discover they are good at sports, music, or working with computers. Less fortunate students will develop competence by being good at disrupting class, getting in trouble, having sex, selling drugs, or committing crimes. Needs for competence and achievement can be facilitated by giving students responsibility within the classroom and through curricular, instructional, and assessment designs that provide for academic success (addressed in the next several chapters) (Strahan, Smith, McElrath, & Toole, 2001). A sense of competence and achievement is a critical component of an early adolescent's personal and social identity (NMSA, 2001b, 2003b; Vatterott, 1999).

The Search for Identity

The second important developmental task of early adolescence is the search for identity (NMSA, 2001a; Mandeville & Radcliffe, 2002). Identity is the central theme of adolescence. In resolving the conflict of identity and role confusion, the young adolescent struggles to define not only his or her personal identity (Who am I?), but also his or her social identity (How do others perceive me?) (Havinghurst, 1976; McDaniel, Necochea, Rios, Stowell, & Kritzer, 2001; Stevenson, 2002). The search for personal identity could best be described as the search for a unique sense of self, independent of family (George & Alexander, 2003). Early adolescents' need to be their own people often causes them to be critical of and feel embarrassed by their families and to try to distance themselves from their family socially (Inlay, 2005). In spite of these impulses, however, most early adolescents attempt to reconcile their new identity with their family identity, simultaneously seeking both independence and acceptance from their family (Kellough & Kellough, 1999; Vatterott, 1999). Early adolescents may appear to be distant from their families, but in reality, confidential surveys show that approval from their families and time spent with their families are very important to this group. Their quest for unique identities produces many of the emotional characteristics that cause them to be sensitive and unpredictable (Kellough & Kellough, 1999; Stevenson, 2002).

Emotional Characteristics of Early Adolescents

- **Early adolescents experience mood swings.**

The term *rollercoaster emotions* has been used to describe the emotional states of early adolescents (Inlay, 2005). They may go from feeling wildly happy to being very upset within a few hours, due partly to erratic hormonal surges and partly because, in the words of an early adolescent, "it's tough figuring all this out" (George & Alexander, 2003; Vatterott, 1999). The emotional and social life of middle school is a high-stakes game and early adolescents' egos are what's at stake. Early adolescents make many decisions about their day-to-day lives while at the same time making many mistakes. Their emotional reactions may seem out of proportion to the situation to which they're reacting (Kellough & Kellough, 1999; Milgram, 1992). The feelings they experience are intense and sometimes overwhelming, leading to some inconsistencies in emotional control and some childlike regressions. The intensity of emotions at this age may explain why early adolescents have a penchant for melodrama (Manning & Bucher, 2001; Price, 2005).

- **Early adolescents are preoccupied with their own development.**

The search for identity produces a strong **egocentrism**, or preoccupation with self (Elkind, 1981; Manning & Bucher, 2001). Early adolescents spend a considerable amount of time focused on and thinking about the dramatic changes that are taking place in their bodies and their lives (McDaniel et al., 2001). This often makes them insensitive to the concerns of others. This egocentrism leads to the phenomenon David Elkind (1981) calls the **imaginary audience**. Because early adolescents are so concerned and focused on themselves, they believe everyone else is as concerned about them as they are (Kellough & Kellough, 1999; Stevenson, 2002). In public they feel as if they are continually under scrutiny and are fearful of being criticized. This belief sometimes reveals itself in a form of paranoia—as when a boy or girl walks by a group of people who are laughing and is sure they are laughing at him or her (Milgram, 1992; Vatterott, 1999).

- **Early adolescents suffer from fragile self-esteem.**

Unsure of their identities and how others are reacting to them, early adolescents suffer from frequent bouts of negative self-esteem (George & Alexander, 2003; Havinghurst, 1976). In their awkward journey to identity, they make some mistakes and are often confused about what to do. Their fragile self-esteem makes them hypersensitive to criticism. They may perceive criticism when none was intended and their feelings can be easily hurt. Self-esteem issues often cause early adolescents to seek attention as a way of feeling validated and respected or feeling a sense of worth (Manning & Bucher, 2001; Vatterott, 1999). Early adolescents need to be noticed and to be heard.

- **Early adolescents want to be adult but also long for childhood.**

Adulthood brings many privileges but also much anxiety. Early adolescents often aren't sure they are ready for adult responsibilities and enjoy the retreat to the securities of childhood. This confusion causes what some people call *fence straddling*, going back and forth from mature adult behaviors to childish behaviors (Kellough & Kellough, 1999; Milgram, 1992).

> A middle level student might still love his teddy bear but want his own room. She may sit on her dad's lap but just die if he held her hand in public. . . . She might demand a ride to school because it is raining but asked to be dropped off a block away from the main entrance before she is seen with a parent. He may cry in his bedroom then mock his sister for crying. (Milgram, 1992, p. 21)

As their sense of self is emerging as unique and separate from others, early adolescents try on different social roles (Manning & Bucher, 2001). They may fantasize, daydream, or rehearse different roles in their imagination (Stevenson, 2002). They enjoy experiencing different roles vicariously through movies, television shows, and books. One day they may choose to be quiet and shy, and on another day, loud and obnoxious (Kellough & Kellough, 1999; Vatterott, 1999). They often behave in certain ways for the sole purpose of seeing how it feels and what reactions the behavior brings from others. This *role experimentation* is consistent with their emerging cognitive abilities to experiment, analyze, and draw conclusions (Havinghurst, 1976; Manning, 1993).

STUDENTS' VOICES

About Identity Versus Role Confusion

"The hardest thing about being this age is that you are a little different every day. Your personality changes. You also change physically."

Chad, eighth grade

"The hardest thing is that I am sort of in between phases of my life. I'm not a teenager, but I'm not a child either."

Tamika, sixth grade

Social Characteristics of Early Adolescents

In their search for identity, early adolescents must define not only their personal identity (Who am I?) but their social identity as well (What groups define me? What is my purpose in the world?) (Havinghurst, 1976). They need to be accepted as the unique people they are, yet they also need to be accepted by and belong to a group (McDaniel et al., 2001; Stevenson, 2002).

- **Early adolescents search for sophistication.**

    With early adolescents' development of identity also comes a search for sophistication ("How do adults act? What kind of adult do I want to be?") (Elkind, 1961; Van Hoose, Strahan, & L'Esperance, 2001). In this search, early adolescents try to integrate role model ideals into their own sense of self and their own unique value system to project the image of the ideal adult they want to be (McDaniel et al., 2001). In order to do this, they need to spend time with adults other than their parents (Pitton, 2001). They need to practice relating to adults *as adults* to find their own sense of adult sophistication (Powell, 2001). Early adolescents could be said to be *socially naïve.* They are unfamiliar with exactly how adults relate to each other and how they act in certain situations (George, Lawrence, & Bushnell, 1998). A *pseudosophistication* is often obvious when early adolescents attempt to act adult and to use adult vocabulary and mannerisms (Elkind, 1961). Note the obvious pseudosophistication in the student's choice of words and use of lengthy sentences in the following quote.

Student's Voice

An Example of Pseudosophistication

"I wish teachers would remember to open up their classrooms by providing tangible activities to involve students our age. By doing this, my studies would improve greatly because it's easier to learn when you don't have to sit so long, and do things other than just studying out of books."

Mohammed, eighth grade

When teachers interact with middle school students as adults, they help them to develop social graces. One-on-one small talk with students in the hall or during lunch gives early adolescents the chance to practice casual adult conversation (Vatterott, 1999). When teachers initiate conversation by asking about a student's weekend or if he or she watched the big game on television last night, they model the art of polite conversation that early adolescents need to practice (Van Hoose et al., 2001). When a middle school student engages a teacher in conversation, it is a way of practicing an important social skill. It may seem trivial to adults, but such casual conversations are very affirming to early adolescents and very necessary for their social development (Strahan et al., 2001; Powell, 2001).

Think back to when you were an early adolescent. Who do you remember practicing the art of conversation with—teachers, club sponsors, aunts and uncles, your friends' parents? Where do you remember those conversations taking place?

- **Early adolescents reconstruct their relationships with adults.**

In their search for social identity, early adolescents try to modify their relationships with adults (Havinghurst, 1976; Manning & Bucher, 2001). They begin to move their allegiance from adults to peers, first by gaining independence from their parents (Inlay, 2005), and second by renegotiating their relationships with other adults to be less subordinate and more equal (Havinghurst, 1976; Kellough & Kellough, 1999). Early adolescents realize that adults are not perfect, that they have faults. They waste no time in finding adults' faults and are quick to point them out. Relationships with adults, including their parents, are no longer based on hero worship—adults have to *earn* respect now (Milgram, 1992). Teachers are no longer automatically respected because of their authority—students decide whether they are *worthy* of respect. At the same time, they are eager to establish themselves as adults and they strongly desire the approval of adults, especially their parents and other adults to whom they feel close (Kellough & Kellough, 1999).

This whole process changes how early adolescents view authority (Havinghurst, 1976; Manning & Bucher, 2001). If they ever had blind allegiance to authority, it is fading fast. They question the right of people in authority to make the rules and they have a strong sense of justice (Kellough & Kellough, 1999). They will become quite indignant when they feel they have been treated unfairly. Early adolescents frequently believe that people in positions of authority are treating them unfairly because their concept of fairness and justice is so concrete, so black and white (Havinghurst, 1976; Stevenson, 2002). Understanding the gray areas is hard for them, but it is an important lesson for them to learn. When students believe that someone in authority has treated them unfairly, it is important to listen to their concerns (Mendes, 2003). In the real world, authority will be unfair at times, and early adolescents need to understand how adults seek retribution in the real world when they believe they have been treated unfairly. An appeal process should exist that allows students to air their concerns about how they have been treated. In many middle schools, students have been told they may meet with the assistant principal if they believe that a teacher or another adult has treated them unfairly. In most cases, few students actually take advantage of the privilege, but the fact that such appeals are available helps to maintain a positive relationship between students and authority in the school.

- **Early adolescents place a high priority on friends and social achievements.**

As early adolescents detach from adults, they become increasingly dependent on peer group approval (Manning & Bucher, 2001; George et al., 1998). They place

Friendships play an important role in self-esteem.

an extraordinary emphasis on friends and social achievements, as if they realize this is one of the very important tasks of adolescence (Kellough & Kellough, 1999; Scales, 1999). They realize that part of being a competent adult is having friends and the approval of a social group (Havinghurst, 1976). Self-esteem is built by their interactions with others—they need the approval of peers but also the approval of adults. They can become very anxious about their social interactions—it's as if every event redefines their self-worth. Their fragile self-image requires frequent social feedback (Daniels, 2005). Early adolescents tend to dwell on social errors to evaluate how much damage was done to their social image (Milgram, 1992).

STUDENTS' VOICES

About Friends

"Another hard thing is 'fitting in.' Everyone wants to feel like they belong but since we're just starting to figure out who we really are it's hard to find out where we belong."

Kate, seventh grade

"I worry most about friends. I always worry whether they're mad at me or they don't want to be friends with me."

Latisha, eighth grade

"I think the hardest thing about being my age is peer pressure. Thinking about what people think about ourselves."

Karen, eighth grade

- **Early adolescents are susceptible to peer pressure.**

Early adolescents' strong need for peer acceptance makes them vulnerable to peer pressure, risk taking, and challenging authority (George & Alexander, 2003). Just as early adolescents try on roles, they also try on friends. They may switch their allegiance from one clique to another frequently, and friendships are fickle (Stevenson, 2002). Best friends today could be enemies tomorrow and best friends again two days later. The creation of a caring community within the classroom and team provides a healthy, wholesome way for young adolescents to form friendships (Pitton, 2001; Scales, 1999; Stevenson, 2002). An early adolescent's identification with a group, roles in society, and acceptance by others all serve to further define his or her individual identity (George & Alexander, 2003). Social identity is influenced by needs for love and belonging, beyond what family can provide (Sagor, 2002; Vatterott, 1999). Acceptance ("people like me just the way I am") and membership ("I'm part of a group, we are like a family") are critical to the development of identity and a positive self-concept in young adolescents (Kellough & Kellough, 1999). It is through the integration of the many influences in their lives—peers, family, and other adults—that young adolescents integrate their personal identity with a social identity (Vatterott, 1999).

REFLECTIVE QUESTION

What do you remember about the social groups in school during your early adolescence? What group did you belong to? What group did you want to belong to?

The Development of Sexuality

The development of sexuality creates an added dimension in the early adolescent's relationships with the opposite sex. Personal identity is not complete without a sexual identity—adopting an appropriate sex role is another major developmental task for early adolescents (Havinghurst, 1976; George & Alexander, 2003). Sex role includes not only how a man or woman dresses and behaves, but also what their hobbies and interests are and how they interact with and what kind of relationships they have with the opposite sex. Finding comfort in an appropriate sex role is a complicated task for today's early adolescent. Sex roles for men and women are not as clear-cut as they used to be. Both sexes have more options, yet it seems as though there is always someone who will disapprove of the choices that early adolescents make (NMSA, 2003b). As they experiment with different hobbies and interests, early adolescents observe closely the reactions of adults and peers about the appropriateness of their choices. In this sense, girls have a much wider range of acceptable choices than boys do. How much disapproval will a girl sense if she decides to pursue sports or aspire to be a scientist? How much disapproval will a boy sense if he pursues dance or gardening as a hobby? It is not surprising that many early adolescents retreat to the security of traditional sex roles.

As an extension of their experimentation with *social* roles, both boys and girls try on different *sexual* roles—being assertive or submissive, flirting or being shy (Scales, 1991, 1999). It is not uncommon for a middle school girl to be sweet and demure one day and the next day to play the role of a sexy vamp. As they experiment, early adolescents learn from peer and adult reactions to their behavior (NMSA, 2003b). As they try to understand the role sexuality plays in everyday life, girls especially learn that sex is power.

Same-sex friendships are the norm at this age (Stevenson, 2002). Since early adolescents are preoccupied with discovering their own identity, it's logical that many of them have no desire to deal with the opposite sex yet (Van Hoose et al., 2001). When pushed by adults or peers into dating or opposite sex relationships, early adolescents often wind up placing too much importance on the relationship as an achievement and investing too much self-esteem in the outcome. Crushes on members of the opposite sex (peers or adults) are common and often represent the opposite sex ideal to an early adolescent (Steinberg & Levine, 1997). Same-sex crushes are also common, not in the sexual sense but because the person represents an ideal—exactly the kind of man or woman, boy or girl, that the early adolescent wants to be. Early adolescents often feel guilty about same-sex crushes, not realizing that it is more about ideal identities than it is about sex (Steinberg & Levine, 1997).

The development of sexuality brings with it different issues for boys and girls (Havinghurst, 1976). For girls, this is a time of anticipation about menstruation, a fascination with the idea that she now has the potential to create and carry life in her body (Omvig, 2000). At the same time this produces a feeling of vulnerability now that she *can* become pregnant. Faulty information about how pregnancy occurs causes early adolescent girls much anxiety. They may fear they are pregnant from some innocent encounter, simply due to a lack of accurate knowledge about how pregnancy occurs (Omvig, 2000). On the other hand, sexually active girls can become pregnant and not realize it for months. Stories of early adolescent girls going into labor and not realizing they are pregnant, incredulous as it sounds, are perfectly believable. Early adolescent girls can go six months between periods (Van Hoose et al., 2001). Add to that fact a rapidly changing body (breasts getting larger, hips widening), and the relatively low birth weight of babies born to young girls, and the scenario becomes credible.

Unfortunately, some girls also see motherhood as the path to identity and competence ("I may not be good at other things but I can be good at being a mom" or "A baby is someone who will love me unconditionally"). Early adolescent girls who are not academically successful and who have few positive social relationships seem to be at greatest risk for early sexual involvement and pregnancy (Omvig, 2000).

For boys, the development of sexuality brings a testosterone overload, which triggers increased aggression and the need for physical release. Frequent erections, nocturnal emissions, and sexual thoughts can bring about feelings of being out of control sexually (Milgram, 1992). The abundance of testosterone during puberty is evident in an increase in horseplay, fighting, and physical risk taking (Lacayo, 2000).

Gay and lesbian children encounter special problems in the development of their sexuality (Manning & Bucher, 2001). It is not uncommon for early adolescents, both heterosexual and homosexual, to experiment with members of the same sex. Such experimentation does not *make* a child gay (Steinberg & Levine, 1997). A number of studies indicate that there is a genetic basis for homosexuality (Frieman, O'Hara, & Settle, 1996). Many adult homosexuals acknowledge that they knew their sexual orientation at a young age, while others did not come to know until their adolescence or adulthood (Steinberg & Levine, 1997). Many gay and lesbian students are confused about what to do about their sexuality, due to conflicting cultural messages (Kantrowitz & Wingert, 1999). Homosexuality, once in the closet, is increasingly being accepted, both socially and legally (Cloud, 2005). On one hand, *tolerance* of homosexuality has increased. On the other hand, so has *intolerance*. Positive role models now exist for homosexual children, but they also see much hatred and prejudice (Manning & Bucher, 2001). Whether a gay or lesbian child chooses to be open about his or her sexuality or to keep it secret, early adolescence is a difficult time. These children need as much affirmation and support as possible (Cloud, 2005; Steinberg & Levine, 1997).

What Are the Implications of Social and Emotional Development for Instruction?

- **Make the social needs of early adolescents a high priority in the classroom.**

Middle school students have a very strong developmental need for socializing and positive social feedback (NMSA, 2001; O'Steen, Cuper, Spires, Beal & Pope, 2002). Early adolescents *will* find a way to get those social needs met (Sagor, 2002). Teachers who fail to recognize the importance of social needs and to plan for them are often frustrated by excessive student talking, note passing, and socializing (Milgram, 1992). Teachers who incorporate conversation, group assignments, and other social opportunities into their classroom activities have fewer problems with excessive student talking and students socializing at inappropriate times (Sprenger, 2005; Wolk, 2003).

STUDENTS' VOICES

About Social Needs

"I wish they [teachers] knew how we like to have fun and be with friends more. Actually I think they know. If they knew they might let us talk more and work with partners."

Ling, eighth grade

"I wish teachers would realize that it's really hard not to talk in class if you have some friends in that class too. I try not to talk, but it is really hard for me!"

Samantha, seventh grade

- **Make the personal relationship between the teacher and student a high priority.**

Students are eager to interact with adults on an equal social plane (practicing to be adults) (Kellough & Kellough, 1999). Teachers should take a few minutes each day to interact with students as they would with other adults—engage in small talk, ask them about their lives, or talk about school or community events (Powell, 2001; Strahan, Smith, McElruth, & Toole, 2001; Wolk, 2003). When friction develops between students and teachers, repair of the teacher-student relationship should be a priority—much as if there were a problem with a coworker. If the teacher-student relationship is very strained, the student and the teacher may benefit from a break from each other for a day. Students should also have the opportunity to interact with adults outside of class through clubs or other planned activities (NMSA, 2001; O'Steen et al., 2002; Hoffman & Levak, 2003). The teacher-student relationship will be discussed in detail in Chapter 4.

TEACHER'S VOICE

About the Personal Relationship between Teacher and Student

"There are kids, you can tell when they walk in, just from body English, facial expressions that they're having a bad day. Those are things you've got to pick up. This one girl walked in yesterday and she had that black cloud over her head, she was having a bad day. Somebody had stolen her shoe at lunch and then hid it, which sounds like a goofy thing, but she was *furious* about it. And so you just take some time, you give her a hug, you sit her down, you make her feel a little better and for two weeks she'll remember that. She's never going to be out of line a day in my class."

Greg Bergner, seventh grade Unified Studies
Parkway Central Middle School

REFLECTIVE QUESTION

Do you remember a special teacher from the sixth, seventh, or eighth grade who made you feel good about yourself? How did that person do that?

- **Nurture student self-esteem.**

Students should have a variety of opportunities for academic success (NMSA, 2001b; O'Steen et al., 2002). Teachers should remember to greet students by name and try to have persistent daily contact with as many as possible (Manning, 1993; Mendes, 2003). Frequent small group work will allow students to receive positive social feedback from peers (Brown, 2002; Hoffman & Levak, 2003). Self-esteem can be nurtured by lessons that incorporate discussions and opportunities for students to voice opinions (Pitton, 2001; Hoffman & Levak, 2003). As much as possible, individual students should be recognized for specific skills, abilities, and accomplishments.

- **Teach healthy handling of emotions.**

Early adolescents need help in gaining self-control and they need to practice socially approved methods for relieving tension (Kellough & Kellough, 1999). Teachers can model these skills by showing students what *they* do when frustrated or angry, and showing students how to use humor to diffuse tension (Hall & Hall, 2003; Mendes, 2003). When students are having difficulty gaining control, they should be allowed to leave the room with a bathroom pass or what some teachers call a *get-a-grip* pass. These can be permanent passes that hang on the wall—that the student can use when needed. The ultimate goal is for the student to initiate his or her own time-out (Hall & Hall, 2003). Some teachers create errands for students or use a preestablished time-out area like the counselor's office or workroom. These techniques allow students to regroup without a loss of face. In the most extreme of cases, students may need a *mental health day* (a day off without penalty) or the option of a shortened day.

- **Help students with social problems.**

When middle school students are having problems socially or emotionally, they have trouble focusing on academics. They need help in analyzing emotional situations logically and objectively and they need skills to solve social problems (Havinghurst, 1976; Strahan et al., 2001). There are several social and emotional lessons that early adolescents need to learn, such as understanding the behavior of others, dealing with peer pressure and authority, and deciding when to seek help from adults (see Figure 3.1). These lessons may require a few minutes of one-on-one time with students, but they will help to reduce the recurrence of problems in the future (Hall & Hall, 2003). Numerous social skills programs are available to teach these lessons more formally. They often contain printed materials or exercises that can be given to students.

→ IMPACT OF CULTURE ON THE PROCESS OF EARLY ADOLESCENT DEVELOPMENT

Puberty has always been a time of great change as children transition between childhood and adulthood. Historically, there have always been children who have made the transition easily and others who have experienced more difficulty. Changes in

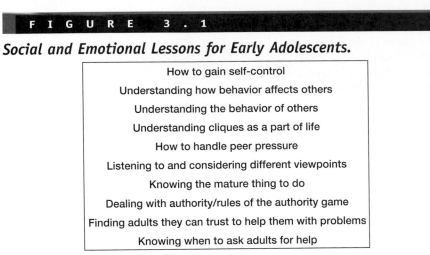

FIGURE 3.1

Social and Emotional Lessons for Early Adolescents.

How to gain self-control

Understanding how behavior affects others

Understanding the behavior of others

Understanding cliques as a part of life

How to handle peer pressure

Listening to and considering different viewpoints

Knowing the mature thing to do

Dealing with authority/rules of the authority game

Finding adults they can trust to help them with problems

Knowing when to ask adults for help

our society and culture over the last 50 years have converged to make the process of puberty today even more challenging for more children than ever before (George & Alexander, 2003; Manning & Bucher, 2001).

Social Forces That Make Adolescence More Challenging Today Than in Previous Generations

Changes in Family Environments

A significant societal change affecting early adolescents has been the change in the typical family structure (NMSA, 2003b). Between 1950 and 1985 the divorce rate in the United States more than doubled and 50 percent of all marriages now end in divorce (Kirn, 2000). This trend has led to more children living with single parents or stepparents and an increase in blended families when single parents remarry. The economic effects of the high divorce rate and fathers who do not pay child support have resulted in more children than ever living below the poverty level (Carnegie Council on Adolescent Development, 1996). More women today work outside the home than ever before. In the mid-1970s just over half of the mothers of children aged 8 to 14 were in the workforce; today that figure is over 75 percent (Kantrowitz & Wingert, 1999).

The increase in single-parent households, working women, and two-career families have resulted in children of this generation spending less time with their parents than in any previous generation (Carnegie Council on Adolescent Development, 1996; Tell, 2000). Even when families are home together, they may not eat meals together and may be engaged in solitary activities as opposed to family activities. In the 1960s when families had only one television set and few choices of programs, the family watched family shows together. Today 50 percent of seventh to twelfth graders have a television set in their rooms and 18 percent have their own VCR or DVD player (Davies, 1993; Schlozman, 2003), allowing them more solitude and less interaction with their families. Family counselors today encourage families to schedule family time and to reinstitute family meals as a means of reconnecting with their children.

The Weakening of Community and Extended Family

Not only do children spend less time with their families than ever before, but they also may have less involvement with their extended families (Taffel, 2001). Families today move more frequently and extended families are more likely to be separated by great distances. Children of divorce may be especially affected by family moves (Kirn, 2000). In unfriendly divorces, children may lose contact with half of their extended family—grandparents, aunts and uncles and cousins—because the custodial parent has cut all ties with the noncustodial parent. In other cases they may be moved several states away. The impact of moving on children of divorce has prompted courts in some states to limit such moves without input to the court from the child's other parent.

In general, the population of the United States is more transient today than ever before. Families move more often and over greater distances than at any other time in our history. This increased mobility has led to less stable communities (Tell, 2000). It is not unusual for some middle schools to experience a turnover of 20 percent of its students over the summer—that is, to lose 100 to 200 students who are replaced by 100 to 200 new students. Add to that the reality of more working women and two-career families, and the result is more people who don't know their neighbors and fewer personal connections for children growing up in the community (Carnegie Council on Adolescent Development, 1996). "Because of the social changes of the past 25 years, teens today have spent more time alone than any other generation. They are missing a coherent sense of community" (Tell, 2000, p. 13).

An Increase in the Diversity of Family Values

If "it takes a village to raise a child," in earlier generations the village was raising the child. One thing that bonded communities together was a set of shared values—adults seemed to agree about what was best for children. In some communities today, that sense of community and shared values still exists; in other communities it is sorely lacking (Taffel, 2001). A growing diversity in values and lifestyles has contributed greatly to the erosion of a sense of community in many neighborhoods (Tell, 2000).

In previous generations, mainstream America seemed to agree about issues like honesty, respecting authority, obeying the law, premarital sex, and childrearing. Children received similar messages about right and wrong from their school, church, home, and neighborhood. It was simpler then for parents to agree about what was right for children and thus easier to take responsibility for other people's children. The 1960s "do your own thing" generation marked the beginning of a diversity of family values that continues to widen. Conformity does not hold the same satisfactions that it once did. Parents today value their individuality and their individual freedom to set their own standards about childrearing (Taffel, 2001). The result is that today there is little standardization among parents about childrearing (Tell, 2000). A broad diversity of opinions exists about such things as whether children should attend church, be paid for chores, or have curfews. Mainstream America cannot agree on whether children should be spanked, what clothing is too sexy for adolescent girls, when teenagers should date, how much supervision children should have, and whether it's okay to search a teen's room. Morality varies from one home to the next and children often receive conflicting messages about appropriate behavior (Taffel, 2001; Tell, 2000).

The diversity of parenting styles can be illustrated through opposites. Some busy parents who feel guilty about not spending enough time with their children try to compensate by buying them things, leading to overindulged children and the "bribery theory of child rearing" (Kantrowitz & Wingert, 2000). Other parents tightly control their children's access to money and closely supervise their children's purchases. In some families, the power structure is very traditional, with the adults making all the decisions (Taffel, 2001). Other families function more democratically, with children having much say over day-to-day decisions (like what to have for dinner) and having substantial input about major household purchases and family trips (Kantrowitz & Wingert, 1999). Some parents exert great control over what television, music, and games children consume and other parents don't. Some parents model narrower, more traditional male and female roles and other parents model broader, more equitable male and female roles. Some parents teach their children tolerance, some teach them racism. All this diversity leads to a wide spectrum of parental opinions on practically any issue that involves children (Taffel, 2001). The development of community is compromised when groups of parents have difficulty finding common ground.

REFLECTIVE QUESTION

What privileges do you remember negotiating for when you were an early adolescent? Did your aunts and uncles and other children's parents have the same rules as your parents?

Disappearing Rites of Passage

During puberty, most cultures provide some rites of passage that signal the child's entry into the adult world. When homogeneity exists in parents' values, it is easier as a culture to maintain rites of passage. When all the parents agreed that age 14 was the appropriate time for girls to wear makeup, it became an informal rite of passage for teenage girls. The increased diversity of parental values has resulted in a loss of informal rites of passage in our culture (Elkind, 1981). Puberty is a transformation that benefits from formal ritual, yet few formal rituals exist today. Religious confirmation, and bar and bat mitzvahs are some of the only remaining formal rituals that usher adolescents into the adult world (Kessler, 2000).

Efforts to create rites of passage in the culture are difficult to enforce due to diversity of parental opinions. Movie industry ratings are a prime example. Some parents won't allow their 14-year-old to watch PG-13-rated movies and other parents take their 10-year-old to R-rated movies. Parental advisories exist on music with explicit language and content, but access to such music varies widely among families.

The lack of formal rites of passage makes it difficult for early adolescents to judge when they are expected to have reached a certain level of maturity (Kessler, 2000). The lack of agreement about the simplest of privileges (staying home alone, dating) has led to some early adolescents being thrust into adult situations before they are ready (Elkind, 1981). The lack of conformity among families also makes it more difficult for adolescents to judge what's age-appropriate and makes it easier for them to negotiate for looser restrictions that may not be in their best interest (Taffel, 2001). In addition, a diversity of sexual values and the blurring of traditional sex roles have combined to further complicate the process of puberty for early adolescents.

The Blurring of Traditional Sex Roles

The adopting of an appropriate sex role was a relatively simple task in previous generations when sex roles were distinctly and clearly defined—women cooked and cleaned, men did yard work and heavy chores. Acceptable careers for women were housewife, teacher, nurse, or secretary. Women did not ask men for dates. Over the last 30 years, those traditional roles have become blurred. A great diversity of acceptable options now exist for both men and women, but that diversity does not come without some ambivalence and some confusion (Steinberg & Levine, 1997). Today in our culture, grown men and women collectively struggle with the definition of their sex roles. Married couples with two careers renegotiate the traditional roles of husband and wife. Working parents struggle to find a balance in sharing household responsibilities. More women than ever are remaining unmarried and the number of women who are single parents by choice has risen dramatically (Edwards, 2000).

This adult ambivalence about sex role complicates early adolescents' search for their own sex role identities. Girls are told they can be anything they want, can do anything they want. While this may appear to be less restrictive for girls, it also sets up more conflict. How traditional a girl should she be? Will others approve of the choices she makes? In many ways, the choices for boys are less diverse. It may now be acceptable for girls to become doctors, but is it equally acceptable for boys to become nurses? Should men be tough and not show emotion or should they be more in touch with their feelings? Girls are more likely to be applauded for their nontraditional choices while boys are more likely to be ridiculed or to be questioned about their sexual orientation (Steinberg & Levine, 1997). Given the diversity of messages and opinions they receive, adopting an appropriate sex role is a confusing task for today's early adolescent.

Diversity of Sexual Values

Gone are the days when sex was discussed only behind closed doors and societal taboos about premarital sex and illegitimate children were widely accepted. Not only is sex discussed more openly today, but the rules have also changed about appropriate behavior (Taffel, 2001). The absolute standards of good and bad have been blurred. The modern woman, no longer powerless, seems to have earned the privilege of being sexually aggressive. Premarital sex and giving birth to babies out of wedlock, once taboo and morally condemned, is so prevalent now it has been accepted by many people as mainstream (Stodghill, 1998).

Less Supervision, More Freedom

The forces of changing family environments, a weakening of community and extended family, and a diversity of family values about privileges have converged to result in less supervision and more freedom for today's early adolescents (Taffel, 2001). This can be a dangerous combination—early adolescents naturally seek independence from their parents yet they still need their parents' supervision (Stodghill, 1998). At the middle school level parent involvement in school activities and, consequently, parents' influence in their children's lives in general, drops off. Seventy-five percent of parents of nine-year-olds claim high or medium involvement in school activities, while only 55 percent of parents of 14-year-olds do so (Wulf, 1995). Middle school students are old enough to stay at home alone after school and many do. With numbers of working parents, this may mean leaving early adolescents unsupervised for several hours. This becomes a prime time for early adolescents to engage in risk-taking behavior like experimenting with drugs, alcohol, petty crime, or sex (Mertens, Flowers, Mulhall, & Fuhler, 2003). For example, most sexual intercourse for early adolescents takes place between the hours of 3 P.M. and 8 P.M. on school days (Omvig, 2000).

Media—The New Community

More freedom, less supervision, and less time spent with family dilutes the impact of family and community on early adolescents (Kantrowitz & Wingert, 1999). The pervasiveness of media in today's culture—the influence of television, movies, music, and teen magazines—confers a power to media as a cultural value setter that has the potential to outweigh the influences of family and community (Carnegie Council on Adolescent Development, 1996; Schlozman, 2003). Media has become the new community for many of today's early adolescents:

> By age 18 a young person will have seen 350,000 commercials and spent more time being entertained by the media than any other activity except sleeping. Little wonder then that the media are referred to as "the other curriculum" or a "parallel school system." (Davies, 1993, p. 28)

About one-fourth of adolescents are considered to be heavy television viewers, watching more than five hours of television on weekdays (Kantrowitz & Wingert, 1999). By the age of 18 a child will have seen 100,000 beer commercials. Middle school students listen to two to three hours of music per day, some of it containing explicit lyrics. Music videos popular with adolescents contain heavy sexual content (Taffel, 2001). For all of the sexual messages to which early adolescents are exposed, they receive many that are titillating, but very few that deal with contra-

Media has a powerful influence on early adolescents.

ception, diseases, the emotional effects of sexual involvement, or personal responsibility (Davies, 1993). Researchers have concluded that children's consistent exposure to violence in the media increases their tendencies toward aggressive behavior (Schlozman, 2003). The popular media contributes to a culture of violence that is especially harmful to adolescent boys.

The most disturbing influence of the media is that it is a "total disclosure medium" (Postman, 1982). It often exposes early adolescents to adult information that they may not be mature enough to understand (Gibbs, 2005). Often experienced without the benefit of adult explanation, this exposure can be stressful for early adolescents, distorting their view of the world and pushing them to grow up too quickly (Lounsbury & Vars, 2003). Recent concerns about the impact of media have precipitated a new examination of societal controls that may be necessary to protect our youth from media overexposure.

Special Risks for Today's Early Adolescents

In 1996, the Carnegie Council on Adolescent Development published *Great Transitions*, the results of a nine-year study on the status of young adolescents. The report alerted the public that at least one-fourth of all adolescents are at high risk to become "lifelong casualties" of risk behaviors such as chemical abuse and premature sexual activity, damaging their chances for a productive future. More recent studies indicate a "vulnerable" period between ages 11 and 13 after which risk behaviors increase markedly. The following statistics outline some of the special risks for today's early adolescents:

- 41% of eighth graders have had at least one drink.
- 19.5% of eighth graders have been drunk.
- 16.5% of eighth graders have tried marijuana.
- 24% of eighth graders have had sex.
- 17% of eighth grade boys and 38% of eighth grade girls have "seriously considered attempting suicide." (Stevens and Griffin, 2001)

SUMMARY

Early adolescents are at a complex stage in their emotional and social development. They are struggling to define their identity, to fit in socially, and to feel a sense of competence in their lives (Havinghurst, 1976). Popular culture, with its diverse messages, complicates the decisions early adolescents have to make in their journey to responsible adulthood (Davies, 1993; Gibbs, 2005). They often have much freedom with little supervision (Taffel, 2001). They are developing sexually in a sex-obsessed media-saturated culture (Kantrowitz & Wingert, 1999). Yet, in reality, they are still *children* who sound, behave and look like adults but feel and think and hurt like children. Caring educators realize they have a difficult job helping early adolescents grow to adulthood in our country today. Chapters 2 and 3 have detailed the physical, intellectual, emotional, and social changes of puberty and discussed implications for instruction. Chapter 4 will discuss how to create the optimum classroom climate to nurture early adolescent development.

KEY TERMS

egocentrism   imaginary audience
identity versus role confusion   industry versus inferiority

APPLICATION ACTIVITIES

1. In Chapters 2 and 3, you learned about physical, intellectual, emotional and social needs of early adolescents. For each type of need, list one strategy you will use in your classroom to address those needs.
2. Think back to when you were in the sixth, seventh, or eighth grade. Think about your family, school, community, and the society in general during those years. How has the typical family and community changed from then to now? Given what you have learned about the physical, social, and emotional changes of puberty, what changes in our society over the last 50 years make adolescence more challenging today than when you were an adolescent?

3. Read a popular teen magazine or watch a television show popular with teens. How does it accurately portray early adolescents? How does it misrepresent early adolescents? How does it misrepresent the world to its early adolescent viewers?

CHAPTER 4

AN EVIRONMENT THAT SUPPORTS ACADEMIC ACHIEVEMENT

❖ INTRODUCTION

The classroom environment greatly influences the quality and amount of learning that takes place (Scales, 1999; Wessler, 2003). Evidence has existed for some time that a supportive classroom climate not only increases student efforts and academic motivation (Johnston & Markle, 1986) but also improves achievement (Jensen, 1998; Vatterott, 1999). For middle school students, a nurturing and supportive classroom environment is essential for their emotional and social development as well as for academic success (Blum, 2005; Johnson, 1992; Scales, 1999). The critical link between attitude and academic performance is especially evident with middle school students, whose psychological and emotional states are so fragile (Mee, 1997; Strahan, 1994; Vatterott, 1999). As Alfie Kohn put it, "If you want academic excellence, you have to attend to how children feel about school and about each other" (1996, p. 103). This chapter will focus on how teachers can create the optimum environment in the classroom. **The purposes of this chapter are to help you**

- create a classroom climate where students will feel secure.
- organize your classroom to meet student needs for physical and emotional comfort.
- discover strategies that will meet student needs for power and competence.
- nurture personal relationships in your classroom.
- create a sense of community in your classroom.
- consider alternatives to punitive discipline.

Essential Questions

After reading and completing the activities in this chapter, you should be able to answer the following questions:

1. Why is classroom environment so critical for successful early adolescent learning?
2. How can I structure my classroom environment to meet early adolescent needs?
3. How can I empower students to take charge of their own learning?
4. How can I nurture positive relationships among students?
5. How can I create a sense of community in my classroom?

✦ A NEEDS-BASED ENVIRONMENT

Creating a supportive environment for middle school students requires an awareness of and a respect for the developmental needs of early adolescents (Havinghurst, 1976; Scales, 1999; Van Hoose, Strahan & L'Esperance, 2001). As mentioned in Chapter 3, early adolescents have basic human needs for survival, love, and belonging (Daniels, 2005) that are intertwined with identity needs (needs to define oneself and to develop appropriate roles) and needs for competence and achievement (Erikson, 1963; Glasser 1986; NMSA, 2001c). Those needs are best met in a respectful, democratic environment that makes personal relationships a priority (DeVries & Zan, 2003; Wessler, 2003). A classroom environment that supports social and emotional needs also enhances academic success (Blum, 2005; Erwin, 2003; Mertens & Flowers, 2003).

Addressing Survival Needs—Creating a Safe Place to Learn

To meet student needs for survival, the classroom should make students feel safe. A safe classroom is a place where students feel secure and protected from physical danger (Patterson, 2003; Pitton, 2002). That danger could be as innocuous as a shove from another student or as foreboding as the presence of a gun or a knife. Safety is the obligation of everyone in the school—principals, teachers, counselors, secretaries, support staff, and students. Safety requires a comprehensive effort by the entire school population working in conjunction with the community-at-large of families, churches, police, and social agencies (Belair & Freeman, 2000; Curwin & Mendler, 1997; Wolk, 2003).

A nonviolent school is created by developing the sense of a caring community with all people in the school, cultivating nonviolence as a school value and being concerned about the mental health of *everyone* in the school community, both children and adults (Curwin & Mendler, 1997; Hoffman & Levak, 2003). "A safe school is more the result of shared community values and expectations than it is the result of metal detectors or security guards" (Belair & Freeman, 2000, p. 3). Conflict resolution and other types of violence prevention programs have proven useful in some schools, but prevention-only programs have not been as effective as comprehensive programs that also address climate and relationships (Curwin & Mendler, 1997). (School climate will be discussed in Chapter 5.) The best violence prevention is a warm, nurturing environment that keeps kids close (Hoffman & Levak, 2003). A mutually respectful relationship between teachers and students will encourage students to communicate openly with teachers about their concerns (Mendler, 2001; Strahan, Smith, McElrath, & Toole, 2001). Students should also have a way to communicate anonymously to teachers or other school officials. Many schools have suggestion boxes or *bug boxes* (What's bugging you) to allow students to voice concerns. Bullying, threatening, teasing, or ridiculing of others are *not* "just part of middle school," as some people may claim (Belair & Freeman, 2000). Teachers and administrators who refuse to tolerate such behavior and make respect a priority set the parameters of a positive environment (Curwin & Mendler, 1997; Wessler, 2003).

It goes without saying that students should feel secure about their physical safety. Less obvious is the student's need for emotional safety (Inlay, 2005), to be safe from ridicule and embarrassment in the learning process and in daily interactions with peers (Pitton, 2001; Wessler, 2003). A classroom must be a comfortable place to learn, a nonthreatening environment that provides support and learning challenges (Patterson, 2003; Vatterott, 1999). Most teachers prohibit students from threatening or embarrassing others but may fail to protect students from embarrassment in the learning process (Jensen, 1998). Students who feel safe and supported are more willing to take the risk of learning (Fashola, 2005; Van Hoose et al., 2001). The tone of the classroom should be one of unanxious expectation: "I won't threaten you, but I expect much of you," of trust and fairness (Sizer, 1992). The goal is low anxiety and high standards (Barth, 1990). Removing threat from the classroom is one of the most important ways teachers can create a comfortable learning environment (Jensen, 1998; Wessler, 2003). Threats of detention, lowered grades, intimidation, embarrassment, or loss of school privileges are counterproductive to learning (Glasser, 1996; Hall & Hall, 2003). Research suggests that learning suffers when learner anxiety is high and that similar internal reactions occur for all kinds of threat—physical or psychological (Pitton, 2001). "Threats activate defense mechanisms and behaviors that are great for survival but lousy for learning" (Jensen, 1998, p. 57).

REFLECTIVE QUESTION

Reflect on your experiences as a college student. Do you remember situations in which the teacher made you feel threatened or uncomfortable? How did it affect how you felt about the class?

Classroom practices should respect early adolescents' physical needs.

Addressing Physical Needs—Respecting Brain Chemistry

As discussed in Chapter 2, early adolescents have a great many physical needs that affect their psychological well-being and ability to learn on any given day. Many traditional classroom practices for controlling students restrict students physically and reflect a mistrust of students to act responsibly (Kohn, 2001; Vatterott, 1999). Practices such as forcing students to sit in certain positions for long periods of time and not allowing them to use the restroom or get a drink ignore some of their most basic physical needs (Bell, 2003; Jensen, 1998, 2000). How many adults would find such rules acceptable in their own work environments?

The fact that some child might take advantage of the chance to decide when to go to the bathroom is no justification for requiring everyone to ask permission. If it's useful to keep track of who's out of the room, or to limit the number who are gone at any given time, children can take a pass or sign out when they feel the need. Better yet, they can be asked as a class to invent a system that addresses everyone's concerns—theirs for autonomy, the teacher's for structure or limits. (Kohn, 1996, pp. 85–86)

In addition to being inconsiderate, such practices are now physiologically indefensible, based on new knowledge about the brain (Sousa, 1998). Factors affecting the body's physical workings (such as nutrition, exercise, and sleep) influence brain chemistry, which influences the student's ability to learn (Jensen, 1998; Sprenger, 2005). Many learning problems at this age are due to brain chemistry imbalances brought about by the early adolescent's need for food, water, rest, or movement (Jensen, 2000).

The need for food is a basic physical need. Given the metabolic changes of puberty, it's possible for students to eat breakfast and still need to eat again before lunch (Kellough & Kellough, 1999). Middle schools that provide snack breaks for students have observed higher levels of concentration and fewer discipline problems (Erwin, 2003). How many adults would function at peak efficiency in their jobs without their coffee breaks or snacks at their desks each day?

In addition to food, the brain needs oxygen to work efficiently. Oxygen is necessary in order to decode and process information (Fahey, 2000; Jensen, 1998). Providing oxygen to the brain through fresh air, movement within the classroom, and regular physical education are important ways to enhance the brain's ability to learn (Jensen, 2000). Sousa (1998) has shown that after people have been sitting for long periods, the amount of blood that actually reaches their brains is reduced. After 20 minutes of sitting, blood leaves the brain and starts to pool in the seat and the feet. After standing for only 45 seconds, the amount of blood flow to the brain has increased by 15 percent (Sousa, 1998). Allowing students to stand and move every 15 to 20 minutes significantly increases blood flow to the brain and alertness. Middle school experts have long advocated daily physical education for early adolescents, and brain research confirms the wisdom of this recommendation (George & Alexander, 2003). Fresh air in the classroom and the presence of green plants also increase the amount of oxygen available to students (Erwin, 2003; Jensen, 2000).

One of the more surprising findings in the research on the brain has been the essential role of water in brain functioning (Fahey, 2000). The brain is about 78 percent water and quickly becomes dehydrated (Jensen, 1998; Sousa, 1998). For optimum functioning, the brain needs 8 to 12 glasses of water a day (Jensen, 1998). Water is necessary for electrical transmissions in the nervous system to occur; it plays an important role in supplying oxygen to the brain, and even reduces stress:

Dehydration is a common problem that's linked to poor learning. To be at their best, learners need water . . . if water is available in the learning environment, the typical hormone response to the stress (elevated levels of corticoids) is "markedly reduced or absent" (Levine & Coe, 1989). These studies suggest a strong role for water in keeping learners' stress levels in check. (Jensen, 1998, p. 26)

Many teachers have discovered that allowing students to bring water bottles to class has increased attention and on-task behavior (Fahey, 2000). Allowing students access to water can have other positive effects as well (Erwin, 2003). In one school,

> consuming water was a good break strategy for long block-scheduled classes and created a more relaxed atmosphere . . . water in the classroom eased tensions and gave students more freedom . . . active learners needed something to do with their hands and bodies during these longer classes. Water helped. Students had something to manipulate, hold onto, and put into their mouths—water bottles. (Fahey, 2000, p. 61)

In addition to food, water, and movement in the classroom, the brain also needs adequate sleep for maximum performance (Jensen, 1998, 2000; Sousa, 1998). As mentioned in Chapter 2, many early adolescents need more than eight hours of sleep, possibly as much as 10 to 12 hours during growth spurts (Wolfe, 2005). Sleep deprivation interferes with the proper functioning of neurotransmitters in the brain, making learning and emotional control more difficult (Kantrowitz & Springen, 2003; Sprenger, 2005).

These facts about the brain pertain to all brains, young and old. Given the stress of the changes of puberty, it would be logical to assume that the early adolescent body would be especially vulnerable to the physical needs of food, water, exercise, and sleep (Sprenger, 2005). Teachers must be sensitive to those needs when they structure their classroom practices (Stevenson, 2002).

REFLECTIVE QUESTION

What have you learned as a college student about your physical needs in regard to learning? What physical needs affect your ability to learn? What practices at the college level seem out of sync with your physical needs?

Addressing Needs for Power and Competence— Putting Students in Charge

Chapter 1 discussed the importance of empowering students to make decisions in the classroom. In creating the optimum classroom environment, teachers need to attend to early adolescents' need for power and competence (Hoffman & Levak, 2003; Vatterott, 1999). How students feel about learning is greatly influenced by the *power* they perceive they have over the learning process (Erwin, 2003; Glasser, 1986). As they search to define themselves and their adult roles, middle school students have a strong developmental need for power (Havinghurst, 1976; Vatterott, 1999). This need is so strong that in their striving to become adults, early adolescents often engage in power struggles over inconsequential issues (Dreikurs, Grunwald, & Pepper, 1982). Teachers often react with tighter control, when allowing students some power would more effectively meet students' needs and often eliminate power struggles (Glasser, 1986):

The difficulty of relinquishing power, or of realizing the importance of doing so, is evident from the number of adults who spend their days ordering children around, complaining all the while that "kids just don't take responsibility for their own behavior." The truth is that if we want children to "take" responsibility, we must first "give" them responsibility, and plenty of it. (Kohn, 1996, p. 84)

In order for students to experience competence, they must be given power to make decisions directly (Eisner, 2002; Inlay, 2005). This requires a shift in the way teachers and students interact, from "doing to" power to "working with" power within the classroom (Erwin, 2003; Kohn, 2001). Every aspect of life in the classroom should cause us to reflect on what decisions might be turned over to students (DeVries & Zan, 2003; Hoffman & Levak, 2003).

The most basic empowerment gives students opportunities to self-monitor, self-evaluate, and set personal goals (Erwin, 2003; Glasser, 1986). For example, many middle school teachers require students to keep a log of assignments and grades received and to regularly average their own grades. Students are often asked to complete a self-evaluation of a project, allowing them to reflect on the quality of their work before the teacher grades it. Students often have input into which items should be included in a portfolio of their work and how those items should be judged (DeVries & Zan, 2003). (Portfolios and student self-evaluation will be discussed in more detail in Chapter 10.)

In addition to self-evaluation and personal goal setting, middle school students should be empowered in the overall process of daily classroom life (Hoffman & Levak, 2003; Marzano & Marzano, 2003). They should have a voice in classroom rules, make decisions about issues that affect the group, and solve problems through regular classroom meetings (discussed later in this chapter) (DeVries & Zan, 2003; Inlay, 2005). Middle school students should be allowed to take charge of some classroom procedures, materials, and displays and should also have input into curriculum themes and methods of learning and assessments (Kohn, 2001; Marshall, 2002). Student needs of competence and achievement can also be addressed through classroom and extracurricular activities that provide opportunities for creative self-expression, self-definition, reflection, and service to community and school (Keefe & Jenkins, 2002; Scales, 1991). Curricular and instructional designs that meet student needs for competence and achievement are discussed in Chapters 6 and 7.

Love and Belonging—Developing Positive Relationships

Love and belonging could be called *ego needs,* as they so intimately affect an early adolescent's sense of self-esteem and identity. Early adolescents need unconditional love and acceptance and often go to great lengths to attain it. They also need to feel a sense of belonging, of connectedness, of membership in a group (Havinghurst, 1976; Patterson, 2003). These very strong needs are met at the middle school through personal relationships with teachers and other students and through the development of a classroom community (Hoffman & Levak, 2003; Strahan et al., 2001). The success of a student's personal relationships can make the difference between academic success and academic failure (Blum, 2005). Students' relationships with their teachers and with other students are both critical (Hoffman & Levak, 2003; Scales, 1999).

The Teacher-Student Relationship

The teacher-student relationship is the most important relationship influencing academic success (Strahan et al., 2001; Vatterott, 1999). Scales (1999) found that middle schools that nurture positive relationships among students and teachers reap the benefit of more students engaged in learning and consequently, higher student achievement (Hoffman & Levak, 2003; Mertens & Flowers, 2003). The significance of the teacher-student relationship is most obvious with at-risk students, where the *lack* of that connection often impedes motivation (Mendes, 2003). When students perceive that the adults and other students do not care about them, they decide not to care what these people think about them (Hoffman & Levak, 2003; Vatterott, 1999). That produces a feeling of being *disconnected* from the school (Strahan, 1989). That sense of disconnectedness produces apathy (Wehlage et al., 1989) and puts students at risk for academic failure (Hoffman & Levak, 2003; Wessler, 2003). The students put forth little effort to learn because effort may result in failure (Brophy, 1998). Disconnected students do not want to risk failure if they feel they have no support—much like walking a tightrope without a safety net. It's much easier not to try. This apathy results in less effort, which causes poor performance, which in turn produces a lack of teacher motivation to continue to meet student needs. This lack of teacher involvement fuels further student apathy (Mendler, 2001; Vatterott, 1991, 1999).

In spite of this link between teacher-student relationships and the level of student effort, Kohn (1991) noted that the interaction of the teacher and the student is rarely seen as integral to the process of learning. Often students most in need of a personal connection are the ones least likely to get it (Fashola, 2005). In one disturbing study, Waxman, Huang, and Padron (1995) discovered a pattern among teachers in inner-city middle schools of minimal interactions with students:

> Teachers in this study were observed spending very little time interacting with students regarding personal issues, encouraging students to succeed, showing personal regard for students, or showing interest in students' work. These are all areas that have been found to be important for developing positive learning environments where students will become successful learners. (pp. 13–14)

While many have suffered from neglect of or lack of a positive teacher-student relationship, other students experience a history of adversarial relationships that further obstructs the meeting of their needs (Fashola, 2005; Vatterott, 1999). In a survey of 2,000 middle school students, Mee (1997) discovered that many early adolescent students believe adults do not like them and do not trust them. "Students mentioned that they thought grown-ups gave them little, if any respect" (p. 40). Only about 38 percent of sixth graders and 24 percent of eighth graders feel they have a caring climate at school (Scales, 1999).

The teacher-student relationship that best supports achievement is a needs-based one (Vatterott, 1999). How does a needs-based teacher-student relationship differ from the traditional teacher-student relationship? Traditionally the teacher-student relationship has been teacher-controlled (Glasser, 1986; Hoffman & Levak, 2003; Kohn, 1996). The teacher has had all the power, has directed instruction, has initiated conversation, and has made the rules. Teachers may have had a relationship with their classes as groups but not necessarily with individual students. In a needs-based classroom, the teacher-student relationship is more democratic and personalized (see Table 4.1) (Gross, 2002; Wolk, 2003). The purpose of teaching is to engage learners, which involves forming a trusting relationship (Hoffman & Levak, 2003; Patterson, 2003). Students must develop a trust in the teacher to guide them in the learning process and protect them from embarrassment (Pitton, 2001). Learning is a risky business, especially at this age when any failure is a serious blow to the ego (Fashola, 2005; Price, 2005).

A needs-based teacher-student relationship begins with absolute positive regard for all students (Hall & Hall, 2003; Mendes, 2003). All children are entitled to absolute positive regard whether they are dirty, poorly dressed, mean-spirited, ugly, or poor. An affirming teacher communicates to students his or her belief that they can be successful and are worthy of respect, that there are no "bad kids" (Wessler, 2003; Vatterott, 1999). An affirming teacher conveys the message that students with problems such as attention deficit disorder, learning disabilities, or behavioral or emotional problems are just as capable of learning as other students, given the proper conditions (Hall & Hall, 2003; Mendes, 2003; Taylor & Lorimer, 2003). At-risk students *can* be successful and the teacher's belief in that success is a critical factor in overcoming failure orientation (Hensen, 2004; Wehlage et al., 1989). Levin (in Brandt, 1992), speaking of the highly successful Accelerated Schools model, stated "the way you define children has an awful lot to do with the way you work with them" (p. 20).

Students' beliefs about themselves and their learning have a major influence on their ability to learn (Brophy, 1998; Jensen, 1998). Students must experience that teacher optimism through an individual relationship with the teacher (Fashola, 2005; Hall & Hall, 2003). If students are to feel accepted, teachers must first have regular, positive interaction with *all* students in their classroom (Strahan et al., 2001). They must take the time to gain personalized knowledge about students and communicate with them one-on-one (Patterson, 2003). Students who are different culturally or ethnically from the majority may need extra attention to feel cared about (Bell, 2003; Fashola, 2005; Wessler, 2003). Teachers must take time to learn about students' cultural backgrounds, families, and outside interests (Gay, 2004; Hoffman & Levak, 2003; Wolk, 2003). **English as Second Language (ESL) students**, students whose primary language is not English, represent a special challenge. Teachers can start by learning how to say "hello" in their students' native language and by showing they care in nonverbal ways with a smile or a touch (Brown, 2002; Frieman, 2001). Regardless of class size or the amount of time it takes, students must be made to feel that teachers care about them and know them as individuals (Erwin, 2003;

Hoffman & Levak, 2003; Wessler, 2003). The investment of time to develop personal relationships will be repaid in students' motivation, their willingness to ask for help, and their improved academic performance (Bell, 2003; Hrabowski, 2003; Rolin, 2003).

TEACHER'S VOICE
About the Teacher-Student Relationship

"You have to know your kids. That's the number one priority in a classroom. I can tell you what happens when he goes home at night, I can tell you what he likes to do on his free time, I can tell you what his interests are, I can tell you what his strengths are . . . the majority of what I'll do is I'll listen. They all have something to say, they want to talk to you. One kid, he's a White Sox fan. I'll read the sports page every morning, I'll look at the standings in the American League. I don't even like the White Sox, but I'll look just to see what they did because I'll say something to him walking in the door, 'The Sox lost last night, they looked horrible.' The kid's hooked automatically. If I say it to him once in three weeks, he knows that I know he's a White Sox fan. I know something about him and it makes him feel special in that room that day. You can do that once a month. You can pick a different kid once every two to three days, you make their world and they're excited about being in your classroom and they buy into whatever it is you're selling. . . . That's the whole job in a nutshell. You have to be able to make those connections with the kids."

Greg Bergner, seventh grade Unified Studies
Parkway Central Middle School

STUDENTS' VOICES
About the Teacher-Student Relationship

"If you and the student have a good relationship, you know, that will make them want to do the work because they want to please the teacher. But if the teacher's, like, yelling at you constantly, well, 'I don't have to do this work because he's always gonna stay mad at me.'"

Erica, eighth grade

"What do I like about Mrs. Sadler? She doesn't talk to you like a student—she talks to you like a peer."

Marco, eighth grade

The student's statement above is somewhat misleading and illustrates an interesting predicament. Middle school teachers *should* be interested in getting to know the student as a person and they should *interact* with students with the same respect they would with adults (Strahan et al., 2001). In this sense, the relationship can *look* almost like a friendship—but it is not. Teachers cannot truly be *friends* with students—after all, the role of a teacher is **in loco parentis**, acting in place of a parent. These parent-child roles are necessary to enable the teacher to be an authority figure and to make decisions that are in the child's best interest (DeVries & Zan, 2003; Mendes, 2003). Like parents, teachers must sometimes make decisions that are not popular with students. Like parents, teachers cannot be swayed in their decision making by being overly concerned that the student will no longer be their friend. In loco parentis is a role ascribed to the teacher *within the confines of the school experience* (Lemlech, 2002). For instance, inviting students to the movies or to one's home without their parents is inappropriate. It characterizes the relationship as a friendship, which it is not. That's why sexual relationships between teachers and students of any age are so egregious. If teachers are acting in place of parents, a sexual relationship between a teacher and a student violates the incest taboo. It is important for teachers to set clear boundaries with students that characterize their relationship as an adult-child relationship, not a true friendship between adults (Wormeli, 2003).

When teachers develop *individual* relationships with students, not just a relationship with students as a group, they validate the worth of all students and meet strong needs for acceptance, love, and belonging (Hoffman & Levak, 2003; Wessler, 2003). Individual relationships send a message of teacher efficacy, the teacher's belief in his or her ability to influence individual student motivation and achievement (Henson, 2004; Vatterott, 1999).

A positive teacher-student relationship does not imply that children are continually praised and rewarded, but that they are given unconditional support (Hall & Hall, 2003; Mendes, 2003). Johnston (1992) calls it "pervasive caring [where people] are alert to each other's needs and take care of them without fanfare" (p. 87). A caring environment sends three messages: you are valuable, you are able, and you are responsible (Strahan, 1994).

> Warm, caring, empathic adults do several things at once. They provide the child with a benevolent, safe place in which to act. . . . I hope that few educators take seriously the absurd dictum that teachers should display no warmth until well into the school year—after firm control of the classroom has been won. Instead, teachers should establish themselves from the beginning as the students' allies, adults with whom they can work to solve the problems that emerge during the normal course of development. (Kohn, 1991, p. 503)

Students need and want relationships with their teachers (Blum, 2005; Hoffman & Levak, 2003): "Young adolescents want open communication with their teachers and want to engage in real dialogue about their learning and life in general" (Mee, 1997, p. 47). A positive teacher-student relationship creates a personal connection with students (Hoffman & Levak, 2003; Vatterott, 1999). This connectedness, or social bonding, has been shown to be an important factor in student motivation (Arhar, 1992; Inlay, 2005; Strahan et al., 2001). In fact, brain research has shown that positive social feedback from others actually increases certain chemicals in the brain that make us feel good (Jensen, 1998). Personal relationships with students send powerful messages to students about themselves (Dalton & Watson, 1997; Wessler, 2003). They affirm a student's sense of acceptance and membership and allow students to feel respected as individuals worthy of having their needs met (Blum, 2005; Inlay, 2005) (see Table 4.1).

Student-Student Relationships

Although critical to student success, even the best teacher-student relationships will not meet all the needs of middle school students. In addition to the need for personalized attention and unconditional acceptance from their teachers, early adolescents need a sense of membership, of being accepted by a group (Havinghurst, 1976; Hoffman & Levak, 2003; Patterson, 2003). After all, being accepted by a group is a validation of one's personal identity, validation that one is a "good person." Not only is social membership important to the developmental needs of early adolescents, but research also indicates the quality of social relationships at school may impact whether students come to school and what they will learn there (Scales, 1999; Vatterott, 1999).

> For at-risk students in particular, with backgrounds of school failure and lack of support of strong homes and communities outside the school, a strong sense of membership is essential to persistence in school. When identification with social institutions outside of the school is weakened, membership in school becomes critical for adolescent development into adulthood. (Arhar, 1992, p. 149)

Positive peer relationships are a critical component of a nurturing classroom (Good & Brophy, 2003; Hoffman & Levak, 2003). Early adolescents need positive

TABLE 4.1

Traditional versus Needs-Based Teacher-Student Relationships

Traditional	Needs-Based
Teacher relates to class as a group	Teacher relates to students individually
Individual personal relationships unnecessary	Individual personal relationships a priority
Teacher-to-student primary communication	True dialogue between teacher and student
Student input or opinions unimportant	Student input or opinions used for decision making
Teacher's priority is to control students	Teacher's priority is to help students

peer relationships for their social and emotional development (Havinghurst, 1976). Unfortunately, many middle school students lack the social skills necessary to form satisfying relationships with other students. Lavoie (2005) identified seven social traits of popular, well-liked children. Popular children smiled and laughed a lot, greeted others, extended invitations, held conversations, shared, and gave compliments. He observed that some learning disabled children lacked these abilities but that the abilities could be learned with coaching and practice. English as Second Language students can be taught some of these basic behaviors as well. By learning a few key phrases, greetings, and compliments in English, ESL students can begin to develop social relationships in predominantly English-speaking classrooms. It is important for teachers to keep informal social skills instruction as part of their daily routine (Marshall, 2002; Marzano, Marzano, & Pickering, 2003). When students are having problems in peer interactions, it is worth the time to take a few minutes to reinforce positive behaviors and to clarify your expectations about how students should treat each other (Wessler, 2003).

STUDENT'S VOICE

About Student-Student Relationships

"Keeping friends at this age is a real struggle. Everyone is going through emotional changes and a lot of good friends from elementary school are not such good friends anymore."

Leslie, eighth grade

✦ MEMBERSHIP—BRINGING DIVERSE GROUPS TOGETHER

The goals of social membership and positive peer relationships can be challenging in schools with diverse populations (Brown, 2002; Rolon, 2003). Middle school students are already a diverse group by virtue of the rate at which they experience the changes of puberty. Middle school students are diverse in many other ways, all of which affect their ability to gain acceptance from peers, interact appropriately with authority, form their identity, and feel positive about themselves (Brown, 2002; Henson, 2004). A feeling of membership, of being part of the group, thus becomes a primary need for early adolescents (Robertson & Valentine, 2002). Unfortunately, many students in middle school feel marginalized, that they are not represented in our schools or in our curriculum (Hoffman & Levak, 2003; Ladson-Billings, 2001). If they are in the minority, they may find it difficult to buy in to the curriculum and learning—they may not feel like they are a member (Brown, 2002; Fashola, 2005; Rolon, 2003). Many types of differences can create that feeling. Helping all students to feel comfortable and accepted is an important job for middle school teachers (Erwin, 2003; Hoffman & Levak, 2003; Wessler, 2003).

Awareness and Sensitivity First

The first step for teachers in addressing diversity among students is to develop an awareness of differences and to be sensitive to them (Brown, 2002; Robertson & Valentine, 2002; Sapon-Shevin, 2003). Schools will obviously vary in the types and extent of diversity among their students. The most common ways in which students may differ are in socioeconomic status, culture, ethnicity, religion, language, sexual orientation, and disabilities.

Differences in Socioeconomic Status

Socioeconomic status most obviously affects resources. Poorer students may not be able to dress in the latest style or to afford basic school supplies. They may not have money to purchase clothes for physical education or project supplies, to pay for field trips or to eat at McDonald's during a field trip (Payne, 2001). In all fairness, public schools should not *require* students to pay for supplies or field trips. It can be *requested* that students pay for certain instructional supplies or field trips, but teachers should be aware that some students' families will not have the money. In those cases, it is important that students not be stigmatized for their failure to pay. At the very least, teachers or the school administration should make arrangements for funding and find a discreet way to provide that funding (Frieman, 2001). When planning assignments and dealing with families, teachers should not assume that all students have access to cable television, computers, or the Internet (Mendes, 2003). Teachers should not assume that all parents are literate or English-speaking, even if their children are (Brown, 2002; Ladson-Billings, 2001; Payne, 2001). Among different social classes, family roles and responsibilities may vary along with the type of family stress. In some families, students may be responsible for babysitting or preparing meals in the evenings. In other families, students may be overscheduled in many outside activities. Teachers should be aware that not all students have extensive free time to do homework and not all students have a quiet place at home in which to do it (Vatterott, 2003).

Cultural and Ethnic Diversity

Cultural and ethnic diversity is becoming more the norm than the exception in many schools today (McDaniel, Necochea, Rios, Stowell & Kritzer, 2001). Sometimes there is a mismatch between the values of the school and the values of a cultural minority such as African Americans, Hispanics, Asians, or Native Americans (Ladson-Billings, 2001). For example, cultural attitudes about the value of education may vary. Some cultural minorities may associate school success with "acting white" and denying their own culture (Kunjufu, 1988; Ladson-Billings, 2001). Teachers should help students understand how they can be successful in school and still maintain their cultural identity (Hrabowski, 2003). Cultures may differ in how they value cooperation and competition (Brown, 2002; Rolon, 2003). Students who have been raised to work for the good of the group may not understand a more competitive mind-set that prohibits them from helping other students (Hodges, 1995). Within different cultures, patterns of how children interact with adult authority may vary from

A diverse group of students can work together toward common goals.

very democratic to very authoritarian. Views of external authority may vary from suspicious to deferential. For instance, children of some cultures have been taught *not* to make eye contact with an authority figure (such as a teacher) as a symbol of respect (Rasool & Curtis, 2000).

Religious Differences

Cultural or ethnic differences often include religious differences (Gay, 2004). For some students, religion may play a small part or no part at all in their lives; for others religion has a prominent place in their lives on a daily basis. Religious beliefs may influence dietary restrictions, form of dress, or whether students pray before eating lunch or taking a test. Religion may also limit a student's exposure to popular music, movies, and television, and cause parents to be concerned about which novels students read in class. Any of these can serve to make students feel different and excluded from the majority of their peers (Ladson-Billings, 2001; Rasool & Curtis, 2000).

Teachers can be sensitive to religious differences by recognizing religious holidays and rituals of different cultures (Gay, 2004). During popular holidays like Christmas, Easter, and Halloween, the history of holiday rituals can be explained as well as how different cultures celebrate (Skelton, Nigford, Harper & Reeves, 2002). Religion and religious differences should be a part of the curriculum. Ideally, instead of ignoring religion, schools should recognize that religion exists and belongs in the curriculum (Nord & Haynes, 1998). For instance, in Family and Consumer Science class, religious restrictions on diet can be discussed in conjunction with lifestyle dietary choices (such as choosing to be vegetarian or choosing a low fat diet for health reasons). In other classes, the influence of religion on historical events, art, and music can be discussed (Bell, 2003). Teachers must be careful, however, not to endorse the practice of any particular religion (Douglass, 2002).

Language Differences

Language differences can separate students in several ways. Students for whom English is a second language (ESL students) are perhaps the most isolated, especially recent immigrants who are adapting not only to language but also to unfamiliar culture and new environments at the same time (Frieman, 2001; Rasool & Curtis, 2000).

The most successful programs for ESL students respect the student's native language. They allow students to develop skills by learning in their native language and may alternate instruction between English and the student's first language (Gebhard, 2003). If ESL students are grouped with regular students in cooperative learning groups, ESL students can learn language through content (Brown, 2002). Other adaptations for ESL include using pictures, pocket translators, dictionaries, and translating software. Some schools assign ESL students to an extra reading class where they have additional time to learn English vocabulary and practice reading skills (Gebhard, 2003). If teachers can find ways to accept and honor ESL students, they will have developed a way of honoring all cultures in their school.

Other language differences may be more subtle, such as regional or ethnic dialects or slang. Children of poverty often lack a command of what is called the **formal register** of language. The formal register is the standard sentence syntax and word choice of work and school that uses complete sentences and specific word choice (Payne, 2001). While casual conversation uses many nonverbal assists, the formal register relies on sentence structure and syntax for meaning. The lack of familiarity with the formal register is a huge impediment to school success.

> Ability to use formal register is a hidden rule of the middle class. The inability to use it will knock one out of an interview in two or three minutes. The use of formal register, on the other hand, allows one to score well on tests and do well in school and higher education. (Payne, 2001, p. 43)

For example, African American students who speak nonstandard English can be made to feel inferior when constantly corrected or asked to restate answers in standard English (Brown, 2002; Fashola, 2005; Rolon, 2003). Asking students to speak only standard English is often perceived by students as asking them to take on another identity and to deny their culture (Ladson-Billings, 2001; Kunjufu, 1988). It is possible to respect nonstandard English much in the way we respect native language of ESL students—allow students to communicate in their preferred mode during learning, but expect formal assignments to be completed in standard English (the formal register) (Brown, 2002). Children of poverty need instruction in the formal register in order to be successful in school (Frieman, 2001). One suggestion for writing assignments is to ask students to write the way they talk, and then work with students to translate their thoughts into formal language (Gebhard, 2003).

Each teacher must decide where he or she stands on the issue of nonstandard English. If one allows students to speak slang or nonstandard English, there will obviously need to be limits on profanity and expressions that are rude or hurtful to others. If teachers are truly uncomfortable with nonstandard English in the classroom, they should explain carefully and respectfully that they are teaching students standard English as another language, the language of business, the language in which successful people communicate in the world of work (Hrabowski, 2003; Ladson-Billings, 2001).

Gay and Lesbian Students

Middle school is an especially difficult period for gay and lesbian students (Bailey & Phariss, 1996). At a time when early adolescents are discovering their sexual identity and defining an appropriate sex role, gay and lesbian children are also coming to grips with what it means to be different, wrestling with the dilemma of denying their sexuality to fit in, and contemplating how they will live in a straight world (Cloud, 2005). Passing as straight becomes an instinctive survival skill. (Someone once said that gay adolescents learn to be *chameleons*, to blend in when they need to, to change their color to the scenery) (Steinberg & Levine, 1997). To make matters worse, prejudice toward gays and lesbians still exists, even in communities that tolerate racial and ethnic differences (Bailey & Phariss, 1996). Sexual orientation is often a *covert* difference—unless students openly admit their sexual orientation, it is impossible to *know* whether they are gay or lesbian. It is possible, however, for teachers to be vigilant for harassment of students (Frieman, 2001). *Any* student may become a target of harassment because of mannerisms, dress, hairstyle, interests, or choices (such as girls choosing to play football or boys choosing to study theater or dance). Other students need to be made aware that none of these choices *proves* someone's sexual orientation, that it is common for early adolescents to experiment with a variety of roles, and that all people are entitled to respect (Steinberg & Levine, 1997). Peer acceptance must be taught and modeled (Bailey & Phariss, 1996; Sapon-Shevin, 2003).

Teacher's Voice

About Sexual Harassment of Gay or Lesbian Students

"As a teacher, you have to take yourself out of the judgement area. . . . Everyone deserves to feel safe and not be made fun of. That's not a privilege—that's a right.

. . . I try to make them aware of their feelings—it's about empathy. . . . I don't allow the word 'gay' in my classroom."

Mike Hirsch, seventh grade math
Hazelwood Junior High School

Students with Disabilities

Students with physical or mental disabilities may be mainstreamed into the regular classroom or may be assigned to special classrooms or special schools depending on the severity of their disability (Frieman, 2001; Sapon-Shevin, 2003). Many parents of children with disabilities lobby heavily to have their child included in the regular classroom because of the socializing benefit for the child. They want their child to have a normal school experience and to interact with all kinds of children. Students with disabilities often deal with issues of self-esteem and isolation (Frieman, 2001; Sapon-Shevin, 2003). Their interactions with other children help them to feel better about themselves, see beyond their disability, and improve their social skills (Ring & Reetz, 2002; Robertson & Valentine, 2002).

Students with physical and mental disabilities provide a wonderful opportunity for teachers to develop compassionate and caring behaviors in the rest of their students (Robertson & Valentine, 2002). Once students are aware of the type of assistance disabled students require, teachers are often heartened by how readily other students help and support children with disabilities (Ring & Reetz, 2002). Just as disabled children learn to define themselves as more than their disabilities, other children learn to see beyond the disabilities to connect with the disabled children on a personal level (Frieman, 2001; Robertson & Valentine, 2002).

In modifying instruction for the disabled student, the classroom teacher should consult the student's Individual Education Plan and work closely with other support personnel (Henson, 2004). Special education teachers, counselors, psychologists, physical therapists, or occupational therapists may be part of a team that works together to design appropriate physical and academic adaptations for disabled students (Ring & Reetz, 2002). Some students may require only limited adaptations, such as preferential seating, written directions for hearing impaired students or physical adaptations for students in wheelchairs. Students who are severely disabled may require a totally individualized curriculum and may even be accompanied by a full-time aide (Frieman, 2001; Ring & Reetz, 2002).

Classroom as Community

When teachers accept, honor, and celebrate diversity, they help to meet student needs for membership and they have begun the process of creating a community of learners within their classroom (Hoffman & Levak, 2003; Sapon-Shevin, 2003). Barth (1990) popularized the concept of a community of learners as "a place where students and adults alike are engaged as active learners in matters of special importance to them and where everyone is thereby encouraging everyone else's learning" (p. 9). A **learning community** is a place where people work together and pool talents and resources to reach learning goals (Barth, 1990; Erwin, 2003; Tomlinson & Doubet, 2005). In a classroom community, "teachers and students work together in a social environment to develop meaningful learning activities for all students" (Keefe & Jenkins, 2002, p. 444). Positive interactions between students are a priority and the classroom functions as a home-based peer group, providing a familylike security for students as they explore their social identity (Arhar, 1992; Hoffman & Levak, 2003; Wessler, 2003). The classroom as community is

> a place in which students feel cared about and are encouraged to care about each other. They experience a sense of being valued and respected; the children matter to one another and to the teacher. They have come to think in the plural: they feel connected to each other; they are part of an "us." (Kohn, 1996, p. 101)

How do teachers go about creating such a wonderful community in their classrooms? Three basic strategies are useful: involving students in norm setting, helping students get acquainted, and holding regular classroom meetings.

Norm Setting

Norm setting is the process by which students determine how they want their classroom to function, how people should treat each other, and how problems should be solved (DeVries & Zan, 2003; Hoffman & Levak, 2003). Norm setting goes beyond involving students in determining class rules. Rules tend to focus on what students should do and not do, but often say little about how people interact and how they treat each other (Kohn, 2001). Norm setting allows students to frame the classroom climate with values that are important to them, but it also helps them to see that values such as respect and fairness are not the arbitrary inventions of adults (DeVries & Zan, 2003; Erwin, 2003). Norm setting forces students to reflect about how personal interactions in the classroom affect their ability to learn. (Interdisciplinary teams may wish to do norm setting as a team rather than as individual classrooms.) Norm setting should be done within the first few days of class and revisited throughout the school year. Basically, norm setting is accomplished by asking students to brainstorm answers to questions like these: How do we want our classroom to be? What do we need to do so that everyone can learn? How do we want to be treated by the teacher and by other students? What values should guide our interactions? (Dalton & Watson, 1997; DeVries & Zan, 2003).

The simplest way to begin the norm setting process is to present students with a series of open-ended questions such as

"I feel comfortable in a classroom where _____"
"In this classroom I want to be able to _____"
"In order for me to learn in this classroom I need _____"
"I want other people in this classroom to _____"

A good way to start a class discussion about norms could be to ask students to think of big concepts that should be addressed. "When we think about how we want the class to be and how we want to treat each other, what big ideas should we talk about?" One group of sixth graders decided that the four areas the norms should address were respect, helping, caring, and friendships. From there they came up with specific norms like "you should help someone if you see they need help." Suggestions for classroom norms should be discussed and agreed upon by group consensus or voting and should be posted in the classroom (Dalton & Watson, 1997; DeVries & Zan, 2003).

Most teachers have found that middle school students take the process of norm setting seriously and usually set norms similar to those the teacher would set (DeVries & Zan, 2003; Stevenson, 2002). If students would propose inappropriate norms (such as "students should be able to leave the classroom at any time they want"), a large group discussion should allow students to play out the ramifications with some teacher guidance. "Let's think about what might happen if we used that norm. What is the goal of the norm? Is there another way to achieve the same goal?" The teacher obviously maintains the right of veto, but a class discussion should clarify why. When students develop the norms themselves, their commitment to uphold them is much different from their commitment to a set a class rules the teacher could present to them (Dalton & Watson, 1997; Marshall, 2002). One student expressed what she thought would be a good norm.

STUDENT'S VOICE

About Classroom Norms

"We should all learn to live together happily helping each other."

Karen, eighth grade

Getting Acquainted

Because relationships are of such critical importance to early adolescents and because they sometimes lack social skills or confidence, structured ways of getting to know others are essential (Hoffman & Levak, 2003). Community doesn't just happen—it builds a little each day as people grow comfortable with each other (Kriete, 2003; Patterson, 2003; Wolk, 2003). Positive relationships are not only important for social development but they also affect the student's comfort level, motivation, and desire to participate in learning.

Teacher self-disclosure is the first step in getting acquainted (Mendes, 2003). Students need to know some personal information about the teacher. They need to be able to connect at some other level, to feel positive about the teacher as a person (Erwin, 2003; Wolk, 2003). Although some teachers are very private and don't want students to know personal information, they need to find a few things about themselves they can share. Students like to know whether teachers have families and children, what they like to do for recreation, or what their hobbies and interests are outside of the classroom. Self-disclosure is a way for the teacher to signal that he or she is a member of the classroom community, not just the teacher (Mendes, 2003; Scales, 1999).

One teacher writes a letter each year to introduce herself to her fifth grade students. Here are some excerpts from her letter (printed in *Among Friends*, by Dalton & Watson, 1997):

> I want to tell you about myself. I've been a teacher for 18 years and taught at Auburndale for 15 years. . . . I've been married 17 years this November and I have a 13-year-old son. He's in the eighth grade and keeps us busy with basketball and baseball. . . . I like sports, especially baseball, but I don't play any. . . . In my spare time, I enjoy cross-stitching, reading, and hiking. . . . I hate to cook, so don't be surprised to see me out in the many restaurants in our area, especially the pizza places. I know we'll have a great year, and I'm eager to learn about you in your letters!
>
> Sincerely yours,
> Mrs. O'Bryan

One way for teachers to get to know their students is by having them complete a survey similar to the one in Figure 4.1.

Other Getting Acquainted Strategies

Partner Interviews Students ask their partner questions about what they want to know. (Teachers can give students scripted questions or they can make up their own.) They record the information in writing or drawing. Students check with the partner to make sure it's okay to share information. Students present their report about their partner to the class.

Talking Artifacts Students bring in items from home that are special to them, sharing with the class something about themselves. Another way to use this technique is to have students share their artifact with a partner, complete a partner interview, and report about their partner's artifact to the class (from *Blueprints for a Collaborative Classroom*, 1997).

Scavenger Hunt Create a scavenger hunt where students have to talk to others in the room to find a person who fits each of several categories. For instance, students

---

FIGURE 4.1

Getting to Know Your Student Survey.

Student name _____
Age ____

1. What is the hardest thing about being your age?
2. What are you most proud of about yourself? This is not something that you own (like clothes or a bike), but something about you (like a personality trait, talent, or achievement).
3. What do you worry about the most?
4. What are your favorite things to do for fun? What makes them your favorite?
5. What do you like most about school?
6. What do you wish you could learn about in school that they do not teach you?
7. What do you wish teacher knew about people your age?
8. If you could change one thing about the world, what would it be?

have to find someone who is an only child, someone who has a pet, someone who plays a sport, someone who likes to cook, someone who has lived in another state, and so on.

Josette Hochman does two things to help her students get acquainted at the beginning of the year. The first test in her class (about two weeks after the start of the year) is a test of student names—students must know the names of all their classmates. The second activity is the T-shirt activity: students decorate a paper cutout in the shape of a T-shirt with information about themselves. The paper T-shirts are then hung on the wall of the classroom for everyone to read.

Jason Holmes has his students complete a timeline of their life in which they rank the highs and lows of their life. These are posted on the wall in the team area. (See Classroom Activity 4.1 for a sample timeline.) These activities not only help students learn about each other, but they also provide valuable information about students for the teacher.

C L A S S R O O M   A C T I V I T Y   4 . 1

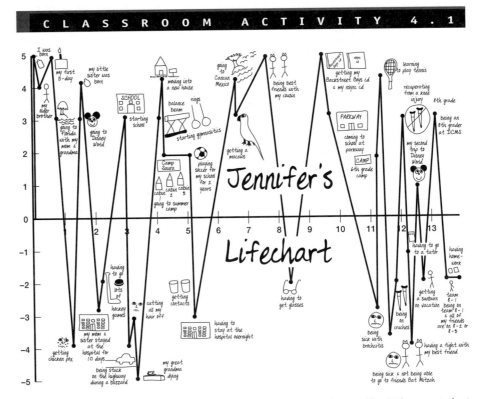

Student timeline and scoring guide Jennifer Weisman–student Jason Holmes, eighth grade Unified Studies Parkway Central Middle School

C L A S S R O O M   A C T I V I T Y   4 . 2

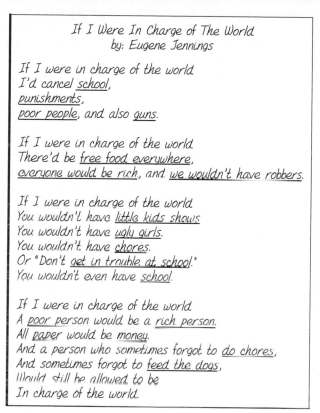

If I Were In Charge of The World
by: Eugene Jennings

If I were in charge of the world
I'd cancel <u>school</u>,
<u>punishments</u>,
<u>poor people</u>, and also <u>guns</u>.

If I were in charge of the world
There'd be <u>free food everywhere</u>,
<u>everyone would be rich</u>, and <u>we wouldn't have robbers</u>.

If I were in charge of the world
You wouldn't have <u>little kids shows</u>
You wouldn't have <u>ugly girls</u>.
You wouldn't have <u>chores</u>.
Or "Don't <u>get in trouble at school</u>."
You wouldn't even have <u>school</u>.

If I were in charge of the world
A <u>poor person</u> would be a <u>rich person</u>.
All <u>paper</u> would be <u>money</u>.
And a person who sometimes forgot to <u>do chores</u>,
And sometimes forgot to <u>feed the dogs</u>,
Would still be allowed to be
In charge of the world.

Eugene Jennings–student
Nicole Shoenweiss and Joda Ferguson
5/6 multiage classroom LeMasters Elementary School

Nicole Schoenweiss and Joda Ferguson gained some insight into their students' lives when they asked them to write their own version of a poem by Judith Viorst. The students first read the poem, then completed a version that had words missing. One student's poem is shown in Classroom Activity 4.2. The student's words are underlined.

 ## REFLECTIVE QUESTION

What do you think the teachers learned about Eugene from reading his poem?

Classroom Meetings

Classroom meetings are a valuable forum for middle school students to share their concerns and opinions and work together to solve problems (Erwin, 2003; Kriete, 2003; McDaniel et al., 2001). They help students develop social competence and enhance their sense of belonging and responsibility in the classroom. Classroom meetings are *not* for the teacher to *tell* students about decisions the teacher has made (Kriete, 2003). Classroom meetings are structured so that students can have real and meaningful input in classroom activities and can work together to solve problems (Strahan et al., 2001). Students should be presented with ground rules for meetings (or generate their own ground rules) such as "no put-downs," "one person speaks at a time," "allow each other to disagree." There are generally three purposes of classroom meetings: planning and decision making, check-in meetings, and problem-solving meetings. Planning and decision-making meetings can be used for such things as planning the next unit of study, making decisions about projects, planning for a substitute teacher, or delegating classroom responsibilities (Kriete, 2003). Interdisciplinary teams may hold planning and decision-making meetings for the entire team to discuss teamwide projects such as science fairs, community service, or field trips. Check-in meetings can be used to discuss what was learned during a certain activity, how students are progressing on a project, or how the class can improve on group work. Problem-solving meetings can be used to brainstorm and solve problems related to classroom learning or social problems like getting along or being respectful to each other. Teamwide problem-solving meetings are especially helpful for problems that affect the entire team (*Ways We Want Our Class to Be*, 1996).

The classroom as community functions differently from a traditional teacher-directed classroom. In a classroom community students have input about things that affect them, they agree about the rules that will govern them, and they cooperate to reach common goals (Stevenson, 2002; Wolk, 2003). A classroom community participates in shared decision making, answering the question, "How do we want our classroom to be?" (Erwin, 2003; Kohn, 2001). A classroom community allows for student membership, ownership, and governance of the classroom (Barth, 1990; Strahan et al., 2001). In a classroom community students have a role in determining how they will learn, what they need to be able to learn, and how they will solve problems that interfere with learning (Dalton & Watson, 1997; Pitton, 2001). In a community, student-student relationships can look very different from those in a traditional classroom (see Table 4.2).

✣ THE ROLE OF COMMUNITY IN DISCIPLINE AND MORAL DEVELOPMENT

A caring classroom or team community not only meets early adolescents' needs for identity and membership but also has great potential as a context in which students can acquire positive moral attitudes and social skills (Kohlberg, 1984; Kohn, 2001; Mandeville & Radcliffe, 2002). According to Kolhberg's theory, the motivation to "do the right thing" is different depending on the extent of a person's moral devel-

TABLE 4.2

Student-Student Relationships: Traditional Classroom versus Classroom as Community

Traditional Classroom	Classroom as Community
Students compete against each other	Students work cooperatively for common goals
Student-student interaction discouraged	Student-student interaction encouraged
Students seek help only from teacher	Students encouraged to ask others for help before teacher
Students' physical needs unimportant	Physical needs of students respected
Threats by teacher used to control	Low anxiety/high standards
No student voice in decision making	Class meetings to establish practices and solve problems

opment. At Kohlberg's level one, children tend to do what's right to receive rewards or avoid punishment. At Kohlberg's level two, children tend to do what's right based on self-interest ("What's in it for me?"). At Kohlberg's level three, children tend to do what's right because they believe they should be a nice person and because they want the approval of the group to which they belong (DeVries & Zan, 2003; Kohlberg, 1984).

Many schools today operate at Kohlberg's level one—the predominant method of controlling students is through reward and punishment (Kohn, 2001). This is most apparent in discipline policies but also pertains to the use of grades, point systems, and honor rolls. Both traditional assessment and discipline reinforce the assumption that the only motive for a child to learn or behave is to receive a reward or to avoid punishment. But educators have learned that children are not lab rats, capable only of receiving rewards and punishments—they are complex human beings with needs for acceptance and belonging (Hall & Hall, 2003). "We cannot assume, as behaviorists did, that children are intrinsically motivated only to satisfy basic physical needs. Children are intrinsically motivated to bond with their caretakers and to fit in with their social group" (Dalton & Watson, 1997, p. 160).

Most recent classroom management programs, with the exception of Canter and Canter's Assertive Discipline (2002), focus on cooperation and community (DeVries & Zan, 2003). Discipline policies based on punishments and rewards (such as Assertive Discipline) can provide temporary compliance, but they work by operating at the primitive level of the brain (survival needs) and the lowest level of moral development (Hall & Hall, 2003). Such policies do little to enhance students' self-discipline or moral development and are often incompatible with early adolescents' developmental needs (Henson, 2004). (Consider the appropriateness of "silent lunches" when children have a strong need to socialize!) Schools that rely on punishment to control students treat students as if they were operating at Kohlberg's level one. It's no wonder students don't behave better. The obedience model of discipline externalizes punishment and makes it easy for students to deny responsibility for their actions (Curwin & Mendler, 1997; Kohn, 2001). When we design discipline to be about obeying rules or pleasing adults we also set up a conflict with the student's need for independence and power and we play into an "us against them" mentality that satisfies students' desire for independence and peer acceptance at the same time (Marshall, 2002).

Adults lament that students don't behave for the good of the group, that they aren't kind, considerate or thoughtful, yet students often feel no obligation to other students because they don't feel any connection to the classroom or school community. If they have no sense of belonging to a community, no input, and no ownership in the school, there is little motivation for them to act for the benefit of the group (Hoffman & Levak, 2003; Pitton, 2002). Kohlberg's level three of moral development assumes the individual is a *part* of the group—students often feel they are not. The development of a classroom community makes students full members of their own society, with opportunities for a democratic voice in ownership and governance (Inlay, 2005; Wessler, 2003). This gives students the opportunity to make moral decisions at level three and at the same time meet their needs in a positive way (DeVries & Zan, 2003; Wolk, 2003).

A classroom or team community can play a role in enhancing students' moral development (Inlay, 2005). Students striving for acceptance by their peers become motivated to do what's good for the group. At Kohlberg's level three, members of the group help to determine what is *good* through their input. This is a democratic process by which an *integration of perspectives* shapes the values and mores of the group (Kohlberg, 1984). In this way, the community allows students to meet their needs for power and peer acceptance at the same time (Hoffman & Levak, 2003; Inlay, 2005). When students are empowered to participate in their own governance, discipline infractions are redefined (Wolk, 2003). Actions are wrong not because they break a rule but because they are *sins against the community* (DeVries & Zan, 2003). Therefore, consequences for infractions are not necessarily punitive, but are focused on problem solving, prevention of future problems, and restitution (Patterson, 2003). After any discipline problem, a primary goal is the repair and restoration of personal relationships (teacher-student or student-student) (Hall & Hall, 2003).

Marshall (2002) proposes one discipline model that is useful in democratic classrooms. His book *Discipline without Stress, Punishment, or Rewards* teaches students about four levels of social development: Anarchy, Bullying, Conformity, and Democracy. He defines each level in terms of how people interact in the classroom and how behaviors affect students as a group. Bullying, for example, occurs when one person believes his needs are more important than the needs of others. Bullying occurs any time a student's actions interfere with the learning of others. Marshall's system for maintaining order in the classroom teaches students to recognize the level at which they are behaving and discussing the action's impact on the group. Instead of rules and punishments, the system focuses on creating a noncoercive environment, developing personal relationships, and asking effective questions to help students self-diagnose. In Marshall's model, student choices, personal reflection, class meetings, and conflict resolution are valuable tools in raising student awareness of the effects their behavior has on the community.

The dilemma of building a moral community is that there will always be tension between individual interests and the good of the community. When decisions are made for the benefit of the group, individuals can't always get their way. This perspective may be difficult for some students, given a popular culture that often promises they can "have it their way" and parents that often value self-interest above the good of the group. Providing a balance between healthy self-advocacy and the good of the group is a necessity in building a democratic school community (Dalton & Watson, 1997; Marzano, Marzano, & Pickering, 2003).

Needs-Based Discipline in a Caring Classroom Community

A classroom or team community that is sensitive to student needs, empowers students, and fosters positive relationships usually has few discipline problems (Hoffman & Levak, 2003). When teachers shift the focus of discipline from adult control to a goal of caring and engaged learners, they change the discipline mind set from control to help (Kohn, 2001; Stevenson, 2002; Wolk, 2003). Discipline in a caring community is respectful of student needs, always maintains student dignity, trusts the good motives of children (that they are capable of acting responsibly), and focuses on the maintenance and repair of personal relationships (Dalton & Watson, 1997; Hall & Hall, 2003).

Interdisciplinary teams often create a discipline plan for the entire team to use. How do teams or individual teachers create a discipline plan that is consistent with the concept of classroom as community? As mentioned in previous chapters, early adolescent behavior is often driven by needs, and children at this age are strongly motivated to meet their own needs (Dreikurs, Grunwald, & Pepper, 1982). Many traditional punishments are in direct conflict with developmental needs and can actually make things *worse* (Kohn, 2001). For instance, if membership is a strong developmental need, punishing students by excluding them from class leads to feelings of rejection and further alienates students from the group. By focusing first on the developmental needs of the student as a possible *cause* of misbehavior, teachers can approach discipline from a desire to help, not a need to control (Dreikurs et al., 1982; Mendes, 2003). Needs-based discipline is the discipline mind-set most consistent with the classroom as community (Erwin, 2003; Hoffman & Levak, 2003).

Several types of needs can drive student misbehavior at this age. Ego needs such as the need for positive attention, to feel part of the group, or to avoid embarrassment are strong motivators for middle school students (Erwin, 2003). Needs for competence, control, and respect are also behind some misbehaviors. Sometimes misbehavior satisfies the simple need to have fun, escape from boredom, or feel a sense of freedom, to make one's own choices (Dreikurs et al., 1982). Inappropriate displays of anger are usually related to hurt feelings, frustration, or fear.

Needs-based discipline strategies focus on **prevention**, **support**, or **interventions**. Punishments are used only as a last resort. The best *prevention* strategies are to

Middle school students have many social lessons to learn.

- create a noncoercive environment (Glasser, 1986; Kohn, 2001).
- make positive relationships a priority (Scales, 1999; Vatterott, 1999).
- have frequent class meetings (DeVries & Kohlberg, 1987; Kriete, 2003).
- give students choice in learning activities (Keefe & Jenkins, 2002; Vatterott, 1999).

TEACHER'S VOICE
About Preventing Discipline Problems

"If students are engaged and like what they're learning, they're less apt to misbehave."

Kerry Brown, eighth grade social studies
Pattonville Heights Middle School

STUDENT'S VOICE
About Preventing Discipline Problems

"I wish teachers knew how it feels to be a teenager today and that they probably went through the same things and just lighten up a little with the stupid rules."

Agostino, eighth grade

Support Strategies

Support strategies are needs-based responses that meet physical, emotional, or social needs. Support strategies seek to identify student needs that may be contributing to student misbehavior (Crone & Horner, 2003). (Special education teachers call them *positive behavioral supports.*) In investigating student problems, teachers search for possible physical, emotional, or social needs that may be precipitating the problem.

Physical Support Strategies   Remember the relationship between physical needs and brain functioning mentioned earlier in this chapter? Rather than punishing students for misbehavior or lack of focus, we need to find ways to *support* their learning by addressing their physical needs. If a student is having trouble paying attention or behaving, an important support strategy is to have the student answer the physical needs questionnaire (Figure 4.2). After learning more about students' physical habits, support strategies may include allowing students to drink water or have a snack before class, allowing them to work in different physical positions, working

FIGURE 4.2

Physical Needs Questionnaire.

These questions will help us find out what may be getting in the way of your learning in this class. Please answer the following questions as completely as possible.
1. How long before this class do you have anything to eat? What do you usually eat at that time?
2. Estimate how many glasses of water (not other drinks) you drink on an average school day.
3. How long can you sit still before you feel like you need to move or get up?
4. What time do you normally go to bed on a school night? What time do you get up? How many hours do you sleep on the weekends?
5. Describe your favorite position to do schoolwork (sitting, standing, lying on the floor, feet up, etc.).
6. What exercise do you get on school days? When do you get that exercise?
7. During which hours in the school day is it easiest for you to concentrate? During which hours is it hardest for you to concentrate?
8. If you could create an ideal school schedule, which classes would you take in the morning and which would you take in the afternoon? Why?

with parents to increase the amount of sleep students get, or having students take a walk or run errands for exercise (Bell, 2003; NMSA, 2001c; O'Steen, Cuper, Spires, Beal & Pope, 2002). Sometimes classroom difficulties can be resolved by changing students' schedules so that their hardest classes are taken at the time of day they are most alert (Sousa, 1998; Jensen, 2000).

Emotional Support Strategies   Emotional support strategies assist students in maintaining their composure and controlling emotions. This can be a difficult process given the hormonal surges and mood swings of early adolescents. Sometimes all students need is a little understanding and sympathy (Mendes, 2003).

Instead of punishing students for being unable to be in control, emotional support strategies allow students time to deal with their frustrations (Hall & Hall, 2003). Students are encouraged to initiate their own time-out or break. Students may be allowed to leave the room for a specified destination (bathroom, counselor, time-out area, other team teacher's room) when they need to regain their self-control. Sometimes students need a break from a class or a teacher for a day or two.

Some students benefit from the formal teaching and practicing of replacement behaviors (Henson, 2004). For instance, if the student is having a problem with inappropriate language, a support strategy might require the student to write down alternative things to say and to practice them with a teacher or peer. Anger workbooks are helpful in getting students to identify and understand situations that bring out their anger. Anger replacement training programs have been successful in teaching students productive ways to handle emotions in the school setting (Curwin & Mendler, 1997).

Social Support Strategies   Social support strategies help students with problems in relationships with other students or with the teacher. When the problem is in getting along with the teacher, the most important concern must be the teacher-student relationship (Hall & Hall, 2003). Teacher-student relationship repair is critical (Strahan et al., 2001). When a student feels unfairly treated or that the teacher dislikes him or her, teacher and student must work together to make amends. Sometimes meeting with a trusted third party (like a counselor or another teacher) is helpful to air concerns (Marshall, 2002). Whether the teacher believes the student's feelings are justified is unimportant. Early adolescent feelings are often unjustified—what matters is how the students *perceive* the situation. Attempting to repair hurt feelings is worth the effort (Mendler, 2001). Some teachers find it easier to have students share concerns in writing first, allowing the teacher time to reflect on the issues.

In one teacher's class, a student with special needs was convinced that the teacher hated him and all other special education students. The teacher was very businesslike and had not taken the time to develop personal relationships with students. For this particular student, that lack of personal attention made him very insecure as a learner, afraid to make mistakes or ask for help. His principal suggested that the teacher and the student ask each other questions via e-mail to get to know each other better. That small amount of personal attention changed the student's perceptions.

When the problem is because the student is in trouble, Marshall (2002) suggests that the teacher ask the student two questions: "Do you know why you are in trouble? Do you think it's personal?" to start the conversation. Often the only repair that is needed is a little one-on-one time with the student (Hall & Hall, 2003; Wolk, 2003). Some teachers will ask students to have lunch with them or to help them in the classroom after school.

Helping students repair student-student relationships is a little more time consuming, but again, a necessary task for middle school teachers. When a student hurts someone in the community, it's important to repair the damage (Wessler, 2003). Some helpful techniques are third party mediation (adult or peer mediators), solving circles (when two students have to work together to resolve a problem), or allowing one student to act as an advocate for another. When student behavior has impacted more than one person, group intervention techniques, in which others talk about how the student has affected them, can be powerful. For some students, social skills instruction is helpful (Marzano, Marzano, & Pickering, 2003). Most counselors are familiar with such programs and can pull small groups of students out of class a few times a week to do formal activities.

Academic Support Strategies Academic support strategies offer positive, proactive approaches to prevent student failure. The most important academic support strategy is "There's no *not* doing it!" (Wormelli, 2003). Most students who receive failing grades at the middle level receive them not because of the quality of their work, but because all work is not turned in. All work must be turned in and students must stay caught up. Some schools have academic labs to which students can be assigned to catch up on work, opportunities for after-school tutoring, or Saturday School programs, all of which send the message that we will not let the student fail by not completing work. Some teachers have students work out a *payback plan*, much like the plans credit managers establish for overspenders. Students develop a plan for how and when they will turn in missing work. If they are really overwhelmed, teachers may be wise to adapt some assignments or give alternative assignments, as they would for students with special needs. Sometimes academic support means rethinking the tasks and the workload for individual students (Hensen, 2004).

Interventions

Sometimes support strategies are inadequate to handle specific discipline problems. Interventions are appropriate when the teacher believes there must be a consequence for student behavior, but does not wish to punish the student. **Interventions** are non-punitive consequences that require students to write about, think about, or talk about their problem (Curwin & Mendler, 1997). What's the difference between a punishment and an intervention? Intention and attitude—how the intervention is explained and carried out reveals both to the student. The intent of a punishment is to hurt and the attitude is one of power over, of "I'll show you who's boss." The intent of an intervention is to allow the student to regain control, reflect on his or her actions, repair damage, or perform retribution (Hall & Hall, 2003; Marshall, 2002). The attitude of an intervention is one of help, respect, affirmation, shaming the deed rather than the person, and forgiveness.

For instance, if a student has just had an emotional meltdown complete with temper tantrum, a punishment could be to suspend the student for the day. An intervention could be to verbalize to the student that he or she is having a very bad day and would benefit from some rest and a chance to think through what caused the tantrum. The student could be asked to reflect on the problem and to write out how he or she could have handled the situation differently. Both the punishment and the intervention would send the student home for the day, but the intervention demonstrates that the *action* rather than the student is bad, and it forces the student to think through some problem solving.

Discipline in the middle school is a learning experience. Early adolescents don't possess the social and emotional knowledge that adults have (Daniels, 2005). Discipline requires scaffolding and support just like other learning does (Marzano, Marzano, & Pickering, 2003). Teachers need to teach middle school students about self-control, relationships, and problem solving and shift the focus of discipline from control to relationships (Hall & Hall, 2003).

Summary

A supportive classroom environment is critical to successful learning for middle school students. Early adolescents are needy—the environment of the classroom must satisfy those needs before students can concentrate on learning. The optimum environment is one in which the classroom functions as a caring community (Hoffman & Levak, 2003). A caring classroom community empowers students to take charge of their own learning, provides an emotionally safe place to learn, nurtures the personal relationships between teacher and student, and fosters positive relationships between students (Mendes, 2003; Wessler, 2003). The caring community of the classroom can assist students in their moral development and support them in their efforts to be self-disciplined.

Key Terms

English as Second Language (ESL)
   students
formal register
in loco parentis

interventions
learning community
norm setting
support strategies

APPLICATION ACTIVITIES

1. Compare the descriptions of traditional teacher-student relationships and needs-based relationships shown in Table 4.1. Do the descriptions of the two types of teachers remind you of teachers from your past? What specific practices or personality traits do you remember about the teachers? How did they make you feel as a learner?

2. Choose a specific cultural or ethnic minority group (such as African-Americans, ESL students, gays or lesbians) that you are interested in learning more about. Read at least two articles about that group. What specific things will you do to make those students more comfortable in your classroom?

3. Design your own set of questions or use the survey in Figure 4.1 to learn more about a group of middle school students. You may survey students in a classroom or give the survey to early adolescents that you know from your family, friends, or community.

PART II

THE STRATEGIES

In Part One you gained knowledge about the unique characteristics and needs of early adolescents and how those needs form the rationale for middle school philosophy. You learned that middle school organizational structures such as teaming and advisory time exist in response to the unique needs of early adolescents. This knowledge about early adolescents is important but inadequate to prepare you to teach effectively at the middle level. In addition to knowledge about early adolescents, effective middle school teachers need tools to plan curriculum and instructional strategies to facilitate learning. Part Two provides the tools you need to develop your teaching skills and to become an effective middle school teacher.

What skills do effective middle school teachers possess? *Effective middle school teachers focus on long-range planning, extrapolate the big ideas within the curriculum, and prioritize curriculum content.* This section will make you aware of the goals and aims of the middle school curriculum and the organizational features that support it. It will guide you through a process of long term planning, show you how to integrate standards into curriculum planning, and offer strategies for the planning of individual learning activities.

Effective middle school teachers know that early adolescents learn best through activities, and they understand how to reach curriculum objectives through activity-based teaching. This section offers many concrete examples of learning activities and shows how activities can be differentiated to address students' learning differences.

Effective middle school teachers use assessment as feedback about learning. They understand that assessment provides feedback not only about learning, but also about the effectiveness of one's teaching. The chapter on assessment challenges the reader to examine the limitations of traditional grading and to appreciate the value of performance assessments.

And finally, *effective middle school teachers reflect on their personal beliefs and attitudes.* The concluding chapter discusses how teacher beliefs and attitudes influence teacher success in the classroom.

When you have completed this section, you should be able to meld the knowledge of early adolescents' unique needs gained in Part One with the activity-based teaching tools illustrated in Part Two to create quality learning experiences for early adolescents.

CHAPTER 5

THE MIDDLE SCHOOL CURRICULUM

❖ INTRODUCTION

In previous chapters, we discussed the ways that cultural forces affect early adolescent development. Social forces, accountability issues, and the nature of the world of work also impact curriculum decisions (Gross, 2002; Waks, 2002). Those curriculum decisions include what should be learned, how it should be learned, and what is considered relevant and meaningful content for early adolescents (Caskey, 2002). This chapter will attempt to clarify what makes a quality middle school curriculum and illustrate how appropriate curriculum can assist in meeting the developmental needs of early adolescents (Lounsbury & Vars, 2003; Stevenson, 2002). This chapter will also examine the goals of a student-focused curriculum and how the curriculum can be organized schoolwide to best meet these developmental goals (Vatterott, 1999). **The purposes of this chapter are to help you**

- to become aware of the social forces that can affect the middle school curriculum.
- to understand developmentally appropriate goals for the middle school curriculum.
- to become aware of how curriculum is typically organized at the middle school.
- to become familiar with examples of developmentally appropriate curriculum.
- to understand the role of school climate and the cocurriculum in meeting the developmental needs of early adolescents.
- to understand the role of teaming, block scheduling, and grouping options in facilitating student-focused curriculum.

Essential Questions

After reading and completing the activities in this chapter, you should be able to answer the following questions:

1. What role do standardized tests and concerns for academic rigor play in the content of middle school curriculum?
2. How do middle schools balance the need for challenging curriculum with emotional and social needs?
3. How has the progressivist nature of middle school philosophy been misinterpreted? How does the progressivist middle school philosophy influence the goals of the middle school curriculum?
4. How do the various components of middle school curriculum address specific developmental needs?
5. How would you characterize a high-quality middle school curriculum?
6. How can schools create the optimum school climate?
7. What are the characteristics of a high-quality cocurriculum at the middle school?

✦ FORCES IMPACTING MIDDLE SCHOOL CURRICULUM

The curriculum of the middle school—what knowledge and skills are to be learned—is influenced by forces larger than the school itself (Gross, 2002; Waks, 2002). These forces affect decisions teachers and principals make about what content is taught, what textbooks are used, what teaching methods are encouraged or discouraged, and how student learning is measured. These forces also affect what our goals are for the curriculum and how we reach those goals (discussed in Chapter 6) (Beane, 1999, 1999b, 2001; George, 2002). It is important to be aware of these forces and to understand the ways in which these forces influence curriculum in our schools. Although many forces impact the middle school curriculum, the most significant are the curriculum alignment with standards, overemphasis on standardized test scores (Bracey, 2003; Pate, 2001), the legacy of caring in the philosophy of the middle school (Dickinson, 2001; Gross, 2002), the most recent anti–middle school movement, (McEwin, Dickinson & Jacobsen, 2005), and the ensuing debate about academic rigor (Anfara & Waks, 2000, 2002).

Curriculum Alignment with Standards

State-mandated standards have been one of the most pervasive forces affecting the middle school curriculum (Bracey, 2003; Pate, 2001). State standards are usually developed in concert with educators and reflect broad outcomes that educators want all students to achieve. State standards help to raise achievement for all students and are beneficial because they force us to focus on education's long-range outcomes (Marshall, 2003; Rose & Gallup, 2003). Typically standards are general and the major task of the school is to reorganize curriculum to align with the state standards. In schools with a well-articulated comprehensive curriculum, aligning the curriculum to meet state standards is a relatively simple task. In some states, however, standards are so detailed and specific that aligning local curriculum becomes a cumbersome task (Marshall, 2003; Scherer, 2004b). In addition, some schools have no formal curriculum on record and have not organized or sequenced curriculum content by grade level or course. For those schools, aligning curriculum to meet state standards may require extensive curriculum development. Unfortunately, schools with poorly developed curriculum are often schools with limited financial resources, making it more difficult to tackle the time-consuming task of curriculum alignment (Scherer, 2004b). Because state standards affect the organization of curriculum and long-range planning, they will be discussed more fully in Chapter 6 on curriculum planning.

Overemphasis on Standardized Test Scores

To measure how well schools are performing and how many students are reaching academic standards, standardized tests are developed or adopted by each state. Schools tend to rely heavily on the state-mandated standardized tests as a measure of their success. If those tests are well aligned with state standards, they can provide teachers with valuable feedback. Unfortunately, many state assessments are not well aligned to state standards (Bracey, 2003; Marshall, 2003; Meier, 2002). Yet, in spite of such mismatches, scores on state-mandated tests are regularly reported by the media as evidence that state standards are or are not being met by individual schools or school districts. This practice often leads to an overemphasis on test scores by politicians, parents, and community leaders and the belief that higher standardized test scores indicate a more rigorous curriculum (Rose & Gallup, 2003; Vogler, 2003). Political pressure to do well on standardized tests can weigh heavily on teachers and can cause them to needlessly narrow their curriculum (Lounsbury & Vars, 2003; Scherer, 2004b). Teachers and principals often attempt to counter this pressure with convincing arguments about the goals they believe to be most important for students (Anfara & Stacki, 2002; Pate, 2001; Perkins-Gough, 2004). The movement to create a test-driven curriculum works in concert with other forces such as the anti–middle school movement and pressure for increased academic rigor to exert powerful influence on curriculum decisions (Gross, 2002; Scherer, 2004b). Because standardized tests can affect the curriculum in such an intimate way, their impact on specific curriculum content will be discussed more fully in Chapter 6.

Caring

Previous chapters discussed the importance of meeting the developmental needs of early adolescents and the importance of climate in providing the optimum environment for learning. The affective curriculum, the curriculum that is experienced by students through policies and procedures, strives to meet the emotional and social needs of students as a prerequisite to academic learning (Van Hoose, Strahan, & L'Esperance, 2001). This attention to *care* has historically been part of the middle school's unique academic mission (George, Stevenson, Thomason, & Beane, 1992; Gross, 2002). The middle school movement has focused strongly on meeting the emotional and social needs of early adolescents. In our zealousness to implement more caring practices, however, some middle level educators have neglected to emphasize the importance of achievement (Erb, 1995). In our efforts to protect and nurture self-esteem, some educators either enabled or ignored academic failure, inadvertently deemphasizing academics (Dickinson, 2001). In fact, the overemphasis on *caring* in the middle school movement over the years has often wrongly been interpreted as being anti-academic (Beane, 1999). A focus on caring and promoting self-esteem does not absolve educators of our academic commitments, nor should they impede us from fulfilling our academic duties. As discussed in Chapter 4, school and classroom climate serve as mediators to the learning process. Caring is merely the milieu in which students experience the curriculum (Strahan, Smith, McElrath, & Toole, 2001). If educators care about early adolescents, they realize the necessity of academic success in meeting developmental needs (NMSA, 2001b; Vatterott, 1999). As Tom Erb once stated: "If you care enough, focus on academics" (Erb, 1995).

The Anti–Middle School Movement

In a way, the middle school has become a victim of its own success (Beane, 1999; Erb, 1999). As intermediate schools have increasingly been renamed *middle schools* (with or without the accompanying child-centered philosophy and organizational structures), the term *middle school* has in the minds of many noneducators come to represent *all* intermediate schools. That is, in the minds of many, the middle school has become as generic as elementary school or high school. Given the general criticism of public education today, it is not surprising that an entire level of schooling is currently under attack (Beane, 1999), so much so that some large urban systems are abandoning the middle school model and returning to K–8 schools (McEwin et al., 2005; Wallis, 2005).

Seeking to become more effective schools for early adolescents, many intermediate schools implemented the structures of middle school such as teaming, block scheduling, exploratory programs, and advisory programs (Lounsbury & Vars, 1978). Unfortunately, those changes were often made without an understanding of the underlying philosophy that the structures were meant to make possible (Dickinson, 2001). In the past, middle schools have often been viewed merely as a collection of programs and their success judged by the presence or absence of these programs (Williamson & Johnston, 1999). Yet often these structural changes have occurred without any real change in the philosophy of the school, the curriculum of the school, or attitudes of the teachers. This has resulted in numerous middle schools that someone once said have "all the parts without the heart" (Dickinson, 2001). It is easy to understand how some outsiders could see little value in the organizational innovations they came to know as middle school and mistakenly believe the K–8 school is automatically better (Wallis, 2005).

The Academic Rigor Debate

The mission of the middle school to provide for the emotional and social needs of children has been criticized for creating schools that lack academic rigor (Anfara & Waks, 2000). Caring is often viewed as a code word for "watering down" (Erb, 1999), as if the act of caring was incompatible with a challenging curriculum (Gross, 2002). Caring and rigor are not a dichotomy; it is not impossible for the two to exist in the same school (Anfara & Waks, 2002; Raebeck, 1992). While critics may believe attention to emotional needs is inconsistent with rigor or high levels of learning, recent brain research reveals just the opposite—that there is a critical link between emotion and learning (Jensen, 2000; Pitton, 2001; Sousa, 1998). The academic rigor debate is fueled by several views of academic rigor. Again, critics are often unfamiliar with what actually happens in the learning process and their views are often indicative of their recollections of schooling from a previous era. The difficulty comes in the way many people define the concept of academic rigor (Beane, 1999).

Rigor is not hours of homework although many define it as hard work. This concept of rigor is closely related to the perennialist philosophy of education that the mind is like a muscle that becomes stronger with exercise. Rigor then becomes work that is hard, that requires one to exert energy. Unfortunately, what many people take for rigor is not necessarily work that is more challenging intellectually (Anfara & Waks, 2002). "Difficulty is often equated to the amount of work done by students, rather than the complexity and challenge" (Williamson & Johnston, 1999, p. 10). More work is a simple way for schools to appear to increase rigor and it requires no additional funding or personnel. Critics who focus on difficulty as important often see hours of homework as a sign of a more rigorous curriculum. The *more is always better* argument ignores quality of work and level of learning required. Rigor to these critics is evidenced by more content piled into the curriculum regardless of the intellectual challenge represented (Erb & Stevenson, 1998; Scherer, 2004b).

Rigor is not a traditional fact-based curriculum taught by traditional methods (Anfara & Waks, 2002). For some people, a rigorous curriculum is evidenced by a fact-based curriculum and the ability to commit large bodies of factual information to rote memory. This is a throwback to a time when memorization defined learning (Thompson, 2002). This definition is usually accompanied by the belief that curriculum should be teacher controlled by a tough taskmaster (Anfara & Waks, 2002).

An accompanying belief is that rigor is indicated by the ability of students to withstand large amounts of passive lecture and to read and do seatwork at length. This reflects the erroneous beliefs that only traditional methods are rigorous and that progressive methods neglect basic skills. These beliefs are related to the somewhat Victorian idea that meaningful learning must be painful, and that if students enjoy learning, it must be frivolous. There is nothing mutually exclusive about joy and rigor (Beane, 2001; Raebeck, 1992).

Curriculum and instruction that produce higher standardized test scores are not necessarily rigorous (Gandel & Vranek, 2001; Neill, 2003). Some standardized tests, especially more recently developed performance-based tests, may require students to demonstrate an advanced level of learning. On the other hand, some standardized tests measure rote learning at a very basic level. In *The Case against Standardized Testing*, Alfie Kohn (2000) builds a strong case that (depending on the nature of the test) too much emphasis on standardized test scores can lead to a curriculum that is less demanding, more focused on rote memory, and not focused on higher level intellectual skills (Bracey, 2003; Meier, 2002).

Rigor is not toughness evidenced by the small number of students who get A's and the large number of students who fail (Raebeck, 1992). Some critics believe that if large numbers of students receive high grades, the curriculum is not rigorous. Assessments can be created that will guarantee a certain amount of failure, but that in no way indicates a rigorous curriculum (Guskey, 2003). In reality, grades can be used to sort and rank learners into categories (and to compare learners with each other) or they can be used to reflect the level of learning students have achieved (Canady, 1993). When grades are designed to reflect level of learning, appropriate learning strategies would produce large numbers of students receiving high grades. Grading and assessment will be discussed in Chapter 10.

The academic rigor debate is more about philosophy than about curriculum (Gross, 2002). Perennialist or essentialist philosophies are primarily concerned with intellectual development. They hold that the function of school is to deal with the intellect. The progressivist philosophy, on the other hand, is a whole child philosophy that believes the school should be concerned with intellectual development as well as social, emotional, physical, and moral development (Gross, 2002). When emotional or social needs of middle school children are addressed, the perennialist will often fear time and energy is being taken away from intellectual needs (as if those needs can't be met simultaneously). Middle school philosophy by its nature is progressivist—that is, the function of the school is to deal with the whole child (Lounsbury & Vars, 1978). But that doesn't necessarily mean that it *takes time away* from intellectual development. Therefore, the intellectual mission of the middle school is not separate from the emotional or social mission (Gross, 2002). Intellectual development is part of an integrated approach to the total development of the child and is, in fact, one of the few certain routes to fulfilling the developmental needs for competence and achievement (Pitton, 2001; Thompson, 2002). Intellectual learning takes place in the *context* of a needs-based environment. The key to intellectual learning at the middle school *is emotional engagement* (Caskey, 2002). Rigor is challenge—but it is not necessarily the same challenge for each student. Given the diverse nature of middle school students, challenging learning experiences will vary for different students. Rigor means challenging each child to reach his or her maximum intellectual capacity.

➔ Aims and Goals of a Student-Focused Curriculum at the Middle Level

Surviving in today's world of school accountability requires middle schools to balance the intellectual needs with personal and social needs. Today's middle school must represent a hybrid of progressivist and essentialist philosophies (Gross, 2002). Therefore the curriculum must simultaneously address all dimensions of a child's development. Many of the goals of the middle school curriculum are best described as meeting students' needs for personal and social development (Bergstrom, 1998; O'Steen, Cuper, Spires, Beal & Pope, 2002). However, the primary charge society has given our schools is the preeminent goal of intellectual development. Today's emphasis on state standards and concern over standardized tests have made that point painfully obvious (George, 2002; Meier, 2002). Although the intellectual mission of the middle school is the charge most readily taken, the progressivist nature of middle school philosophy (to prepare children to live in society) compels us to be concerned about the child's moral development as well (DeVries & Zan, 2003)—about what kinds of people we want them to be (Inlay, 2005; Kohn, 2000). The goals of intellectual development and personal development are not mutually exclusive.

When addressed in an integrated fashion, personal, social and intellectual needs can be met without sacrificing academic rigor (Anfara & Stacki, 2002). There are 10 goals of a student-focused curriculum at the middle level that are encompassed within three major aims: to develop and refine intellectual skills, to assist students in the development of identity, and to assist students in defining their role in the adult world. These are elaborated below.

Aim One: To Develop and Refine Intellectual Skills

Critics often complain that middle schools don't prepare students for high school. Developing and refining intellectual skills is the one *true* way middle schools prepare students for high school. Middle schools prepare students for high school, not by acclimating them to passive lecture and hours of silent reading, but by refining the skills necessary to think abstractly and to learn independently (Lounsbury & Vars, 1978; Perkins-Gough, 2004; Wolk, 2003). Beyond the passive acquisition of inert content, middle school students need opportunities to hone their skills for abstract thought and perfect skills such as reading comprehension, problem solving, and expressing ideas verbally and in writing. To develop and refine intellectual skills, the middle school curriculum needs to meet the four goals discussed next.

Goal 1: To Develop Students as Thinkers, Learners, and Problem Solvers

Middle school students need help in developing abstract thought and analyzing and solving problems (Gross, 2002; Stevenson, 2002; Waks, 2002). To become competent thinkers, learners, and problem solvers, students need to be able to use a variety of tools and to be technologically literate. A good student-focused curriculum provides exposure to abstract activities, abstract discussions, and opportunities for methodical, logic-based problem solving (Powers, Rafferty, & Eib, 2001).

Goal 2: To Help Students Make Meaning, Reflect, and Use Reflection to Make Decisions

As opposed to being passive receptacles of information, middle school students need to be actively involved in constructing their own knowledge (Alexander, 1995; Vatterott, 1999). A student-focused curriculum provides opportunities for students to make meaning from information, to gain understanding through generating questions, to learn from mistakes, to create theories, to form opinions, and to write and talk about their learning (Anfara & Lipka, 2003; Powell, 2001; Thompson, 2002).

Goal 3: To Help Students Make Sense of the World around Them

Middle school students crave an awareness of what's going on in the world. Hungry for understanding, they are intensely curious, like preschoolers, and ask an infinite number of "why" questions (Kellough & Kellough, 1999). A student-focused curriculum provides activities that help early adolescents understand such mysteries as the physical and metaphysical world, the complexities of personal relationships in a variety of social contexts, the formal and informal rules of organizations, and the realities of law and politics (Storz & Nestor, 2003; Wolk, 2003). As students transition into abstract thinkers, they need learning experiences that help them to comprehend the complex nature of the world—that most things are not clearly black and white, but shades of gray (O'Steen et al., 2002; Waks, 2002).

TEACHERS' VOICES

About Developing and Refining Intellectual Skills

"I'm teaching them, more than anything, how to learn. So that no matter what the topic is, they can take this information, go on to something else, and they will have the skills that will allow them to learn whatever it is."

Mike Burgio, seventh grade science
Pattonville Heights Middle School

"We need to be teaching metacognition—for them to monitor what they're thinking. I think that's an important part of problem solving."

Mike Hirsch, seventh grade math
Hazelwood Junior High School

"When a group of students or an individual student says something profound, something that most adults don't even grasp—it could be a theme in history, a pattern or something that's evolved, it could be a basic human right that we take for granted, it doesn't really matter. It's when somebody actually makes a connection to the way our world works, without me making it for them. I think that's the biggest reward."

Kerry Brown, eighth grade social studies
Pattonville Heights Middle School

Goal 4: To Develop in Students the Ability to Learn Independently of Others

Middle school students need to develop the ability and motivation to learn without the assistance and constant supervision of teachers or other adults (Havinghurst, 1976). To be self-supporting in the future, students need to develop self-direction and self-discipline (Stevenson, 2002; Waks, 2002). A student-focused curriculum provides opportunities for individualized research, practice in the management of long-term projects, responsible self-direction, self-discipline, and when necessary, formal instruction of study skills (Storz & Nestor, 2003; Vatterott, 1999).

Many middle school teachers plan instruction that allows students to work independently on a daily basis on a series of long-range tasks. Eighth grade language arts teacher Janet Von Harz structures her class time so that students must plan which learning task they will do each day in order to complete projects on time. She feels strongly about the value of developing self-directed learners.

 ## Teachers' Voices

About Developing Independent Learners

"I think one of the things we tend to do in middle school is baby our students too much. I'm trying to get them prepared for high school where they will have to be more independent learners and they are going to have to take responsibility for each assignment that they are given."

Janet VonHarz, eighth grade language arts
Pattonville Heights Middle School

"My goal is to make them independent thinkers and make some of their own decisions."

Mike Burgio, seventh grade science
Pattonville Heights Middle School

Aim Two: To Assist Students in Developing Identity

The formation of identity (finding oneself) is one of the crucial developmental tasks of early adolescence (Erikson, 1963; Vatterott, 1999). Finding out what you're good at and becoming a unique personality with a positive sense of self are tasks that play heavily in the early adolescent's identity (Scales, 1991; Stevenson, 2002). A student-focused curriculum contributes to identity when it assists students in becoming successful learners and when it helps students recognize and develop talents and interests (McDaniel, Necochea, Rios, Stowell, & Kritzer, 2001). To assist students in developing identity, the middle school curriculum needs to meet goals 5, 6, and 7.

Goal 5: To Nurture within Students an Identity as Successful Learners

Students who have been successful learners need to continue with increasingly challenging material and to maintain a confidence in their ability to learn new concepts and skills (Sagor, 2002). Students with learning difficulties must be convinced that they can be capable learners and that their deficits can be remediated with hard work. English as Second Language students must experience success in their native language until they can learn in English (Gebhard, 2000). Severely handicapped students must be given tasks at which they can be successful (Frieman, 2001). A student-focused curriculum works to remediate students especially in math and reading, the subjects most critical to success in all other academic areas. An appropriate middle school curriculum prioritizes key skills and concepts and utilizes mastery learning to assure success (Anfara & Waks, 2002). Instead of covering a huge amount of content quickly and superficially—"a mile wide and an inch deep"—teachers focus on less content but take more time to be sure that students understand the concepts and have mastered the skills (Marzano, 2003). Less is more—fewer concepts learned well, fewer skills taught, but those skills mastered (Scherer, 2004b). This gives students a solid foundation of basic skills and concepts that allows them to be successful learners in the future. In addition to an appropriate curriculum, nonpunitive grading practices are essential in nurturing success and maintaining motivation for middle school students (Kohn, 1996; Van Hoose, 2001). Academic remediation is absolutely essential to students' continued engagement in school. Decisions to drop out of high school are most often made in middle school, not high school. If students do not become successful learners in middle school, they are likely to have inadequate learner self-esteem to see them through the difficult high school years (Wheelock & Dorman, 1988). (Assessment practices will be discussed more fully in Chapter 8.)

Goal 6: To Discover and Develop Students' Individual Strengths and Talents

As an enhancement to identity, early adolescents need to realize their unique strengths and talents (Havinghurst, 1976; Scales, 1991). Students may know their academic strengths ("I'm good at math") but not look beyond that to see their strengths and talents in other areas. Just as multiple intelligences theory recognizes talents in interpersonal, spatial, or musical areas, a student-focused curriculum allows students the freedom to showcase their unique strengths and talents (Vatterott, 1999). This ultimately results in more well-rounded, multifaceted adults. (Van Hoose et al., 2001; Waks, 2002).

Goal 7: To Assist Students in Developing Wholesome Interests and Leisure Pursuits

Early adolescents define themselves in part by what they are interested in. When students develop healthy, wholesome interests, they build competence and gain positive social feedback. Interests are also a vehicle for meeting social needs. Early adolescents form friendships based on common interests. When middle schools focus on student interests in the regular curriculum as well as the cocurriculum, they assist early adolescents in their search for identity and help them to gain social acceptance from their peers (Van Hoose et al., 2001). Whenever possible, student projects should be designed so that students can explore their own ideas and interests (Vatterott, 1999).

TEACHER'S VOICE

About Developing Student Interests

"In an art class you should see projects where you might be able to tell that they're working on the topic of perspective, but each picture is so individual and so different that you can really tell that the students were allowed to explore their own ideas, were allowed to do the things that interest them and that's really where the connections occur and where they personalize them."

Ed Kastner, art teacher
Wydown Middle School

Aim Three: To Assist Students in Defining Their Role in the Adult World

Consistent with their mission to educate the whole child, middle schools help to prepare students to define their role in a global society (Havinghurst, 1976; Waks, 2002). In preparation for their adult life, early adolescents need to learn to work productively with others, to develop healthy interpersonal relationships, and to appreciate the importance of physical health to personal productivity. They also need to experience a moral and ethical school environment, with opportunities to contribute to the school and the larger community in a positive way (Apple & Beane, 1995). Middle school students need to believe not only that they *can* make a difference in the world, but that they *should* (Beane, 1997; Eisner, 2004; Perkins-Gough, 2004). To assist students in defining their roles in the adult world, the middle school curriculum needs to meet goals 8, 9, and 10.

Goal 8. To Develop Productive Citizens

Early adolescents have a strong desire to be accepted by others and to make meaningful contributions to the group. They are often highly idealistic about what their role in the world should be as adults and may have unrealistic visions of the world of work. The goal of developing productive citizens is an attempt to guide students into being responsible, nonviolent, tolerant adults (Arnold, 1993; Boyer, 1995; Gross, 2002; Perkins-Gough, 2004). Being productive means becoming self-supporting, socially and emotionally healthy people (having friends), and inter-acting positively with others in their world. A student-focused curriculum accommodates this goal through providing students opportunities and guidance in social relationships, by allowing students to reflect on how they will contribute to the world, and by providing them opportunities to explore and evaluate career interests (Anfara & Lipka, 2003; McDaniel et al., 2001).

Adults often say that early adolescents want all the rights of adults without the responsibilities. Yet sometimes early adolescents don't seem to understand the connection between effort and success. In their social naivete and idealism, early adolescents seem to think if they want something badly enough, it will come to pass. When asked what they want to do when they grow up, middle school students often give answers like be a professional football player, rock singer, or movie star. While it is not our job to discourage dreams, it is helpful to guide students in seeing the hard work and skills necessary to reach their dreams and to make meaningful contributions to society (Waks, 2002).

STUDENT'S VOICE
About Developing Productive Citizens

"I wish they would teach us more about real life. Managing budgets, money, organization, job skills and let us see what it's like in the job world."

Leslie, eighth grade

TEACHER'S VOICE
About Developing Productive Citizens

"That's actually my whole point for teaching is to make them better citizens when they get out of here. It's not so they can recite who Paul Revere was."

Kerry Brown, eighth grade social studies
Pattonville Heights Middle School

Goal 9. To Develop Moral, Ethical, and Tolerant Citizens

Early adolescence is a critical stage in a child's moral development (Arnold, 1993; Kohlberg, 1984). Piaget paralleled the intellectual development of abstract thought with the development of moral perspective taking and the development of an ethical sense of self (Cowan, 1978; Havinghurst, 1976). Regardless of their home environment, most early adolescents are advancing in their moral development and see the inherent value of ethics and tolerance (McDaniel et al., 2001). Their strong desire for approval of the group and for approval by adults they respect can facilitate their moral development. When norms are established for fair and ethical actions within the school, the ethical perspective becomes ingrained in the "way we do things around here" (Dalton & Watson, 1997). A student-focused curriculum and school climate should have a *social emphasis*—on caring about the world, contributing to the well-being of others, accepting and honoring differences (Anfara & Lipka, 2003; Kohn, 1991), and developing a *service orientation*—that everyone has an obligation to service as an integral part of their role in the world (Arnold in Bergstrom, 1998; Eisner, 2004; Mandeville & Radcliffe, 2002).

Goal 10: To Develop Physically Healthy Adults

With their increased independence from adults, middle school students make daily decisions that affect their health and may contribute to lifelong health and fitness habits. They need school experiences that promote the development of a wholesome teen lifestyle (Anfara & Lipka, 2003; Gross, 2002). A student-focused curriculum at the middle level encourages physically healthy habits and stress management, a healthy relationship with food and body weight, and a commitment to lifetime fitness (NMSA, 2003a). Middle schools that are concerned about developing healthy adults also have drug education and sex education programs that discourage drug and alcohol use and that encourage students to delay sexual activity (George & Alexander, 2003).

The middle school curriculum encourages health and fitness.

STUDENT'S VOICE

About Developing Healthy Habits

"I wish we could learn more about dealing with stress in school."

Chad, seventh grade

✦ THE NATURE OF MIDDLE LEVEL CONTENT

How do we reach these goals? These goals are best attained through the development of a student-focused curriculum that respects the importance of the student's *personal* connection to the curriculum (Inlay, 2005; Keefe & Jenkins, 2002). The student's personal relationship with the curriculum is essential to student motivation and learning (Vatterott, 1999). In the teacher-focused classroom, the teacher is personally involved with the content but may not help students establish their own personal connection with the content. In the student-focused classroom, the teacher structures the content in a way that allows the student to develop that personal relationship (Tomlinson & Doubet, 2005). That relationship begins when students are actively engaged by the curriculum (Alexander, 1995). Student-driven content is made relevant to student interests, adapted to students' level of readiness, and personalized through paths and choices (Vatterott, 1999).

What does an engaging curriculum for middle level students look like? "Engagement happens when a lesson captures students' imagination, snares their curiosity, ignites their opinions, or taps into their souls" (Tomlinson, 1999, p. 38). In general, the best curriculum is *student-friendly* and could be described as

- a picture that's meaningful—content is focused on big ideas, broad interrelated concepts and principles rather than discrete unrelated facts (Inlay, 2005; Patterson, 2003; Wolk, 2003).
- problem based—students gain knowledge through solving problems that are important to them (Beane, 1997; Waks, 2002).
- process based—students learn content through the honing of important skills, such as writing, research, experimentation (Fuhler, 2003; Wolk, 2003).
- performance based—students show what they've learned through producing knowledge or discourse, creating products or performances, or providing personal reflections (Thompson, 2002; Vatterott, 1999).

Curriculum is the vehicle that enables schools to meet the needs of middle school students. Therefore, the way teachers *organize* curriculum is not as critical as how the student *experiences* the curriculum (Caskey, 2002). For many years middle school advocates believed that only an integrated curriculum could meet the needs of middle schools students. We now are beginning to understand the limits of the integrated curriculum. The simple act of organizing curriculum in an interdisciplinary fashion does not guarantee developmental responsiveness (O'Steen et al., 2002).

Integrated curriculum has often focused only on the external elements of the curriculum (Bergstrom, 1998; Gatewood, 1998), as opposed to integrating the curriculum in the minds of students. The true goal of integration is personal and social integration of the content with the interests and needs of the students. Few schools have come close to that ideal (Beane, 1997).

A student-focused curriculum starts where the child is, with the child's interests and existing knowledge, then leads to the development of adult knowledge in a fuller and more organized form (O'Steen et al., 2002). That is, interests and existing knowledge form the basis for general information, which further develops into formalized knowledge (Anfara & Waks, 2000). The larger priority should be instruction; instruction in many middle schools is still primarily teacher-focused (Gatewood, 1998). A curriculum planned around students' interests and existing knowledge experienced through student-focused instructional methods represents the greatest hope for reaching our goals (Caskey, 2002; Pitton, 2001).

✦ THE FIVE CURRICULA OF THE MIDDLE SCHOOL

The developmental needs of early adolescents are met as students experience five curricula in the middle school:

- The academic curriculum, which includes math, science, social studies, language arts, and learning skills
- The expressive curriculum, which includes courses in the fine and practical arts
- The wellness curriculum, which includes physical education, health, and advisory programs
- The cocurriculum, which includes extracurricular activities, clubs, and service projects
- The affective curriculum, which includes the unstudied curriculum of school climate, policies, and procedures

The Academic Curriculum

The **academic curriculum** is comprised of courses in math, science, language arts, reading, social studies, and learning skills. The academic curriculum of middle school is typically organized around a team of teachers teaching the four core subjects of math, science, language arts, and social studies (George & Alexander, 2003). Often language arts is taught as a two-hour block incorporating language arts and reading. Sometimes language arts and social studies are taught in a two-hour unified studies block. Study skills may be taught as a separate subject, integrated into the teaching of other academic subjects, or taught only as needed. The academic curriculum is expressly tailored to develop and refine intellectual skills (goals one through four) (Lounsbury & Vars, 1978), and is strongly driven by state standards, yet it also helps middle school students in the development of identity and their roles in the adult world (Fuhler, 2003). The best academic curriculum increases student content knowledge and skills through relevant activities that connect learning to prior knowledge, capitalize on student interests, and allow students to be creative (Caskey, 2002; Wolk, 2003). Some examples of a student-focused academic curriculum are described below. (More detailed curriculum examples are described in Chapter 7.)

Examples of Language Arts Curriculum

- Students write and illustrate chapter summaries to summary books. Students are allowed to read these summary books during silent sustained reading time (Nicole Schoeneweis and Joda Fogerson, LeMasters Elementary School).
- Students research a consumer item of their choice and write a consumer report (Janet VonHarz, Pattonville Heights Middle School).
- Students produce a career brochure based on their research of a specific career (Janet VonHarz, Pattonville Heights Middle School).
- Students keep a metacognition log to analyze factors that affect their reading (Jason Holmes, Parkway Central Middle School).
- Students identify characters who exemplify specific virtues and vices in the story they are reading about the Trojan War (Greg Bergner, Parkway Central Middle School).

Examples of Social Studies Curriculum

- Students learn about a historical period by analyzing the music of the period (Mike Holdinghaus, North Kirkwood Middle School).
- Students create an imaginary family living during the Civil War. They keep a journal as if they were a member of that family (Mike Holdinghaus, North Kirkwood Middle School).
- During the *What Causes Revolution?* unit, students act out a play about the Boston massacre, analyze current political cartoons, and do a cause and effect analysis about the American Revolution (Kerry Brown, Pattonville Heights Middle School).
- Groups of students become "experts" on various aspects of the presidential election process. They research their topics and create a Hyperstudio program used by other students to study each aspect of the election process (Tony Ambrose, Parkway Central Middle School).

Examples of Math Curriculum

- Students create boxes by folding pieces of paper of different areas. They fill the boxes with popcorn to measure the volume of the boxes, create a table of averages, and graph the two tables (Pat Johnson, Pattonville Heights Middle School).

- Students write in journals every two weeks to explain what they have learned, describe relationships between concepts they have learned, and respond to specific activities (Pat Johnson, Pattonville Heights Middle School).
- Students create ABC books using math vocabulary words (Stephanie Walton, Pattonville Heights Middle School).
- Prealgebra students make up games about integers to be used by sixth grade math students (Stephanie Walton, Pattonville Heights Middle School).

Examples of Science Curriculum

- Students demonstrate their knowledge of the solar system by creating a *Travel to a Constellation* travel magazine (Debbie Bruce, Parkway Central Middle School).
- Seventh graders brainstorm ideas for the science fair on a poster they give to the sixth graders (Mike Burgio, Pattonville Heights Middle School).
- Students prepare and demonstrate experiments that show the steps in the scientific method (Debbie Bruce, Parkway Central Middle School).
- Students design, build, and launch rockets as a way of learning about force and motion, momentum, and Newton's Laws (Mike Burgio, Pattonville Heights Middle School).

STUDENT'S VOICE

About Academic Curriculum

"I like the rocket because you see those big space shuttles on TV and all this stuff like going into the sky and it's just like a little mini-version of that. But still you feel like you're important and you're progressing. . . . I just really liked it cause it made me feel big."

Maria, seventh grade

TEACHER'S VOICE

About Academic Curriculum

"My whole purpose for being a history teacher is for my kids to learn the lessons of history and how they can apply them to today, so whatever way I can make it reach them and whatever way I can show them the importance of it, I do it; and it's

usually through stuff they discover, not me telling them that it's important. They
have to realize it for themselves that it's an important event or issue to deal with."

Kerry Brown, eighth grade social studies
Pattonville Heights Middle School

Examples of Unique Academic Programs

Cultural Connections   Cultural Connections is a year-long course required of all
sixth graders at Parkway Central Middle School. The curricula of Art, Home
Economics, and Foreign Language are integrated in this course. Students learn about
speaking the language of a specific country, the art of the country, and the food of
the country. They spend a trimester in each of the three subjects and the curriculum
is also connected to the sixth grade social studies theme of Western civilizations.

Math Remediation   Students needing additional help in prealgebra are placed in
Math Remediation which alternates with physical education. Students attend their
regular math class and then receive an additional period of individualized help in the
Math Remediation class (North Kirkwood Middle School).

Saturday School   Saturday School is a voluntary self-help program for students
who need to make up work that has been missed or needs to be redone, or work that
the student needs extra help to complete. A mid-morning brunch prepared by school
administrators and volunteers has become a great time for visiting with the students
and validating their wise decision to take some control and responsibility for their
success in school (Pattonville Heights Middle School) (Vatterott, 1999).

Microsociety Inc.   Microsociety Inc. is a multidisciplinary simulation of a real society with students operating virtually every aspect of the society, including government, law enforcement, and business. West Middle School in Sioux City, Missouri,
has a Microsociety operating in its school. A Constitutional Convention determines
the laws and the *Bill of Rights and Responsibilities*. A monetary system is devised,
businesses established, and a government elected. During the last hour of the day,
students *go to work*. Students earn *money* and spend it at the various businesses.
Student jobs may be anything from reporting news, to running a business (product
or service), to being a judge, policeman, or other government employee.
Microsociety was the brainchild of teacher George Richmond, who eventually established Microsociety Inc. as a nonprofit organization. Microsociety Inc. is currently used in more than 200 schools throughout the country (Vatterott, 1999).

The Expressive Curriculum

The **expressive curriculum** includes courses such as art, vocal and instrumental
music, speech and drama, foreign language, computer science, family and consumer
science (replacing what was once known as home economics), and industrial technology (replacing what was once known as industrial arts) (George & Alexander,

The expressive curriculum helps students discover their unique talents.

2003). Although some states have defined standards for these curriculum areas, many states have not, and these areas are typically not included in standardized tests. The expressive curriculum, once called fine and practical arts courses, are often called exploratory courses at the middle school, since the goal of the middle school curriculum is to allow students to explore a wide variety of courses for short periods of time (Waks, 2002). These courses allow students to appreciate the aesthetic and artistic elements in their world and allow them to express their own aesthetic and artistic interests and talents (Van Hoose et al., 2001). The organization and scheduling of these courses varies greatly among middle level schools, with each type of organization offering its own advantages. In traditional junior high schools, these subjects may be offered as semester-long or even year-long electives, allowing students to choose only a few courses but offering the potential to explore subjects in greater depth. Middle schools typically offer the expressive curriculum organized in an exploratory wheel, with groups of students rotating through a series of 6 to 10 week courses for the year (4 to 6 courses per year), allowing them to experience most of the expressive curriculum. A true exploratory wheel does not offer choice but instead forces all students to be exposed to most of the exploratory courses (George & Alexander, 2003). Many middle schools offer a combination of the forced wheel and elective choices—students may follow an exploratory wheel in sixth and seventh grades with choices in the eighth grade, or students may be scheduled into an exploratory wheel one period a day and have choices of electives another period.

The expressive curriculum plays two important roles in meeting the needs of early adolescents. First, it enables students to discover and develop their individual talents and strengths in areas outside of academics (Bergman, 1992). This is especially crucial to the development of a sense of competence for students who do not excel in academic subjects or who struggle with basic academic skills (Scales, 1991). Second, the expressive curriculum assists students in developing wholesome interests and leisure pursuits (Waks, 2002). It may be the last window of opportunity to develop interest in foreign language and music before students reach high school. The most powerful argument for the forced exploratory wheel is that students often discover an interest in a subject they had no interest in before. The expressive curriculum also offers special opportunity for students to appreciate culture and heritage through art, foreign language, and music (Skelton, Wigford, Harper, & Reeves, 2003). Courses in the expressive curriculum may be called exploratory courses, elective courses, or encore courses (courses that are not core courses). The best expressive curriculum helps students see the cultural value of art and music, learn to express thoughts and emotions in a different form, understand the value of new experience, experiment with their own creativity and budding mental talents, learn more about themselves, and broaden their interest and appreciation of the world around them (Waks, 2002). Some examples of expressive curriculum are described below.

Examples of Expressive Curriculum

- Music: Students learn about rhythm patterns by composing and playing their own original patterns (Kathy Bhat, North Kirkwood Middle School).
- Art: Students learn various art concepts through the design of CD covers, magazine covers, and cereal boxes (Ed Kastner, Wydown Middle School).
- Art: Students design haunted house brochures at Halloween (Ed Kastner, Wydown Middle School).
- Art: During the *Bully project*, students read newspaper articles about bullying, brainstorm ideas, and create a picture that expresses the concept of bullying (Ed Kastner, Wydown Middle School).

Examples of Unique Expressive Curriculum/Programs

- Peer tutoring is offered as an elective class for eighth graders, allowing them to serve their fellow students. The student needing help is pulled out of social studies or science to work with his or her peer tutor (North Kirkwood Middle School).

- Integrated Arts: In the sixth grade, teachers and students in art, drama, music, and technology classes work together for the semester to produce a musical. Students design the sets in art, write the play in drama, create the scripts in technology classes, and compose the music in their music class (Wydown Middle School).
- Conflict mediation is taught to all sixth graders in the family and consumer economics course (Parkway Central Middle School).
- Choices for elective courses include seminars created by academic team teachers on such topics as law, Shakespeare, or ecotechnology, depending on the interests and knowledge of the individual teachers (North Kirkwood Middle School).

The Wellness Curriculum

The whole child emphasis of the middle school makes wellness a priority. The wellness curriculum is designed to promote the physical and mental well-being of students and addresses the crucial goal of developing physically healthy adults (Pateman, 2004). Children in the United States are unhealthier today than they have been in generations. There are higher rates of obesity in young children and teens than ever before in our country's history (Dalton, 2004). This is due primarily to poor diets that are high in fat, too much fast food and snack foods, and too little physical activity (Thompson & Shanley, 2004). Teens also have a higher than acceptable rate of pregnancy, sexually transmitted diseases, and drug and alcohol use (Pateman, 2004). The **wellness curriculum** includes the formal curriculum (physical education, health, and advisory courses) as well as health and nutrition services, counseling, and social services. Middle schools concerned about wellness have a comprehensive health program that approaches physical and mental health problems from a holistic perspective (Carnegie Council on Adolescent Development, 1996; NMSA, 2002). That is, teachers, counselors, administrators, and health care professionals work together to coordinate formal curriculum with school health and counseling services. A comprehensive wellness curriculum helps students cultivate lifetime habits for good physical health as well as strategies for handling stress and promoting emotional health (Erb, 2001; NMSA, 2003). Like the expressive curriculum, courses in the wellness curriculum are typically not influenced by state standards or standardized tests.

The physical education and health component of the wellness curriculum should emphasize individual health needs, the value of good health, and the value of wise decisions (George & Alexander, 2003; Pateman, 2004). The physical education and health curriculum at North Kirkwood Middle School is comprehensive, developmentally appropriate, and student focused. The curriculum recognizes the vast differences in early adolescent physical abilities (and the tendency to be physically uncoordinated) and teaches less about the playing of specific sports and more to lifetime fitness habits and skill development. The health curriculum focuses on decision making and lifetime health habits and helps students understand the dangers of unhealthy diets, substance abuse, and promiscuity. The physical education curriculum emphasizes objectives in physical activity and lifetime wellness, weights and conditioning, gymnastics and tumbling, rhythms and dance, and efficiency of human movement as well as performance in individual and team sports.

The physical education program evaluates students on knowledge and form as opposed to skill level. Assessments reward form rather than strictly results. For instance, in volleyball the student receives points for using the proper form of serving and following the rules, even if the ball doesn't go over the net. In competitive games each student can score only once until all other students on the team have scored.

Examples of Physical Education and Health Curriculum

- Physical education—students learn about physical fitness by calculating their percentage of body fat (Janet Peabody, North Kirkwood Middle School).
- Students alternate days in the fitness center, regular physical education class, and health class, allowing teachers to integrate health lessons with practical applications in the fitness center or gym (Janet Peabody, North Kirkwood Middle School).
- CPR is part of the physical education curriculum and is required of all physical education students at Pattonville Heights Middle School.

TEACHER'S VOICE

About the Wellness Curriculum

"It's really important for physical education to be individualized. We don't test on results, but on form. We don't care that they get it in the basket."

Janet Peabody, physical education
North Kirkwood Middle School

Advisory Programs

The advisory component of the wellness curriculum complements the physical education and health curriculum to meet students' emotional and social needs. Traditional junior high schools often had homeroom periods. The concept of teacher advisory is a similar nonacademic block of time. **Advisory programs** were originally conceived as a method of formalizing a one-on-one advisor-advisee relationship between teacher and student (NMSA, 2001c). The goal was that each child would be known well by at least one adult in the school (Beane, 2001). That adult could function like a *guardian angel*, to look out for the child academically, socially, and emotionally. The adult advisor's role would be that of *advocate*, to monitor the child's academic success and provide emotional support (Stevenson, 2002). The core tenets of the advisory concept are "that each child is known and cared about by an adult, that children and adults establish constructive and productive relationships, and that students and teachers have quality time to work, learn, and talk, with one another" (Williams & Johnston, 1999, p. 12). The goals of the advisor are to nurture within students an identity as successful learners, assist them in becoming productive citizens, and help students negotiate obstacles to physical and mental health and academic success (Connors, 1992; NMSA, 2001c). In an effort to meet those goals, many middle schools use a nonacademic block of time to implement advisory programs. This block of time is similar to homeroom, but is ideally 20 to 30 minutes in length (George & Alexander, 2003). In some schools all staff, including counselors and the school nurse, are assigned a group of student advisees. This allows for lower adult-student ratios but may result in advisors who have little contact with their students at other times of the day. In some schools, all teachers are assigned advisees. In other schools, the academic team shares advisory responsibility for all students assigned to their team (NMSA, 2001c). The last two arrangements result in higher teacher-student ratios, but teachers are more likely to already have a relationship with the student.

The advisory program has become the most controversial component of the middle school program. Some of the issues surrounding this controversy are whether faculty are trained to implement programs with a heavy counseling emphasis, whether communities view advising as the teaching of values and the supplanting of family control over the teaching of values, and whether nonacademic time take away time that should be spent on academics (George & Alexander, 2003). Most failed advisory programs have been the victim of lack of support from parents and teachers. This is often because schools have focused on *advisory as curriculum* and have lost sight of the original goal of the advisory program—for each student to be known well by at least one adult. The advisory program is more of a *personal relationship* than a *program* (Connors, 1992).

It has been said that two kinds of advisory programs are unsuccessful: those that give teachers too much freedom and those that give them too little. The advisory curriculum may vary from nonexistent (with teachers free to spend the time in any way they like), to weekly or monthly themes (friendships, responsible decision making, resolving conflicts, exploring careers), to a highly structured prepackaged curriculum complete with student activities and worksheets about a variety of topics (Connors, 1992; NMSA, 2001c). In programs where the curriculum is nonexistent, some teachers may engage students in meaningful discussions and activities, and other teachers may simply allow the students free time without interacting with them. Under these conditions, it's easy to see how some teachers, students, and parents can perceive the advisory program to be a waste of time. Highly structured programs, such as the Lions Quest program or the Wise Skills program, come complete with structured activities for students. For example, Wise Skills provides writing, research, and journaling activities for each of eight monthly themes and uses character portraits of famous people to illustrate themes (see Figure 5.1, an overview of the WiseLives component of the Wise Skills program).

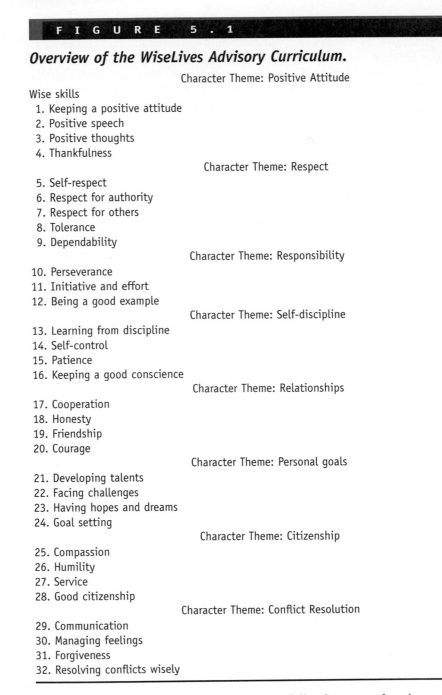

FIGURE 5.1

Overview of the WiseLives Advisory Curriculum.

Character Theme: Positive Attitude

Wise skills
1. Keeping a positive attitude
2. Positive speech
3. Positive thoughts
4. Thankfulness

Character Theme: Respect

5. Self-respect
6. Respect for authority
7. Respect for others
8. Tolerance
9. Dependability

Character Theme: Responsibility

10. Perseverance
11. Initiative and effort
12. Being a good example

Character Theme: Self-discipline

13. Learning from discipline
14. Self-control
15. Patience
16. Keeping a good conscience

Character Theme: Relationships

17. Cooperation
18. Honesty
19. Friendship
20. Courage

Character Theme: Personal goals

21. Developing talents
22. Facing challenges
23. Having hopes and dreams
24. Goal setting

Character Theme: Citizenship

25. Compassion
26. Humility
27. Service
28. Good citizenship

Character Theme: Conflict Resolution

29. Communication
30. Managing feelings
31. Forgiveness
32. Resolving conflicts wisely

Most of the prepackaged programs are essentially character education programs, focusing on values, personal qualities, and decision making. Some prepackaged programs are quite helpful to teachers, especially if they have been designed specifically for early adolescents. Programs that have been created for a generic audience of elementary students may not fit the specific needs of middle school students and students may complain that the activities are dumb or babyish. The most successful advisory programs seem to be those developed by the faculty of the school to meet the special needs of their students. These programs often used prepackaged programs as resources without adopting them in their entirety.

Middle schools utilize the advisory block of time in a variety of ways (see below). Some schools use advisory time for cocurricular activities or community service (George & Alexander, 2003). When advisory time is assigned to the academic team, teachers may chose to use certain days for advisory activities and other days for academics (NMSA, 2001c). For instance, the team may use an advisory period for students to study for this week's social studies test, time for students to work on science fair projects, or time for a guest speaker. Some teams use one advisory period a week for silent sustained reading or study hall. The time can also be used to incorporate other nonacademic programs that would be taught during the school year. Below are some topics or programs schools may implement during the advisory period.

Advisory time belongs to the students, and their interests should be considered in planning the activities (Connors, 1992; Pitton, 2001). Students may want to learn more about a topic related to recent unit of study or they may enjoy discussing favorite books they are reading. They may want to choose a series of careers and arrange guest speakers. They may enjoy using the newspaper to find current events they wish to discuss. Or they may want to spend some time sharing things about themselves, such as hobbies, pets, or travel. Any of these topics could be acceptable uses of advisory time.

Although a formal commitment of time for advisory activities is ideal, it is possible to meet the goals of the advisory program without formal advisory time. Many of the goals can be met through the development of personal relationships

Academic Uses of Advisory Time

Study skills instruction	Individual academic monitoring
Academic lab/remediation period	Silent sustained reading
Homework help	Study hall

Nonacademic Uses of Advisory Time

Understanding puberty	Sexuality education
Understanding others	Drug education
Friendships	Multicultural education
Social skills	Career education
Manners/etiquette	Decision making
Communication skills	Goal setting
Conflict resolution	School improvement projects
Peer pressure	Community service activities

between teachers and students, school climate considerations, and some formal one-on-one academic monitoring. "The most successful advisement programs emphasize personal contact between student and advisors along with continuing support of the student in his or her academic program and personal adjustment to school" (Keefe & Jenkins, 2002, p. 443). At Parkway Central Middle School, for instance, counselors practice what is called developmental guidance. Counselors present lessons on study skills, stress, and test anxiety in the academic teams. They meet with students four times during September and October. Teams can request specific topics based on their students' needs.

✦ THE COCURRICULUM

The **cocurriculum** includes all extracurricular clubs, sports, and activities offered to students through the school. Extracurricular activities are called the cocurriculum to emphasize that they are integral to the educational program. "*Cocurricular* reinforces the idea that any activity sponsored by the middle level school is linked to core academics and supports the goals of the school" (Galletti, 1999, p. 1). The cocurriculum is meant to complement and complete the academic, expressive, and wellness curriculum and to work in concert with them to meet the goals of the middle school (Feinstein, 2003). The goals most strongly addressed by the cocurriculum are the goals of developing strengths and talents, developing interests, becoming productive moral citizens, and being physically healthy (Holloway, 2002). The cocurriculum allows students to explore interests that they are unable to fully explore within the regular schoolday. It provides opportunities for students to socialize with peers outside of home and to broaden friendships to include friends of other cultures and social classes. The cocurriculum can be a powerful force in socializing new students, severely handicapped students, and ESL students and creates a sense of belonging that enhances engagement in the learning process during the schoolday (Holloway, 2002).

The cocurriculum also meets a need of parents and the community by providing wholesome supervised social activity for early adolescents between the hours of 3 p.m. and 6 p.m. For children of poverty, after-school activities are often a safe haven from dangerous neighborhoods and turbulent home environments (Mertens, Flowers, Mulhall, Fuhler, 2003). Many children of poverty are forced to stay inside after school, further limiting their socialization. Nationwide, an estimated five million to fifteen million children—one-third of all 12-year-olds—are left unsupervised in the afternoon, putting them at significantly greater risk of truancy, low achievement, obesity, and behaviors that can lead to substance abuse, promiscuity, and delinquency. Middle school children who spend considerable time after school alone felt less academically able and had lower esteem than other children (Mertens et al., 2003). The rate of violent crime among juveniles triples between 3 p.m. and 8 p.m. (Pride, 1999, p. 20). The cocurriculum meets a critical need in many communities for students who are too old for babysitters but often not ready for total freedom (Feinstein, 2003).

Cocurricular programs are organized and offered in a variety of ways, most commonly after school two to four days a week. Many middle schools have found it difficult to sustain a viable after-school cocurricular program without providing after-school transportation. If after-school transportation is a problem, clubs can be offered weekly or biweekly during the school day. One way this can be accomplished is by shortening each class period by 5 or 10 minutes and holding club meetings at the end of the day. Some schools obtain private funding to assist them in the cost of offering after-school programs.

Ideally, the staffing of cocurricular programs should be done by classroom teachers or other adults who work in the school. This provides students with the chance to interact with teachers outside of the classroom and meets valuable needs for adult role models (Holloway, 2002). In most schools the sponsoring of cocurricular activities is voluntary. In some schools teachers are paid a stipend for sponsoring any cocurricular activity and in other schools only athletic coaches are paid. In many middle schools, sponsors are not paid but sponsoring is often assumed to be part of the teacher's professional responsibility in educating the whole child. Sponsoring cocurricular activities is a wise teacher investment of time that allows teachers to get to know students outside of the regular classroom (Wormeli, 2003). However, each teacher must weigh the time required to sponsor activities against his or her professional need to provide good instruction and personal need for down time. Beginning teachers often delay sponsoring activities until after their first semester or first year of teaching, or choose to co-sponsor an activity with an established sponsor.

When effectively structured and implemented, middle level cocurricular programs can be a valuable asset in meeting early adolescents' developmental needs (Feinstein, 2003). These programs, when effective, are characterized by four elements:

- Effective cocurricular programs are *age appropriate*. They reflect a knowledge of student needs and are success oriented.
- Effective cocurricular programs are *inclusive*. That is, they are flexible enough and offer sufficient variety to allow all students to participate. Inclusive programs reflect the cultural and ethnic diversity of the school and are not limited to students who can afford uniforms or materials.
- Effective cocurricular programs are *balanced*. Activities represent student interests in the academic, expressive, and wellness curriculum. The activities offered are viewed as similar in scope and importance (i.e., not only sports are viewed as important).
- Effective middle level cocurricular programs are viewed as *legitimate*. They are perceived by students to be fair, worthwhile, positive experiences. Cocurricular programs allow students to engage in active, meaningful activities (Galletti, 1999).

Types of Cocurricular Clubs and Activities

Intramural and Interscholastic Sports   One of the most common cocurricular activities is **intramural sports**, in which students play on noncompetitive teams against others in their school, and **interscholastic sports**, competitive teams that represent the school in play against teams from other schools. Traditional interscholastic sports, when modeled after collegiate and professional sports, may not be developmentally appropriate for middle school students (NMSA, 2001d). When interscholastic sports place winning above everything else, cut low-performing players, bench others, and glorify a few star athletes, the programs become detrimental psychologically to many of the participants. Early adolescents have a wide range of athletic ability. When all players are expected to perform at the same level, given the differences in the timing of their physical development, students who begin puberty earlier are more likely to be rewarded with a position on the team. Students who develop later and lack the physical strength and size of early maturing students may feel inadequate. When the interscholastic team is one of the only cocurricular activities offered, students have difficulty meeting their needs for membership and belonging (George & Alexander, 2003).

In addition, sports are physically quite risky for early adolescents because their rapidly growing bones and muscles are fragile and can break easily. Early adolescents are especially at risk for breakage in the bones' growth plates and for tears in muscles, tendons, and ligaments stretched tight by rapidly growing bones (McEwin & Dickinson, 1997). Approximately one-third of all sports injuries now occur in children aged 5 to 14. Many of those injuries are overuse injuries caused by overtraining and long playing seasons. Football is the most dangerous of interscholastic sports for early adolescents, with the highest incidence of injuries of all sports at the elementary, middle school, and high school level (McEwin & Dickinson, 1996). It has been said that a seven-year-old is safer playing football than a seventh grader.

Intramural sports, in which teams play only other teams within the school, are much more developmentally appropriate for middle school students. Intramural programs accept all players, regardless of skill level, and in a well-designed program offer a variety of sports for both boys and girls (NMSA, 2001d). Intramural programs should deemphasize winning and losing and focus on skill development, teamwork, and having fun. Many schools organize intramural teams around the interdisciplinary teams the students are assigned to, further enhancing the student's sense of membership within the team (George & Alexander, 2003). Typical intramural programs may include such sports as flag football, volleyball, soccer, softball, and basketball. More inclusive programs may offer fitness activities that are noncompetitive such as a jogging club, African dance, jump rope team, or aerobics.

Academic Clubs   Clubs that focus on academic areas can be used as enrichment, remediation, or just for fun. The recent emphasis on standardized test achievement has prompted many middle schools to establish after-school programs for remediation or tutoring. Such programs are an excellent way to help students academically and can provide an important service to promote academic success. They should not, however, become so pervasive that they prevent students from participating in nonacademic activities. Care must be taken that academic remediation does not supplant cocurricular programs meant for personal enrichment and enjoyment. The goal of the cocurricular program is to diversify and enrich learning experiences for early adolescents, not to extend the academic school day (Pride, 1999). The purpose of academic clubs is to tap students' interest in math, science, social studies, language arts, or computers and to allow them to explore those interests. Typical academic clubs may include such options as creative writing, school newspaper, yearbook, international students club, book club, history club, biology club, environmental club, math games club, and fun with computers.

Special Interest Clubs   Special interest clubs may complement the expressive curriculum or may focus on other interests of students. In many middle schools groups of students are allowed to start a club based on their special interest, provided they have an adult sponsor. Special interest clubs that complement the expressive curriculum may include choir, orchestra, jazz band, art club, ceramics, Spanish club, student theater, or cooking club. Clubs that focus on other interests could include the newcomer's club, the photography club, gardening club, babysitters club, chess club, travel club, or videography club.

Service/Student Government   Middle school students are at a unique stage in their moral development to benefit from the act of service (Blum, 2005; Eisner, 2004; Perkins-Gough, 2004). Many middle schools require students to do a prescribed number of hours of community service. Service may be to community groups such as senior citizen homes or homeless shelters or may take place within the school. With supervision, students of this age are capable of making decisions and handling many of the details of parties, dances, fund raisers, and other special school projects. In one middle school, the student council decided they wanted to paint the student lockers. They asked local businesses to donate the paint, arranged for adult supervision, and painted the lockers on weekends. Other service to the school could include such activities as planting flowers, working in the library, tutoring other students, serving as peer mediators, or serving as aides at the elementary school. In some schools each cocurricular club takes responsibility for some area of service.

Student government should be elected by a method that represents all students, such as representatives elected by homeroom or advisory groups, and should represent all ethnic and minority groups as well as both girls and boys. Student governments should have the power to identify and solve school problems and make recommendations to the administration (Vatterott, 1999). At Mount View Middle School each grade level has its own town council, with two representatives from each advisory class. Each town council meets monthly to discuss proposals, concerns, or needs. An adult advisor attends those meetings and communicates with grade-level teachers. The town councils plan and implement social events and community service (Vatterott, 1999).

Affinity Groups/Support Groups   An *affinity group* is group of students who share a specific cultural, racial, or ethnic affiliation and meet together to discuss common problems and to offer support to one another. An affinity group uses the common experience of its members to focus on issues of culture, race, religion, or ethnicity (Aguilar & Gross, 1999). The school forms *support groups* to help groups of students deal with specific problems such as divorce, death, chemical abuse, or eating disorders. Support groups are most often organized and led by school counselors or other counselors trained in the specific problem.

Unique Cocurricular Programs

Rose Court is a club available to seventh and eighth grade girls at Kettering Middle School. Parents and administrators work together to provide workshops and field trips about careers, self-esteem, and leadership. The group holds seminars about social and political issues, does community service, and conducts a rite of passage cotillion planned by parents, teachers, and students (Peters, 1999).

Making It Happen is an extracurricular program at Wydown Middle School that focuses on academic achievement, school membership, and ownership. Originally designed for African American students, the program is now open to any student. Teachers serve as mentors and involve students in a number of activities to enhance school membership and group togetherness. Each student is assigned a tutor, a local college student. Students in need of a computer in their home can receive a used computer donated to their family.

Aim High is a mandatory academic support program at Parkway Central Middle School for students identified as having academic difficulties after the first six weeks of school. The program meets twice a week after school. Students receive tutoring and suggestions for improving their academic standing. Tutors in the program are high school students, seventh and eighth graders or classroom teachers.

School News is a morning "news" program written, produced, directed, and broadcast by students via closed circuit television at Mirror Lake Middle School (Blahous & Voss, 1999).

The Affective Curriculum—School Climate

In Chapter 4, we discussed creating the optimum *classroom climate*. The **affective curriculum** is the **school's climate**—what the student experiences emotionally and socially while at school but *outside* the classroom. A positive school climate is experienced by students as warm, caring, and supportive. It is evidenced by positive attitudes, a sense of ownership, and pride—the school is a place where students and teachers want to be (Blum, 2005). A negative school climate is experienced by students as unfriendliness, alienation, and disconnection (Vatterott, 1999). Although schools often attempt to formalize the affective curriculum through mission statements and policies, the true affective curriculum is what is actually experienced by the student in day-to-day interactions with people and procedures (Powell, 2001). School climate is critical at the middle school level because of the fragile nature of student attitude and its impact on motivation and achievement (Blum, 2005; NASSP, 1985). The affective curriculum also has the potential to provide valuable experiences that will help students become productive, ethical citizens (Mandeville & Radcliffe, 2002). A positive affective curriculum helps the middle school meet its goals by meeting the early adolescent's basic needs for acceptance, belonging, recognition, and responsibility (Hoffman & Levak, 2003; Vatterott, 1999).

Creating a Positive School Climate

The creation of a school culture is more dependent on the behavior of adults in the school than on characteristics of students, the economic climate of the community in which the school is located, per-pupil expenditures, physical facilities, or a host of other demographic or environmental variables (Vatterott, 1999). The building principal is the most influential person in determining climate. He or she, along with other administrators, clearly sets the tone and expectations and reinforces the climate of a school. Creating a positive climate requires attention to some basic school practices (Vatterott, 1999). Discussed below are nine practices that help promote a more positive school climate at the middle level.

1. *Create small communities for learning.*

The 1989 report by the Carnegie Council on Adolescent Development, *Turning Points*, recommended that middle schools reduce the size of the group to which students belong. The most common way this is done is by assigning students to interdisciplinary teams of two to four teachers from the core academic areas of math, science, social studies, and language arts (George & Alexander, 2003). For instance, a group of four teachers shares the same 120 students. A two-person team might share 50 to 60 students. For most of the day, that group of students shares the same schedule. Other practices that attempt to create smaller houses or schools within one large school may assign all seventh graders to one group of teachers, all eighth graders to another group of teachers. Buildings with large enrollments often stagger class dismissal times so that smaller numbers of students are moving at any one time.

2. *Reinforce group identities.*

Once the size of the group has been reduced, schools must establish and reinforce group identities. Teams or houses need territory to create identity. As much as possible, classes for a team or grade level should be in the same area or hall. Those areas should be designated for those groups (i.e., the eighth grade hall or the Team 7 West area). If possible, student lockers should be assigned in their territory and bulletin boards and wall space in the territory should belong to the group. Team or grade-level identities are encouraged through team names, newsletters, displays, or special activities. Some teams enjoy creating T-shirts, pins, logos, or slogans to reinforce their identities (Vatterott, 1992).

3. *Respect and celebrate diversity.*

Schools that respect diversity make students comfortable by allowing them to express their culture, religion, or ethnicity in their dress, language, and actions. Teachers model an acceptance of diversity by being eager to learn about individual students' culture and practices (Bell, 2003; Brown, 2002). Differences in cultures are incorporated into the curriculum whenever possible (Ladson-Billings, 2001). Respect for others is an absolute, and verbal intimidation, or gender or racial slurs, are never tolerated (Erb, 2000; Sapron-Shevin, 2003).

4. *Make sure each student is known well by at least one adult.*

This may be accomplished through a formal advisor-advisee relationship or through a more informal commitment of faculty. Either way, the purpose is to provide each student with a guardian angel, who oversees the student's academic and social progress (Vatterott, 1992).

5. *Provide opportunities for students to spend time with teachers outside the classroom.*

The best middle level schools have a varied cocurricular program of after-school clubs and intramurals that give students the opportunity to socialize with teachers and other students. School picnics, carnivals, or field days also are excellent ways for students and adults to get to know one another better (Stevenson, 2002; Vatterott, 1992).

6. *Give the students authentic power.*

A representative student government allows students input into rules and ownership of school activities (Hoffman & Levak, 2003). Students can be responsible for such tasks as reading the daily bulletin, monitoring halls, and caring for school facilities and school supplies. Students from each team can take responsibility for team bulletin boards, hallways, and specific areas of the school grounds (Vatterott, 1992).

7. *Engage students in community service projects.*

Community service is an excellent vehicle through which students can gain responsibility and receive positive recognition (Blum, 2005; Hoffman & Levak, 2003). With adult supervision, students should be allowed to create and manage service projects such as recycling, visits to senior citizens homes, fund-raising sales, or neighborhood cleanups.

8. *Give awards and recognition for a wide variety of achievements.*

In some schools, only a few outstanding scholars and athletes receive all the awards. A good middle school recognizes a large number of students for all types of accomplishments (Van Hoose et al., 2001). Awards can be given for participation in clubs, perfect attendance, good citizenship, community service, or academic performance. Out-of-school accomplishments and interests can be recognized through daily bulletins, letters to parents, or personal congratulations from principals or teachers. The goal is that all students feel recognized for some positive accomplishment (Hoffman & Levak, 2003).

9. *Reward collegiality, positive attitudes, and positive actions of staff.*

The principal promotes a positive school climate by encouraging teachers and support staff to work together to improve conditions in the school. By modeling positive expectations, discouraging negative attitudes, and rewarding collegiality, the principal acts as the head of the family to reinforce the value of a positive environment. By meeting teacher needs for support and belonging, principals maintain conditions that make it easier to meet student needs. According to a popular middle level writer, "If you don't feed the teachers, they eat the students!" (Connors, 2000).

10.   *Pay attention to the physical appearance of the school.*

A clean, well-maintained building sends a powerful message to parents, students and teachers. It says that people care about and value the school. When a shortage of funds limits proper maintenance, parent or student groups may be able to donate their time to paint, do repairs, plant flowers, or maintain grounds. Local businesses often will donate materials or services free or at a reduced cost if they receive recognition. Opulent settings are not necessary for a positive school climate. It is more important that a school look clean and that its hallways reflect the importance of students by displaying student work. First impressions about school climate are strongly influenced by the appearance of the school. Although cosmetic improvements alone are rarely enough to improve a poor school climate, improvement of school appearance is a good place to start because results are fairly immediate and often dramatic (Vatterott, 1992).

Planning positive school practices requires specific attention to the students' emotional needs for acceptance, belonging, responsibility, and recognition (Blum, 2005). Creating caring school practices like those listed above requires schools to reflect on the *messages* that students derive from their interpretations of those school practices. Students who experience a positive school climate share some basic attitudes or beliefs about the way they relate to the school and the people in it (Vatterott, 1999). By examining those beliefs we can better understand how to create a climate that encourages such beliefs. Knowing what students perceive as caring makes it possible for us to create an environment in which students thrive. Figure 5.2 lists student beliefs, attitudes, and behaviors that relate to the basic needs of acceptance, belonging, responsibility, and recognition. Some specific school practices that reinforce such beliefs in the students' minds are listed in Figure 5.3. Those examples illustrate attitudes and practices that communicate the message of *pervasive caring*. These school practices and others like them provide opportunities for students to meet their emotional needs in healthy, positive ways rather than in negative ways. The examples in Figure 5.3 also reflect *teacher behaviors*. Teacher behavior is by far the most influential factor in creating student beliefs and behaviors.

School climate is really nothing more than the feelings the school people and practices convey to the students (Vatterott, 1991). In short, one can study climate by looking for the feelings the school seems to evoke. As we assess school practices to determine their effect on students, we must ask ourselves two questions: What practices in our schools encourage students to believe they are accepted, part of a group, responsible, and special? (Hoffman & Levak, 2003). What practices discourage such beliefs?

FIGURE   5 . 2

Positive Student Beliefs and Attitudes.

Beliefs and attitudes about acceptance
Students believe the school is for people like me.
Students believe their culture and religion are respected.
Students believe mistakes will be forgiven.
Students believe their opinions are valued.
Students feel comfortable expressing feelings.
Students believe they are some teacher's favorite kid.

Beliefs and attitudes about belonging
Students feel that they are a member of the school.
Students can name friends in the school setting.
Students socialize with other students outside of school.
Students identify themselves as members of a school-sponsored group (team, club, etc.).
Students feel comfortable participating in school activities.
Students can name someone they could discuss confidential problems with at school.
Students believe they are missed when absent.

Beliefs and attitudes about responsibility
Students know how to influence school policy and believe they can.
Students believe their concerns about school problems will be listened to.
Students believe they can be trusted to handle equipment, grade papers, and so on.
Students have a role in preparing assignments, assisting in peer tutoring, and self-evaluation.
Students voluntarily care for school or classroom property.
Students believe they are capable of self-control.

Beliefs and attitudes about recognition
Students believe they have special talents.
Students believe teachers know them as a person.
Students believe they are successful in more than one class.
Students feel positive behavior is rewarded. (Vatterott, 1999)

Positive School Climate Examples

- Parkway Central Middle School has a display case that belongs to the ESL students and features pictures and information about a different ESL student each week. The ESL students have made presentations about their program to the school board and the school has sponsored a family literacy night for ESL parents.
- Pattonville Heights Middle School serves about 20 children from a local children's home. With a grant from the state of Missouri, the school hired a full-time teacher to act as a teacher liaison to the children's home. The teacher liaison monitors these students' progress through daily contact with the students and their teachers. Since the inception of this program, those

students' academic achievement and behavior have shown marked improvement.

- Parkway Central Middle School offers an ambassador's program in which seventh graders call and welcome new sixth graders, a newcomer's club for new students, a club for enriching race relations, and a peer teaching program in which high school students teach self-esteem lessons to the middle school students.

F I G U R E 5 . 3

Positive School Practices.

School practices that encourage acceptance
Student have opportunities to show off special talents and skills.
Teachers listen to student opinions.
Teachers do not allow students to ridicule others.
At-risk students are assigned to advisors for one-on-one help.
Teachers accommodate different learning styles.
Teachers treat all students with equal respect.

School practices that encourage belonging
Opportunities are given for teachers and students to socialize outside class.
Multiple types of nonacademic activities are available for students (games, contests, etc.).
A large number of students participate in cocurricular activities.
Teachers and students proudly display badges of membership.
Teachers are knowledgeable about individual students' interests.

School practices that encourage responsibility
Students have opportunities to influence school policy.
The student council has an advisory role in school governance.
Students represent the school through community service.
Routine classroom duties are rotated among all students.
Students have the opportunity to determine consequences for their actions.
An appeal process is available for decisions students believe are unfair.

School practices that encourage recognition
Students are recognized in ways such as the following:
Formal awards and ceremonies
Recognition of nonacademic achievements such as citizenship, attendance, service, improvement
Publicity for out-of-school achievements
Talent shows or other opportunities for students to showcase special talents
Attention to special needs of individual students
Recognition of student birthdays
  (Vatterott, 1999)

REFLECTIVE QUESTION

Think of the last time you visited a school. What were your impressions about the school's climate? How did the people and the environment make you feel? What people or things helped to form your impressions? How did the physical appearance of the school affect your impression?

↠ ORGANIZATIONAL STRUCTURES THAT FACILITATE CURRICULUM GOALS

How the schoolwide curriculum is organized can either enhance or undermine a school's ability to reach curriculum goals. The typical middle school organizational structures of teaming and block scheduling are designed to support the goals of the middle school curriculum (Anfara & Lipka, 2003). The structures themselves do not assure developmental responsiveness—simply organizing teachers and students into teams or changing the schedule does not guarantee that schools will use those structures effectively (Erb & Stevenson, 2000; Lounsbury, 1992). When properly utilized, teaming and scheduling have the potential to facilitate the goals of the middle school curriculum (Flowers, Mertens, & Mulhall, 2003; Pitton, 2001).

Interdisciplinary Teams

The interdisciplinary team is the pivotal organizational feature of the middle school (Vars, 1993). No other practice in the middle school has a greater potential to meet early adolescents' needs (Anfara & Lipka, 2003; NMSA, 2004). **Interdisciplinary teams** assign a group of students to a group of two to five academic teachers who are responsible for the academic instruction in the four core subjects—math, science, social studies, and language arts. Reading teachers or special education teachers may also be part of the team. The students spend most of their day with their team of teachers, often seeing them for reading and advisory or large group time as well as the four core subjects (George & Alexander, 2003).

How Teams Are Organized

School administrators typically assign students to teams during master schedule development. Usually all students within one grade level are assigned to one or more teams depending on the average class size desired and the number of teachers available. For instance, if there are 100 seventh graders and an average class size of 25, one team of four teachers would be assigned all 100 students, or two teams of two teachers each would be assigned 50 students to each team. If there are 300 seventh graders, they could be assigned to two teams of teachers, giving each team 150 students, or if enough staff were available, they could be assigned to three teams of teachers, giving each team 100 students each. Given the number of students and teachers in a grade level, administrators may create some four- or five-person teams and some two- or three-person teams. In four- or five-person teams, each teacher is usually responsible for one of the four core subjects and possibly the teaching of reading. It is not uncommon for all teachers on a team to teach reading. In smaller teams, each teacher may teach two or more core subjects. Smaller teams usually require the teacher to prepare lessons for more subjects, but many teachers prefer smaller teams because they deal with fewer students (NMSA, 2004).

In the assignment of students to teams, balance is an important consideration (Lounsbury, 1992). Most schools attempt to balance teams racially, ethnically, and across ability groups. That is, certain groups of students are intentionally divided across all teams so that one team doesn't house a majority of students from one racial or ethnic group, or so that all the special education students or all the gifted students aren't assigned to one team. This allows each team to reflect the diversity of the school as a whole (George & Alexander, 2003). On the other hand, sometimes specific groups, such as ESL students or severely handicapped students, may be *intentionally* placed on the same team to make it easier to provide specialized service. For instance, Parkway Central Middle School actually identified a group of at-risk sixth graders whom they assigned to a small, two-person team for the purpose of providing more hands-on, one-on-one learning activities.

Balance is also an important concept in the selection of teachers for each team. Normally, faculty have significant input on the teams administrators assign. When deciding which combination of teachers will make the most effective interdisciplinary team, administrators must balance teachers' strengths and weaknesses, teaching styles and philosophies, and teaching experience.

The Philosophy behind Teaming

The philosophy behind teaming can be explained through three concepts: family ownership, learning community, and group problem solving. Family ownership refers to the idea that teachers working as a group feel an obligation to mentor their assigned group of students beyond their own classroom and share a common concern for student welfare (George et al., 1992). Team teachers keep informed about what happens to their students outside of the team and outside of the school. They are concerned about the children's physical, social, and emotional well-being in addition to how they are doing academically (Stevenson, 2002). They approach student problems holistically, much as a parent would, using all their knowledge about each child's life (Beane, 2001).

The team functions as a learning community when students work together to help each other, when they take responsibility for one another, and when they develop a group identity (Patterson, 2003). A team functions almost like a surrogate family or surrogate peer group. "The team constitutes an extended family of sorts within which students can form primary social affiliations. . . . At its best, the team serves as a positive answer for students' need to belong to a sanctioned and defined social group" (George, Stevenson, Thomason, & Beane, 1992, p. 59). Team building and team spirit activities are important because they reinforce this group identity (George & Alexander, 2003; Stevenson, 2002). Students enjoy naming their team, picking team colors, and creating team logos or slogans. Other team activities may include publishing a team newsletter, maintaining a team display case, or competing against other teams in sports, academic competitions, or service activities.

Group problem solving is an important aspect of teaming (Lounsbury, 1992). A team's teachers work together to solve individual student problems, brainstorm the best way to teach certain concepts, and support each other. Because they oversee a large group of students, they often work with principals or counselors to solve problems that develop at the building level. Students also participate in group problem solving through class and team meetings.

Implementing the Team Concept Successfully

Implementing the team concept successfully requires time, space, autonomy, and commitment (Lounsbury, 1992). Each is essential for meeting students' needs.

Successful Teams Need Planning Time   Most schools that organize students and teachers into interdisciplinary teams assign team teachers two planning periods, one for individual planning and one as a team assignment period (sometimes called TA) for team planning. The team planning period is absolutely critical for the success of a team (Flowers et al., 2003). Teams that do not have a team assignment period simply do not have time to fully implement the team concept. However, adding a team planning period is an expensive option for schools because more teachers must be hired to supervise students. In schools in which teams do not have a team assignment period, team members may meet on their own time before or after school or during their lunch period. If team members are assigned the same class period for their personal planning, they may decide to give up some of their personal planning time to meet as a team.

Successful Teams Need Space   In order to establish a team identity, teams need an area that is exclusive to them. Ideally, all team classrooms are in the same hallway or area of the building. Student lockers are assigned in the same hallway and bulletin boards or display cases located in the area are dedicated for that team. Teams need a territory that allows them to create a space that reflects the needs and personality of their team (NMSA, 2004).

Successful Teams Need Autonomy   Administrators need to grant team teachers the autonomy to make decisions about their schedule, the grouping of students, and curriculum. If the team's classes are scheduled in a block of time (such as periods 1 through 5), team teachers should be allowed to rearrange the schedule of team classes or create large blocks of time within that schedule to accommodate special activities (Hackman, 2002). Team teachers should also be allowed to regroup students for specific needs. For instance, suppose all students in the team are grouped into four math classes of 25 students each, and the math classes are taught during periods one, two, three, and four. The team teachers decide a small group of students are doing so poorly that they need more individualized instruction. The team teachers could decide to regroup their students so that the first period class has only 10 students and periods two, three, and four has 30 students each. Teachers may also want to group students who have problems into the same class or to change specific students' schedules to improve their chances for academic success.

Teachers should also have the autonomy to make curriculum decisions (George & Alexander, 2003). Although the framework of the curriculum and standards are usually defined for teachers, teams should have the freedom to organize their curriculum in a way that makes sense for their students, adapt curriculum to maximize the possibilities for academic success for their students, find connections between the individual subjects they teach, and engage in long-range planning for the year.

Successful Teams Are Committed to the Team Concept   Successful teams not only have time together, space together, and autonomy, but they also share a commitment to get along, compromise, and be productive (Stevenson, 2001). Teachers are not necessarily born to be team members. They each have their own philosophy and theories about children and learning. They each enjoy the freedom of being in charge of the total learning experience in their classroom—the curriculum, the climate, and the rules and procedures (Pickler, 1992). But being a team member requires compromise, an openness to other viewpoints, and the ability to reach a group consensus, always keeping in mind what is best for the students (George & Alexander, 2003). In those ways, being a team member is similar to getting along in a marriage or a family. It requires a long-term commitment, a realization that everyone can't always get his or her way, and that sometimes what's good for the group is not necessarily good for everybody. Teams evolve slowly—it takes time to feel comfortable together, to learn to trust each other, and to figure out how to get along. Positive team members support and listen to each other, keep the group focused on their long-range goals, respect diverse opinions, and treat each other with patience and understanding (Pickler, 1992).

What Teams Do

The interdisciplinary team provides an organizational framework that facilitates academic and behavioral monitoring, the development of personal relationships, and a consistency of rules and procedures among team teachers (Lounsbury, 1992). The team structure allows teachers to coordinate assignments and tests, plan interdisciplinary projects, and work together to help individual students with academic, personal, or social problems. Teams of teachers that share a team planning period in addition to their personal planning period provide the maximum benefits for students (Mertens & Flowers, 2003). Interdisciplinary teams that do not have a team planning period are seriously handicapped in their efforts to help students. Interdisciplinary teams work through six major functions, discussed below.

Providing a Home Base   Team teachers' classrooms are usually adjacent to or across the hall from each other. Students spend most of their day in that small area of the building. Student lockers are in that area, as well as team bulletin boards or display cases. Ideally, students begin and end their day in the team area (Connors, 1992).

Standardizing Procedures   Teams usually standardize discipline and grading policies and rules about tardiness, classroom materials, paper headings, rest room use, locker visits, late work, and other procedures to create less confusion for students (Pickler, 1992).

Coordinating Homework, Projects, and Tests   One of the most valuable aspects of teaming is coordinating classwork so students are not overburdened. Teams often select certain days for homework in certain subjects, schedule only one major test each week, and organize a team calendar to spread out due dates for big projects (Pickler, 1992).

Monitoring Individual Student Success   Teams work proactively to monitor student academic and behavioral success. They may review gradebooks every week or two to see which students are having academic problems and they may schedule after-school help sessions. If a student is having behavioral problems, the team may consult with counselors, school social workers, or principals. They pool their knowledge of the student and may select one teacher to work with the student one-on-one (Stevenson, 2002). They may schedule a team conference with the student or the student's parents to share their concerns. They may change the student's schedule within the team to improve his or her learning environment or to separate problem students. They may schedule students to stay after school and rotate the supervision among the team members.

Integrating Curriculum   Students internalize learning better when they see the connection to other learning. Team members become familiar with the curriculum in each of two to five subject areas taught within the team. They look for areas of overlap across the subjects and they sequence their individual curricula to connect with those of the other teachers on the team. They create thematic units that interrelate the content in each of the subjects (Alexander, 1995; Beane, 1997). (Integration will be covered in greater detail in Chapter 7.)

Grouping Students for Learning   Because the team is responsible for instruction of a large number of students during several class periods a day, they have many options for grouping students that can facilitate academic success. Teams can vary the size of instructional groups based on students needs. Within the team, teachers can reorganize students for short periods of time to remediate or challenge specific groups of students (Tomlinson, 2003). As mentioned earlier, if several students in more than one class are struggling with the same math concepts, those students can be temporarily be regrouped into one math class (NMSA, 2001a). The team may decide to keep this class smaller in size than the other three or four math classes. This *within-class grouping* is temporary and *skill-based* as opposed to the permanent status of ability grouping.

The Team Meeting Agenda

Team planning time can be used for a variety of tasks, but most of the time is generally taken up on the following types of issues:

Academic monitoring of individual students or groups of students—May include students who are failing or whose performance is declining, students whose performance is improving, changes in adaptations for special education students, or students who are missing work.

Behavioral concerns with individual students or groups of students—May include discipline problems within or outside the team, concerns about social or emotional problems of individual students, or concerns about relationships between groups of students.

Communications with parents—May include general communication about the team calendar, procedures, or upcoming projects, progress reports, positive phone calls or notes about improving students, calls or notes about discipline problems, or requests for a parent-team conference.

Communications with support personnel—May include discussion and group problem solving with the school counselor, social worker, principal, nurse, or other teachers about individual students or groups of students.

Coordination of tests, homework, or assignments—Usually accomplished with a team calendar to avoid overburdening students.

Coordination of supervisory responsibilities—May include discussion of hall monitoring, lunch duty, dismissal, or scheduling of after-school help sessions.

Establishment of team policies—May include standardization of grading, late work policies, class rules, work for absent students, and revisiting of such policies for individual students.

Coordination of team activities or long-range projects—May include planning for field trips or guest speakers, advisory activities, or the use of advisory time.

Integration of curriculum—May include the connection of individual lessons in two or more subjects, coordination of lessons to connect with lessons in exploratory classes, or planning of interdisciplinary units (George & Alexander, 2003).

Teams are normally expected to maintain a team meeting log or meeting minutes to document how they are spending their team meeting time. Figure 5.4 illustrates the diversity of items a team may deal with during a typical week of team meetings. Figure 5.5 can be used as a team planning tool.

→ SCHEDULING OPTIONS

Middle schools generally operate with one of three basic types of schedule. The traditional departmentalized schedule (most often seen in junior high schools and high schools) divides the school day into six to eight periods of equal length, usually resulting in periods of 50 to 60 minutes. This schedule offers few advantages to middle schools hoping to implement student-focused, project-based instruction (Hackmann & Valentine, 1998; NMSA, 2001a). Figure 5.6 shows a typical departmentalized schedule.

F I G U R E   5 . 4

Team Meeting Log.

Monday

- Filled in team calendar for the next two weeks of homework assignments, projects, tests, and quizzes.
- Reviewed records of students whose grades have been slipping. Determined students whose parents should be called. Divided calls among team members.
- Many students seem to be missing assignments and there has been more paper in the halls lately. Scheduled locker cleanout and folder organization for Friday during advisory period.

Tuesday

- Held IEP conference for Melissa Baker with Melissa, Melissa's parents, special education teacher, and assistant principal.
- Called parents of students identified Monday.

Wednesday

- The students have been extremely loud and boisterous returning from lunch. Teachers in that hallway have complained that it is disturbing their classes. Scheduled class meetings during advisory today to brainstorm solutions to the problem.
- Started work on Ancient Civilizations interdisciplinary unit for next month.

Thursday

- Organized letter to parents and permission slip for next week's team field trip to the Science Center. Checked on bus request and called parent volunteers.
- Held team conference with Juan Perez and his grandmother about his behavior problems and missing work.

Friday

- Met with counselor and assistant principal about persistent problem of two groups of girls (led by Tiffany Rubenstein, Latisha Jones, Maria Chevez, and Angel Washington) who are spreading rumors about each other. Counselor and assistant principal will meet with the girls.
- Discussed concerns about Peter Kowalski. He has not been bathing regularly or wearing clean clothes. Students are refusing to sit by him. Checked with the school nurse—she will contact parents and talk with Peter.

The second type of schedule is the **flexible block schedule**. The flexible block schedule organizes the interdisciplinary team time into a large block of time (NMSA, 2001a). For instance, students may be assigned to their interdisciplinary team for the first four class periods of the day. This gives the team teachers the freedom to organize the schedule in different ways for different purposes (Wunderlich, Robertson, & Valentine, 2002). They may choose to divide the time equally (one class period for each academic subject), or they may combine class periods to allow for a two-hour lab or activity. The flexible block schedule allows team teachers to

F I G U R E   5 . 5

Team Planning Period Tool.

Total number of minutes available for planning per week   225

**Number of minutes
allocated per week**   **Topic**

—————   Academic monitoring of individual students
—————   Behavioral concerns with individual students
—————   Communications with parents
—————   Communications with support personnel (Counselor, social
                 worker, principal, nurse, other teachers)
—————   Coordination of tests, homework, assignments
—————   Coordination of supervisory responsibilities (breaks, hall
                 monitoring, dismissal)
—————   Establishment of team policies (grading, discipline policies)
—————   Coordination of team activities or long-range projects
—————   Integration of curriculum (Interdisciplinary units, related
                 activities)
—————   Other topic your team deems important
—————   Unscheduled time for unplanned problems

* *

Daily schedule

	Topic	Number of minutes
Mondays (45 minutes)	——————————	——————————
	——————————	——————————
	——————————	——————————
	——————————	——————————
Tuesdays (45 minutes)	——————————	——————————
	——————————	——————————
	——————————	——————————
	——————————	——————————
Wednesdays (45 minutes)	——————————	——————————
	——————————	——————————
	——————————	——————————
	——————————	——————————
Thursdays (45 minutes)	——————————	——————————
	——————————	——————————
	——————————	——————————
	——————————	——————————
Fridays (45 minutes)	——————————	——————————
	——————————	——————————
	——————————	——————————
	——————————	——————————

FIGURE   5 . 6

Departmentalized Schedule.

Time	Class Period	Teacher Schedule	Student Schedule
8:00–8:45	1	Math—group 1	Math
8:50–9:35	2	Team planning period	Exploratory
9:40–10:25	3	Reading	Science
10:30–11:15	4	Personal planning period	Physical education
11:15–11:45	Lunch	Lunch	Lunch
11:45–12:30	5	Math—group 2	Social studies
12:35–1:20	6	Math—group 3	Reading
1:25–2:10	7	Math—group 4	Language arts
2:15–3:00	8	Advisory	Advisory

FIGURE   5 . 7

Flexible Block Schedule.

	Time	Class Period	Teacher Schedule	Student Schedule
Academic block—periods 1–4	8:00–8:45	1	Math— group 1	Math
	8:50–9:35	2	Math— group 2	Science
	9:40–10:25	3	Math— group 3	Social studies
	10:30–11:15	4	Math— group 4	Language arts
	11:15–11:45	Lunch	Lunch	Lunch
Reading/advisory block—periods 5–6	11:45–12:30	5	Reading	Reading
	12:35–1:20	6	Advisory	Advisory
	1:25–2:10	7	Personal planning period	Physical education
	2:15–3:00	8	Team planning period	Exploratory

combine all students on their team for field trips or guest speakers without interfering with the student's schedule outside of the team. Interdisciplinary activities can be team taught. The flexible block schedule allows more time for creative scheduling for individual students (NMSA, 2001a). An individually adjusted schedule can benefit a student in numerous ways such as changing the time of day a student takes his or her hardest subject, separating two students who disrupt class when

FIGURE 5.8

Alternating Day Block Schedule.

Day A

Time	Class Period	Teacher Schedule	Student Schedule
8:00–9:35	1	Math—group 1	Math
9:40–11:15	2	Math—group 2	Science
11:15–11:45	Lunch	Lunch	Lunch
11:45–1:20	3	Personal planning period	Physical education
1:25–3:00	4	Reading	Reading

Day B

Time	Class Period	Teacher Schedule	Student Schedule
8:00–9:35	5	Math—group 3	Social studies
9:40–11:15	6	Team planning period	Exploratory
11:15–11:45	Lunch	Lunch	Lunch
11:45–1:20	7	Math—group 4	Language arts
1:25–3:00	8	Advisory	Advisory

they are together, or allowing a student to remain in one subject for two class periods. Figure 5.7 shows a flexible block schedule.

The third type of schedule, called the **alternating-day block schedule** or the **eight-block schedule**, is quickly gaining popularity at the high school level but is also used in middle school (Hackmann, 2002; Smith, 2002). This type of schedule holds classes in large blocks of time, 90 minutes or more, with fewer classes each day. Typically, students are assigned to eight classes, attending four classes each day, each for 90 minutes or more (NMSA, 2001a). The eight-block schedule fits nicely with project-based instruction, allowing students to cover topics in greater depth, but it is not effective for 90 minutes of lecturing or passive instruction. Larger blocks of learning time are generally popular with students and teachers and are consistent with the latest research on how the brain learns best (Hackmann & Valentine, 1998; Wunderlich et al., 2001). An alternating day schedule is shown in Figure 5.8.

Organizational structures such as teaming, grouping, and scheduling options are the vehicles for reaching the goals of the middle school curriculum. They often allow schools more freedom and flexibility in creating the conditions that maximize student engagement and student success (Hackmann, 2002; Smith, 2002).

SUMMARY

While the pressures of society and accountability threaten to control curriculum, middle level educators need to remember the aims of the middle school curriculum—to develop and refine students' intellectual skills, to assist students in the development of identity, and to help them define their role in the adult world. These aims are best met through creating a personal connection between students and the curriculum. The curriculum should be designed with the unique needs and interests of early adolescents in mind. Developmentally appropriate curriculum for early adolescents is relevant to their lives, built around activities and student-focused instructional methods, taught through varied strategies, success oriented, and individualized. The cocurriculum and the affective curriculum (school climate) are complements to the regular curriculum and may either enhance or detract from it.

KEY TERMS

academic curriculum
advisory program
affective curriculum
  (school climate)
alternating-day block schedule
  or eight-block schedule
cocurriculum

expressive curriculum
flexible block scheduling
interdisciplinary teams
interscholastic sports
intramural sports
wellness curriculum

APPLICATION ACTIVITIES

1. Review the examples of math, science, language arts, and social studies curricula in this chapter. In what ways do they differ from a traditional curricula? How do they differ from the curriculum you experienced in school?

2. Review the examples of expressive curriculum in this chapter. In what ways do they differ from a traditional curriculum? How do they differ from the expressive curriculum you experienced in school?

3. Review the examples of a wellness curriculum in this chapter. In what ways do they differ from a traditional curriculum? How do they differ from the curriculum you experienced in school?

4. Review the examples of a cocurriculum in this chapter. What common characteristics do you see in the content of these cocurricula?

5. Match each item in the team meeting log (Figure 5.4) with one of the task categories in Figure 5.5.

6. Form a team with two to five of your classmates. Create a fictional team—choose the grade level of your students (grade 6, 7, or 8) and generally describe your student population. Choose a team name and logo.

   Assume your team has a 45-minute period each day (Monday through Friday) for team meetings. Your team must prioritize how you will use your team time. Use the list of activities in Figure 5.5 to decide how much time to allocate for each activity per week. For instance, if your team decides that communications with parents is more important than coordination of curriculum, you will allocate more time for that activity. Then decide on a general schedule of activities for the week. For example, you may need to spend 20 minutes each Monday on curriculum, or allow 15 minutes daily to discuss behavioral concerns.

CHAPTER 6

❦

MAKING DECISIONS
ABOUT CURRICULUM

✧ INTRODUCTION

In Chapter 5, we discussed the general goals of the middle school curriculum, how the curriculum may be organized within the school, and how the curriculum can assist in meeting developmental needs of early adolescents. The ultimate goals of the curriculum at the middle level should be to develop students as thinkers, learners, and problem solvers; these goals should allow students to assume responsibility for their learning and help them in the formation of their identity by encouraging an emphasis on student interests, strengths, and talents (Caskey, 2002; Eisner, 2004; Vatterott, 1999). To achieve these goals, teachers must understand the relationship between curriculum, instruction, and assessment in the instructional planning process and why, given the current emphasis on standards, results must drive curriculum planning (Bracey, 2003; Wiggins & McTighe, 1998). Curriculum planning requires teachers to consider their long-range goals for students, to incorporate state and local standards, and to think carefully about the enduring understandings they want students to internalize (Danielson, 2002). Once they have determined the specific results they wish to achieve with their curriculum, teachers can begin to design student-focused activities that will facilitate meaningful learning for middle school students (Anfara & Stacki, 2002; Gross, 2002). **This chapter will help you**

- to reflect on curriculum content that is meaningful to middle school students.
- to analyze the relationships among curriculum, instruction, and assessment and how those relationships influence curriculum planning.
- to understand the role of standardized tests in curriculum planning.
- to appreciate the necessity of results-driven curriculum planning.
- to clarify your own long-range goals for student learning in your content area.
- to practice incorporating state and national standards in curriculum planning.
- to delineate important principles, concepts, and processes in your content area.

Essential Questions

After reading and completing the activities in this chapter, you should be able to answer the following questions:

1. What relationships should exist among curriculum, instruction, and assessment in the curriculum planning process?
2. Why *should* results drive curriculum planning for today's classroom?
3. How can teachers incorporate standards into their planning without teaching the test?
4. What four questions should teachers consider when determining long-range goals?
5. What is the role of state and national standards in the curriculum planning process?
6. How should teachers use local curriculum documents in the curriculum planning process?
7. What concepts, principles, and ideas do you believe to be most important in your subject area?
8. How does the use of essential questions help teachers focus their curriculum planning?

✦ CURRICULUM, INSTRUCTION, AND ASSESSMENT

How do we create curriculum that engages students and develops their strengths and talents? We must first understand the relationship among the components of the teaching-learning experience—curriculum, instruction, and assessment. **Curriculum** is usually considered the *content* to be *learned* (Vatterott, 1999). This content may be comprised of facts (whales are mammals), concepts (the process of photosynthesis), principles (matter can change forms), attitudes (we should be concerned about the environment), or skills (drawing conclusions from data) (Tomlinson, 1999). The curriculum is "what a student should come to know (facts), understand (concepts and principles), and be able to do (skills) as a result of a given segment of study" (Tomlinson, 1999, p. 43). **Instruction** is the *set of learning experiences or activities* students participate in for the purpose of learning (Vatterott, 1999). Instruction could be hearing a lecture, engaging in a discussion, participating in cooperative learning, reading the textbook, doing an experiment, creating projects, or doing any other activity that causes learning to take place. **Assessment** is the method used to determine the extent to which learning goals are achieved (Wiggins & McTighe, 1998). Methods of classroom assessment may include paper and pencil tests, projects, performances, student exhibitions, or evaluation of student portfolios. Recently, standardized tests have come to play an important role as assessment (Bracey, 2003). Before we can make decisions about curriculum, we need to rethink the traditional relationship among curriculum, instruction, and assessment and consider an alternative relationship that is more appropriate for today's classrooms and today's students (Anfara & Stacki, 2002; Gross, 2002).

❖ THEN AND NOW: THE EVOLUTION OF TRADITIONAL PLANNING

The traditional relationship among curriculum, instruction, and assessment has existed for years and still influences teacher planning today. Traditionally the curriculum revolves around factual information the student is expected to retain and communicate to the teacher on a paper and pencil test (Patterson, 2003). Traditional teachers typically employ direct instruction, presented by the teacher to the students as a group. After presenting the content to the students, teachers create tests to measure how much content the student remembers (Gross, 2002; Vatterott, 1999).

In this traditional method, all students are expected to learn the same content in the same way (Gross, 2002). The teacher transfers the curriculum content to the student, much like a person pouring beans (the curriculum) into a jar (the student). To assess learning, the teacher then measures the amount of content (curriculum) the student has retained, that is, how many beans are in the jar (Vatterott, 1999). In this traditional mode, the method of instruction is the same for all students but the results differ from one student to the next. Traditional teachers expect that some students will not learn, and some student failure is acceptable to them; it is considered almost inevitable (Levine, 2003b). Sadly, this style of teaching is still commonly used (Patterson, 2003). This traditional relationship among curriculum (C), instruction (I), and assessment (A) could be illustrated in this way:

C (curriculum)→I (instruction—the teacher)→A (the test)

In this traditional relationship, the curriculum drives instruction, which determines assessment. Planning for instruction is driven by curriculum content and assessments are often created as an afterthought, *after* instruction had taken place (Vatterott, 1999).

REFLECTIVE QUESTION

If your goal is for all students to be successful learners, what inherent flaws do you see with the C→ I → A relationship?

Limitations of Traditional Planning

The traditional conceptualization of the teaching-learning process just discussed may have been acceptable in years past, but it fails to serve the needs of today's students (Anfara & Stacki, 2002). The current standards and standardized test movement grew in part out of the realization that the traditional methods of using curriculum, instruction, and assessment produced many students who lacked basic skills and basic knowledge (Marshall, 2003).

The emphasis on state standards and standardized test results has forced schools and teachers to be more accountable for learning (Gross, 2002). Schools today demand that students know more than just facts; they must be able to *show* what they have learned (Elmore, 2003). Schools demand success for more students and teacher accountability for student learning. Schools want results; learning is no longer *optional*. Teachers are expected to educate a more diverse population of students who are expected to do well on performance-based assessments (Brown, 2002; Marshall, 2003).

Results-Driven Planning

To meet the needs of today's students and the demands of accountability, a fundamental shift must occur in what drives instruction (Vatterott, 1999). The traditional relationship of curriculum, instruction, and assessment must change (Gross, 2002). Instead of the curriculum driving instruction and assessment, the *results* we wish to achieve in the learner become the starting point that directs everything else (Danielson, 2002; McTighe & Thomas, 2003). Those results may be influenced by state standards. The *results determine the assessment, which directs instruction.* Compared to the traditional planning process, this is a **backward design** (a term coined by Wiggins and McTighe, 1998), and could be illustrated in this way:

R (results)→A (which shows evidence of the learning result)
→I (learning task—the student)→C (content)

In backward design, the results of learning determine assessments, which direct the selection of instructional methods. The desired results of learning are determined first, and assessments are designed to reflect the results all students should achieve (McTighe & Thomas, 2003). Instructional methods and resources are selected based on the evidence that assessments require (Guskey, 2003). This model, in which instruction is driven by results, is much more appropriate for today's classroom than the content-driven model (Vatterott, 1999). Backward design is a good conceptual beginning when our goal is for all students to reach a certain level of academic

Learning tasks are planned around individual needs.

success. For instance, if the result the history teacher wants is an understanding of the impact of historical events on present-day events, the assessment might require students to make those connections in an essay. Instruction would then be tailored to those connections as opposed to a factual lecture on the names and dates (Guskey, 2003).

Results-Driven Planning in the Student-Focused Classroom

There is nothing inherently student focused or constructivist about backward design (Brown, 2002; Vatterott, 1999). If the results one hoped for were rote memorization of facts, that could easily be achieved by teacher-directed instruction, with all students learning the same way (Daniels & Zemelman, 2004). While this model doesn't necessarily lead to student-focused instruction, Chapter 7 will illustrate how the model can be used to develop student-focused lessons.

In adapting backward design for use in the student-focused classroom, results become the common goals that all students are expected to reach (Vatterott, 1999). Those common goals represent broad conceptual knowledge and skills as opposed to factual content (Patterson, 2003). Our current knowledge of learners tells us that all students do not learn in the same way. Therefore, if all students are to reach the same common goals, learning tasks must be planned around individual needs (Brown, 2002; Strong, Silver, Perini, & Tuculescu, 2003). In the student-focused classroom, this results in many different types of learning tasks chosen by different students. Student-focused instruction is not something that is *done to* the student but is the creation of activities that facilitate learning (Eisner, 2004; Vatterott, 1999). Individual adaptations result in individualized content (Cetron & Cetron, 2004). In other words:

R (results)→A (assessment)→filtered through the needs
of students→many I's (differentiated instruction)→many
C's (differences in curriculum content experienced)

This does not mean students experience no common curriculum. All students are expected to achieve similar results. Those common results are the common curriculum (Gross, 2002; Vatterott, 1999). In other words, students experience unique content on their journeys to common goals (Cetron & Cetron, 2004).

To illustrate the differences, in the traditional teacher-focused classroom, Teacher A delivers the content of climate zones through lecture and reading and tests the students on the knowledge. All students are exposed to the same content. In the student-focused classroom, Teacher B is also teaching about climate zones. In Teacher B's class, students may choose which climate zone to report on (polar, temperate, or tropical). The learning task (also the assessment) is an exhibit that requires students to explain the climate's impact on plant and animal life, the climate's relationship to the industry and economics of the region, variations in temperature, and so on. Each group of students presents their exhibition to the class. During the learning task, each student learns detailed information about one climate zone. Students also listen to and observe the exhibitions about the other two climate zones. So while each student experiences one of three pieces of content in detail (one of the three climate zones), they all learn the broad concepts about the relationship of climate to geography, plant and animal life, industry, and economics of the region. The teacher's focus is on achieving the broad conceptual goals, not on content coverage (Vatterott, 1999).

REFLECTIVE QUESTION

How do you predict student learning about climate zones in the student-focused classroom will differ from student learning about climate zones in the traditional classroom? Why is the backward design more appropriate than the traditional design for today's classrooms?

✦ THE ROLE OF STANDARDS AND STANDARDIZED TESTS IN CURRICULUM PLANNING

How do teachers determine the results they want for their students? If results drive planning, how important are state-mandated standards and standardized tests in the planning process? To begin with, every state has defined standards and the public widely supports the use of standards as a vehicle for school improvement (Bracey, 2003). A general attitude exists that our expectations for children have been too low; that the more we expect from children, the more they will achieve; and that standards can help raise those expectations (Anfara & Waks, 2002). In recent surveys, the majority of parents wanted schools to continue to implement standards and the majority of teachers agreed that standards were a move in the right direction (Gandal & Vranek, 2001; Rose & Gallup, 2003).

Standards can be a positive influence in many ways. They can be helpful in refining our long-range goals and in helping us see the big picture of our curriculum

(Marshall, 2003; Scherer, 2001). They may show us broader outcomes than we had envisioned or remind us of important content or skills we may have omitted. They have the potential to raise achievement for all students by encouraging teachers to prescribe remedies for students who perform poorly (Scherer, 2001; Vogler, 2003). On a broader scale, standards have the potential to be the catalyst for improvements in both curriculum and instructional strategies (Kluth & Straut, 2001; Marshall, 2003).

Given the public visibility and political popularity of standards, it is unlikely that schools will abandon them, and it is a certainty that standards will significantly impact the curriculum planning process (Cetron & Cetron, 2004). Standards have been a powerful tool in shifting the focus of teacher planning from curriculum content to results (Gross, 2002; Marshall, 2003; Scherer, 2001). In an effort to improve education and increase accountability for learning, states created standards to articulate the *results* of instruction that all students should achieve. States then created or adopted *assessments* (standardized tests) in an effort to evaluate whether students were reaching those standards (Cawelti, 2003). Those standard-based *results* and *assessments* impact the *results* and *assessments* that teachers determine as they plan their curriculum (Guskey, 2001). Before teachers can begin the planning process, they must become familiar with their state standards (George, 2002). Only then can they determine what role standards and standardized tests will play in their planning (Elmore, 2003; Vogler, 2003).

Examples of General State Standards

Two types of standards may be stipulated at the state level: *general state standards* that span across all subject areas and *content standards* that are specific to a content area. The goals shown in Figure 6.1 represent the general standards for the state of Missouri (Missouri Department of Elementary and Secondary Education, 2000). In Missouri's standards, each goal is accompanied by several more specific standards students should be able to demonstrate. Figure 6.1 lists only the first four standards for each goal.

Examples of Content Standards

Many states also have content standards by subject area (see Figure 6.2), often reflecting standards set by professional associations such as the National Council for Social Studies, the National Council of Teachers of Mathematics, the National Council of Teachers of English, and the National Science Teachers Association. Standards determined by national professional associations are readily available from those organizations.

State standards vary in detail and organization (Marshall, 2003). Kentucky's standards, for example, contain both general and content goals and standards, and list standards for art, practical living, and vocational studies. Kentucky's standards also include two learning goals that are not tested by the state's academic assessment program. These goals are shown in Figure 6.3 with a sampling of more specific standards for each goal.

A Sampling of General State Standards

The Show-Me Standards for the State of Missouri

GOAL 1: Students in Missouri public schools will acquire the knowledge and skills to gather, analyze and apply information and ideas. *Students will demonstrate within and integrate across all content areas the ability to:*

1. Develop questions and ideas to initiate and refine research.

2. Conduct research to answer questions and evaluate information and ideas.

3. Design and conduct field and laboratory investigations to study nature and society.

4. Use technological tools and other resources to locate, select and organize information.

GOAL 2: Students in Missouri public schools will acquire the knowledge and skills to communicate effectively within and beyond the classroom. *Students will demonstrate within and integrate across all content areas the ability to:*

1. Plan and make written, oral and visual presentations for a variety of purposes and audiences.

2. Review and revise communications to improve accuracy and clarity.

3. Exchange information, questions and ideas while recognizing the perspectives of others.

4. Present perceptions and ideas regarding works of the arts, humanities and sciences.

GOAL 3: Students in Missouri public schools will acquire the knowledge and skills to recognize and solve problems. *Students will demonstrate within and integrate across all content areas the ability to:*

1. Identify problems and define their scope and elements.

2. Develop and apply strategies based on ways others have prevented or solved problems.

3. Develop and apply strategies based on one's own experience in preventing or solving problems.

4. Evaluate the processes used in recognizing and solving problems.

GOAL 4: Students in Missouri public schools will acquire the knowledge and skills to make decisions and act as responsible members of society. *Students will demonstrate within and integrate across all content areas the ability to:*

1. Explain reasoning and identify information used to support decisions.

2. Understand and apply the rights and responsibilities of citizenship in Missouri and the United States.

3. Analyze the duties and responsibilities of individuals in societies.

4. Recognize and practice honesty and integrity in academic work and in the workplace.

FIGURE   6 . 2

A Sampling of Content Area Standards

Show-Me Standards

Social Studies

In Social Studies, students in Missouri public schools will acquire a solid foundation which includes knowledge of:

1. Principles expressed in the documents shaping constitutional democracy in the United States.
2. Continuity and change in the history of Missouri, the United States and the world.
3. Principles and processes of governance systems.
4. Economic concepts (including productivity and the market system) and principles (including the laws of supply and demand).

Science

In Science, students in Missouri public schools will acquire a solid foundation which includes knowledge of:

1. Properties and principles of matter and energy.
2. Properties and principles of force and motion.
3. Characteristics and interactions of living organisms.
4. Changes in ecosystems and interactions of organisms with their environments.

Mathematics

In Mathematics, students in Missouri public schools will acquire a solid foundation which includes knowledge of:

1. Addition, subtraction, multiplication and division; other number sense, including numeration and estimation; and the application of these operations and concepts in the workplace and other situations.
2. Geometric and spatial sense involving measurement (including length, area, volume), trigonometry, and similarity and transformation of shapes.
3. Data analysis, probability and statistics.
4. Patterns and relationships within and among functions and algebraic, geometric and trigonometric concepts.

Communication Arts

In Communication Arts, students in Missouri public schools will acquire a solid foundation which includes knowledge of and proficiency in:

1. Speaking and writing standard English (including grammar, usage, punctuation, spelling, capitalization).
2. Reading and evaluating fiction, poetry and drama.
3. Reading and evaluating nonfiction works and material (such as biographies, newspapers, technical manuals).
4. Writing formally (such as reports, narratives, essays) and informally (such as outlines, notes).

FIGURE 6.3

Kentucky State Standards Not Assessed by the State

Goal 3: Students shall develop their abilities to become self-sufficient individuals

3.4 Students demonstrate the ability to be resourceful and creative.

3.5 Students demonstrate self-control and self discipline.

Goal 4: Students shall develop their abilities to become responsible members of a family, work group, or community, including demonstrating effectiveness in community service.

4.2 Students use productive team membership skills.

4.5 Students demonstrate an understanding of, appreciation for, and sensitivity to a multi-cultural and world view.

REFLECTIVE QUESTION

Kentucky's goals 3 and 4 are not addressed in the state's academic assessment program. Speculate as to why.

Aligning Curriculum with Standards

Most schools today invest a considerable amount of time and energy aligning the curriculum with standards (George, 2001). Many teachers have no problem aligning their curriculum and planning instruction with state standards, especially when the standards are fairly general (George & Alexander, 2003). If the standards are performance based and focus on higher level thinking skills, as with the Missouri and Kentucky standards, it's possible that they will be similar to our own long-range goals and may fit nicely with the results we want for our students (Scherer, 2001). But this may not always be the case. Standards may be too specific, with hundreds of detailed facts that fail to focus on higher level learning (Kohn, 2000). Standards may also be so vague as to offer little help at all. They may not be performance based, making it difficult to use them to plan results-based instruction (Marshall, 2003). The most common problem in aligning curriculum with standards is the sheer number of standards. Some states specify 75 to 100 pages of standards for each subject at each grade level. Robert Marzano, a prominent researcher of educational standards, believes that the amount of content covered in standards should be reduced and the number of standards be cut by about two-thirds (Marshall, 2003; Scherer, 2001). When the list of standards is 100 pages long, it will be necessary to prioritize the list for our individual classroom. When standards are poorly written and out of sync with the needs of our specific community, it may be unwise to allow state standards to exert too heavy an influence on our planning (Caskey, 2002; Marshall,

2003). Standards should inform instruction, but each teacher must decide how much they control the curriculum (McDaniel, Necochea, Rios, Stowell, & Kritzers, 2001).

Tests That Attempt to Measure Standards

While many teachers would have no problem planning instruction around their state's standards, an overemphasis on the *tests designed to measure the standards* often causes problems (Bracey, 2003; Marshall, 2003). Teaching to standards and having students do well on *the test* are often two very different things. Standardized tests vary widely in quality and in their ability to truly and objectively measure state standards (Bracey, 2003; Meier, 2003). In some states, the tests fail to address the breadth and depth of the content and skills in the standards (Gandel & Vranek, 2001). Ideally, such tests should be performance based, requiring students to actually demonstrate skills or knowledge (such as writing a paragraph, or showing how they solved a problem). But good performance-based tests are time-consuming to grade and there are often problems with the reliability of the grading (Meier, 2003). Some states that were initially committed to performance-based standards found them too subjective to evaluate and have reverted back to multiple-choice exams that focus on low-level learning (Brooks & Brooks, 1999). That can result in a mismatch between standards that reflect higher level thinking skills and tests that measure low-level factual knowledge (Neill, 2003). What the test actually measures may then be quite far removed from the original standard (Bracey, 2003; Gandal & Vranek, 2001; Meier, 2002).

The Dilemma of Teaching to the Test

With the drive for increased teacher accountability, state-mandated testing has become increasingly problematic (Lounsbury & Vars, 2003; Meier, 2002). When high-stakes testing is tied to funding or other incentives, teachers are often pressured to ignore their own goals for students and plan all instruction around only the state-mandated test (Kohn, 2000; McDaniel et al., 2001).

Even when the standards reflect high-stakes testing, teaching to the test requires tough choices and prioritizing of content (Elmore, 2003; Gross, 2002). When teachers focus too much on state tests, they run the risk of reducing the curriculum "to only that which is covered on tests, and this constriction limits student learning" (Brooks & Brooks, 1999, p. 20). In fact, an overemphasis on standardized test content can actually result in *less* meaningful learning (Kohn, 2000; Neill, 2003). Teachers who narrow the curriculum to match the test often neglect student-focused instruction, abandoning critical thinking, and sacrificing in-depth learning (Anfara & Stacki, 2001; O'Neil & Tell, 1999). There seems to be a tendency to use direct instruction in an effort to *pour the knowledge in* before test time (O'Steen, Cuper, Spires, Beal, & Pope, 2002; Patterson, 2003). This often results in fragmented content that students have difficulty connecting and making sense of. Brain research confirms that this is *not* the path to meaningful learning. It is possible for students to be *taught the test*, to do well on the test, and still have accomplished no meaningful long-term learning (Neill, 2003). On the other hand, it is also possible to prioritize essential skills and knowledge contained on the test and to create rich and challenging learning experiences that enable students to perform well on the test (Pate, 2001).

Should Teachers Teach to the Test?

It is not necessary to abandon other important curriculum goals to prepare students for standardized tests (Pate, 2001; Scherer, 2004). Kohn (2000) and others have argued that students can spend a relatively short amount of time on the content and format of the test and do as well as students in an entire year of *test-preparation* curriculum.

Teachers should spend some time reviewing previous test results, look for general areas where their students consistently perform poorly, and make some adjustments in their teaching. For instance, performance-based tests often rely heavily on reading and writing skills (George, 2002). If many students are poor readers and poor writers, literacy skills should be emphasized in all curriculum areas by creating activities that give students practice in such skills as word attack, expressing relationships between things or ideas, and using standard English.

Within an interdisciplinary team, the language arts teacher can incorporate many of these skills in interdisciplinary activities that use content from the other academic areas (Beane, 1997; Stevenson, 2002). These skills can easily be integrated across the curriculum without sacrificing other curriculum content (O'Steen et al., 2002; Pate, 2001). Many teachers claim that tests contain unfamiliar vocabulary that hampers student performance and take care to integrate that vocabulary into their curriculum. In addition to reading, writing, and vocabulary, teachers can adjust their curriculum to emphasize specific skills or content that is problematic. One teacher added Canada to her geography curriculum because the state test had questions related to Canadian provinces. Students were familiar with the geography principles in the test questions, but because they were unfamiliar with the concept of provinces, many could not answer the question correctly. The teacher was still able to teach the geography concepts already in her curriculum, but she made a small adjustment in content to familiarize her students with the concept of Canadian provinces.

The best policy seems to be to integrate concepts that are covered on the standardized test into the regular curriculum throughout the year, as opposed to teaching the test concepts in isolation (Mertens & Flowers, 2003; O'Steen et al., 2002). In some schools, the regular curriculum is completely abandoned in the month prior to the standardized test as teachers drill students on the test curriculum. Teachers who do that typically don't have much success. Students quickly distinguish between the *test prep* (typically drill, memorization) and the *real curriculum* and often expend little effort learning the test curriculum. Many teachers are aware of the test, integrate test objectives into their curriculum over the entire year, and still maintain the integrity of their district curriculum (Pate, 2001; Vogler, 2003).

Teacher Mike Hirsch creates student-focused activities for his math students that help to prepare students for the standardized tests and also reflect his school district's curriculum. His math students use the USA Today Web site (**www.usatoday. com**) to access "snapshots," graphs depicting statistical surveys. His students complete a variety of learning tasks related to the graphs (see Classroom Activity 6.1).

Helping Students Test Better

Although *teaching the test* is generally ineffective in improving student test performance, there's nothing wrong with making sure students are familiar with the test format. Some teachers provide sample questions that students can practice with prior to the test. Other teachers make their classroom tests similar in format to the standardized test, so students are accustomed to recording answers in a particular fashion. But addressing format alone will yield only some improvement. Teaching students how to answer a specific type of question without teaching mastery of the skills necessary to get the correct answer typically doesn't result in much improvement of scores.

It is equally vital that teachers impress on students the importance of the test (George, 2001; Vogler, 2003). Many teachers lament that students don't take the test seriously. Students need to understand that state test results do reflect on the school and on them as students and that the results may influence funding or accreditation. Schools may challenge students with incentives to improve last year's scores and reward students after the testing period with parties or free time (George, 2001).

And finally, the physical condition of the student during test taking is critical. The biochemistry of the brain is strongly affected by several factors (Sousa, 1998). Students and parents must be educated about the importance of a full night's sleep and a good breakfast prior to the test (Wolfe, Burkman, & Strong, 2000). During the testing period, students should have access to water and high carbohydrate snacks. Water and glucose are beneficial in promoting optimum brain performance (Jensen, 1998). Exercise during testing breaks is equally important to promote circulation to the brain (Bell, 2003; Sousa, 1998).

In summary, standards and standardized tests are a reality for today's teachers (Marzano, 2003; Scherer, 2001). Teachers must be familiar with standards, be aware of how their students are performing on standardized tests, and review test results carefully. They must then consider that information when designing their curriculum (Gross, 2002; Elmore, 2003). Standards and standardized test results are only one piece of information teachers take into account when making decisions about what and how to teach (McDaniel et al., 2001; Pate, 2001).

REFLECTIVE QUESTION

What do you know about the standardized tests in your state? How do teachers you know integrate test preparation with their regular curriculum? How can you prepare students for standardized tests with student-focused methods?

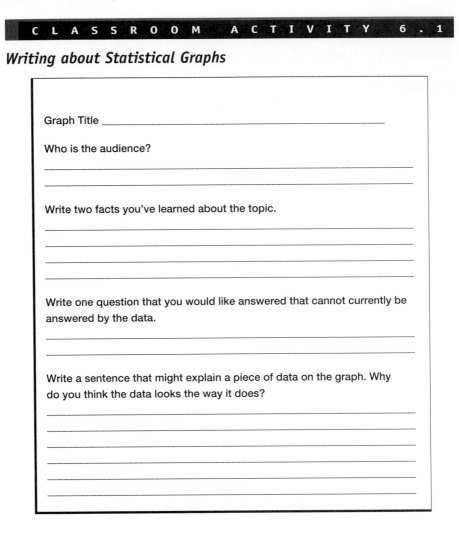

C L A S S R O O M   A C T I V I T Y   6 . 1

Writing about Statistical Graphs

Graph Title _____

Who is the audience?

_____

_____

Write two facts you've learned about the topic.

_____

_____

_____

_____

Write one question that you would like answered that cannot currently be answered by the data.

_____

_____

Write a sentence that might explain a piece of data on the graph. Why do you think the data looks the way it does?

_____

_____

_____

_____

_____

_____

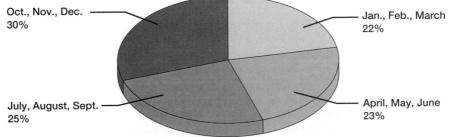

The seasons for books

When people buy the most books

Oct., Nov., Dec.
30%

Jan., Feb., March
22%

July, August, Sept.
25%

April, May, June
23%

continued

Writing About Statistical Graphs

Describing Data

Write two sentences about what the graph shows. Use the words more and same (or least, less, most, none . . .).

Tell us what this graph is about.

Use numbers to describe the data displayed on the graph.

Use fractions (or ratios or decimals) to describe the data displayed on the graph.

Analyzing Data

What conclusions can you draw from the data?

Why do you think the data looks the way it does?

Compare two pieces of data from the graph. What conclusions can you draw from the comparison?

Does the data look the way you expected it to look? Why or why not?

Writing Problems About Data

Write a story problem that another student could solve using the data.

Write a question that can be answered by looking at the data.

Reflecting on the Process

Which type of graph was used to represent the data (line, pictograph, circle, double bar . . .)? Was this type of graph a good choice? Why or why not?

Do you think this graph was easy or hard to construct? Why?

What types of decisions did the USA TODAY designers need to make to create this graph?

List some things you might do differently if you had constructed this graph.

Mike Hirsch, seventh grade math
Wentsville Middle School

✦ STEPS IN CURRICULUM PLANNING

Suppose you are a new teacher about to begin the school year. You've been given a copy of your state's standards, your district curriculum guide, and a textbook for the course you will teach. Where will you begin? How will identify the results you hope to achieve? Efficient planning for an entire school year requires long-range as well as short-range goals and a view of the big picture as well as specific lessons (Caine, Caine, & McClintic, 2002). Backward planning requires teachers to maintain a focus on the *results* they hope to achieve while organizing curriculum content to that end (McTighe & Thomas, 2003). The backward planning process consists of five steps. The first four steps are discussed in detail in this chapter; the fifth step is covered in Chapter 7.

- Step 1: Determine *long-range goals* (through personal reflection, examination of state and national standards and local curriculum documents).
- Step 2: Organize curriculum content around *big ideas*.
- Step 3: Organize big ideas into *enduring understandings*—clusters of concepts, principles, or ideas that you want students to understand.
- Step 4: Determine *essential questions* that are important for students to be able to answer after they have completed the course of study.

- Step 5: Design *student activities* that produce learning necessary to answer the essential questions.

Step 1: Determining Long-Range Goals—Four Questions

The idea of organizing curriculum around results may seem foreign to some established teachers, especially if their past pattern of planning has been content driven. Thinking about content first (not results) can become a habit. Teachers who are accustomed to planning this way must fight the inclination and shift their perspective on the curriculum planning process (Danielson, 2002). In order to think in terms of the *results* we want from the curriculum, we must be willing to think about long-range goals. What do we want our students to know or be able to do as adults (Caskey, 2002; Patterson, 2003)? Until we step away from the daily coverage concerns (and think beyond the standardized test) we fail to focus on the ultimate goals of the curriculum and we often fail to *connect* the curriculum with the real world (Pate, 2001). Developing this new perspective requires us to ponder four significant questions that go to the heart of why we teach, what we teach, and who we are as teachers. These four questions ask us to consider what our students will be like as adults (Eisner, 2004; Scherer, 2004a).

- What do we want students to know and why do we want them to know it?
- What do we want students to understand and how well do they need to understand it?
- What do we want students to be able to do and how well do they need to be able to do it (Wiggins & McTighe, 1998)?
- What do we want students to value, believe in, or fight for in the adult world?

As teachers, we will not all agree on the answers, but the answers should have a significant impact on the assessments, curriculum, and instruction we plan. Each of these questions requires careful reflection before we begin the process of planning curriculum.

1. What do we want students to know and why do we want them to know it?

Answering this question takes us to the heart of our educational philosophy and our personal relationship with the content (Beane, 1993, 1997). All of us treasure specific knowledge within our field. But given the limitations of our time with our students, which knowledge is most important for them to know (Eisner, 2004; Hirsch, Kett, & Trefil, 2002)? If the seventh grade social studies curriculum includes ancient civilizations, what about ancient civilizations is important for students to know? Traditional planning (thinking of content first) may lead teachers to assume that it would be important for students to know the names of Greek gods and the history of battles between civilizations. But are these facts that would be valuable for students to know as adults (Caskey, 2002)? (As a contestant on *Jeopardy*, perhaps!) Would it

THE FAR SIDE®   By GARY LARSON

Math phobic's nightmare

be more important for students to understand the role ancient civilizations played in the creation of frameworks for cities and governments that still persist today?

Knowledge of specific facts, concepts, or principles may serve either instrumental or intrinsic purposes (Anfara & Waks, 2002). Instrumental knowledge is knowledge that is useful in our lives, such as the ability to read and write, or the ability to use math for shopping or bill paying. A knowledge of the writings of Shakespeare, on the other hand, may have little utility in everyday life but may be considered intrinsically valuable—that is, valuable for its own sake. Philosophically, teachers' views span a continuum from those who believe that instrumental knowledge is most important to those who believe that much knowledge is valuable strictly for its own sake (Eisner, 2004). Teachers whose philosophy leans toward perennialism or essentialism tend to have a longer list of intrinsic knowledge they believe to be important, whereas progressivists or social reconstructivists tend to have a longer list of instrumental knowledge (Anfara & Waks, 2002; Gross, 2002). Thus we find a difference of opinion among language arts teachers as to whether it is essential to study classic literature or whether contemporary literature is just as valuable. Social studies teachers disagree as to how important names and dates are, and science teachers argue about the importance of knowing the periodic table.

REFLECTIVE QUESTION

Think about the content of the subject area you teach or are being trained to teach (i.e., language arts, science, music, physical education). What knowledge in your field do you believe is intrinsically important? What knowledge is important for instrumental reasons?

The problem with intrinsic knowledge is that if teachers love their content, they could believe that *all of it* was intrinsically valuable to know! *The New Dictionary of Cultural Literacy: What Every American Needs to Know* (Hirsch, Kett, & Trefil, 2002) represents an exhaustive compilation of what the authors believe to be intrinsically valuable knowledge. Although much expanded from Hirsch's earlier version, some critics claim Hirsch's work does not adequately reflect the cultural diversity of America. Lists of intrinsic knowledge alone provide little guidance for learning. What exactly are learners required to *do* with the knowledge? How much should they know about the topics (Caskey, 2002)? Should they merely be familiar with the topics, know detailed information about them, or understand relationships and contexts of specific topics? Instead of providing a dictionary of basic topics, a more important approach would probably be to ask "Is there some knowledge inherent in the content that all educated people should know?" "Is there essential knowledge in the field that is necessary for continued learning in that field?" "Should what we want students to *know* focus more on concepts and principles and less on discrete facts?" (Beane, 1993, 1997). Obviously, what teachers believe to be important instrumental and intrinsic knowledge will vary from person to person and change with the times. Do most teachers still value sentence diagramming and long division? Should students still memorize the capitals of the states?

TEACHER'S VOICE

About Intrinsic Knowledge

"I don't test on dates. I have dates on my board, so they basically understand it was the 1760s and 1770s but I'm not going to ask them what happened on March 5, 1770, and make them say that was the Boston Massacre. It doesn't matter. Why did it happen? That's what matters—and I think that's what the kids want to know too."

Kerry Brown, eighth grade social studies
Pattonville Heights Middle School

REFLECTIVE QUESTION

What content do you remember being required to learn that you felt had no intrinsic or instrumental value?

---

2. What do we want students to understand and how well do they need to understand it?

Students may understand an idea at many different levels. Teachers often think their students understand a concept when they are able to deliver the right words, definitions, or formulas, but recitation of a memorized definition is no evidence of understanding (Vatterott, 1999). Actually, being able to give examples of a concept often indicates more understanding than giving a definition. Understanding requires more than just knowing about or being familiar with a concept (Tomlinson, 1999). True understanding usually requires students to be able to use and adapt what they know in a new context (Fuhler, 2003). A student who understands something can

- Explain it clearly, giving examples;
- Use it;
- Compare and contrast it with other concepts;
- Relate it to other instances in the subject studies, other subjects, and personal life experiences;
- Transfer it to unfamiliar settings;
- Discover the concept embedded within a novel problem;
- Combine it appropriately with other understandings;
- Pose new problems that exemplify or embody the concept. (adapted from Barell, 1995, in Tomlinson, 1999, p. 38)

Teachers will disagree about what concepts and principles require understanding and at what level. Is it important for students to merely *be aware of* the causes of the Civil War, to be able to *analyze* the relationships between events, to *compare* differences in political attitudes then and now, or *predict* what might have happened if the outcome of the war were different (Marzano, Pickering, & Pollock, 2001)? Do students need a general understanding of how the circulatory system works or the ability to explain relationships between lifestyle and heart disease? Do they need to understand the chemistry involved in the transfer of oxygen from the lungs or simply know that it happens?

TEACHER'S VOICE

About Understanding

"It's extremely important to know why conflict happens. . . . I think if they can just grasp the sense that there's always more than one side to the story. That's one of the most valuable lessons they can take into the real world, is that it's not just my view, it's not the only credible one."

Kerry Brown, eighth grade social studies
Pattonville Heights Middle School

3. What do we want students to be able to do and how well do they need to be able to do it?

The increased use of performance assessments reflects a trend in curriculum away from the mere acquisition of content knowledge toward the development of skills that will allow students to be productive citizens (Caskey, 2002; Cawelti, 2003; Fuhler, 2003). If we continue to focus on what our students need to be able to do as adults, many of the answers to the question above will be generic skills that are not specific to one subject area. Some examples of generic skills that consistently show up in standards are abilities to problem solve, use technology effectively, organize information, and communicate ideas. Skills may also be subject specific, such as using the scientific method, converting fractions to decimals, or being creative in art or music. (See Figure 6.4 for an example of some subject-specific skills from the California Language Arts Standards.) Again, teachers will disagree about which skills are most important and how well students should be able to perform those skills. What specific computer skills should students master? How much math should students be able to do "in their head"? How close an estimate is close enough? How good does a work of writing have to be? What is an acceptable reading level for a high school graduate? The answers to these types of questions will shape each teacher's long-range goals (Caskey, 2002).

4. What do we want students to value, believe in, or fight for in the adult world?

Even when we try, it is impossible for teachers *not* to impart values to our students. Many of our personal values are communicated through the way we run our classrooms, treat others, and enforce rules (Doyle, 2003). Values such as equality, justice, charity, neatness, cooperation, and competition are clearly communicated on a daily basis. But we also impart values in the curriculum that we teach (Beane, 1993; Eisner, 2004; Powell, 2001). From the grand to the mundane, the way curriculum is communicated to students showcases our opinions about any number of concepts, ideas, or principles (Danielson, 2002; Goodlad, 2004). Within the context of our curriculum through our teaching, we communicate our opinions about the positive or negative value of such ideas as civil disobedience, government

F I G U R E   6 . 4

English Language Arts Content Standards for California Public Schools, Grade 6

Reading

1.0 Word Analysis, Fluency, and Systematic Vocabulary Development

Students use their knowledge of word origins and word relationships, as well as historical and literary context clues, to determine the meaning of specialized vocabulary and to understand the precise meaning of grade-level-appropriate words.

Word Recognition

1.1 Read aloud narrative and expository text fluently and accurately and with appropriate pacing, intonation, and expression.

Vocabulary and Concept Development

1.2 Identify and interpret figurative language and words with multiple meanings.

1.3 Recognize the origins and meanings of frequently used foreign words in English and use these words accurately in speaking and writing.

1.4 Monitor expository text for unknown words or words with novel meanings by using word, sentence, and paragraph clues to determine meaning.

1.5 Understand and explain "shades of meaning" in related words (e.g., softly and quietly).

2.0 Reading Comprehension (Focus on Informational Materials)

Students read and understand grade level-appropriate material. They describe and connect the essential ideas, arguments, and perspectives of the text by using their knowledge of text structure, organization, and purpose. In addition, by grade eight, students read one million words annually on their own, including a good representation of grade-level-appropriate narrative and expository text (e.g., classic and contemporary literature, magazines, newspapers, online information).

Structural Features of Informational Materials

2.1 Identify the structural features of popular media (e.g., newspapers, magazines, online information) and use the features to obtain information.

2.2 Analyze text that uses the compare-and-contrast organizational pattern.

Comprehension and Analysis of Grade-Level-Appropriate Text

2.3 Connect and clarify main ideas by identifying their relationships to other sources and related topics.

2.4 Clarify an understanding of texts by creating outlines, logical notes, summaries, or reports.

2.5 Follow multiple-step instructions for preparing applications (e.g., for a public library card, bank savings account, sports club, league membership).

intervention, capitalism, cultural diversity, the environment, the ethics of science, space exploration, classic literature, poetry, a persuasive argument, the media or the metric system. The following "Teacher's Voice" includes an excerpt from a letter to his eighth grade students in which Mike Holdinghaus shares some of his desires for them.

Teacher's Voice

About What We Want Students to Value, Believe in, or Fight for in the Adult World

"The world is full of mystery and things to wonder about. . . . How could one small man—Gandhi—force a very powerful country to do what he wanted just by refusing to eat? How could a sloppy democracy in the midst of a depression rise up to defeat Hitler's hate? . . . How is it that a simple woman from Montgomery, Alabama, can sit down on a bus and, through her example, start a civil rights movement that expanded overseas and eventually led to the end of communism in Russia? . . . It may be abstract or seem unbelievable, but we need you to be a good citizen. Every student we lose to boredom or drugs or thugdom makes it more difficult for the rest of us to live decent lives. Each of you that decides to pay attention to the news, to read newspapers, to watch so that your government treats people with respect and honors the wishes of all levels of society, each of you who debates issues with your parents and stays curious will make democracy and good government more likely in the future. There is a real race between good and evil and you're part of the race whether you want to be or not."

Mike Holdinghaus, eighth grade social studies
North Kirkwood Middle School

Student's Voice

About What We Want Students to Value, Believe in, or Fight for in the Adult World

"We should help the world grow in a positive way. This should be changed because there's too many wars and starvation, which shouldn't exist in our world."

Jonathan, seventh grade

Step 2: Organizing Curriculum Content around Big Ideas

Once we have thought through our long-range goals, our next step will be to put those goals aside and to examine the existing curriculum (Vogler, 2003). The long-range goals will influence our planning in Step 3. Even though we are planning based on results, it is easier to organize the curriculum by content to give us a frame-work for planning (Marzano, 2003).

Working within the Existing Curriculum:
Using Local Curriculum Documents

Just as we considered state and national standards in planning our long-range goals, so too must we consider the local curriculum of our school district (Danielson, 2002). Our goals do not exist in a vacuum—we want results to drive instruction but we still need to work within the confines of the curriculum provided to us by the school district in which we work.

Teachers have a moral and legal obligation to follow local curriculum documents, if such documents are available to them. The extent of curriculum development will vary from district to district, due to resources available for curriculum development, state mandates, and the amount of resistance to change in communities (Doyle, 2003). Even the best curriculum documents have limitations. Some will be based on outcomes, others will contain only content, and others will combine outcomes and content. Local curriculum is always subject to interpretation, is sometimes outdated, and may not reflect community or state standards (Marshall, 2003).

Some local curriculum documents may specify outcomes by subject area but not be articulated by grade level within those subjects. If the local curriculum is not articulated by grade level, teachers may receive guidance from state standards articulated by grade level (Marshall, 2003). In many states, accountability efforts may mandate that the state determine grade-level expectations, even if they are derived from the grade-level tests given by the state. If state guidelines are not available, teachers may need to work with others in their building or district to create a logical sequence of specific outcomes by grade (Perkins-Gough, 2004). Given the limitations of local curriculum documents, effective use of them requires teachers to

- interpret existing curriculum documents using knowledge of the content field.
- separate out statements that are references to implementation strategies as opposed to content (i.e., the student will utilize technology in a language arts class).
- discard extraneous information from the existing curriculum documents in order to focus on essential content (Perkins-Gough, 2004).
- make decisions with conviction that reflects the needs of the population of students.
- make decisions about the results we wish to achieve with the curriculum, based on the long-range goals we have chosen.

Even though our goal is to plan curriculum around results, many school districts still organize curriculum by content. Even in schools in which written documents do not exist, tradition often stipulates that certain content be taught at each grade level (this is frequently based on textbook adoptions for those grade levels). If curriculum content specific to grade level exists in our school district, we are usually wise to plan around it as we focus on results.

School District Curriculum Guide: Major Learnings in Social Studies, Grade 6

To illustrate the process of using local curriculum documents, let's assume we have been assigned to teach sixth grade social studies. We will use the sixth grade social studies curriculum from the Parkway School District (1999) in Chesterfield, Missouri (shown in Figure 6.5). Parkway is a large school district in St. Louis County fortunate enough to resources for curriculum development. Their curriculum has been aligned with the Missouri Show-Me Standards in Figures 6.1 and 6.2.

How Two Groups of Teachers Organized Content around Big Ideas

In its current state, it would be difficult to plan instruction from the curriculum shown in Figure 6.5. Organizing the curriculum around big ideas is a crucial step to-

---

FIGURE 6.5

Major Learnings in Social Studies Grade 6, Parkway School District

Title of the Textbook: World Regions
MAJOR THEME FOR THE YEAR (overarching theme for the entire year in social studies) The study of the nature of geography, people, government, and economy of major regions of the world.

Geography Review
Unit 1 The United States and Canada (geography, history, citizenship, economics, multi-cultural)
Unit 2 Latin America (geography, history, citizenship, economics, multicultural)
Unit 3 Western Europe (geography, history, citizenship, economics, multicultural)
Unit 4 Eastern Europe and Northern Asia (geography, history, citizenship, economics, multi-cultural)
Unit 5 Middle East & Northern Africa (geography, history, citizenship, economics, multi-cultural)
Unit 6 Sub-Saharan Africa (geography, history, citizenship, economics, multicultural)
Unit 7 Southern and Eastern Asia (geography, history, citizenship, economics, multicultural)
Unit 8 The Pacific (geography, history, citizenship, economics, multicultural)

Major Learnings for the Year
1. Know the distinctive governments, cultures, and economies of the United States and Canada.
2. Know that peoples of Latin American have developing economies, a rich mix of cultures/traditions.
3. Know that Western Europe's 24 nations have democratic governments, and developing economies.
4. Know that E. Europe and N. Asia are experiencing changes in government and economies.

continued

5. Know that most economies in the Middle East and N. Africa are based on agriculture and oil.
6. Know that Sub-Saharan Africa is rich in tradition and developing in this post-colonial period.
7. Know that S. & E. Asia have some of the oldest cultures, populated countries, and varied governments and economies.
8. Know that the Pacific region includes both Australia and Antarctica, as well as many islands.

Major Skills

Geography: understanding latitude and longitude, understanding map projections, relating elevation and climate, reading maps of different scales, reading time zone maps, reading contour maps

Thinking: decision making, distinguishing fact and opinion, recognizing bias, determining point of view, determining accuracy of information, drawing conclusions, asking questions, discussing views

Study Skills: reading time lines, reading graphs and charts, using reference sources, using primary and secondary sources, reading climographs, reading political cartoons, reading newspapers, varied reading/writing related to social studies content

Technology: using the CD-ROM, Adventure Time and others, video clips, Internet site resources http://www.mmschool.com; and other technologies

---

Citizenship:

Making a Difference —recognizing the contributions of individuals and groups to the "common good"

Viewpoints— considering/supporting viewpoints

Foundations—recognizing democratic documents/principles

---

ward allowing teachers to focus on results (Marzano, 2003; McTighe & Thomas, 2003). Two groups of teachers were given the curriculum document shown in Figure 6.5 as a starting point and were asked to define the *big concepts that we want students to understand* for the sixth grade social studies curriculum.

The two groups who completed the task approached it with different mind sets that, interestingly, yielded very different results. The first group, practicing middle school teachers, began immediately to organize the content based on the order in which they would teach the units. "We would start by teaching the United States and then Canada, and then Latin America." The *big ideas* to them were represented by the chunks of content, information to be delivered. It was almost as if it *never occurred to them* what the broad conceptual knowledge was—they thought only in relation to what they wanted students to *know* about the content. This was not surprising, knowing that so many teachers still begin planning with content. Thinking in this way, it was easy to see how they arrived at the *big ideas* as the unit topics listed in the curriculum document: United States, Canada, Latin America (see Figure 6.6).

This is a fairly typical result when teachers are accustomed to focusing on content first, instruction second, and assessment last. This seems most expedient when

FIGURE 6 . 6

Curriculum Map Organized by Unit Topics

The United States and Canada
Latin America
Western Europe
Eastern Europe
Middle East and Northern Africa
Sub-Saharan Africa
Southern and Eastern Asia
The Pacific

FIGURE 6 . 7

Curriculum Map Organized by Big Ideas

Government
Culture and multiculturalism
Geography
Economics
Critical thinking
Study skills
Technology
Citizenship

time is short and instruction must be planned for each day. This curriculum organization makes it fairly easy to teach factual content (and follow the textbook) but may not allow students to grasp the big concepts that permeate the curriculum (Seif, 2004).

The second group of teachers were also asked to define the *big concepts that we want students to understand* for the same curriculum document. These teachers were pre-service teachers with little planning experience. When asked to organize the curriculum in terms of big concepts they actually had less trouble seeing the bigger picture than many of the practicing teachers (see Figure 6.7).

Organizing the curriculum around chunks of content (Figure 6.6) does not define the broad conceptual learning. When the curriculum is organized around big ideas (such as economics, governments, or cultures in Figure 6.7), it frees the teacher's perspective to think more in terms of broad student outcomes and less in terms of content (Marzano, 2003; Seif, 2004).

Step 3: Organizing Big Ideas into Enduring Understandings

Wiggins and McTighe (1998) suggest that we prioritize curriculum content by first thinking of the broadest organization of knowledge within our field as a large circle. That circle contains all the knowledge that we believe is *worth being familiar with*. Within the large circle is a smaller circle that contains the content that we believe is *important to know and do* within this field of learning. Finally, inside the second circle is an even smaller circle that focuses on **enduring understandings** (see Figure 6.8):

> The term "enduring understandings" refers to the big ideas, the important understandings, that we want students to "get inside of" and retain after they've forgotten many of the details. . . . Enduring understandings go beyond discrete facts or skills to focus on *larger concepts, principles, or processes* (emphasis added). As such, they are applicable to new situations within or beyond the subject. (Wiggins & McTighe, 1998, p. 10)

Enduring understandings are the general results we hope to achieve (Marzano, 2003; Seif, 2004). (Later, we will refine those enduring understandings by writing more

FIGURE 6.8

Prioritizing Curricular Content.

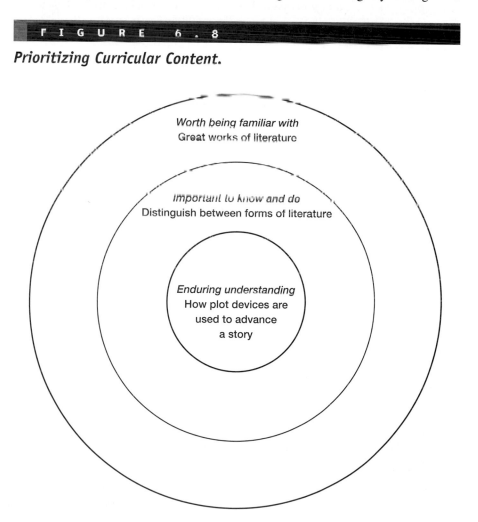

specific essential questions and objectives.) For example, a language arts teacher may want his students to be familiar with great works of literature, be able to distinguish between various forms of literature, and have an enduring understanding of how plot devices are used to advance a story (see Figure 6.8).

Each big idea within your curriculum content must be further clarified (Caskey, 2002; Seif, 2004). What are the *concepts, principles, or processes* that we want students to understand and be able to do (Marzano, 2003)? To define the enduring understandings, return first to your long-range goals—what you want students to know, understand, and be able to do. Focusing on *concepts, principles, or processes* we want the students to understand helps us to think in terms of outcomes as opposed to factual content (Seif, 2004).

It is easier to determine enduring understandings from big ideas than from unit topics. The big ideas form the basis for further defining the enduring understandings (*concepts, principles, and processes*). For example, as the social studies teacher reflects on the big idea of citizenship he or she could arrive at some of the enduring understandings listed below.

Enduring Understandings for the Big Idea of Citizenship

- Immigrants must earn the right of citizenship.
- In a democracy, individual freedoms must be balanced with what is good for the larger group.
- Citizen participation is necessary for the survival of democracy.
- Citizen participation in government balances the power of the government.

(These enduring understandings are also shown in the Curriculum Planning Template, Figure 6.11, at the end of the chapter.) This initial conceptualization of the curriculum in no way restricts the organization or sequencing of content within the course. Organizing the content around enduring understandings (concepts, principles, or processes) merely helps teachers focus on the *outcomes* they want students to have achieved as a result of the course. Teachers may still choose to organize and sequence the content as shown in Figure 6.6, but they should plan instruction around enduring understandings as opposed to purely factual information.

REFLECTIVE QUESTION

What enduring understandings (concepts, principles, or processes) would students need to have learned to complete Classroom Activity 6.2?

CLASSROOM ACTIVITY 6.2

Creating a New Solar System

In this activity students will be allowed to work in groups of two or three or may choose to work alone. Materials that will be available to the students are resource books on topic, large sheets of paper, markers, crayons, colored pencils, and a diagram of the solar system. This activity will require one hour for brainstorming, creating a drawing, and deciding which activity the group will do, and one hour to complete the chosen activity.

Students are to assume the identity of an alien from a far away solar system. Within your group use the following questions as a guide to creating your alien solar system. Write down all ideas and be descriptive and creative. After you have a good idea of how your solar system will look, create a drawing of your planet and solar system.

1. What is the name of your alien?
2. What is the name of your planet and solar system?
3. How many planets are in your solar system?
4. How do the planets revolve around your solar system?
5. How do the rotational orbits of your planet differ from orbit of the earth?
6. How many moons revolve around your planet?
7. Do you have seasons on your planet and what are they like?
8. What is your atmosphere made up of?
9. What kinds of creatures inhabit your planet?

Now that you have created your alien solar system, choose one of the following activities:

A. You have been asked to appear on a talk show. The host of the talk show has asked you to describe your solar system and your home planet. Include in your interview how earth and your home planet compare and contrast. Write a script for the talk show and include the drawing of your planet and solar system.
B. Write a scientific paper that describes the alien solar system and home planet that you come from. Compare and contrast your alien solar system to the earth's solar system. Include the drawing of your planet and solar system.

Elizabeth Baker
Karen Giedeman
Michael Geoffic

Step 4: Determining Essential Questions

Enduring understandings have helped us to focus on results. After we have organized content with enduring understandings, we can maintain our results focus by determining **essential questions** about the content (Jacobs, 1997; McTighe & Thomas, 2003; Wiggins & McTighe, 1998). Essential questions are broad questions that represent the knowledge students should have gained at the end of a unit of study (Caskey, 2002).

> How do we more deliberately and practically design units and courses to develop student understanding? How might we take a mass of content knowledge and shape it to engage and focus student inquiry? One key design strategy is to build curriculum around the questions that gave rise to the content knowledge in the first place. (Wiggins & McTighe, 1998, pp. 26–27)

Essential questions represent the learning that remains when students have forgotten low-level factual information (Caskey, 2002; Danielson, 2002). Essential

Essential questions guide the creation of student learning activities.

questions are questions that students can't answer after a few lessons and the answers to which were never explicitly taught—only inferred or left up to the student to synthesize. The use of essential questions is a design strategy to help us maintain our focus on results as we organize content and a device to stimulate our creativity and to enable us to reflect upon the ultimate outcomes of the curriculum (McTighe & Thomas, 2003; Seif, 2004). One set of essential questions for the seventh grade social studies curriculum is shown in Figure 6.9.

FIGURE   6 . 9

Essential Questions for Seventh Grade Social Studies

Big Idea: Government

Essential Questions

What are the characteristics of the different types of governments?

How does a government relate to its people?

How does a government effect the economy?

What principles shape constitutional democracy in the United States?

continued

Big Idea: Culture and Multiculturalism

Essential Questions

In what ways do people show or illustrate culture?

How are different cultures established?Why is it important to appreciate different cultures?

How does diversity affect a nation?

Big Idea: Geography

Essential Questions

How does geography relate to culture and economy in the lives of people?

What strategies do you use to read and interpret maps?

Big Idea: Economics

Essential Questions

What are the characteristics of an economy?

How are the economies of different nations similar or different from one another?

In what ways does the government control or affect the economy?

Big Idea: Critical Thinking

Essential Questions

How do the decisions of individuals and leaders affect the community?

How is fact distinguished from opinion?

Big Idea: Study Skills

Essential Questions

What strategies should be used for reading and evaluating information?

What conclusions can be drawn from evaluating data?

Big Idea: Technology

Essential Questions

What is the importance of using technology in society?

How can we use technology to better understand our world?

Big Idea: Citizenship

Essential Questions

What contributions can individuals or groups make to the common good?

How is citizenship important to a nation?

What is the importance of active citizenship?

Step 5: Designing Student Activities

Essential questions allow us to form a conceptual map and that allows us to organize results into units and activities (Caskey, 2002; Marzano, 2003). From the essential questions we will generate more specific results (to be written as objectives) that will guide the creation of student learning activities (Seif, 2004). (Step 5, the writing of objectives and the designing of learning activities, will be discussed fully in Chapter 7.) In order to see the complete planning process, it will be helpful to offer a brief discussion of step 5 here. We can organize results into five types of learning:

- Facts—discrete bits of information that we believe to be true
- Concepts—categories of things with common elements that help us organize, retain, and use information
- Principles—rules that govern concepts
- Attitudes—degrees of commitment to ideas and spheres of learning
- Skills—the capacity to put to work the understandings we have gained (Tomlinson, 1999, pp. 38–39)

For instance, suppose we focus on one essential question from the seventh grade social studies course shown above, "What principles shape constitutional democracy in the United States?" From that question we could generate the following results (written as objectives) that we want all students to achieve:

- The student will be aware of the rights listed in the Bill of Rights (fact).
- The student will identify and explain basic constitutional rights and liberties of U.S. citizens (concept).
- The student will explain how laws protect the primary democratic values implicit in the U.S. constitution (principle).
- The student will formulate a position and use relevant and logical arguments to support the position (skill).
- The student will appreciate the connection between rights of citizens and responsibilities of citizens in a democracy (attitude).

After determining the specific results, we would then design the student activities that could help students reach the results listed above (Caskey, 2002; Seif, 2004). Possible learning activities for the essential question "What principles shape the constitutional democracy in the United States?" include these: writing a letter to a new immigrant explaining his or her basic rights as guaranteed by the U.S. Constitution, using real-life examples to illustrate each right; and finding stories in the newspaper that illustrate constitutional rights issues, finding one story for each right in the Bills of Rights.

Curriculum Planning Template

Step in the planning process	Subject area example 7th grade social studies	Your subject area
Step 1 **Long-range goals**	**7th grade social studies** long range goals	
What students should know		
What students should understand		
What students should be able to do		
What students value or believe in		
Step 2 **Big ideas**	**Big ideas for** **7th grade social studies**	Record 8 big ideas from your subject area in the column below.
	Government	
	Culture and multiculturalism	
	Geography	
	Economics	
	Critical thinking	
	Study skills	
	Technology	
	Citizenship	
Step 3 **Enduring understandings**		
Enduring understandings for the one big idea	(One big idea from step 2) Citizenship *Enduring understandings for Citizenship*	Choose one big idea you listed in step 2. Write it here. List at least 3 enduring understandings for that big idea in the column below.
	Immigrants must earn the right of citizenship.	
	In a democracy, individual freedoms must be balanced with what is good for the larger group.	
	Citizen participation is necessary for the survival of democracy.	
	Citizen participation in government balances the power of the government.	
Step 4 **Essential questions**		Choose one enduring understanding from step 3. Write it in the box below.
(choose one enduring understanding from step 3)	In a democracy, individual freedoms must be balanced with what is good for the larger group.	

continued

	Essential questions.	Write 2 essential questions for that enduring understanding.
Essential questions for that one enduring understanding	How are basic rights protected and limited by the constitution?	
	What principles shape the constitutional democracy of the United States?	
Step 5: designing student activities		Write one essential question here.
(choose one essential question from step 4)	How are basic rights protected and limited by the constitution?	
Possible student activities for that one essential question	Write a letter to a new immigrant explaining his or her basic rights as guaranteed by the U.S. Constitution. Use real-life examples to illustrate each right.	
	Find stories in the newspaper that illustrate a constitutional rights issue. Keep searching until you have one story for each right in the Bills of Rights.	

SUMMARY

The traditional method of planning instruction based on curriculum content has serious limitations for today's teachers (Levine, 2003b; Patterson, 2003). The political popularity of standards and standardized tests has shifted the focus of curriculum planning to a backward design that begins with the desired results of instruction (Brown, 2002; Gross, 2002). Results-based curriculum planning requires teachers to determine long-range goals and to organize content around big ideas, enduring understandings, and essential questions (Wiggins & McTighe, 1998). This chapter has detailed the first four steps in the curriculum planning process. This process requires teachers to think carefully about the long-range impact of their curriculum and to make decisions about the role state and local standards will play in their teaching (Danielson, 2002; Marshall, 2003). It requires them to analyze, organize, and prioritize curriculum content and to reflect seriously on the big ideas they want their students to internalize (Caskey, 2002; Eisner, 2004). The activities of this chapter have allowed you to practice the first four steps in the curriculum planning process which have included the following:

- Determine long range goals (step 1).
- Review local curriculum documents and organize content by big ideas (step 2).

- Prioritize content by which concepts, principles, and processes are most critical for enduring understanding and integrate state and local standards into planning (step 3).
- Use essential questions to clarify results (step 4).

Once teachers have organized content and clarified results for their curriculum, they are ready to design student activities (step 5) that will enable their students to reach the results. This step of curriculum planning will be covered in Chapter 7.

KEY TERMS

assessment	enduring understandings
backward design	essential questions
curriculum	instruction

APPLICATION ACTIVITIES

1. The general standards shown in Figure 6.1 stipulate that they should be integrated across all subject areas. Select one of the four academic subject areas (math, science, language arts, or social studies) and evaluate each general standard for how easily you believe it could be integrated into that subject area. Circle "easy to integrate" if you believe the standard would be easy to integrate into your subject area, circle "difficult to integrate" if you believe the standard would be difficult to integrate into your subject area, or circle "not sure" if you are not sure.

   Goal 1
   Standard 1 easy to integrate   difficult to integrate   not sure
   Standard 2 easy to integrate   difficult to integrate   not sure
   Standard 3 easy to integrate   difficult to integrate   not sure
   Standard 4 easy to integrate   difficult to integrate   not sure

   Goal 2
   Standard 1 easy to integrate   difficult to integrate   not sure
   Standard 2 easy to integrate   difficult to integrate   not sure
   Standard 3 easy to integrate   difficult to integrate   not sure
   Standard 4 easy to integrate   difficult to integrate   not sure

   Goal 3
   Standard 1 easy to integrate   difficult to integrate   not sure
   Standard 2 easy to integrate   difficult to integrate   not sure
   Standard 3 easy to integrate   difficult to integrate   not sure
   Standard 4 easy to integrate   difficult to integrate   not sure

   Goal 4
   Standard 1 easy to integrate   difficult to integrate   not sure
   Standard 2 easy to integrate   difficult to integrate   not sure

Standard 3 easy to integrate   difficult to integrate   not sure
Standard 4 easy to integrate   difficult to integrate   not sure

2. Select one set of content standards from Figure 6.2. Create a list of topics that could be taught in that subject to reach the standards listed. Consult a local curriculum guide or middle school textbook in that content area to help you in determining topics.

3. Review the math and language arts content standards shown in Figure 6.2. Then look at Classroom Activity 6.1. Which goals and standards does Mr. Hirsch address with the activities in Classroom Activity 6.1?

4. Select a curriculum concept from Figure 6.1, 6.2, or 6.3 that you want students to understand. Create learning tasks for that concept that would allow students to demonstrate each of the types of understanding listed below.

Curriculum concept _____

Types of understanding	**Learning task**
Explain concept or give examples	_____
Compare and contrast it with other concepts	_____
Transfer it to unfamiliar settings	_____

5. Go to Figure 6.4. Find at least two standards that specify *how well* students should be able to perform a skill. For example: Standard 1.0 Word Analysis, Fluency, and Systematic Vocabulary Development: Students use their knowledge of word origins and word relationships, as well as historical and literary context clues, *to determine the meaning of specialized vocabulary* and *to understand the precise meaning of grade-level-appropriate words.*

6. Review the general standards for Missouri in Figure 6.1. How many of them refer to something students should *know*? How many of them refer to something students should *understand*? How many of them refer to something students should *be able to do*?

7. Write a paragraph about the values you believe your subject area should communicate to students. For example, the love of reading for language arts, respect for the constitution for social studies, or concern for the environment for science.

8. Review Figure 6.8 *Prioritizing curricular content.* Draw your own circle for your content area. List at least three concepts in each of the concentric circles. (You may use any of the standards shown previously for ideas.)

9. Read through Classroom Activity 6.2. Write five essential questions students should be able to answer after completing that activity.

10. Go to your state's Web site and find the standards for social studies, language arts, math, and science. Select one of the four subjects and use the standards to organize the content of those standards into 8 to 12 big ideas. Record those big ideas under step 2 on the Curriculum Planning Template, Figure 6.10.

11. Refer to the Curriculum Planning Template, Figure 6.10. Choose one of the big ideas you previously listed under step 2 of the template. In the space provided under step 3, list at least 3 enduring understandings for that big idea.

12. Refer to the Curriculum Planning Template, Figure 6.10. Choose one enduring understanding you wrote under step 3. Write 2 or 3 essential questions for that enduring understanding.

CHAPTER 7

PLANNING
FOR STUDENT-FOCUSED
INSTRUCTION

➔ INTRODUCTION

In Chapter 6, we organized curriculum by big ideas and focused on the results of instruction by writing enduring understandings and essential questions about our content. How will those big ideas and essential questions guide us in planning units, activities, and daily lessons? Our next step is to take the essential questions we have written and specify results. In this chapter, we will explore how teachers determine the results of learning and how they plan learning experiences. This chapter will illustrate what student-focused instruction looks like day-to-day in the classroom. **The purposes of this chapter are to help you**

- understand the connection between unit and lesson objectives and long-range planning.
- understand the process of validating the results of learning.
- be aware of the factors that teachers consider when making decisions about designing learning experiences.
- appreciate the importance of the student-content relationship.
- design learning activities within the context of student needs and interests.
- think creatively about your content.
- understand the role of constructivist learning in student-focused instruction.
- understand how and why learning activities should be differentiated.
- practice the steps of designing learning activities.
- practice the steps of designing an interdisciplinary unit.

Essential Questions

After reading and completing the activities in this chapter, you should be able to answer the following questions:

1. How does the content of learning influence the results teachers use to show learning?
2. How can the technique of essential questions be used to clarify results?
3. How can results be expressed as behavioral objectives?
4. How can learning activities function as both instruction and assessment of learning?
5. Why is the student-content relationship an important aspect to consider when planning student-focused instruction?
6. What steps do teachers go through in designing student-focused learning activities?
7. What role do enduring understandings and essential questions play in the design of learning activities?
8. What are the ideal characteristics of a student-focused learning activity?
9. In what ways do teachers use learning activities as a means of differentiating learning experiences to meet individual learner needs?
10. How are interdisciplinary learning activities created?

✈ PLANNING UNITS AROUND ESSENTIAL QUESTIONS

At the beginning of each school year or semester, most teachers find it helpful to follow the steps illustrated in Chapter 6 to arrive at the big ideas, enduring understandings, and essential questions for the content of each course they teach (McTighe & Thomas, 2003; Vogler, 2003). They then use that information to plan units. Before planning units, most teachers spend some time mapping out the curriculum for the year (Perkins-Gough, 2004). A curriculum map is a broad plan for the year that shows what concepts will be taught and in what order (Jacobs, 1997). A **curriculum map** organizes big ideas and concepts in a sequential manner (Lemlech, 2002; Marzano, 2003). To create a curriculum map, a teacher consults a calendar and organizes content, specifying large blocks of time for each set of concepts. For instance, in Chapter 6 a group of teachers determined big ideas for sixth grade social studies. Those big ideas were government, culture and multiculturalism, geography, economics, critical thinking, study skills, technology, and citizenship. Figure 7.1 shows how one teacher might organize the curriculum for the school year using those big ideas. The study of the United States is shown in the greatest detail. Later units about other regions would contain similar content.

F I G U R E   7 . 1

Sixth Grade Social Studies Curriculum Map

September
Introductory unit (2 weeks)
> Get acquainted activities
> Course overview
> Introduction to study skills
>> Strategies for reading and evaluating information
>> Concept mapping, graphic organizers
>> Note-taking, test-taking skills

The United States (late September through December)
Geography (2 weeks)
>> Understanding latitude and longitude
>> Reading time zone maps
>> Reading contour maps

October
History of the United States (4 weeks)
>> Role of geography in history
>> Significant events in American history

continued

How history is recorded
   Distinguishing fact and opinion
   Determining point of view
   Determining accuracy of information

November
Government and economics (4 weeks)
   Founding principles of United States government
   Foundations—democratic documents/principles
   Characteristics and structure of democracy
   Basic principles of economics

December
Citizenship ($1^1/_2$ weeks)
   Bill of rights
   Rights and responsibilities
   Role of active citizenship
   Community service
Culture and multiculturalism ($1^1/_2$ weeks)
   Diversity in a democracy
   Recognizing and dealing with bias
   Respecting and celebrating diversity
   Cultural rituals and holiday celebrations

January–May
Latin America (3 weeks)
   Geography, History, Citizenship, Economics, Culture
Western Europe (3 weeks)
   Geography, History, Citizenship, Economics, Culture
Eastern Europe and Northern Asia (3 weeks)
   Geography, History, Citizenship, Economics, Culture
Middle East and Africa (3 weeks)
   Geography, History, Citizenship, Economics, Culture
Southern and Eastern Asia (3 weeks)
   Geography, History, Citizenship, Economics, Culture
The Pacific (3 weeks)
   Geography, History, Citizenship, Economics, Culture
Culminating Countries Activity (2 weeks)

This teacher chooses to organize the curriculum by geographic regions and to begin with an extensive series of units about the United States as a way to introduce basic concepts of geography, government, economics, and culture. By beginning with the country with which students are most familiar, the teacher can illustrate concepts with examples from the students' everyday lives. Those concepts would then be reinforced in the shorter units about other world regions.

Study skills, critical thinking skills, and technology skills are integrated into each unit and taught as needed for specific learning activities. Citizenship and culture units are intentionally scheduled prior to winter break so students can perform community service and learn about cultural traditions related to the holidays.

In Figure 7.1, unit ideas are mapped out first and essential questions for each unit are determined later. In some cases, one broad essential question may form the basis for a unit. To illustrate, it may be helpful to see how one teacher plans a unit around his essential question "What causes revolution?"

TEACHER'S VOICE

About Unit Planning

"We start off with the ten main events of the Revolutionary War. Then we do a two-day play on the Boston Massacre. I go over political cartoons at least once a week on current events and since we've been talking about perspective and point of view the whole year, they learn that it's not just the American version of the revolution, and it's not just the Palestine version of what's happening in the Middle East, so they're really aware of two sides of a conflict right now. One of the things they do is draw a political cartoon about the Boston Tea Party. They did the cartoon from the American colonist's point of view.

We're doing two kinds of evaluation. I'll have them do a debate against each other on whether they felt America was justified in revolting and that's the real student-driven assignment. Because this is tested so heavily in the standardized test, I'm also going to give them the standard quiz."

Kerry Brown, eighth grade social studies
Pattonville Heights Middle School

Mr. Brown's unit is a typical student-focused unit—not very many short, daily lessons—mostly activities alternated with other methods such as direct instruction, cooperative learning, discussion, reading (Gabler & Schroeder, 2003; Henson, 2004) (methods that will be discussed in Chapters 8 and 9).

✦ WRITING OBJECTIVES FOR UNITS AND LESSONS

Essential questions help us to frame the content of individual units (Wiggins & McTighe, 1998). But in order to plan specific activities and lessons, we must relate the essential questions to the specific results we wish the students to achieve (Good & Brophy, 2003; Marzano, 2003; Marzano, Pickering & Pollock, 2001; Wiggins & McTighe, 1998). Those results will be influenced by our long-range goals, state standards, and to some extent, standardized tests.

Results are expressed in relation to **objectives**. **Objectives** are statements that specify what we want the students to know or be able to do at the conclusion of a learning experience or unit (Gronlund, 2000; Kellough & Kellough, 1999). Objectives are important tools that focus our planning and assessment on results of learning (Cawelti, 2003). Objectives are always written in student terms—"The student will be able to . . ." and reflect the type and extent of learning desired (Jacobsen, Eggen, & Kauchak, 2002).

Objectives can be used to describe **cognitive, affective,** or **psychomotor** learning (Gronlund, 2006; Jacobsen et al., 2002). **Cognitive objectives** refer to the development of intellectual knowledge or skills, such as knowing the difference between half and whole notes, understanding the parts of a paragraph, or being able to divide fractions (Bloom, 1984; Gabler & Schroeder, 2003). **Affective objectives** refer to the development of attitudes or values about the content, such as appreciating classical music, caring about the environment, or enjoying a well-written story (Henson, 2004; Kellough & Kellough, 1999). **Psychomotor objectives** refer to the development and perfection of physical skills, such as the ability to play a musical instrument, serve a tennis ball, or type quickly and accurately (Gronlund, 2000; Kellough & Kellough, 1999; Schurr, 1989). Teachers of academic subjects will most often write cognitive objectives.

Levels of Cognitive Objectives

Cognitive objectives generally describe one of five levels of cognitive learning: knowledge, comprehension, application, analysis, synthesis, or evaluation (Bloom, 1984). The type of learning required in each of the six levels is described below (Gabler & Schroeder, 2003; Gronlund, 2000):

Knowledge: Remembering or recognizing something previously encountered
    without necessarily understanding it.
Comprehension: Understanding, explaining, or interpreting information.
Application: Using knowledge in a new situation to solve a problem.
Analysis: Breaking something down into its components or inferring meaning.
Synthesis: Creating something new by combining new ideas.
Evaluation: Making defensible judgments that are based on knowledge.
(Jacobsen et al., 2002; Kellough & Kellough, 1999; Woolfolk, 1990)

Samples of each level of objective are shown in Figure 7.2.

These cognitive levels are arranged in a hierarchy that moves from simple (knowledge level) to more complex learning (evaluation level), but the categories are not meant to be discrete. It is often difficult to pinpoint exactly which of the six levels a particular objective fits. The primary purpose of the hierarchy is to help teachers focus whenever possible on higher level learning (Henson, 2004; Kellough & Kellough, 1999). Every activity or lesson will not necessarily address all six levels of learning. In addition, it would be a fallacy to assume that all learning must proceed linearly from the simplest to the most complex. Constructivist teachers have found that it is often preferable to give students an application or evaluation task for which they have little prior knowledge (Gabler & Schroeder, 2003; Henson, 2004). Students are then required to complete the low-level learning in order to solve that higher level problem (Simon, 2002). The low-level learning now has more meaning and context because its purpose is central to completing the higher level task (Brooks, 2004; Perkins, 2004). For example, Mike Burgio's science students built

F I G U R E   7 . 2

Sample Objectives

Knowledge level

The student will be able to list 10 parts of a cell.

The student will recall typical Spanish greetings.

The student will be able to locate Germany on a world map.

Comprehension level

The student will be able to explain how glaciers are formed.

The student will be able to divide fractions.

The student will be able to classify words as adjectives or adverbs.

Application level

The student will be able to use the scientific method to solve a problem.

The student will be able to find the area of a triangle.

The student will be able to write a persuasive essay.

Analysis level

The student will be able to categorize animals based on their characteristics.

The student will determine which method to use to solve a math problem.

The student will analyze a piece of writing to determine point of view.

Synthesis level

The student will design a travel brochure for a region of the world.

The student will generalize about the relationships between environment and animal adaptations.

The student will plan a trip for settlers to travel the Oregon Trail.

Evaluation level

The student will evaluate a diet for nutritional value.

The student will critique a piece of writing for style and content.

The student will defend a position on a political issue.

---

and launched rockets *before* they completed the worksheet with the formal definitions of force and momentum.

Types of Content Objectives Address

Objectives also specify one of five *types of content* that we want students to learn.

- Facts—discrete bits of information that we believe to be true.
- Concepts—categories of things with common elements that help us organize, retain, and use information.
- Principles—rules that govern concepts.

- Attitudes—degrees of commitment to ideas and spheres of learning.
- Skills—the capacity to put to work the understandings we have gained (Gabler & Schroeder, 2003; Jacobsen et al., 2002; Tomlinson, 1999).

When you write objectives for units or lessons, you should consider all five types of learning, even though they all may not be included (Gronlund, 2000). What concepts and principles do students need to understand to form the framework for the unit? What factual information is needed for students to understand those concepts and principles? (Marzano et al., 2001). What attitudes do you hope to develop in students about the content? What skills should students master related to the content? (Henson, 2004; Kellough & Kellough, 1999).

Suppose we are planning a unit about constitutional rights. The unit will focus on the essential question "What principles shape constitutional democracy in the United States?" From that question we could generate the following results (written as objectives) that we want all students to achieve:

- The student will be aware of the rights listed in the Bill of Rights (fact).
- The student will identify and explain basic constitutional rights and liberties of U.S. citizens (concept).
- The student will explain how laws protect the primary democratic values implicit in the U.S. constitution (principle).
- The student will formulate a position and use relevant and logical arguments to support the position (skill).
- The student will appreciate the connection between rights of citizens and responsibilities of citizens in a democracy (attitude).

REFLECTIVE QUESTION

Which of the six levels of learning does each of the above objectives represent?

After determining the specific objectives for the unit, we will plan activity-based lessons to help students reach the objectives (Henson, 2004; Gabler & Schroeder, 2003). Examples of possible learning activities for a unit about constitutional rights include these:

- Research a particular time in history when basic rights were denied or infringed upon for a particular group. Present an oral or written report of your findings.
- Use the Bill of Rights to defend an individual or group accused of breaking the law in a current or past news story. Present your defense to the class.
- Write a persuasive essay defending your position on this statement: "In this country, 13-year-olds do not have all the constitutional rights guaranteed by the Bill of Rights." Support your ideas with examples.

How Will We Know If Students Are Reaching Our Objectives?

Objectives are validated by assessments (Henson, 2004; Kellough & Kellough, 1999). Assessments are used as evidence of how well objectives have been reached (Gabler & Schroeder, 2003; Marzano et al., 2001). Ideally, student-focused instruction allows curriculum, instruction, and assessment to be integrated in such a way that the assessment and the learning experience are combined (Vatterott, 1999). If the learning experience is successful, the result is a product that can be assessed to determine if learning took place (McTighe & Thomas, 2003). That is, to complete the assessment task requires learning by the student. The *result* of the successful completion of the activity, the product, serves as the *evidence* of learning (Guskey, 2003). The primary action of the classroom therefore becomes not the *teacher's* delivery of inert content, but the *interaction of the student with the content* (Eisner, 2004; Vatterott, 1999).

✦ HOW DO TEACHERS DESIGN LEARNING ACTIVITIES THAT ALSO ASSESS LEARNING?

In order to design learning activities that also assess learning, teachers must first identify desired results, and then determine what assessment will serve as evidence of those results (Danielson, 2002; Elmore, 2003). Traditional measurement of learning has often relied on paper and pencil tests as evidence of results (Patterson, 2003; Wiggins & McTighe, 1998). We now know that teachers can evaluate learning using other types of evidence, objective and subjective, such as projects, interviews, observations, or portfolios (Gabler & Schroeder, 2003; Henson, 2004). Teachers select the kind of evidence to use based on the types of results they want (Danielson, 2002; McTighe & Thomas, 2003).

Teachers make decisions about desired results based on what they want students to know, understand, and do (Marzano, 2003). Teachers must make decisions about the depth of learning that is preferable and the importance of specific curricular content (Caine, Caine, & McClintic, 2002). In Chapter 6 (Figure 6.8), we distinguished between content that students should be familiar with, content that is important to know and do, and content worthy of enduring understanding (Wiggins & McTighe, 1998). Before planning activities, teachers must first reflect on the kinds of learning they want to take place (Danielson, 2002; Marzano et al., 2001). If they merely want students to be familiar with information or to commit content to rote memory (such as multiplication tables), they may create a simple game that will help students remember those facts and then may evaluate the learning with a paper and pencil test (Caskey, 2002). If, on the other hand, they are interested in their students being able to understand and apply information, they will probably want to design performance tasks that require students to create a product or presentation (Fuhler, 2003; Vatterott, 1999).

The desired results of learning (rote memory versus understanding or application) determine the type of assessment a teacher will select, and the type of assessment

FIGURE 7.3

Curriculum Priorities		Assessment Types
Worth being familiar with	⟶	Traditional quizzes and tests (paper/pencil)
Important to know and do	⟶	Traditional quizzes and tests (paper/pencil)
Enduring understanding	⟶	Performance tasks and projects (complex, authentic)

determines the type of learning activity the teacher will design (Danielson, 2002; Marzano et al., 2001). Lower levels of learning such as awareness or basic knowledge may be measured by paper and pencil tests, whereas higher levels of learning may require application tasks (Vatterott, 1999). Wiggins and McTighe (1998) illustrate this concept with the diagram shown in Figure 7.3. (Assessments will be discussed fully in Chapter 10.)

CLASSROOM ACTIVITY 7.1

The Day (24–Hours) before the Chapter 5 Test

Lesson 1—"Success at Jamestown"
What do I know about Lesson 1? *I know about the people (John Smith, King James, John Rolfe, and Pocahontas)*
What do I need to study for Lesson 1? *I still need to study the changes in government and the House of Burgesses.*

Lesson 2—"The Pilgrims at Plymouth"
What do I know about Lesson 2? *I know about the first Thanksgiving, and I know about the Indians. (Squanto and Samoset)*
What do I need to study for Lesson 2? *I need to study the hard times at Plymouth. Lesson 2 is the lesson I know the best because a national holiday is named from them (Thanksgiving).*

Lesson 3—"The Settlement of New England"
What do I know about Lesson 3? *I know about the Great Migration, which was the migration to America by English Puritans during the 1630s.*
What do I need to study for Lesson 3? *I need to study the New England Way. I also need to study the towns in Colonial New England. This is the lesson I know the least because it is so long.*
I will receive a 90% on the Chapter 5 Test, and with corrections, I think I will have a 95%. I predict I will receive a 92% to 100% on the essay questions.

by
Abby Robison   Jason Holmes
8th grade student   eighth grade Unified Studies Teacher
Parkway Central Middle School   Parkway Central Middle School

What evidence can be used to show that learning has occurred? Is there a product or presentation that shows both that learning has occurred and that the objective has been met? Sometimes the learning experience also provides evidence of learning (McTighe & Thomas, 2003; Vatterott, 1999). If the learning activity and the evidence can be the same, that is ideal. If the learning activity and the evidence (the assessment) are two different events, how can the learning activity be structured to help prepare the student to succeed at the assessment? For example, Jason Holmes's students take paper and pencil tests to assess their learning of social studies reading. Their learning activities include chapter reading and drawing illustrations to summarize their chapter knowledge. To prepare them to take the paper and pencil test, students complete the activity shown in Classroom Activity 7.1 the day before the test. The test is the assessment, but all the previous learning experiences prepare students for the assessment.

If the evidence of learning is a student project as opposed to a paper and pencil test, learning activities are needed to prepare the student to complete the project (Vatterott, 1999). To illustrate this process, let's review one teacher's plan for a unit. Mr. Bergner outlined concepts and created activities and assessments for his unit on the Trojan War described in Classroom Activity 7.2.

The low-level learning of vocabulary was accomplished with worksheets and was assessed by a vocabulary list and a matching quiz. The concepts of virtue and vice required a deeper understanding—students were asked to apply their knowledge of the virtues and vices by giving their opinion of which characters in the *Iliad* exemplified each virtue and vice (Classroom Activity 7.3)

These and other tasks gave students the necessary conceptual learning to allow them to complete the final project, a synthesis task in which groups of students created Hyperstudio projects about specific groups of Greek or Trojan gods (Classroom Activity 7.3).

C L A S S R O O M   A C T I V I T Y   7 . 2

Mr. Bergner's Plan for the Trojan War Unit

This is an in-depth unit on the history and literature of Classical Greece emphasizing the unique contributions of Greece concerning the *nature and potential of man*. It focuses on man's more noble virtues and ignoble vices as exemplified in political development, economics, warfare, literature, cultural development in Ancient Greece. The real outcome of this unit of study will be insight and reflection upon the nature of man at the dawn of the 21st century.

Activities will include map study, vocabulary, reading an adapted version of the *Iliad*, and student research about people and gods of Greece, people and gods of Troy. Students will also research the history of Greece and create multimedia presentations in which students demonstrate their understanding of concepts.

Greg Bergner
seventh grade Unified Studies teacher
Parkway Central Middle School

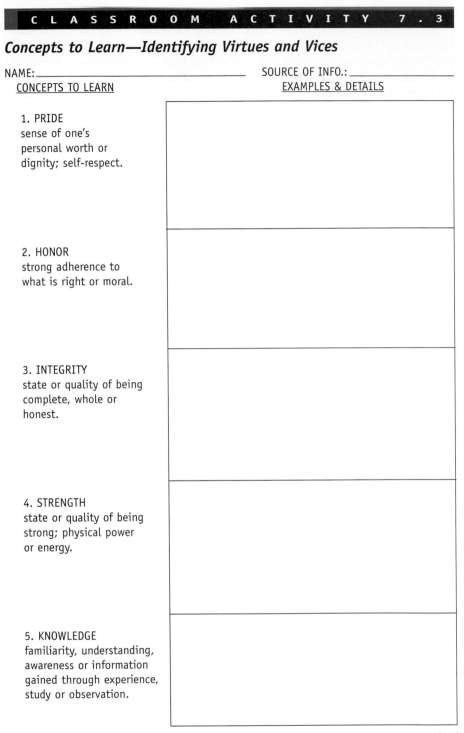

continued

NAME:_____   SOURCE OF INFO.:_____

<u>CONCEPTS TO LEARN</u>   <u>EXAMPLES & DETAILS</u>

1. ARROGANCE
full of unwanted or
overbearing pride;
conceited.

2. GREED
excessive, selfish
desire to have or
acquire something,
usually wealth.

3. JEALOUSY
fearful or suspicious of
losing something to
someone else
(especially the love of
another person).

4. IMPULSIVE
inclined to act without
planning or reflection.

5. VANITY
excessive pride with
one's appearance,
abilities or
accomplishments.

Greg Bergner
seventh grade Unified Studies teacher
Parkway Central Middle School

TEACHER'S VOICE

About Student Enthusiasm for Classroom Activity 7.3

"The novel they read was a watered-down version of the *Iliad*. They had to look for examples of positive and negative concepts of human behavior (Classroom Activity 7.3). Usually they had to fill in three out of the five boxes on each side. We started every day in Unified with a discussion of the sheets and the two chapters they read, 15–20 minutes. They loved it! They learned almost all their Greek gods just by reading the story. They're coming into class saying 'Poseidon's a jerk! I probably shouldn't phrase it that way.' 'No, that's great!' I'd say. They're coming in fuming, 'Aries, I can't believe he did that in that chapter.' And I said, 'This is awesome!'"

Greg Bergner, seventh grade Unified Studies
Parkway Central Middle School

REFLECTIVE QUESTION

What essential questions should students be able to answer after completing the Trojan War Unit?

→ WHAT LEARNING PRINCIPLES ARE IMPORTANT WHEN PLANNING STUDENT-FOCUSED LEARNING ACTIVITIES?

When you plan student-focused learning activities, it is important to keep in mind three basic principles that form the foundation of the student-focused philosophy: Learning is constructivist, students need a personal relationship with the content, and learners are unique.

Learning Is Constructivist

As discussed in Chapter 1, constructivism is the belief that learning occurs as the child constructs meaning by connecting new concepts to existing knowledge structures (Brooks & Brooks, 1993, 1999; DeVries & Kohlberg, 1987; Piaget, 1954, 1970). Constructivism is a style of learning that is social, active, and creative and requires higher level thinking (Caine et al., 2002; Henson, 2004). Constructivist learning may involve simulation, reflection, or manipulation of objects and ideas (Perkins, 1999, 2004). The way students interact with the curriculum becomes as important as their interaction with the teacher (Anfara & Waks, 2002; O'Steen, Cuper, Spires, Beal, & Pope, 2002; Vatterott, 1999). Proponents of constructivism believe

Constructivist activities lead to deeper understanding of concepts.

that students can't learn passively and that passive learners don't really learn things permanently (Gabler & Schroeder, 2003; Henson, 2004). Passive learners may be able to remember low-level factual information long enough to do well on tests, but they have not internalized the learning into their long-term memory (Alpert, 2004; DeVries & Zan, 1995; Patterson, 2003).

When deeper understanding or conceptual knowledge is the goal, constructivist learning activities are preferable (Brooks & Brooks, 1993, 1999; Brown, 2002a; Findley, 2002). But constructivist learning is time consuming, so most teachers prioritize content that requires deep understanding and can best be served by constructivist tasks (Vatterott, 1999). For instance, if a math teacher wants students to be able to solve equations using pi, he or she may simply present the formula for finding the area of a circle. If the teacher wants students to have a deeper understanding, a more constructivist activity may be helpful. Classroom Activity 7.4 describes a constructivist activity to help math students understand the concept of pi.

Circle Pi

1. Students are given 20 circles of different dimensions.

2. They measure "across" and "around."

3. Then the teacher introduces the terms *circumference* and *diameter*. Then the students divide the "around" by the "across" to see what they get.

4. They make a chart of their answers, graph their answers and are able to see the approximations to pi.

Pat Johnson
eighth grade math teacher
Pattonville Heights Middle School

TEACHER'S VOICE

About Constructing Knowledge in Classroom Activity 7.4

"We're trying to prove pi. I didn't tell them we were trying to prove pi until the end. I said, 'Let's see. If we take the *around* and divide by the *across*, what are we going to get?' When you look at the chart of their answers, some came close to pi and a few were exact. They see where pi came from, rather than just recall and remembering."

Pat Johnson, eighth grade math
Pattonville Heights Middle School

After the activity, students reflect on their learning by answering these questions in their math journal: "Describe the relationship between the circumference of the circle, the diameter, and pi. Do you see a pattern in your graph? If so, describe the pattern." The journal writings can be used to assess what students learned during the activity (Perkins, 2004).

Constructivism is a helpful way of defining or clarifying student-focused instruction, but student-focused instruction is not always constructivist (Vatterott, 1999). It would be ideal if it could be, but some content doesn't lend itself to constructivist learning. In some cases, low-level awareness of concepts or rote memory of factual information is all that is necessary or desirable (Anfara & Waks, 2002; Marzano, 2003). Even so, student-focused activities can be designed to make such low-level learning meaningful and enjoyable (Caskey, 2002; Gross, 2002). For instance, Nicole Schoenweis and Joda Fogerson's students learned about idioms by producing an idiom book in which they drew pictures about idioms.

Here are some other examples of activities that can be used for low-level learning:

- Write a story or newspaper article showing you know the meaning of the 15 vocabulary words for the week.
- Make up a jeopardy game that covers the list of main ideas at the end of the chapter.
- Produce a model of a human cell with household items that approximate the shapes and proportions of the parts.

Students Need a Personal Relationship with the Content

Truly engaged learners have a *personal* relationship with the content they are learning (Brooks, 2004; Perkins, 2004; Scherer, 2004; Thompson, 2002). The student-content relationship must be developed and nurtured, much like the relationship between the teacher and the student (Keefe & Jenkins, 2002; Strong, Silver, Perini, & Tuculescu, 2003; Vatterott, 1999). Early adolescents are emotional beings who need an emotional involvement with the content (Pitton, 2001). (Remember, emotion drives attention, which drives learning (Alpert, 2004; O'Steen et al., 2002; Sylwester, 1995).

Most teachers enjoy a personal relationship with their content. They often have great passion for their subject, relish the idea of learning more about it, and enjoy talking about it and sharing it with others. If they are lucky, that enthusiasm is contagious—their students catch it (Alpert, 2004; Price, 2005; Strong et al., 2003). Middle school students have great potential to become excited about content if they have some control over what they learn and how they learn it (Mee, 1997; Vatterott, 1999).

Middle school students are most likely to be emotionally engaged by content when they are allowed to give their opinion, solve a problem that is important to them, compete with others, imagine possibilities, or be creative (Intrator, 2004; Mee, 1997; Vatterott, 1999). Students connect personally with content when they identify with people or feelings, connect the content to something in their everyday life, or use the content to understand the world around them or to wrestle with moral or ethical dilemmas (Beane, 1997; Pate, 2001; Simon, 2002).

This personal connection to the content helps students meet developmental needs for identity and competence (Keefe & Jenkins, 2002; Pitton, 2001; Vatterott, 1999). Through that connection, students help define their own interests, further develop those interests, and sometimes find new leisure pursuits (Waks, 2002). By finding a way to be successful with the content, they feed their need for competence (Gross, 2002; NMSA, 2001; O'Steen et al., 2002). Table 7.1 contrasts the traditional teacher-content relationship with a student-content relationship.

Jason Holmes, eighth grade Unified Studies teacher at Parkway Central Middle School, helps students connect personally with the content when he teaches about the slave trade. Mr. Holmes places a slave box in the front of his room. The

TABLE 7.1

Teacher-Content Versus Student-Content Relationships

Teacher-Content Relationships	Student-Content Relationships
Teacher has primary relationship with the content	Teacher mediates the relationship between the content and student
Curriculum does not reflect the diverse cultures of the students	Students are allowed to learn through culturally relevant materials
No attempts made to connect curriculum with students' personal lives	Students' personal connection with content is the priority
Students have no input on curriculum tasks	Students' opinions and input are used as motivation and in planning learning tasks
All students learn the same way	Students have choices of tasks and learning paths

Mr. Holmes's "slave box."

slave box is a wooden box 36" wide × 30" deep × 32" high—built to the exact size of boxes used to transport slaves to America. Students are given the opportunity to get inside the box to reflect on what it must have been like to be a slave. See above for pictures of Mr. Holmes's "slave box."

Josette Hochman, eighth grade Unified Studies teacher at Parkway Central Middle School creates personal connections at the beginning of the year with the

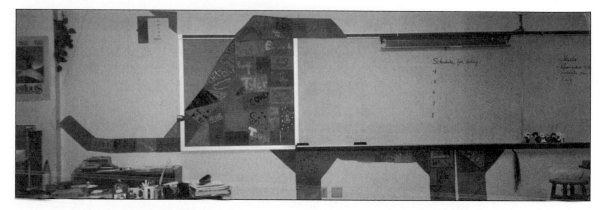

The Elephant in Josette Hochman's eighth grade classroom.

poem "Six blind men and the elephant." She gives each student a sheet of colored paper. The sheets are various colors and shapes and students decorate their papers with their names, making it uniquely theirs. They combine the sheets of paper on a bulletin board to form the shape of an elephant. Ms. Hochman uses the exercise along with the poem to discuss the concept of perspective. The "elephant" remains on the wall for the year (see photo).

Greg Bergner titled his unit on American History "The Teenage Years" to connect the growth and development of the United States to the turbulence of adolescence. Students choose from a list of over 60 people from history to interview and from a list of over 30 events on which to report. They also make a timeline and map. (See Classroom Activity 7.5)

Mike Hirsch knew that his seventh grade students liked to make paper airplanes and that they enjoyed convincing others of their point of view (about just about anything!). He decided to capitalize on those interests to teach the properties of central tendencies and the use of statistics. Classroom Activity 7.6 describes his method of teaching his students about central tendencies.

Teachers' Voices

About Personal Connections to the Content

"They had to present this advertising campaign to me, supposedly the president of this company, that wanted to buy 100 million of their paper airplanes. The funny part about it was—you know how businesses take statistics and kind of bend the truth; they don't lie but they're not telling the whole truth—I found the students doing the exact same thing. It was really great."

Mike Hirsch, seventh grade math
Hazelwood Junior High School

Historical Person Official Interview Form

1. Name of the person(s) being interviewed: _____

2. Fill out the chart below answering the interview questions from the perspective of the individual being interviewed. If you don't know the answer, make something up based on your knowledge of political, social, and economic history of these "Teenage Years."

Interview Question	Response
1. Where were you born?	
2. What is your birthdate?	
3. Did you have a big family?	
4. Tell me about growing up when you were young.	
5. Did you attend school and if so, what type of school was it?	
6. Did you have any chores when you were growing up?	
7. What did you do for fun when you were young?	
8. What place do you think you serve in history?	
9. Can you offer any suggestions to future generations based on what you experienced in your lifetime?	
10. Would you consider your life one of privilege or one of hardship?	
11. What type of controversial events surround your life?	
12. What are you most proud of in your life?	
13. Are there any events in history that affected your decisions in life?	
14. What methods of transportation did you used to use?	
15.	
16.	

continued

Historical Event Official Big Picture Report

Name _____ **Date:** _____

1. Name of Important Event: _____ 2. Date of Event: _____

3. Name at least three important people associated with the event and briefly describe his or her role (Attach extra sheets if you need more room)

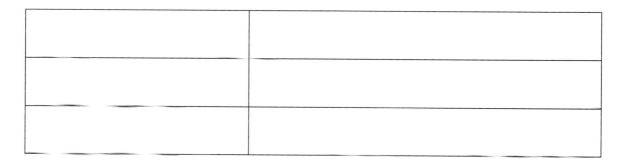

4. How did this event affect the political and/or social environment of this era (1820–1850)?

5. How did this event affect the future events in the twentieth (1900s) and twenty-first (2000–present) centuries?

6. Create a diagram that shows the sequence of events leading up to the event. Describe any major influences, problems, or dreams of those involved that led up to this event. Draw the diagram on an 8½ by 11 sheet of paper and attach to this form.

Greg Borgner
seventh grade Unified Studies teacher
Parkway Central Middle School

"In Unified Studies, novels can relate to what you're studying in history. I just gave my kids a novel, *Captain's Dog*, taken from the point of view of Lewis's dog on the Lewis and Clark journey. The kids critiqued the book—was it a good book, a bad book—and the one kid said 'I loved it, I'm a dog person.' I guarantee you, you ask them about the facts of the Lewis and Clark journey and they know everything there is to know because they read that book."

Greg Bergner, seventh grade Unified Studies
Parkway Central Middle School

Learners Are Unique

Chapter 2 made us aware of the diversity of interests, abilities, and learning profiles among middle school students. We learned that students have preferences in the way they like to learn and that effective learning tasks lend themselves to being differentiated (Eisner, 2002; Gross, 2002; Pitton, 2001). Student-focused learning activities

C L A S S R O O M   A C T I V I T Y   7 . 6

Paper Plane Activity

Students first learn how to arrive at the three measures of central tendency (mean, median, and mode). Working in teams, students design their own paper airplanes, fly them, record the distances their planes fly on a flight data sheet, and calculate the team mean, median, and mode. Each team then gives a presentation to the CEO (the teacher) and Board of Directors (the rest of the class) of a toy company interested in buying millions of these paper airplanes. Each team must decide which measure of central tendency to use in their presentation in order to present their product in the best light.

Mike Hirsch
seventh grade math teacher
Hazelwood Junior High School

offer students choices that allow them the freedom to work from their strengths and create presentations or products that reflect their unique characteristics (Brown, 2002; Levine, 2003). Student-focused learning activities not only facilitate learning but they also help students discover and develop their individual strengths and talents (NMSA, 2001c; Pitton, 2001; Storz & Nestor, 2003).

Classroom Activity 7.7 is a good example of an activity that can be differentiated for unique learner interests and learning styles.

C L A S S R O O M   A C T I V I T Y   7 . 7

Literature Closure Activities

Pick from the following activities for your Literature Set Closure Project. Please be sure to get teacher approval on the project you have selected before you get started. Available points are listed next to the assignment and the grading scale is at the bottom of the sheet.

Drama

1. Dramatize an incident or an important character alone or with a partner. (2)
2. Create a video that depicts a portion or all of the story. (2)
3. Do a radio announcement to publicize the book. (1)
4. Write a play based on the continuation of the story or a new adventure for the characters. (4)

Art

1. Create a jacket for the book, complete with illustrations, title, and additional comments. (1)
2. Make a diorama (shoe box or the like) to show the setting of your favorite part of the story. (2)
3. Make puppets and present a play based on the book. (3)

continued

Writing

1. Keep a diary of one of the characters in the story, using first person. (4)

2. Write a letter to the author telling why you like the book, your favorite parts, and what you would have done with the plot. (2)

3. Be a newspaper columnist. Write a review for a book selection. (1)

4. Explain how the story might have ended if a key character or incident has changed. (5)

5. Write a biography of the leading character using information from the book. (4)

6. Write an essay describing the character's personal changes or conflicts during the story. (5)

7. Construct a story map to show the plot, setting, and major events and write an essay describing the map. (4)

Research

1. Research any subject on the book and how it affects the main character. Write a two- to four-page paper. (5)

Grading Scale:

A—10 or more points

B—8–9 points

C—6–7 points

D—4–5 points

F—3 points or below

Greg Bergner

seventh grade Unified Studies teacher

Parkway Central Middle School

TEACHER'S VOICE

About Unique Learners and Classroom Activity 7.7

"For the literature closure activities, there are different things that tap into kids' strengths. . . . Whatever it is they want to do to prove to me that they read the book . . . they know what their strengths are and they'll say 'I don't write very well but I can draw really well so I'm gonna take this choice of drawing. . . . I'm gonna draw you a picture of what happens at the end.'"

Greg Bergner, seventh grade Unified Studies

Parkway Central Middle School

REFLECTIVE QUESTION

What differences in learners does the Literature Closure Activity address?

→ HOW DO TEACHERS DESIGN STUDENT-FOCUSED LEARNING ACTIVITIES?

They Redirect the Time and Energy of Planning and Assessment

Teachers will often say that designing student-focused lessons is more time consuming than planning a lecture. In the traditional teach and test system, in which the teacher presents information, gives an assignment for reinforcement or practice, and tests students, teacher-focused instruction seems efficient in the amount of content that can be "covered" in a short amount of time (Kohn, 2001; Patterson, 2003). The teacher typically spends some time preparing the lecture and creating the test, and then more time afterward grading assignments and tests (Gross, 2002; Vatterott, 1999). Designing student-focused learning activities requires teachers to *redirect* time and energy (Brooks, 2004; Vatterott, 1999). In student-focused instruction, teacher time and energy is directed away from content presentation and grading papers and into the development of meaningful activities and assessments (Alexander, 1995; Keefe & Jenkins, 2002). In student-focused instruction, most time and energy is spent up front, planning the learning activities and rubrics (Vatterott, 1999). Most teachers agree that when activities and rubrics are designed up front, supervision of the learning activities is less demanding.

For her eighth grade Unified Studies class's European/African Project, Shannon Burger spent time up front designing descriptions of project options, a list of research questions for students to use to gather information, a project proposal form, and a project evaluation scoring guide. She gave her students the information in advance, which made project work easier. Classroom Activity 7.8 shows the student choices for the European/African project.

In reality, planning student-focused instruction should require no more teacher time and energy than planning traditional teacher-focused instruction (Vatterott, 1999). In student-focused instruction, as students take more responsibility for their own learning, teachers spend less time lecturing, less time and energy struggling to motivate students, and more time structuring and individualizing learning experiences (Cetron & Cetron, 2004; Eisner, 2004).

C L A S S R O O M   A C T I V I T Y   7 . 8

European/African Country Project

Choices for European/African Project

Name _____

A. Hyperstudio Stack—Pairs of students develop and produce a Hyperstudio Stack that will provide information on the country of their choosing. They will research and then display information on the physical features, climate, government, economy, people and history, education, arts, and recreation. Students will have access to a computer to produce the Hyperstudio Stack at school.

B. News Magazine—Pairs of students will design, write, and publish a magazine that will provide information on the country of their choosing. They will research and then design, write, and publish a magazine providing information on the physical features, climate, government, economy, people and history, education, arts, and recreation. Other information can be included in magazine style. Illustrations, maps, graphs, etc., are required; the magazine can be bound at school.

C. ABC Book—Pairs of students will write and publish an ABC book that will provide information on the country of their choosing. They will research and then design, write, and publish an ABC book providing information on the physical features, climate, government, economy, people and history, education, arts, and recreation. Each page will contain a letter of the alphabet with a concept that relates to the country explained on that page. Illustrations are required; the book can be bound at school.

Shannon Burger
sixth grade Unified Studies teacher
Parkway Central Middle School

TEACHER'S VOICE

About Redirecting Time and Energy

"When you structure things ahead of time, supervising the learning activities is a breeze."

Shannon Burger, sixth grade Unified Studies
Parkway Central Middle School

They Think Creatively about Their Content

Creativity requires risk taking and relaxation. It was once said that creativity requires "getting your pushy left brain out of the way." In other words, you can't think too logically or narrowly. Creativity is often enhanced by outside stimuli—looking through books, magazines, even television shows or movies related to the content. The Internet is an endless resource for stimulating creativity. By searching for sights about specific content, teachers often find not only activities but also new ways of looking at the content. Teachers often come up with creative ideas through open-minded brainstorming, after which they review their ideas, keeping some and discarding others.

The following questions may be helpful in stimulating teacher creativity.

Questions to Stimulate Creativity

1. What are my students interested in? (music, sports, computers, animals?) For example, baseball batting averages could be used to teach about central tendencies. Song or rap lyrics could be compared to styles of poetry.
2. What do my students like to do? (drawing, acting, experimenting, making things?) For example, students could write a role play about the westward expansion or build a working model of a volcano.
3. How can I "hook" my students emotionally? (Gabler & Schroeder, 2003). For instance, one teacher started a unit on human biology with a calf's brain on her desk.
4. Can I relate the content to a pattern or schema they already know? For example, the structure of the atom has been explained using the analogy of a neighborhood and gangs: The atom is the neighborhood, the electrons are the "elected " gang who circle the neighborhood, the neutrons are the "negative dudes," and the protons are the "positive dudes."
5. In other words, how can I tie my content to their interests and feelings?

Nicole Schoenweis found that traditional book reports were not very successful for her students. Nicole and her co-teacher Joda Fogerson decided to get creative in the way they assigned book reports. They gave students book report handbooks that included several unusual types of book report projects. Each handbook included a calendar of due dates for the year, a glossary of types of fiction and nonfiction, and a supply list for each type of book report. Classroom Activity 7.9 lists the categories of book reports.

TEACHERS' VOICES

About Thinking Creatively about Content

"The reason we started doing more performance-based book reports, we had the nonfiction form, the fiction form, and the kids turned in trash. And so we felt like 'we're not affecting their reading, they're not turning things in. They're not excited about it.' Even the best kids were turning in garbage. So we sat and took about 30 hours to create these 16 book reports for the packet. And they know at the begin-

C L A S S R O O M   A C T I V I T Y   7 . 9

Book Report Handbook

Book Report Categories

All projects will be first demonstrated/explained in class
on the first Monday of each two-week cycle.

9 FICTION	BOOK REPORT PROJECT	DUE DATE
(REALISTIC) FICTION	Story Element Mobile	SEPT. 24
SCIENCE FICTION	Character Trait Poster	OCT. 22
HORROR	Triorama	NOV. 24
MYSTERY	Filmstrip*	JAN. 14
HISTORICAL FICTION	Story Trails	FEB. 11
FANTASY	Story in a Can*	MARCH 10
CLASSICAL	Book Billboard (poster)	APRIL 6
NEWBERY AWARD WINNER	Newbery Book Report*	MAY 19
FICTION (FREE CHOICE)	Scrapbook Book Report	JUNE 2

7 NONFICTION	BOOK REPORT PROJECT	DUE DATE
INFORMATIONAL	Artifact Box*	OCT. 8
BIOGRAPHY	Biography Book Report*	NOV. 5
HISTORY	Timeline in a Can*	DEC. 10
NONFICTION (FREE CHOICE)	5 types of Poems	JAN. 28
NONFICTION (FREE CHOICE)	Road Map	FEB. 25
NONFICTION (FREE CHOICE)	Paper Bag Report	MARCH 24
NONFICTION (FREE CHOICE)	Report form	MAY 5

* These book report projects are more challenging and may require additional time
and parent/guardian assistance.

Nicole Schoenweis and Joda Fogerson
fifth/sixth multiage teachers
LeMasters Elementary School

---

ning of the year when they're going to need a piece of poster board, when they're
going to need that shoe box."

Nicole Schoenweiss, fifth/sixth multiage
LeMasters Elementary School

"Most of my ideas I think of on my own. Sometimes I'll be reading journals or a
book and all of a sudden I'll say 'Hey, that sounds like a cool idea—how can I take
that and use it at my grade level?' I've read things in reading and they do an activity that is a wonderful activity but it's not used in math, so I'll take it and modify it."

Mike Hirsch, seventh grade math
Hazelwood Junior High School

They Involve Students in Planning

Most teachers who plan student-focused instruction use student input (Caskey, 2002; Pitton, 2001). Research supports the many positive benefits this practice has for students, including an increase in student motivation and retention of learning (Alexander, 1995; Henson, 2004; Pate, 2001). Teachers involve students in planning curriculum in a number of ways:

1. They find out what students already know about a topic of study.

Many teachers ask students to fill out a KWL chart like the one shown below at the beginning of a unit (Alpert, 2004). This gives the teacher information about students' prior knowledge and what they are interested in about the topic (Fuhler, 2003). This experience helps validate learners' previous knowledge and is motivating because it reinforces their view of themselves as successful learners (Caskey, 2002; Mee, 1997).

KWL Chart

K (what do I know about _____?)	W (What do I want or need to know?)	L (What did I learn?)

2. They learn what questions students have about the content.

Student questions are helpful in organizing content and can be used to maintain interest throughout the unit (Alpert, 2004; Pitton, 2001; Simon, 2002). One way of using student questions is to have students write questions on index cards, then ask them to help sort the questions into like categories. This starts the students thinking about how the information for the topic is organized, and may even give the teacher ideas for how to structure the unit (Alexander, 1995). The teacher can then answer the questions at the time they fit into the appropriate lesson. Student questions can also be used to guide individual student research (Storz & Nestor, 2003; Vatterott, 1999).

3. They ask students for input about how they might learn about the topic and how learning activities could be evaluated.

Students often have great ideas for how they might structure their own learning (Caskey, 2002; Pate, 2001; Pitton, 2001). Questions like these are useful for getting student input: What do we need to know and how might we go about finding out? How can we organize this unit? How can we tell that we have learned what we need to know? Students can help identify what makes a good project and can be involved in the design of rubrics for projects (Alexander, 1995; Fuhler, 2003).

4. They ask students to reflect on their own learning.

Self-reflection causes students to process their learning, think through what they have learned, and identify gaps in their learning (Powell, 2001; Tomlinson, 2003). Reflection allows students to use higher level thinking skills of synthesizing content, constructing meaning, and evaluating their own learning processes (Alexander, 1995; Lemlech, 2002; Stevenson, 2002). Reflection is also a valuable resource that helps teachers evaluate students' levels of understanding. Pat Johnson uses journals to help students reflect on their learning and as a tool for evaluation. See Classroom Activity 7.10 for a description of an activity and the journal questions to which students responded.

✦ STEPS IN CREATING STUDENT-FOCUSED LEARNING ACTIVITIES

Some steps teachers might go through in planning student focused learning activities are listed below:

Structuring the Activity

The teacher begins by determining objectives for the activity, the pattern of instruction (group instruction, then the learning task, then the follow-up or in-depth activities), and a preliminary time schedule.

Volume of a Cube Activity

Each group of students receives a square of graph paper.
Each group cuts different size squares out of each corner.
(group 1 cuts out 1×1 squares, group 2 cuts out 2×2 squares)
This gives each group a different size figure capable of being folded into a box.

They then determine how many popcorn kernels fit into each size box.
The class makes a table of the numbers of popcorn kernels.
Then they make a table of the actual volume of the boxes.

They graph the two tables and see how similar they are.

After the activity, they reflect in their math journals by answering the following questions:
Describe the relationship between the popcorn average and the actual volume.
What dimensions must you consider when finding the volume of a box?

Pat Johnson
eighth grade math teacher
Pattonville Heights Middle School

Determining a Method for Evaluation

The teacher may create a rubric that includes criteria and quality rankings for each of the criteria. Students may be asked to help create the rubric or offer suggestions for how the activity will be evaluated (Alexander, 1995; Fuhler, 2003). Rubrics are not the only method of evaluation that can be used. Observations, checklists, portfolios, or more traditional evaluations could also be used (Gabler & Schroeder, 2003; Henson, 2004). (Specific types of evaluations will be discussed in Chapter 10.) It is important that teachers think through what information should be used as evidence of learning.

Assembling Resources or Reference Materials Necessary for the Student to Complete the Activity

Resources may include textbooks, newspapers or news magazines, Internet and software resources, or names and addresses of people or agencies. Materials for projects may include such items as poster board, construction paper, glue, tape, markers, or scissors.

Setting up Learning Stations

Learning stations could include computers to access information, equipment to do experiments, or simply designated spaces to spread out the reference material to avoid student congestion. Assigning areas for group work or for construction of games may also be helpful. (Learning stations will be discussed in more detail in Chapter 9.)

Teaching the Skills Necessary to Complete the Task

This could include how to write a personal letter, persuasive essay, or research paper; how to create a Hyperstudio project; how to use lab equipment; or how to complete a specific procedure.

Monitoring the Students As They Work on the Task

Teachers should monitor student work on a daily basis, preferably with a visible timeline for the completion of each stage of the unit (Marzano et al., Vatterott, 1995). One way to monitor progress is to write the steps of a project on squares of colored paper that are placed around the perimeter of a bulletin board, like squares of a board game. Students can then be given small paper circles that they write their names on. The circles can be moved from one square to the next as the student completes each stage of the project. This becomes a visible reminder of their progress.

STUDENT'S VOICE

About Long-Term Projects

"The long-term projects I like better; they're just easier for me, instead of, like, it's due tomorrow."

Nick, seventh grade

TEACHER'S VOICE

About Long-Term Projects

"You have to stagger when the assignments come in. Part of it is the middle school brain—if they have five things to do at once and if you make that due date at the end of three weeks, they're gonna freak out at the end of the three weeks and leave it all 'til the last minute. If I tell them the first part is due at the end of the first week and the second part is due at the end of the second week it breaks it into smaller chunks for them and it seems to work a little easier."

Greg Bergner, seventh grade Unified Studies
Parkway Central Middle School

→ WHAT DO GOOD LEARNING ACTIVITIES LOOK LIKE?

Good learning activities keep passive methods to a minimum (Alexander, 1995; Daniels & Zemelman, 2004). They are designed for active learning, meet students' social and emotional needs, and when possible, include hands-on, concrete experiences. The ideal learning activity capitalizes on students' personal and social concerns and is rich in personal relevance (Beane, 1993; Gross, 2002; Moulds, 2004). Projects that utilize the arts are especially appropriate as they allow for creativity and personal expression, and allow students to communicate their identity in a unique manner (Waks, 2002). Ideal characteristics of learning activities are summarized below.

Ideal Characteristics of Learning Activities

Allow student choice
Permit student autonomy
Require application of skills or content
Integrate more than one subject
Allow for a "personal signature"
Culminate in a project that is presented or displayed
(Vatterott, 1999)

Ideal Characteristics of Learning Activities

Ideal learning activities are integrated, allow for student choice and autonomy, require application and personal signature, and culminate in a project (Vatterott, 1999). Many learning activities do not share all of these ideal characteristics. The goal in activity design is to *maximize* the use of these characteristics.

Student Choices

Students should have more than one choice in how and what they learn (Caskey, 2002; Erwin, 2003; Fuhler, 2003; Glasser, 1998; O'Steen et al., 2002; Storz & Nestor, 2003). Choice can be as simple as allowing students to choose which 10 math problems out of 20 that they want to do. Choice can also involve creating several different options for students (Allington, 2002). For instance, students may choose which climate zone to report on (polar, temperate, or tropical), which aspect of Chinese culture to research (Confucianism, changing role of women, history of Chinese communism), or which poem to read. Students may choose a question they would like to answer that relates to a topic they just studied and identify sources of information to guide their research. In this case, all students learn the same general concepts about climate zones or Chinese culture, but they do so by focusing on a specific area that is of interest to them. By allowing students to choose and complete different learning experiences and on different schedules, students may not all create the same product, but they should be able to reach the same goal (Allington, 2002; Tomlinson, 2003).

Students may be given a choice to work alone or with others.

Student Autonomy

Students should have some freedom in the way they learn (Arnold, 1993; Caskey, 2002; Tomlinson, 2003). For instance, a student may have the freedom to read, listen to a tape or lecture, or watch a video to learn information. During a written assignment, students may have the freedom to work at a desk or a table, to sit on the floor, or to work standing by a bookshelf. During a group assignment, students may have a choice of working within a large group, with only one person, or working alone. In general, students should have freedom to move about and interact with others in the learning process whenever possible (Erwin, 2003).

Application of Skills

Ideal learning activities deemphasize low-level factual content in favor of broad conceptual knowledge and skills that enable students to think critically and creatively to solve problems (Alpert, 2004; O'Neil, 1990; Perkins, 2004). For instance, instead of memorizing the types of governments and their characteristics, students at Parkway Central Middle School designed their own country, complete with type of government, climate zone, and terrain. They determined what industry it would support, compiled laws, and with the help of a computerized program in music, wrote a national anthem (Vatterott, 1999). After being introduced to linear equations, Mike Hirsch's students had to *apply* their knowledge about linear equations during the activity shown in Classroom Activity 7.11.

Integration of Content

Curricular content should be organized around relevant themes with clusters of interdisciplinary concepts rather than a subject-based sequential list of factual information (Deane, 1993, 1997; Caskey, 2002; Lounsbury, 1992; O'Steen et al., 2002). For instance, when sixth graders at Willard South Elementary studied ancient Egyptian civilization, they practiced basic math skills using Egyptian numerals, researched the culture, read mystery books with mummies as the central characters, and mummified chickens with oil and spices to demonstrate the embalming process (Vatterott, 1999). Many of Jason Holmes's students traveled frequently, so he decided to create an interdisciplinary activity for his students related to their travels. An excerpt of the activity is shown in Classroom Activity 7.12.

Allowing for a Personal Signature

Just as signatures are unique, assignments that allow for a personal signature give students the freedom to make a project unique, unlike anyone else's (Easton, 2002; Eisner, 2002; Erwin, 2003; Intrator, 2004). *Writing to Learn*, a type of instruction that allows students to write about things that are meaningful to them, typifies this concept (Atwell, 1987). In one special education class at Osage Beach Middle School, seventh graders created and dictated a Christmas story to the teacher, who helped them correct grammar and sentence structure as she wrote the story on the board. Students checked the dictionary for spelling, copied the story, designed a cover, and later read the story to a fourth grade class (Vatterott, 1999). Kathy Bhat allowed her students a personal signature by asking them to create their own

C L A S S R O O M   A C T I V I T Y   7 . 1 1

Linear Equation Cards

Each team is given a different equation to solve. Equation cards made by the teacher are dealt face down to each team member. Each student will receive at least one sequence card. Number 2, for example, will start by laying his or her card face up on the table. Then number 3 will place his or her card in the proper sequence (before or after number 2's card). Then number 4 will place his or her card in the proper sequence, etc., until all cards have been played. If a mistake has been made, the team will discuss and correct the mistake, placing the incorrect card in the correct sequence. The team will then teach the rest of the class their problem by writing it on the board with each team member explaining his or her part of the solution.

<u>Materials needed</u>: One <u>different set</u> of 3 × 5 cards with an equation and the sequential steps to solve the equation for each team.

Here are examples of two card sets varying in degree of difficulty.

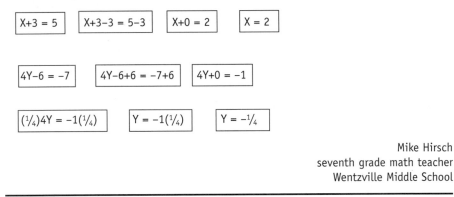

Mike Hirsch
seventh grade math teacher
Wentzville Middle School

---

melodies. One student's work is shown in Classroom Activity 7.13. Mike Burgio's science students personalized the appearance of the rockets they built to learn basic concepts of physics. Classroom Activity 7.14 shows the requirements for the rocket project portfolio and how students analyzed their rockets' perfor-mance. Both of these tasks also allowed students to make choices to personalize the assignment.

STUDENT'S VOICE

About the Personal Signature

"For the rockets you got lots of choices, you got to choose, this isn't really important, but like the paint, what you made it out of. But then it's original—it makes it your rocket and you're really proud of it when it gets done instead of like, it looking like everyone else's."

Julie, seventh grade

C L A S S R O O M   A C T I V I T Y   7 . 1 2

So You Get to Go on a Trip

Lucky you! How fortunate you are to gain such an experience.
This assignment is designed to help you make the most of your trip.
One way to use your experience is to make and use a journal.
In a journal, you will concentrate on what you see and experience, then you
will report the experiences. Journals may include feelings, but in a journal, you will
report experiences that you want to share with classmates, teachers, and readers.

Here are some of the requirements for this activity:

Before the trip

Write a statement of expectations or plan for the trip.
Draw a map and/or write the planned itinerary for the trip.

During the trip

For each day of the trip write a memory—an essay, a story, or a poem.
Draw at least one more map.
Make at least two drawings from the trip.

After the trip

Write an epilogue—recall the best parts, the biggest problems, and how you
resolved problems. Explain what you learned by taking this trip. Minimum
length 300 words.

Math

Total the number of miles covered during the trip. Make bar and circle graphs
of percentage of mileage and percentage of time in each mode of travel
(car, airplane, taxi, etc.).

Science

Record weather information each day. Indicate how you gathered information
to decide what clothing to pack.

Jason Holmes
eighth grade Unified Studies teacher
Parkway Central Middle School

Project Templates

It is not always easy to create student-focused learning activities that exemplify the
ideal characteristics. Generating the initial concept for the activity is often the most
difficult task. The project templates shown in Figure 7.4 can be used as starting
points for the creation of student-focused activities.

Music Composition Starter Activity

Student Music Composition Starter

Step 1: Write a 6–8 measure rhythm pattern

Step 2: Test notes for your rhythm pattern. Choose those you like the best.

C BA GA F# F# CA G G FE DD C DC G AC A G F E DC

Step 3: Write your composition on staff paper.

Step 4: Play your composition!

Paige Viedringhaus
6th grade student
North Kirkwood Middle School

Sample Music Composition Starter

Step 1: Write a 6–8 measure rhythm pattern (see example)

Step 2: Test notes for your rhythm pattern. Choose those you like the best. (See example)

Use your note chart!!

C E E E DEF   G   A A A A G G DF D D   GA A   C
     G   BCB E   C   B

Step 3: Write your composition on staff paper. (see example)

Step 4: Play your composition!

Kathy Bhat
sixth grade music teacher
North Kirkwood Middle School

C L A S S R O O M   A C T I V I T Y   7 . 1 4

Rocket Project Description

Portfolio requirements

Analysis of rocket performance

Rocket Project-Portfolio

Goals

1. Develop a better understanding of Force and Motion
2. Calculate speed, acceleration, momentum, force etc.
3. Explain Newton's 3 Laws
4. Build and Launch a Model Rocket

1. Photographs with description of what's happening in the picture with dates.
2. Magazine Cover Page—Colorful and Creative
3. Table of Contents
4. Colorful Drawings related to project
5. Comis Strip about Newton's Laws or something similar
6. 2 page typed Fictional Story about space travel, rockets, future etc.
7. Calculations—speed, acceleration, momentum, force etc. Must show all work.
8. Blue prints showing actual size and parts of rocket using metric units
9. Charts/Graphs/Data Tables
10. Journal Notes that document what happened throughout the project-organized, neat, colorful etc.
11. Song/Poem related to force, motion, rockets, outer space, Newton's laws etc.
12. Letter written to NASA or some other space agency requesting material about rockets or history of space travel

Analysis of Rocket Performance

Directions—Write out the answers on a separate piece of paper and use complete sentences. Neatness Counts! You may use your book to help answer questions 4 and 5. Pages S11-S55

1. Describe what happened to your rocket before, during, and after the launch of your rocket. Be Specific and give details!
2. If a member of the NASA space agency asked you to build another model rocket, what would you do differently to improve the performance of your rocket?
3. Reflect on this project and share some of your own personal feelings about the importance or enjoyment of this project and why you would or would not recommend this project to other students.

continued

4. Using your rocket as an example, explain what the following terms mean in your own words. Force, acceleration, velocity, and momentum.

5. In your own words, explain how you think a rocket works. Hint: Use the parts of the rocket and Newton's three laws to help you.

Mike Burgio
seventh grade science teacher
Pattonville Heights Middle School

❖ USING LEARNING ACTIVITIES TO DIFFERENTIATE INSTRUCTION

Middle school teachers who care about the success of all of their students adapt instruction to meet individual needs (Allington, 2002; Eisner, 2004). Instruction is **differentiated** when it is flexible enough to meet the needs of a variety of learners. **Differentiated instruction** is instruction that is adapted in content, process, or product to meet the needs of a variety of learners (Tomlinson, 2003). Activities that exemplify the ideal characteristics automatically offer differentiation (Allington, 2002; Vatterott, 1999). (Differentiation will also be addressed in some of the strategies in Chapter 9.) Just as not all student-focused learning activities include all the ideal characteristics discussed earlier, not all activities lend themselves to differentiated instruction (Tomlinson, 1999).

Why Do Teachers Differentiate?

Instruction is differentiated to meet three types of student needs: differences in **readiness, interest,** or **learning profile** (Allington, 2002; Bean, 2002; Tomlinson, 1999).

Readiness refers to a student's ability to understand concepts or to a student's skill level with a particular learning task (Tomlinson & Eidson, 2003). Students with limited readiness may need more direct instruction, practice, concrete experience, or simpler reading (Allington, 2002). More advanced students may benefit from more challenging tasks or the opportunity to explore topics in greater depth (Tomlinson, 2003). For example, Debbie Bruce differentiated her microscope test for her regular and challenge students. Regular students were given a test with many matching questions, while the challenge students were expected to provide the same information from memory in fill-in-the-blank questions. The test for the regular students evaluated more basic knowledge while the test for the challenge students evaluated more critical thinking skills.

Interest refers to a student's curiosity or passion for specific concepts or skills related to the curriculum (Bean, 2002; Tomlinson & Eidson, 2003). Ed Kastner teaches principles of art by allowing his students to create CD covers, cereal boxes, and magazine covers. Mike Holdinghaus differentiates for student interest when he allows students to select a genre for a radio show (see Classroom Activity 7.15).

Learning profile encompasses differences in the way students like to learn and learn most easily (Tomlinson & Eidson, 2003). Differences in the learner's pre-

F I G U R E   7 . 4

Six Project Templates

1. Talk show script/enactment

   Identify a theme for the show; compose the scripts, list of guests, and interviews; and present to the class.

   EXAMPLES: Interview characters from To Kill a Mockingbird

   Interview important people from a period of history

2. Board game

   Create a board game that shows the steps in a process, or progression of a series of events.

   EXAMPLES: The path of food through the digestive system, what led to a war, steps in solving a mathematical or scientific problem.

3. Role-play

   Create roles and dialogue for characters to illustrate a process or show an analogy of a relationship.

   EXAMPLES: How a bill becomes a law (with senators, representatives, the bill), how blood carries oxygen through the body (train and train stations).

4. Models

   Build a model that illustrates a concept or use skills learned in class to build a model.

   EXAMPLES: Use math concepts to build a doll house, determine how much flooring, wallpaper to buy; build a model showing what causes a flood.

5. Mini-museum or museum display

   Make a display with descriptive signs that illustrates a process or concept or synthesizes information about a concept.

   EXAMPLES: A display describing the various forms of rocks, a display depicting the significant events during a specific presidency.

6. Small business

   Create a small business in which you make and market a product or service. Costs and overhead must be computed and the business must be able to make a profit. Apply math and economics concepts learned in class.

   EXAMPLES: Paper cups decorated and filled with popcorn, note delivery service, custom music tape service (recording favorite songs on CDs) (Vatterott, 1999).

ferred method or modality of learning such as Dunn and Dunn's learning styles and Gardner's multiple intelligences theory were discussed extensively in Chapter 2. For instance, some students may prefer writing activities, while others may prefer to create models or games. Classroom Activities 7.7 and 7.8 are differentiated for learning profiles.

Radio Show or Studio Project

Mr. Holdinghaus lists the cultural changes of the 1920s on the board, including women's right to vote, prohibition, the Red Scare, jazz, Ida B. Wells's expose of lynching. The students take two or three class periods to research, write, rehearse, and rewrite their shows. Large boxes are placed in front of the class to separate the radio players from the audience. Each group goes behind the boxes and produces their show.

Mike Holdinghaus
eighth grade social studies teacher
North Kirkwood Middle School

TEACHER'S VOICE

About Differentiating with Classroom Activity 7.15

"I encourage humor, music, editorials, poetry, and sports reporting as genres of radio shows. I've had students play saxophones, write original poetry, and show off their dramatic sense by using great voices and sound effects in their presentations. One advantage that comes for struggling students is that they get four or five reviews of the material in an entertaining way on the day before the test, so test scores are strong on this unit and I think their memory of the era will last because they both construct their own shows and listen to four others."

Mike Holdinghaus, eighth grade social studies
North Kirkwood Middle School

How Do Teachers Differentiate Instruction?

To differentiate instruction, teachers modify **content, process, or product** (Tomlinson, 1999). **Content** is what the teacher wants the student to learn and the materials they use to learn it (Classroom Activity 7.15 differentiates content). **Process** is the activity or method the student uses to learn (Classroom Activity 7.12 differentiates process) and the **product** is what the student creates or completes that shows what he or she has learned (Tomlinson & Eidson, 2003) (Classroom Activity 7.13 differentiates products).

When Should Teachers Differentiate?

Teachers may differentiate the curricular elements of content, process, or product based on the needs of specific students at any point in a lesson, but differentiation is not possible, or even desirable, all the time. Tomlinson provides a good guideline to follow: "Modify a curricular element only when (1) you see a student need and (2) you are convinced that modification increases the likelihood that the learner will understand important ideas and use important skills more thoroughly as a result" (Tomlinson, 1999, p. 11).

➔ INTERDISCIPLINARY LEARNING ACTIVITIES

Interdisciplinary learning activities are activities that address content in more than one subject area (Nesin & Lounsbury, 1998). They may be activities that last a single day or more than a week. Learning activities that integrate more than one subject area offer several advantages to both teachers and learners. Interdisciplinary learning activities have a positive effect on student achievement (Findley, 2002; Lounsbury, 1992; Mertens & Flowers, 2003; Thompson, 2002). They help the brain make connections, increase the relevance of content to students, and allow teachers to teach to several objectives at once. **Interdisciplinary units** are units of study organized around a theme that integrate content from more than one subject area (Beane, 1993, 1997). Interdisciplinary units usually last one to two weeks but can last longer.

Most middle school principals expect their academic team teachers (language arts, social studies, math, and science) to create and implement at least one interdisciplinary unit per year. Many middle school principals have much higher expectations for interdisciplinary activities, such as integrating reading and writing across all curriculum areas (Mertens & Flowers, 2003). It is not uncommon for teachers of elective subjects to also be required to collaborate with other teachers in planning interdisciplinary activities. Planning and implementing interdisciplinary activities is a time-consuming process (Caskey, 2002), that most middle school teachers do during their regular or team planning time. Ideally, schools should allow teachers staff development days or extra pay during the summer to work on interdisciplinary planning. However, financial concerns often prohibit this from happening.

The process of developing interdisciplinary activities begins with finding connections between concepts or skills of one subject area and concepts or skills of another subject area (Beane, 1993, 1997; Lounsbury, 1992; O'Steen et al., 2002). It is important that teachers find legitimate connections, not create fake connections. Activities for different subject areas should flow together naturally. When integration has to be contrived, it is counterproductive (Caskey, 2002). Interdisciplinary activities about apples may be interesting, but if the content is not related to the regular curriculum, it may not be an appropriate theme.

Choosing Themes for Interdisciplinary Units

The first step in planning an interdisciplinary unit is to identify a theme (Lemlech, 2002). Beane (1993, 1997) identified three sources of themes for middle school interdisciplinary activities: content embedded, major social problems, or early adolescent concerns. Content embedded themes begin with a concept or skill that is already part of the curriculum—the theme is embedded in the existing curriculum. A unit planned around the Civil War, the solar system, or fractions starts with a content embedded theme. Major social problems (such as racism, poverty, or pollution) or early adolescent concerns (such as peer pressure or personal fitness) can also provide sources for themes. Ideally, selected themes should be broad and socially significant, and should incorporate both early adolescent and social concerns (Beane, 1993, 1997; O'Steen et al., 2002). For instance, the theme of conflict resolution would encompass the social problem of global conflict as well as the early adolescent concern of peer conflict and gangs. The theme of identities would encompass both cultural diversity and the early adolescent concern of personal identity. The theme of justice would incorporate laws and social customs with the early adolescent's concerns and problems of dealing with authority. In one instance when middle school students were allowed to choose their own themes for an interdisciplinary citizenship education project, they chose such important topics as school violence, homelessness, handicapped awareness, and animal rights (Vatterott, 1999).

These three sources of themes (content embedded, major social problems, early adolescent concerns) provide an excellent starting point for brainstorming themes, but are certainly not the only sources of ideas (Beane, 1993, 1997). Many excellent themes would not fit into one of those three categories. Themes such as baseball, the Olympics, or designing amusement park rides have produced excellent content-rich interdisciplinary units. Many beginning teachers find it easiest to begin with content embedded themes, usually finding social studies and science content the easiest place to begin. Since language arts and math are more skill based, it is easy to create tasks that apply those skills to the social studies or science content in a content-embedded unit. Several of the activities in this chapter that were created by Unified Studies teachers began with content embedded social studies themes that then required students to apply language arts skills in their project work.

Methods for Developing Interdisciplinary Themes

Before themes can be developed into units, teachers must brainstorm content that is appropriate for that theme. There are two helpful methods for beginning the creative process of planning an interdisciplinary activity. The simplest is the subject wheel, which starts with the theme in the center (Lounsbury, 1992). Teachers then brainstorm content that relates to the theme for each of the subject areas they are trying to integrate. An example of a subject wheel is shown in Figure 7.5.

The second method for generating ideas for an interdisciplinary unit is called the concept activity wheel (Beane, 1993, 1997; Lounsbury, 1992). With this method, after choosing a theme, the teachers brainstorm components, issues, causes, or results of the theme. Then they brainstorm meaningful student tasks or activities—activities that they consider significant (Moulds, 2004). They brainstorm these activities without regard to specific subject areas. Then for the third step, they determine what content knowledge or skills are necessary to complete the activities. Only then do the teachers think about the content or skills in their subject areas. This process is illustrated in Figure 7.6.

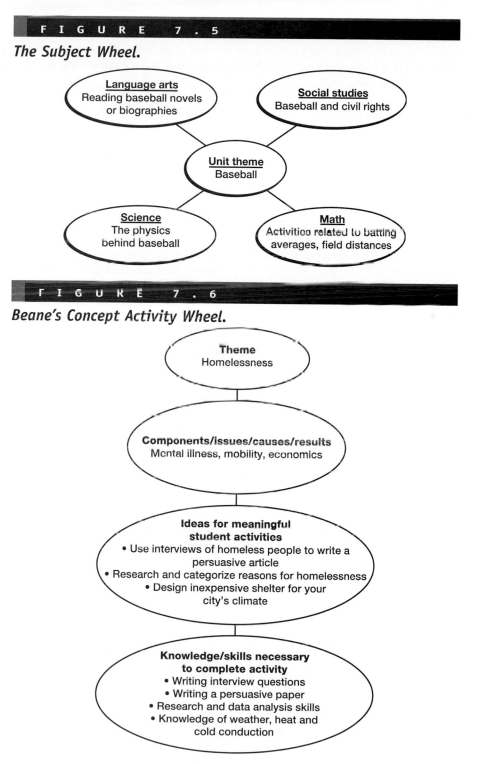

FIGURE 7.5

The Subject Wheel.

FIGURE 7.6

Beane's Concept Activity Wheel.

Components of an Interdisciplinary Unit

A plan for an interdisciplinary unit usually consists of an overview, overarching understandings or goals, descriptions of learning activities, and a **culminating activity** (Nesin & Lounsbury, 1998).

Components of an Interdisciplinary Unit

Overview

Overarching understandings or goals

Descriptions of learning activities (what the students will do)

Description of culminating activity (a student product or presentation)

A culminating activity is a task that occurs at the end of the unit and requires students to synthesize their learning (Moulds, 2004). Culminating activities are structured so that students demonstrate their learning through a presentation or a product (Alpert, 2004; Koetsch, D'Acquisto, Kurin, Juffer, & Goldberg, 2002). By this criterion, guest speakers or field trips are not culminating activities. In Gloria Sadler's State of the Children Project, students researched the state of children in a specific country. They collected statistics about such items as income, nutrition, and life expectancy in that country. They then determined solutions for improving conditions there and drafted resolutions to present to the United Nations. The culminating activity was a Global Summit in which they proposed resolutions in a mock United Nations Summit that was televised on the school's closed circuit network. Classroom Activity 7.16 shows the scoring guide for the student research and the resolution form.

Sample Interdisciplinary Units

More complete versions of these units can be found in Appendix II.

C L A S S R O O M   A C T I V I T Y   7 . 1 6

State of the Children Project

State of Children Project Rubric

RESEARCH: Choose a country . . . . _____ 10 pts.

GNP . . . . _____ 10 pts.

Natural Resources . . . . _____ 10 pts.

Education (Literacy etc.) . . . . _____ 10 pts.

Life Expectancy . . . . _____ 10 pts.

Health/Medical (Immunizations) . . . . _____ 10 pts.

Per Capita Income . . . . _____ 10 pts.

Safe Water/Sanitation . . . . _____ 10 pts.

Nutrition . . . . _____ 10 pts.
  (Infants with low birth weight/wasting)

Infant Mortality Rate . . . . _____ 10 pts.
  (Deathrate under 5)

% of Population Below the Poverty Level . . . . _____ 10 pts.

How Have Conflicts/Tensions Affected . . . . _____ 10 pts.

Arbitrary Setting of Boundaries . . . . _____ 10 pts.

Effects of Imperialism/Colonialism/Nationalism . . . . _____ 10 pts.

State of Children . . . . _____ 25 pts.
  (Your conclusion)

Two of the Above Shown in a Graphic Organizer . . . . _____ 25 pts. ea.

TOTAL POINTS . . . . . . _____ 215 pts.

All of the above information will be presented in a two-page typed paper. The two
  graphics will be attached to the final copy.

Gloria Sadler
eighth grade social studies teacher
Wydown Middle School

C L A S S R O O M   A C T I V I T Y   7 . 1 7

Thrill Rides of Learning Interdisciplinary Unit

Overview

This two week unit integrates content from math, science, and language arts around the
theme of designing a theme park. Students use writing and presentation skills to write commercial scripts and to design a brochure for the park. They apply the concepts of perimeter,
area, and map reading to the design of a map for the theme park. They apply Newton's laws
of motion to study what happens in various park rides. They also use knowledge of environmental science to assess the impact of the theme park on the environment. The unit culmi-
nates in students presenting their brochure, a model of a park building, and their commercials to the class.

Art content could also be integrated in this unit by having students create pop art
sculptures to be used in the park. Business content could also be integrated in this unit by
having students create a marketing survey to determine the most popular types of rides and
analyzing the costs of running a park.

Essential Questions

• Why is writing for diverse audiences an important language arts skill?

continued

- Why is speaking clearly and expressively, and using appropriate articulation important when giving an oral presentation?
- How do Newton's laws affect our daily movements?
- What is the importance of knowing how to maximize or minimize a shape's area in the real world?
- Is there a correlation between a shape's area and its perimeter? Why or why not?

Selected Learning Activities in Language Arts

- Writing a commercial script using persuasive writing techniques (includes prewriting, peer editing of initial drafts, revisions, proofreading)
- Writing a history of the theme park and a list of rules for park guests (prewriting, editing, revisions, proofreading)
- Creating a brochure for the park (includes the history, list of rules, and the map created in math class)

Learning Activities in Math

- Constructing a model of a building for the theme park, given a restricted perimeter
- Designing a center garden for the theme park—no more than 5,000 square feet, with three different flower gardens, a fountain, and at least 500 square feet of sidewalk.
- Constructing a map of the theme park—each map must contain a minimum of six roller coasters, four theme rides, ten food vendors, and eight stores. Students are free to include more if they like. Attractions must have names that relate to the theme of the park. For this map they have as much space as they would like to use.

Selected Learning Activities for Science

- Newton's first law of motion

Examples will include the behavior of coffee in a coffee cup while the person holding it is riding in a car, and how seat belts provide an unbalanced force that takes the passenger from a state of motion to a state of rest. Students will generate examples of this law that they might encounter in an amusement park.

Hands-on Activities: Experiments with Slinky Toys, Dominos, Marble Ramps

- Environmental science

Selecting a particular part of the country where they will build their theme park, students will use the Internet and library sources to learn about plants or wildlife that would be displaced by the park. They will develop a plan to keep wildlife in the park, use landscaping to preserve plant life, and other ways to minimize the park's impact on the environment.

Culminating Activity

The students will present their theme park concept to the class. During this presentation the teams will show the brochure, model, and commercial script.

This unit was adapted from a larger unit designed by Amy Ennenbach, Rick Neal, Derek Sizemore, Brian Fisher, and Garrett Lawrence, preservice teachers at University of Missouri–St. Louis.)

```
C L A S S R O O M   A C T I V I T Y   7 . 1 8
```

Media Literacy Interdisciplinary Unit

Overview

This two-week unit integrates content from social studies, language arts, health, and economics around the theme of media literacy. Its goal is to make students more aware of the power of the media to influence their opinions, their self-image, and their personal habits, as well as how they spend their money. Students will learn how to analyze media for specific propaganda techniques, intended audience, and intended goal. Students will also learn about the history of government regulation of the media.

Essential Questions

- How do television advertisements affect gender stereotypes?
- Why do advertisers use propaganda techniques?
- What elements make an advertisement more appealing to its audience?
- Why is the government involved in the media?
- How do television advertisements reflect current cultural attitudes and values?
- How do you analyze the message in an advertisement?
- What kind of budget is required for television advertisements?
- What kind of nutritional choices are television advertisements persuading you to make?

Selected Learning Activities for Language Arts

- Fact versus opinion

    How advertisers use facts and opinions

    Students practice sorting statements into fact or opinion groups

    Students develop totally factual advertisements

- Students develop and videotape commercials for products using specific propaganda techniques

Selected Learning Activities for Social Studies

- "What does the sponsor want the consumer to do?"

    For homework, students watch and record types of commercials. They make a bar graph showing types of products advertised and the goal (get the consumer to buy product, stay in school, etc.)

- History of government regulation of media

    What commercials we don't see on television (firearms, tobacco, pornography) and why they are censored

    Public safety and truth in advertising laws

Selected Learning Activities for Health

- How television advertising affects personal health

    Most common body types portrayed in television advertising

continued

Gender stereotypes in the media

Relationships between stereotypes, self-esteem, body image, and violence

- TV diet

  Students will analyze the number of fast food, junk food, and health-oriented commercials on television

- True value meals

  Students will analyze nutritional information pamphlets from fast-food restaurants to assess the nutritional value of meals. They will also use a decision-making grid to make healthier choices from the fast food menu

Selected Learning Activities for Business

- Air time—students create an ad, define where the ad would play, how often, why they chose that time slot
- Budget—students create a budget for marketing their product in an advertising campaign

Culminating Activity

The students will create a responsible advertising campaign that reflects what they learned in class. The product must be a positive product used by responsible consumers. The students create a storyboard, written script, and a written justification that shows what they have learned in the two-week unit. The advertisements will be videotaped and presented on the final day of the unit.

(This unit was adapted from a larger unit designed by Colleen Hill, Robyn Haug, Erika Nelson, and Jane Stokes, graduate students at University of Missouri–St. Louis)

Summary

Planning for student-focused instruction requires teachers to focus on results, to engage in outcome-based planning, and to respect the essential student-content relationship (Danielson, 2002; McTighe & Thomas, 2003; Vatterott, 1999). Learning activities that both teach and assess learning are ideal. Creating student-focused activities requires attention to the interests and needs of students, prioritizing of content, and shifting of time and energy to more up-front planning (Brown, 2002). Learning activities should allow for freedom and choice, focus on application, and culminate in a product or presentation (Brooks, 2004; Vatterott, 1999). Whenever possible, learning activities should respect differences in learner readiness and profiles and connect with content in other subjects (Tomlinson, 2003). The learning activities showcased in this chapter have provided concrete examples of student-focused instruction in action.

Key Terms

affective objectives
cognitive objectives
culminating activity
curriculum map
differentiated instruction
interdisciplinary learning
   activity

interdisciplinary unit
interest
learning profile
objectives
psychomotor objectives
readiness

Application Activities

1. Review Classroom Activities 7.1 to 7.6. For any two of the activities, list specific ways students are personally connected to the content.

2. Review the summary of the seven ways of teaching in Chapter 2, Table 2.5 (page 48). Using one of the curriculum topics from Chapter 6 or a topic from one of the Classroom Activities in this chapter, brainstorm a set of learning tasks that would allow students choices in at least four of the seven intelligences.

3. Revisit Classroom Activity 7.8. What resources and materials would need to be assembled for the European/African Project activities?

4. Review Classroom Activities 7.1 through 7.10. How many of them allow student choices?

5. Classroom Activity 7.11 requires students to apply the content they have learned. What other Classroom Activities in this chapter require students to apply the content they have learned?

6. Most of the Classroom Activities in this chapter contain some but not *all* of the ideal characteristics, yet they are all good examples of student-focused activities. Pick five of your favorite Classroom Activities at random and complete the chart below to see how many of the ideal characteristics they share.

Classroom Activity	Ideal Characteristic	yes	no	not sure
_____	Student choice			
_____	Student autonomy		_____	
_____	Requires application of skills or content		_____	
_____	Integrates more than one subject		_____	
_____	Allows for a personal signature		_____	
_____	Culminates in a project that is presented or displayed		_____	

7. For each of the project templates in Figure 7.4, think of a concept in your content area that students could use to complete that type of student activity. (Refer to the Classroom Activities in this chapter or the standards from

Chapter 6 if you need content ideas.) Create one learning activity for each template. You may use a different content topic for each template or use the same content topic for more than one template.

8. Some Classroom Activities do not lend themselves to being differentiated. Again, that does not mean they are not excellent student-focused learning activities. For each Classroom Activity in this chapter check to see if content, process, or product is differentiated:

   Which Classroom Activities differentiate content?
   Which Classroom Activities differentiate process?
   Which Classroom Activities differentiate product?

9. Select a Classroom Activity from this chapter that is specific for one subject area and create related activities in at least two other subject areas.

10. Review the section "Choosing themes for interdisciplinary units." Select a theme suggested in that section, a theme suggested by one of the Classroom Activities in this chapter, or an original idea of your own. Complete a subject wheel (see Figure 7.5) with at least three subjects for your theme. Try several different subject areas. If you have difficulty brainstorming activities for three subject areas, try a different theme. (Teachers often brainstorm several themes before finding one suitable for the subjects they are trying to integrate.)

11. Review the section "Choosing themes for interdisciplinary units." Select a theme suggested in that section, a theme suggested by one of the Classroom Activities in this chapter, or an original idea of your own. Complete a concept activity wheel (see Figure 7.6) with at least three subjects for your theme. Try at least two different themes. Determine which theme provides the richest content experiences.

12. Compare the subject wheel activity you completed in Application Activity 11 with the concept activity wheel activity you completed in Application Activity 12. Which activity felt more creative? What advantages does each method offer?

13. Using the examples shown in Classroom Activities 7.17 and 7.18 and the template on page 237, create a plan for student activities for two or more subjects for a 3–10 day interdisciplinary unit of your choice. (You can use Chapter 6 and this chapter for content ideas or come up with your own.) Include in your plan brief descriptions of learning activities (what the students will do). Activities should allow for student choices in content, process, or product. The culminating activity should be a student product or presentation.

CHAPTER 8

SELECTING TEACHER-FOCUSED STRATEGIES

✦ INTRODUCTION

In Chapter 7 you learned how to design student-focused learning activities. Activity-based learning is most appropriate for middle school students, but it would not be wise to attempt to design activities for all types of learning. Middle school teachers need to use a variety of instructional strategies, both student focused and teacher focused, to teach the broad range of facts, concepts, principles, skills, and attitudes in the curriculum (Gatewood, 1998; Lemlech, 2002). This chapter will discuss criteria for selecting instructional strategies and describe a variety of teacher-focused strategies. It will also examine the limitations inherent in teacher-focused strategies, and how some of these typically passive techniques can be made more active. Chapter 9 will discuss student-focused strategies. **The purposes of this chapter are to help you**

- apply a set of student-focused principles in the selection of instructional strategies.
- become aware of the value and limitations of specific teacher-focused methods.
- understand the structure of lessons using various teacher-focused methods.
- adapt teacher-focused methods to be more "student friendly."
- use teacher-focused methods judiciously.

Essential Questions

After reading and completing the activities in this chapter, you should be able to answer the following questions:

1. What factors should guide my choice of instructional strategies?
2. For what type of content is direct instruction most effective?
3. What are the limitations of the direct instruction method?
4. How can teachers increase student voice in instructional activities?
5. What skills are necessary in conducting effective student discussions?
6. What factors should be considered in creating a positive climate for questioning?
7. How does wait time affect student learning?
8. What strategies are important for the effective use of questions?
9. How can written assignments be made more appealing to students?
10. What are the most effective ways to use reading and writing as learning tools?

→ ORGANIZING PRINCIPLES FOR SELECTING INSTRUCTIONAL STRATEGIES

As teachers make decisions about instructional strategies, several principles should guide the decision-making process. These principles are consistent with the philosophy of student-focused instruction, what we know about the developmental nature of the early adolescent, and what scientists have discovered about the how the brain learns.

Principle 1: The choice of instructional strategy should be based on learner outcomes.

When teachers are choosing the most appropriate strategy for a lesson, they should focus on the type of learning they wish to occur, not which strategy is easiest or fastest (Anfara & Waks, 2002; Marzano, 2003; Wiggins & McTighe, 1998). Teacher-focused strategies such as lecture (a form of direct instruction) are often the simplest strategies to plan and they allow the teacher to cover a large amount of material in a short period of time (Brown, 2002; Lemlech, 2002). These strategies may be perfectly appropriate if the desired outcome for a particular lesson is for students to have a general awareness of information or an overview, but inappropriate if the desired outcome is for students to apply information or perform a skill (Fuhler, 2003; George & Alexander, 2003). For each type of content (facts, concepts, principles, generalizations, or skills), teachers must determine what they want students to know or be able to do with that content, and at what level of mastery they want the students to perform (Powers, Rafferty, & Eib, 2001; Stevenson, 2002). Does the content lend itself to student-focused methods or projects? Student-focused methods are ideal but may not always be feasible depending on the outcome desired. The student outcome should help to determine whether teacher-focused or student-focused methods are more appropriate (Lemlech, 2002; Marzano, 2003; Powers et al., 2001).

Principle 2: Learner outcomes must be <u>prioritized</u> and those priorities affect the teacher's choice of instructional strategy.

Practicing teachers learn quickly that there is never enough time to teach everything they want to teach in the depth they want to teach it (McTighe, Seif, & Wiggins, 2004). One of the hardest tasks for teachers is continually reprioritizing curriculum—limiting the amount of time they have to teach a specific concept and making decisions about the depth of learning that is possible given the limitations of time (Brooks, 2004; Danielson, 2002; Marzano, 2003). That limitation of time often influences which instructional strategy a teacher will select—teacher-focused methods are often less time consuming but result in less depth of learning (Manning & Bucher, 2001; Vatterott, 1999). Learning at a knowledge or understanding level is often less time consuming than learning at the level of application.

Principle 3: The selection of strategies must be <u>balanced</u> to create a variety of learning experiences.

Students need variety in their learning experiences (Brown, 2002; Henson, 2004). This means that teachers should strike a balance between teacher-focused and student-focused strategies; between small group projects, independent work, and whole class instruction; and between paper/pencil and hands-on activities (Powers et al., 2001). Most teachers use a variety of strategies within a unit of study.

Principle 4: Learning experiences should be <u>engaging</u>.

As teachers make decisions about instructional strategies, they should ask themselves, "How can I make it *fun*?" Although not all learning can be fun, it can certainly be made interesting and engaging (Caskey, 2002; Gross, 2002; Scherer, 2004). Tomlinson (1999, 2003) spoke of the importance of providing students with "respectful tasks," learning activities that respected students' intellect, interests, and needs.

Keeping the principles of outcomes, priority, balance, and engagement in mind, teachers must be knowledgeable about a variety of both teacher-focused and student-focused instructional strategies (Henson, 2004; Lemlech, 2002; Perkins, 2004). Many beginning teachers rely on teacher-focused strategies because they experienced those strategies, the strategies are familiar, and therefore easier to use (Jacobsen, Eggen, & Kauchak, 2002). Given that, I will begin my discussion of teaching strategies with the most familiar—traditional teacher-focused strategies.

✦ DIRECT INSTRUCTION

Direct instruction is a teacher-controlled method in which the teacher presents information or demonstrates a skill (Kellough & Kellough, 1999). Direct instruction

Demonstrations are one type of direct instruction.

can be used to provide factual information to students, to introduce or explain a concept (especially new or unfamiliar concepts), to teach or demonstrate a skill, or to provide a synthesis of information for students (George & Alexander, 2003; Marzano, Pickering, & Pollock, 2001). Student-focused teachers often use direct instruction to introduce a unit of study, rely heavily on student-focused activities for learning, and use direct instruction again at the end of a unit to help students synthesize the information. Kerry Brown uses direction instruction at the end of his unit on the Revolutionary War.

TEACHER'S VOICE

About Direct Instruction as Synthesis

"Someone needs to pull the pieces together; that's my job for today—to make sure that they get it. I wanted them to read about, write about, and do political cartoons about the Revolutionary War. But then it's my responsibility as a teacher to make sure that I've presented the information as to why it really happened. I can't just let them put their pieces together and leave it like that, if some of the links are missing."

Kerry Brown, eighth grade social studies
Pattonville Heights Middle School

Although direct instruction is useful for presenting factual content, overviews and summaries, or to demonstrate a skill, many students are limited in their ability to learn from traditional direct instruction (Jensen, 2000; Levine, 2003b). Direct instruction is often heavily focused on delivery of information verbally, making it easy for auditory learners, but more difficult for learners who prefer to learn visually or kinesthetically (Erwin, 2003; Sousa, 1998). Direct instruction also often proceeds in a linear fashion, favoring logical sequential learners over learners who view things holistically (Brown, 2002; Reif, 1993).

REFLECTIVE QUESTION

What positive and negative things do you remember about your experience with direct instruction as a student?

Special Considerations When Using This Method

Because direct instruction can be so passive for students, it is easy for students to remain uninvolved—the biggest potential problem with direct instruction is boredom (George & Alexander, 2003; O'Steen, Cuper, Spires, Beal, & Pope, 2002). Therefore, when using direct instruction, it is best to divide content into small chunks or to divide skills into small steps (Manning & Bucher, 2001). This way, lecture or other passive instruction can be limited to shorter periods. Teachers should give an overview and outline of what information will be covered to help students see the big picture and to cue students as to when passive instruction will be over. **Graphic organizers**, visual outlines that show the organization of lesson information, either on the board or on a handout, are extremely useful for students as they try to mentally organize the information (Fisher, Frey, & Williams, 2002; Fuhler, 2003). Teachers should check for understanding every few minutes, asking questions and soliciting responses from the entire group ("raise your hand if you think the answer is yes") or by asking questions that a few students answer and other students indicate whether they agree or disagree with the answer (Lemlech, 2002).

Cosmetic concerns are especially important for effective direct instruction (Henson, 2004). A well-modulated voice, used to convey enthusiasm and to emphasize key points, is one of the teacher's most valuable tools for direct instruction. The pace of the lesson must be kept brisk but not rushed (Good & Brophy, 2003), and teachers must maintain eye contact with all students and move around the room to keep students' interest (Intrator, 2004). Props such as visual aids or music are always helpful. Visual organizers are especially important and the use of color (on transparencies or with colored chalk) also adds welcome interest. Inattention to cosmetic concerns can diminish the effectiveness of even the best-planned direct instruction lesson (Henson, 2004).

The 12-Minute Rule

Given the attention span of the average middle school student, a good rule of thumb for direct instruction is that the teacher should not talk for more than 12 minutes without someone else talking (Vatterott, 1999). When it is necessary to use direct instruction, time should be a critical factor:

> Cut the length of focused attention time expected or required. Remember that the human brain is poor at non-stop attention. As a guideline, use 5–7 minutes of direct instruction for K–2, 8–12 minutes for grades 3–7, and 12–15 minutes for grades 8–12. After learning, the brain needs time for processing and rest. In a typical classroom, this means rotating mini-lectures, group work, reflection, individual work, and team project time. (Jensen, 1998, pp. 48–49)

Janet Von Harz quickly realized that it was impossible for her students to process very much information at one time during direct instruction.

TEACHER'S VOICE

About Limiting Direct Instruction

"It's too fast. That's one of the things about lecture. I don't think kids this age are ready for total lecture mode."

Janet Von Harz, eighth grade language arts
Pattonville Heights Middle School

If teachers create an open climate in their classrooms where students are encouraged to ask questions, it is possible that student questions may successfully maintain the 12-minute rule. If not, teachers should have open-ended questions ready to insert in a lecture or presentation to solicit audience interaction (Lemlech, 2002). In general, teachers should use dialogue with students to break up teacher talk and use student input to advance the lesson (Powell, 2001). Questions such as "What should I do next in the math problem?" or "Can anyone find the mistake I've made?" help to keep students actively involved in direct instruction. Given the need middle school students have for activity, teachers should also limit their *total* time lecturing to no more than 20 minutes per hour (Vatterott, 1999). This forces the teacher to create more student-focused activities.

TEACHER'S VOICE

About Limiting Teacher Talk During Lecture

"When I say lecture, it's more like a Socratic lecture. It's not me talking the whole time, it's me asking questions and pulling the information out of them that they should already have. It's a big form of review."

Kerry Brown, eighth grade social studies
Pattonville Heights Middle School

Structure of a Teacher-Focused Direct Instruction Lesson

A typical teacher-focused direct instruction lesson may follow the Madeline Hunter lesson model (Cawelti, 2003; Lemlech, 2002) (see Figure 8.1). The lesson begins with some sort of focusing event, followed by a statement of the objective. The teacher then provides information to the students verbally or with visuals, models the objective by demonstrating what students are to do, checks for understanding, gives students a task to do that is monitored (called guided practice), and then has the students perform a task on their own (called independent practice) (Jacobsen et al., 2002; Lemlech, 2002). This model can work well when you are teaching students

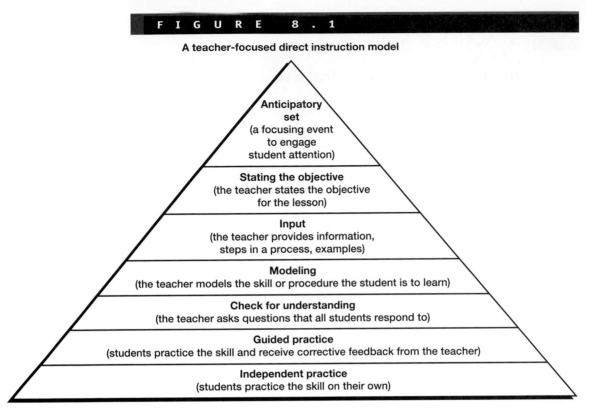

FIGURE   8.1

A teacher-focused direct instruction model

Anticipatory
set
(a focusing event
to engage
student attention)

Stating the objective
(the teacher states the objective
for the lesson)

Input
(the teacher provides information,
steps in a process, examples)

Modeling
(the teacher models the skill or procedure the student is to learn)

Check for understanding
(the teacher asks questions that all students respond to)

Guided practice
(students practice the skill and receive corrective feedback from the teacher)

Independent practice
(students practice the skill on their own)

Adapted from Lemlech, 2002

math, language skills, or physical skills (such as how to serve a tennis ball) but may not be as effective for other kinds of learning (Kellough & Kellough, 1999).

Structure of a Student-Focused Direct Instruction Lesson

When it is necessary to use direct instruction, the model shown in Figure 8.2 is more student friendly than the teacher-focused lesson in Figure 8.1. In this model, a "hook" activity at the beginning of the lesson gets students interested in the topic (Fuhler, 2003). The hook could be a thought-provoking question on the board, a physical prop, a picture or cartoon, or audio- or videotape (Gabler & Schroeder, 2003). Mike Hirsch uses a warm-up activity (see Classroom Activity 8.1) on the board as a hook. Students complete the activity when they first come into the room before direct instruction begins. Most students copy the warm-up from the board, but some students who need extra time to do the activity receive the warm-up printed on a page.

The hook is followed by a short direct instruction using an organizer. The teacher uses dialogue to break up teacher talk, limiting teacher talk to 12 minutes (Vatterott, 1999). Then the students move into an application task, simulation, or game using the information from the direct instruction (Caine, Caine, & McClintic,

Student-focused direct instruction lesson model

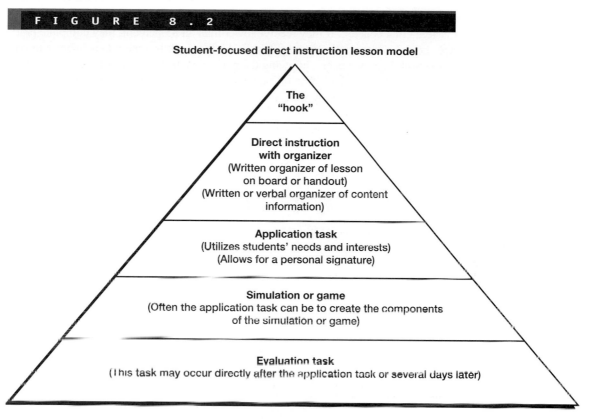

Vatterott, 1995

2002; Fuhler, 2003). At some point after the application task, an evaluation task is completed that allows the teacher to assess student learning. Stephanie Walton's students create math books as an evaluation task after learning about integers (see Classroom Activity 8.2). Shannon Burger's students draw a timeline of India (see Classroom Activity 8.3) as an application task.

Direct instruction does not have to be delivered by the teacher. Janet Von Harz knew she had to help her students master concepts of grammar, but found grammar tedious to teach. So she devised a method of independent work in which students could practice and test when they were ready. All students take a 12-part diagnostic test over basic grammar and mechanics. This test determines which areas they have mastered and which areas they have not. Stations are set up for each test area with instructional sheets that explain the grammar rules. For instance, if the student has not mastered the rules for subjects and predicates, he or she goes to the station for subjects and predicates, and studies the instructional sheet: *Lesson 7 Subjects and Predicates*. Every Monday students have the opportunity to take mastery tests in each of the 12 areas. Students practice and review the rules on their own and take the individual mastery tests only when they think they are ready. If they received an

85 percent or higher on Mastery Test I for that concept, they are considered to have mastered that concept. If they receive lower than an 85 percent, they complete practice sheets and later take Mastery Test II. All the work is done independently by the students at their own paces, allowing them more control over their learning and freeing the teacher to work one-on-one with those who need individual attention. Classroom Activity 8.4 shows a sample lesson for the grammar area Subjects and Predicates.

TEACHER'S VOICE
About Self-Paced Direct Instruction

"I don't think the kids like to be lectured to and when I was doing things like that I don't know that they were learning any better. When I grade their mastery tests, I sit down with them and I explain to them what they did wrong and give them strategies. If they're doing something wrong with the commas and the dependent and independent clauses, we're having this dialogue with each other. It's not like I'm up there saying, "*This* is a main clause.""

Janet Von Harz, eighth grade language arts
Pattonville Heights Middle School

The Issue of Student Voice

The biggest problem associated with the use of direct instruction is its overuse (Kain, 2003). When teachers use direct instruction too often, it results in too much teacher talk and too little student voice in the classroom (Vatterott, 1999). One of the

CLASSROOM ACTIVITY 8.1

Math Warm-Up

1. A sentence that has an = is called an _____ .
2. A _____ is a value that makes the open sentence true.
3. Find the solution to the equations.
   a) $x + 7 = 15$ $x =$_____
   b) $3y = 15$ $y =$_____
   c) $z - 13 = 3$ $z =$_____
   d) $2x + 3 = 11$ $x =$_____

Mike Hirsch
seventh grade math teacher
Wentzville Middle School

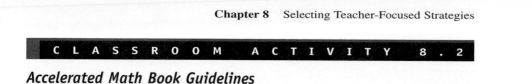

Accelerated Math Book Guidelines

Names _____

Accelerated Math Book Guidelines

You will create a book to be used by other students as a reference book when learning to work with integers. The following items must be included in your book.

1. cover .... _____ 10 pts
2. table of contents .... _____ 10 pts
3. definitions and example of the words:

    integer .... _____ 2 pts

    variable .... _____ 2 pts

    equation .... _____ 2 pts

4. order of operations

    *explain the correct way to solve problems that have
    many operations .... _____ 5 pts

    *5 practice problems .... _____ 5 pts

5. Adding integers

    *rules and examples .... _____ 5 pts

    *5 practice problems .... _____ 5 pts

6. Subtracting integers

    *rules and examples .... _____ 5 pts

    *5 practice problems .... _____ 5 pts

7. Multiplying integers

    *rules and examples .... _____ 5 pts

    *5 practice problems .... _____ 5 pts

8. Dividing integers

    *rules and examples .... _____ 5 pts

    *5 practice problems .... _____ 5 pts

9. Adding and subtracting equations

    *examples .... _____ 5 pts

    *2 practice problems .... _____ 5 pts

10. Multiplying and dividing equations

    *examples .... _____ 5 pts

    *2 practice problems .... _____ 5 pts

11. A correct answer key for ALL practice problems .... _____ 10 pts

continued

12. Overall neatness and creativity . . . . _____ 10 pts

YOUR POINTS _____

POINTS POSSIBLE   110

DUE ON _____

Stephanie Walton
seventh grade math teacher
Pattonville Heights Middle School

CLASSROOM ACTIVITY 8.3

Student Samples of Timelines of India

TIMELINE OF INDIA

HW = ①Read 514-517
Add 2 or more dates
②Draw pictures of each date
4/3/2001

Ape

Bf
P

British Portuguese Dutch French claimed India theirs
1500

East India Company
-formed by British
British → traded gold + silver
India → traded cotton, silk, tea

British   Indians

British
RULES

British overcame French for India
1760

Indians are upset with British rule
1. Outlaw Hinduism
2. tried to convert to Christianity
3. high taxes for farmers
1850

Sepoy Rebellion Indian Soldiers forced to use rifles greased with pork and cow fat
1857

India becomes a British colony
-controlled
 · foreign + military affairs
 · court system
- ruled by appointed officials
- "widespread racism"
1858

COLONIZED

Mohandas Gandhi was born
1869

India won independence led by Gandhi
India -Hindus Pakistan -Muslim (Islamic law)
1947

FREE INDIA

Gandhi was killed by extremist (Hindu)
1948

GHANDI   ALMOST DICTATOR

Indira Gandhi took on almost dictatorial powers, because economic + political problems began increasing
1970

Thrown

David Rosenfeld

David Rosenfeld—student
Shannon Burger
sixth grade Unified Studies teacher
Parkway Central Middle School

```
C  L  A  S  S  R  O  O  M      A  C  T  I  V  I  T  Y     8  .  4
```

Self-Paced Grammar Packets

Lesson Seven: Subjects and Predicates

1. The subject of the sentence is a word, phrase, or clause that identifies the performer of the action. It is the topic, the thing the sentence is about.
   Ex.   *Tom* threw the ball.
            Tom is a noun, the performer of the action.
         The poor thing collapsed of exhaustion.
            The poor thing is a noun phrase performing the action. *Thing* is the subject noun.
   The subject noun is called the simple subject. In our exercises, it is the simple subject we will ask you to identify.

2. Although in most sentences the subject begins the sentence, sometimes the subject will follow an introductory phrase or clause.
   Ex.   In the afternoon, *I* usually take a nap.

3. In interrogative sentences (questions), the subject often comes after part of the verb.
   Ex.   Did *you* eat your peas?

4. In many imperative or exclamatory sentences (direct commands), the subject is often not expressed but is *understood* to be "you."
   Ex.   Eat your peas.
         (You) Eat your peas.

5. In *passive voice* sentences, the subject is the receiver of the action rather than the performer. Still, it is the topic or focus of the sentence.
   Ex.   *Bill* was hit by the ball.

6. When searching for the simple subject, first cross out all prepositional phrases. The simple subject is *never* in a prepositional phrase. Remembering this rule will eliminate many problems in identification of subjects and also in writing.
   Ex.   ~~In the morning~~ one ~~of the sailors~~ got sick.
         The subject is *one* **not** sailors.

7. The predicate of the sentence is everything in the sentence that is not the subject or part of the subject. It contains the verb and its modifiers and complements.
   Ex.   Simon *cried.*—verb
         Christine *hugged Paul.*—verb, direct object
         John *gave Sue the ring.*—verb, indirect object, direct object

   The verb, with any helping verbs, is called the simple predicate. In the exercises we ask you to circle the simple subject and underline the simple predicate.
   Ex.   In the morning, Frank <u>will give</u> you the details.

continued

8. Simple predicates, or verbs, describe an action, *or* they signify a state of being.
   Ex.   walk, run, jump, throw, break   Ex.   am, is, are, was, were

9. In the active voice, they may be used alone.
   Ex.   You *walk* to the store.
          Elroy *is* my best friend.

10. In the passive voice they may be used together.
    Ex.   The bat *was broken*.

11. Other verbs that may be used alone or used as helping verbs are as follows:
    Ex.   have, has, had, may, might,
           will, would, can, could, shall, should
           do, does, did, must, must have
    He *has* my bat.
    He *has broken* my bat.

12. Sometimes the predicate is split.
    Ex.   <u>Are</u> you <u>leaving</u> now?
           When <u>did</u> Frank <u>see</u> you?

13. In complex and compound sentences, each clause has its own simple subject and
    simple predicate.
    Ex.   When the rain <u>stops</u>, we <u>will go</u> home.
           The team <u>played</u> well, but the other team <u>was</u> too strong.

14. Some sentences have compound simple subjects and/or compound simple
    predicates.
    Ex.   The boys and girls <u>wrote</u> their names on the board.
           The sailors <u>chipped</u> and <u>painted</u> the ship.
           The boys and girls <u>sang</u> and <u>danced</u> all night.

15. "Not" or "n't" is always an adverb, and it is **never** part of the simple predicate.

Janet Von Harz
eighth grade language arts teacher
Pattonville Heights Middle School

---

most pervasive indicators of a teacher-focused classroom is the predominance of
teacher talk and the control of student talk (Patterson, 2003). Kohn (1993) views the
practice as an American tradition.

> One of the most disquieting things about American education is the emphasis
> placed on being quiet. If we attend to all that is not being said by students, we
> realize that the absence of children's voices occurs by design and is laboriously

enforced. Talking is called 'misbehaving.'. . . Teachers who depart from this norm by letting them talk more freely are said to have lost control of their classrooms (a marvelously revealing phrase). (p. 213)

In 1984 John Goodlad observed that, on average, 70 percent of class time was taken up by teacher talk, most of it telling, not requiring a student response. This problem persists in many classrooms. The chronic problem of teacher talk and student silence has created many passive students at the middle level (Vatterott, 1999). The more and the longer teachers talk, the fewer questions students ask, the less confident they are to initiate interaction with the teacher, and the less confident they are that what they say matters (Kain, 2003; Shor, 1992). Many students seem resigned to the pattern, saying in essence, "You're the boss; if you want to do all the talking, we'll just watch."

Student voice is the antithesis of direct instruction. The use of the term *voice* in the discussion of classroom learning is both symbolic and literal (Brown, 2002; Powell, 2001). Broadly defined, **student voice** indicates students' ability to have input into such things as classroom rules and procedures, curriculum themes, and methods of learning and assessment (Vatterott, 1999). As teachers adapt direct instruction to be more student focused, they begin by encouraging student voice in the literal sense (Perkins, 2004). Obviously, some teacher talk is necessary. Providing explanations of concepts, instructions for assignments, and coaching advice are all justifiable uses of teacher talk. But students need dialogue and interaction to meet their social needs (Caskey, 2002; Jensen, 2000). If the goal is student responsibility for learning, students must be allowed to talk about their learning (Brooks, 2004; Storz & Nestor, 2003). The pattern of interaction in the classroom needs to include more dialogue between teachers and students, and more talking to learn (Sprenger, 2005). By limiting teacher talk to no longer than 10 minutes at a time, and no longer than 20 minutes within a class period, teachers are forced to plan more student-focused activities, more student talk and teacher listening, and more teacher-student dialogue (Vatterott, 1999). Brain research indicates that students process and organize information by talking (Jensen, 2000; Sousa, 1998).

 ## STUDENT'S VOICE

About Talking to Learn

"When you talk about it more, it gets more in your head and when you do it for fun, it attracts more of people's memory."

Nick, seventh grade

CLASSROOM ACTIVITY 8.5

Interactive Notebooks

Mrs. Burger's World Regions Class Interactive Student Notebooks
THE BASICS OF THE INTERACTIVE NOTEBOOKS

What is the purpose of the notebook?
The purpose of the interactive notebook is to enable you to be a creative, independent thinker and writer. Interactive notebooks will be used for class notes as well as for other activities where you will be asked to express your own ideas and process the information presented by this class. As you work with the notebook, it becomes a portfolio of your work, thoughts, and beliefs. This notebook is different from traditional notebooks due to the fact that it provides activities for a variety of learning styles, mixture of the Multiple Intelligences, and tasks are geared to how our brains learn best.

Left Side/Right Side at a Glance

Left Side
Student Output
POPs and ROCs

POP = Preview or Process
assignments, information, etc.
**preview what you will be learning
**process what you have learned
**use illustrations, diagrams, flow charts, poetry, cartoons, color, etc. to show your understanding of new content
**explore opinions, clarify values, wonder "what if" about new ideas

ROC = Required Outside Credit
**must have 3 per unit for an "A". . . 2 per unit for a "B". . . 1 per a unit for a "C". . . you must have all required assignments, too.
**relate the content to what we are studying

OPTIONS:
1. NEWS ARTICLES—
   cut out/stick in/write a half page summary, how it relates to class and your opinion about it
2. POLITICAL CARTOONS—
   cut out/stick in/write a half page summary, how it relates to class and your opinion about it
3. PERSONAL RESPONSE/QUESTIONS—
   write a half page (or more) response to activities or assignments we are doing in class (positive or negative)
4. PARENT/RELATIVE RESPONSE—
   have anyone 18 or older read and respond to any of the POP questions or just respond to your work in the notebook
                THEY MUST SIGN IT!
5. MOVIE REVIEW—
   watch a movie that relates to our current topic of study. Fill out the Movie Review Sheet and stick it in notebook.
6. POWERFUL PICTURE—
   find a powerful picture (from a CD Rom, book, magazine, or your own drawing) that relates to your right side notes/stick it in/write a half page (or more) explanation of what the picture is trying to show and your thoughts about it. If drawing your own pictures you must have at least five colors.

See Appendix II for a complete copy of student handouts.

Right Side
Teacher Directed Input
NOTES

NOTES FROM LECTURES, MOVIES

**students take notes during lectures and class activities
**book and outside reading notes are recorded here
**this information should be regarded as "testable" and should be structured so that key ideas and concepts are clear.
**HERE I STAND = teacher required activities where the student states conclusions are supports opinions.

Shannon Burger
sixth grade Unified Studies teacher
Parkway Central Middle School

Teachers can increase student voice in classroom activities by using some of the following methods:

- Use student questions to guide and organize instruction. Ask students to list questions they have about the topic and use them to organize the lesson for the day.
- Encourage students to generate and lead discussions. Student-generated discussions allow students to interact with the content, examine it from various perspectives, and voice their opinions.
- Use dialogue with students to advance the lesson. For example, have students tell the next step in a process, find a deliberate mistake, or give their opinions about a concept just presented.
- Ask thought-provoking questions that force students to use previously learned information to analyze and answer questions.
- Have students summarize the class hour in groups, pairs, or by individuals, accepting all reactions and opinions.
- Ask for student input into the organization of units, types of assignments, schedules, or classroom problems (Strahan, Smith, McElrath, & Toole, 2001; Vatterott, 1999).

One unique method for encouraging student voice and dialogue between teacher and student is through the use of interactive notebooks. **Interactive notebooks** allow students to express their opinions about class discussions or readings and also allow teachers to respond in writing to student comments. Shannon Burger uses interactive notebooks with her Unified Studies students. See Classroom Activity 8.5 for an example of interactive notebooks.

✦ CLASS DISCUSSION TECHNIQUES

The use of class discussions is another way to increase student voice. Class discussions are a popular technique with middle school students when they are allowed to become actively involved in the discussion, and when they are able to play with and manipulate ideas (Mee, 1997; Vatterott, 1999). Discussions can provide valuable practice in abstract thinking and reflection in a low-risk, ungraded setting. Middle school students enjoy sharing ideas and opinions and the chance to react emotionally to topics or scenarios (Sprenger, 2005; VanHoose, Strahan, & L'Esperance, 2001). They enjoy practicing their abstract thinking skills by arguing and can learn much about constructing and defending their arguments through a well-monitored discussion (Lemlech, 2002; Storz & Nestor, 2003).

Discussions have many valuable purposes:

- Discussions facilitate the student's individual interpretation of information.
- Discussions allow students to reflect on previous learning.
- Discussions assist students in analyzing or synthesizing information.
- Discussions solicit student opinions or reactions to previous learning.
- Discussions provide a forum for attacking problems.

Discussions are most valuable to learning because they improve student thinking (Sousa, 1998). The discussion of information helps students to construct their understanding of information by causing them to reflect on and think about it (Caskey, 2002; DeVries & Zan, 2003). It assists students in metacognition, thinking about their own thinking. Discussions also allow the externalization of thinking—the teacher can see the pattern of their students' thinking (Arends, 2000). Teachers can use discussions to assess what students are learning, how completely they understand a topic, and how well they are processing what is being taught (Perkins, 2004). As teachers assess student understanding, they can give students feedback if they observe misconceptions or faulty reasoning (Sprenger, 2005).

Special Considerations

A civil discourse requires students to practice some valuable conversational skills— skills that many middle school students are just learning (Stevenson, 2002). Therefore, part of the teacher's task in discussion is to help students learn those skills and to guide them in their use (Gabler & Schroeder, 2003; Lemlech, 2002). Students need help in communicating ideas clearly, listening carefully to other's ideas, asking good questions to learn more about another person's viewpoint, and reconciling opposing opinions (sometimes agreeing to disagree) (George & Alexander, 2003). The skills that students practice during discussions are skills that are necessary in their daily social interactions (Brown, 2002).

Student participation requires an open climate in which students feel comfortable sharing their ideas and feel they have the freedom to state their mind (Brown, 2002; Lemlech, 2002). Ground rules must be established so that only one person is speaking at a time (many teachers use a small ball to toss to the next speaker). Students must also understand that while they may disagree, they must be respectful of others' opinions. Teachers must be able to remain nonjudgmental, even when they do not agree with students and must help students see both sides of an argument (Gabler & Schroeder, 2003).

Teachers should consider whether the physical arrangement of the seating in the classroom is conducive to free flow of discussion (Kellough & Kellough, 1999). Some teachers like to move desks into a U or a circle, so everyone can see everyone else more easily. However, some students feel very exposed in these seating arrangements and are more comfortable in a traditional arrangement of rows or tables. If furniture is difficult or impossible to move, some teachers simply have students stand in a U or a circle around the perimeter of the room (Gabler & Schroeder, 2003).

The biggest challenge in a class discussion is to facilitate the participation of all students (Intrator, 2004; Jacobsen et al., 2002). It is not uncommon for a few articulate "high talkers" to dominate a discussion and intimidate the shyer students from participating (Lemlech, 2002). Several techniques are helpful to balance the participation in discussion:

- Have students discuss topics in pairs or small groups prior to the whole class discussion.

- Respectfully refuse to call on high talkers ("Juan, you've talked quite a bit; let's get someone else's opinion").
- Ask shyer students to comment or give their opinion about a previous comment ("What do you think, Courtney?").
- Ask the whole group questions that require a response ("Raise your hand if you agree with Paul's statement. Raise your hand if you disagree").

Structure of Discussion Lessons

Typically, in teacher-directed discussions, the teacher decides on the topics to be discussed and all remarks must go through the teacher (Vatterott, 1999). In a student-focused discussion, it is possible for students to generate topics and questions for discussions and for discussions to be conducted by students with teacher monitoring but with little direct teacher intervention (DeVries & Zan, 2003). The structure of the lesson for a discussion should begin with a pre-discussion exercise. This exercise could consist of a task ("Brainstorm all the ways the environment influences animal survival") or a question that students should respond to ("Why did most colonists come to America?"). Sometimes teachers use a KWL chart (tell me what you want to learn about the topic) or a free write (what thoughts you have about the story). The pre-discussion exercise is best done individually at first, but students may move into groups afterward to share or expand on their ideas.

Small groups are very helpful to facilitate maximum participation of students (Gabler & Schroeder, 2003). Many students will share ideas in a small group that they would not share in a whole class discussion. When group members then contribute the group's ideas to the whole class, more student ideas are shared (Brown, 2002). Shy students who dislike speaking in front of the whole class can have another student in their small group communicate their ideas.

Small and whole group discussions require guiding questions to advance the discussion (Lemlech, 2002). Teachers can create guiding questions or students can create the questions in their small groups and the teacher can then write and organize them on the board. Or there can be some combination, where the teacher offers very broad questions and allows students to add more specific questions. Guiding questions provide a structure and sequence for discussion (Gabler & Schroeder, 2003). However, free-flowing discussions often digress to topics further down the list. Teachers must be prepared to decide when the digression is a teachable moment (and go with the flow) and when topics or questions are being discussed prematurely without being allowed to evolve from other ideas (Jacobsen et al., 2002).

What Is the Role of the Teacher in a Discussion?

The role of the teacher in discussion is to encourage all students to participate, to keep the discussion moving at a brisk pace, and to keep the discussion focused in the direction of the lesson. The teacher accomplishes that by

- refocusing and redirecting students to the next topic when appropriate.
- visually organizing individual students' contributions on the board or overhead.

- restating students' ideas in other terms to clarify them for the class.
- prompting or encouraging students to clarify or extend their ideas ("keep talking, tell me more").
- encouraging other students to clarify or extend a student's ideas.
- correcting misconceptions or faulty reasoning.
- playing the devil's advocate. (Lemlech, 2002)

REFLECTIVE QUESTION

Think back to classes in which you remember having lively discussions. What do you remember about the behavior of the teacher? How did he or she encourage or maintain that free-flowing exchange of ideas?

☇ STUDENT AND TEACHER QUESTIONING TO ADVANCE LESSONS

In a teacher-focused classroom, teachers typically ask questions of students, often requiring only one response per question and often requiring only low levels of recall. In a student-focused classroom, both teacher and student questions can be useful tools for meaningful, higher level learning (Bell, 2003; Storz & Nestor, 2003).

Questions can be used for several purposes related to learning: to evaluate student understanding, to test student memory or recall, or to challenge students to think. The goal of questioning determines which type of question is most appropriate (Jacobsen et al., 2002; Kellough & Kellough, 1999; Lemlech, 2002).

Types of Questions

An easy way to categorize types of questions is in terms of Bloom's taxonomy: knowledge, comprehension, application, analysis, synthesis or evaluation (Gabler & Schroeder, 2003; Kellough & Kellough, 1999). Knowledge level questions are *right there*, meaning the answer is explicitly found in class notes or the text (Raphael & Pearson, 1982). "Who was Patrick Henry?" or "What is 12 × 12?" are knowledge-level questions. Knowledge-level questions are good for review of rote memory information but really don't require students to think (Jacobsen et al., 2002). Answering knowledge-level questions is low risk in one way—students either know the correct answers or they don't. There's no personal risk involving the creation of an answer or interpretation. On the other hand, if students have not memorized the information required, they can sometimes feel like the loser on a game show. At the same time, when knowledge questions have obvious answers that everyone seems to know, middle school students are sometimes hesitant to answer.

Questions at the comprehension, application, or analysis level require under-standing, such as "How do you explain the reaction after the ammonia nitrate was added?" Raphael and Pearson (1982) called questions of this type *think and search*. These questions require the student to understand concepts, to identify information necessary to answer the question, and to integrate ideas (Jacobsen et al., 2002; Muth & Alvermann, 1992).

Synthesis or evaluation questions are *on your own* questions. These questions require students to think at the highest level—requiring reasoning and personal judg-ment. "What's the moral of the story?" or "What might happen if . . . ?" questions require students to synthesize information and use original, creative thinking. Though teachers often perceive this type of question as high risk for students, stu-dents often prefer open-ended questions that have many possible correct answers (Gabler & Schroeder, 2003). Questions that may have multiple responses also offer greater group participation (Bell, 2003).

Creating a Positive Climate for Questioning

To effectively use questions to enhance learning, teachers must create an open and respectful climate in their classroom (Lemlech, 2002). Students need to feel com-fortable responding to questions, knowing that even if they give a wrong answer, they will be treated with respect (Gabler & Schroeder, 2003). A critical aspect of maintaining a nonthreatening climate is the teacher's ability to dignify incorrect an-swers ("that's close," "not exactly," "that has some value as _____"). Another im-portant skill is that of prompting (Jacobsen et al., 2002). When students give vague or partially correct answers, prompting guides them in the direction of the correct answer or allows them to give more information so that they can come closer to an acceptable response (Bell, 2003; George & Alexander, 2003).

The phrasing of questions must also be considered. Questions that are non-threatening are ones that the student perceives to be "easy" to get right or that have several possible correct answers (Jacobsen et al., 2002). Consider the difference in how the following questions might be perceived:

"What is the definition of an asset?" (This is the most threatening—it sounds like only a dictionary definition will be correct.)

"Can someone give me an example of an asset?" (Examples are usually easier to provide than a definition, and of course there is more than one correct answer.)

"What do you think might be an example of an asset?" (This question is less definite, open to individual interpretation, "think" sounds like one's opinion.)

Maintaining a nonthreatening climate for questioning requires teachers to think carefully about using questions for classroom management. Using questions for classroom management can be effective when the intent is to reengage students. When the group's attention is waning, teacher questions should be interesting, struc-tured so that several students can respond, and should be used to create student dis-cussion. When questions are used to test the group to see who has been paying at-tention, they are often viewed as punishing or manipulative. Teachers who frequently feel compelled to use questions for classroom management should reexamine their choice of instructional strategies. When the goal is to reengage an entire classroom of students, *all must think* strategies (discussed later in the chapter) or asking students to think of questions to ask are effective techniques.

Questions should never be used to catch students off guard and embarrass them for not paying attention (Kellough & Kellough, 1999). When the goal is to reengage an individual or small group of students, the best strategy is as follows: Alert the student or group of students, using a name first—"Marco, I have a question for you." Do not refer to the fact that they have not been paying attention. Out of respect for the student, the teacher should start the question with the student's name. When a teacher asks, "What does the author mean in that passage, Marco?" the first word the inattentive student hears is his name, with no clue as to what the question was. Ask an open-ended or opinion question that you are sure the student can answer even if he or she was not paying attention during the last few minutes.

REFLECTIVE QUESTION

Do you remember a teacher who was particularly good at asking questions? What made you feel comfortable about answering? Do you remember a class in which you hesitated to answer questions? What was it about the teacher or the questions that intimidated you?

The Importance of Wait Time

Wait time is the amount of time teachers wait after asking a question before calling on someone to answer or rephrasing the question (Gabler & Schroeder, 2003). One of the most effective skills teachers can master to improve questioning is to *wait after asking a question*. Research indicates that the average amount of time a teacher waits after asking a question before calling on a student is one second (Jacobsen et al., 2002). Several problems are associated with this short wait time. First of all, the students whose hands shoot up after just one second are the students who process information the most quickly. The slower, more methodical thinkers never get the opportunity to raise their hands. Short wait times reward the fastest processors while punishing the slower processors. Second, as soon as someone is called on to answer the question, everyone else breathes a sigh of relief and stops thinking about the question (Lemlech, 2002). Short wait times mean that students who process more slowly never have to think. They are quickly rescued from responsibility by the faster processors.

What Happens When Teachers Wait Longer?

Research indicates that when teachers wait at least three seconds, many positive things happen: Student responses to the questions are longer, more students respond, and teachers receive fewer "I don't know" answers (Arends, 2000; Gabler & Schroeder, 2003). In addition, while the teacher is waiting, students continue to think about the question. As students think, they often ask questions about the question. Extended wait time gives students more time to formulate their answers and increases their confidence in responding (Bell, 2003).

How to Wait

When asked why they call on students so quickly, most teachers indicate they are fearful of the pace of the lesson lagging, but many also admit to feeling uncomfortable with the dead silence (Gabler & Schroeder, 2003). Longer wait time is an acquired skill that most teachers learn by literally watching the clock before calling on students (while trying to maintain eye contact with students at the same time). Teachers learn to use the three to five seconds to read student faces to determine whether they need to clarify or reword questions. If the teacher feels that not enough students know the answer, then the question can be rephrased, but rephrasing is no substitute for wait time (Gabler & Schroeder, 2003). Rephrasing a question before students have had a chance to process the question usually just results in more confusion. If teachers are in doubt as to whether they have given students adequate wait time, it may be better to *repeat* the question first. Then if there is still inadequate response, the teacher can *rephrase* the question (George & Alexander, 2003). Teachers who have difficulty with longer wait times sometimes find it easier if they ask students to write down their responses before answering.

Strategies for Improving Questioning

The strategies below offer the most success and participation for students and extend student talk.

- *All must think* **strategies.**
  - Ask students to raise hands when they have an answer and keep their hands up until at least half of the class has an answer. Don't call on the first hand that goes up.
  - Alert students ("everyone be prepared to answer this").
  - Call on several students to answer in succession without commenting on their answers.
  - "How many of you know the answer? Raise your hands."
  - "How many agree with John's answer? Raise your hands."
- **Individualize questions for different students**
  - Change the level of difficulty—give some students easier questions (George & Alexander, 2003).
  - Let anxious students know that they will be called on next ("Melissa, the next question will be for you").
- **Extend student answers with follow up probes** such as:
  - "Why?" "How do you know?" "Give your reasons." "But what about _____?" "What do you mean by _____?" "Could you give me an example?" "Tell me more." "Keep talking" (George & Alexander, 2003; Lemlech, 2002).

Procedures for a Gallery Walk

Gallery Walk

Materials needed:
Large sheets of newsprint or poster board (one for each question)
Colored markers (a different color for each group)

Procedure:
The teacher places large sheets of newsprint or poster board around the room. These can be taped to walls, put on tables, or placed in any configuration as long as they are separated by enough room to let groups discuss and answer their questions without interfering with other groups' interactions.

On each paper the teacher writes a different challenge question (at least one for each group that is involved). It is important to use only questions that have several possible answers.

The teacher sets the scenario with a narrative or story about the topic. He/She explains to students that each group will have to visit several stations during the allotted time period and answer a question by writing or drawing on the sheet with their particular colored marker. As students move from station to station they read each question as well as any answers made by previous groups. They must come up with an answer *different* from that of any answers already written by other groups.

The teacher gives students a designated time limit for each question and requires students to move on to the next question when time is called. (Generally it will take less time to answer at the first one or two stations than at the last few, so budget time accordingly.)

When all questions have been answered by the group, answers are then discussed by the whole class. The question sheets with the groups' answers may be fixed to walls in the classroom or in the hall so that the cooperative effort can be shared with others.

Linda Ramsey, Ed.D.
Project Life
Louisiana Tech University

- **Adjust the pace and wait time for questions based on the purpose of the question.**

   Questioning for review or recall of facts should consist of short questions in a fast-paced manner. Questions that are used to promote reflection or analysis need longer wait times.

Other Uses of Questions

A **gallery walk** is an activity in which students rotate in groups through a series of stations, writing answers to open-ended questions on large posters. Gallery walks use questions with several answers to stimulate student thought, evaluate learning, or help students synthesize previous learning. A gallery walk can be used as a learning technique at the beginning of a lesson or as an assessment technique at the end of a lesson. Because groups of students respond to the same questions with different answers, creativity and critical thinking is encouraged. Procedures for a gallery walk are shown in Classroom Activity 8.6 (Silver, 1999).

A question box is an easy anonymous way for students to ask questions about content that has been covered in class (Wiggins & McTighe, 1999). Questions may be about concepts students are confused about, or simply about things the student is curious about that relate to the lesson (Henson, 2004). After students put their questions in the box, the teacher can address questions with the whole class group or with students individually. Throughout this book several methods of using student questions have been illustrated. For instance, in the KWL strategy, students write questions about what they want to learn (Alpert, 2004; Fuhler, 2003). Students may write questions about what they read, or they may write questions for their peers as part of a review process. Student questions may also be used to extend student learning as part of individual research projects or investigative studies.

→ BOOKWORK/PAPERWORK

Although active tasks are usually preferred, there are many times students need to complete written exercises, reading or writing as a learning task. Considered by some to be the most boring of tasks (Mee, 1997), even worksheets and reading can be made more interesting. The ideal characteristics of written activities are the same as for any other learning activities—whenever possible allow students choices, personalize the learning task, and create tasks that allow students to apply skills (Vatterott, 1999).

Worksheets should be short, self-monitored, and visually interesting. For instance, if a chapter worksheet is several pages long, it is helpful to separate it into several short worksheets. When feasible, allow students to complete the work with a partner. Greg Bergner has found it helpful to allow students to work with others.

TEACHER'S VOICE

About Bookwork

"I don't like to have them seated in their desks for immense amounts of time. Get them up working on something. If they need to work on a section review, if they can

Worksheets should be limited to one or two pages.

do it with two other people, it gives them a little control over what they're doing and gives them a little freedom."

Greg Bergner, seventh grade Unified Studies
Parkway Central Middle School

Consistent with early adolescent attention spans, students should be given tasks they can complete in 15 to 20 minutes, perhaps only one- or two-page worksheets. Completing those one or two pages brings students a sense of accomplishment far greater than completing the first few pages of a worksheet that is several pages long. Many students feel overwhelmed with worksheets that are several pages long, even when they know they have several days to complete them. Immediate feedback is another motivating factor. Students should be allowed to self-monitor their work by checking their own work with a key (Perkins, 2004). The physical appearance of the worksheet is another important aspect that affects student attitude and motivation. Middle school students seem to be strongly affected by the visual aesthetics of assignments. They frequently complain about illegible worksheets, blanks too small to write answers, and assignments that "look hard." Teachers should do their best to make assignments visually appealing.

Hints for Creating Visually Appealing Worksheets or Written Exercises

- Make sure type or printing is clear and easy to read.
- Use large blanks or boxes for answers; leave plenty of room to write answers.
- Use graphics or clip art to make the paper look more interesting.
- Leave lots of white space on the page; limit the amount of work required on each page.
- Make printing large enough; use bold, underlines, interesting fonts, or hand printing.
- Break long lists of vocabulary words or definitions into small groups of shorter lists.
- Make it look fun!

Using Textbooks Wisely

The textbook is not the curriculum (McTighe, et al., 2004). In fact, many teachers see a great mismatch between the textbook used in a course and the curriculum mandated by their school districts (Allington, 2002). Beginning teachers must guard against the temptation to plan instruction around the textbook—the textbook is only one resource teachers have for creating learning activities (Allington, 2002; Daniels & Zemelman, 2004). Although the textbook usually provides valuable information and a direct teaching format for facts and conceptual information, learning out of a book is not a substitute for active learning (Daniels & Zemelman, 2004; McTighe et al., 2004). Most teachers use the textbook to introduce students to information, to help students organize information and concepts, and as a resource or background information for application tasks (Bean, 2002).

For students to use textbooks successfully, they must possess certain reading skills. They must be familiar with the vocabulary used in the text, and they must have word attack skills that allow them to gain contextual meaning (to figure things out when they don't know all the words) (Allington, 2002; Stevenson, 2002). At the middle school level, all teachers are reading teachers—that is, all teachers must give students the tools necessary to learn from written material (Bell, 2003; Perkins-Gough, 2004; Schoenbach, Braunger, Greenleaf, & Litman, 2003). Jason Holmes's students are expected to read a minimum of 15 minutes a day and to keep a metacognition log to help them reflect on what factors influenced their reading. They also graph their number of minutes of reading per day. Classroom Activities 8.7 and 8.8 show one student's metacognition log and reading graph.

Many teachers have students do prereading exercises like constructing chapter outlines showing topics and subtopics (Schoenbach et al., 2003). Before students read, teachers may give them lists of vocabulary words with definitions to refer to as they are reading. Jason Holmes uses an Anticipation/Reaction Guide (shown in Classroom Activity 8.9) to get students to think about the reading before they read. Students discuss their anticipations and reactions in pairs before and after they read.

Another useful technique is to divide students into groups before reading and assign each member of the groups a different task. Members may be asked to focus on different topics during their reading, or they may be asked to read different sections of the text, which they will later summarize for the group (Bean, 2002). Other times students might be asked to react to the reading by responding to questions: "What did you like about what you read?" "What bothered you about what you

C L A S S R O O M   A C T I V I T Y   8 . 7

Metacognition Log

Metacognition Logs for September

9-1-2000 (Trial 2)

In trial one and trial two I had the same amount of words per minute. I was reading a book called <u>A Caribbean Mystery</u>, by Agatha Christie. On trial one, I read for pleasure and enjoyment. On trial two, I read as fast as I could, but I had to re-read some parts of the book because I read to fast. The WPM is important because it shows how much the reader increases or decreases. In my case, I stayed the same. The chart we are marking our WPM is neat because it shows our improvement.

(9-5-2000) (Reading over the weekend)

—On Friday I read for 20 minutes after school.

—On Saturday I read for 30 minutes.

—On Sunday I read for 20 minutes.

—And, on Monday I read 30 minutes of my book, and all of the Our Town script.

—Today I want to read over 160 words per minute or more.

(9-6-2000) (Subvocalizing)

Readers can overcome subvocalizing by using a pencil, or your finger. By putting your finger in front of your mouth you are able to tell if you are subvocalizing. Subvocalizing causes us to read slower.

When we subvocalizing our bodies have to read the word, process it through our eyes, and into our brains. Once the word is in our brain we have to process it though our muscles, and into our mouth. It is quicker to read when we only have to process it through our eyes and into our brain.

September 7, 2000

Last night I read in bed. I like to read before I go to bed because it makes me sleepier. Yesterday we learned about the listening behaviors. The three listening behaviors are to sit up straight, don t side talk, and have eye contact with the speaker.

Abby Robinson—student
Jason Holmes
eighth grade Unified Studies teacher
Parkway Central Middle School

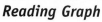

Reading Graph

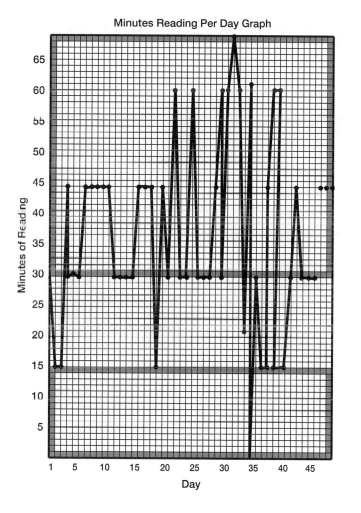

Abby Robinson—student
Jason Holmes
eighth grade Unified Studies teacher
Parkway Central Middle School

C L A S S R O O M   A C T I V I T Y   8 . 9

Anticipation/Reaction Guide

Unified Studies 8
United States History

Directions: In the "before" column, put a plus if you agree or a zero if you disagree with the statement. Be sure to discuss your reason for your response with your partner even though you may not agree. After reading the lesson, put a plus or minus in the "after" column and discuss this answer. Be sure to state your reasons if there is a change. The answers will be discussed in class so be certain to support your answers with evidence from the textbook.

Chapter 10-1 A Union of Thirteen States
Forging a Republic
Before After

Before	After	
+	+	1. At the conclusion of the Revolutionary War the Revolution had not yet begun.
+	+	2. Most Americans agreed that the new country should be a democracy.
0	0	3. Most Americans were suspicious of central state government.
+	+	4. Republicanism stated that the education of women was essential to maintaining individual freedom.
+	+	5. Women ended slavery in Massachusetts by 1783.

Abby Robinson—student
Jason Holmes
eighth grade Unified Studies teacher
Parkway Central Middle School

---

read?" "What connections can you make to previous reading in this class?" "What questions do you have about what you read?" (Beck & McKeown, 2002).

Efficient student reading requires active monitoring techniques such as outlining or graphic organizers (Bean, 2002; Fuhler, 2003). Fill-in-the-blank worksheets are often ineffective at generating real learning—most middle school students have become quite adept at completing such worksheets without doing assigned reading and without internalizing much knowledge. Graphic organizers are a much more effective method to guide student's interpretation of material (Fisher et al., 2002). Asking students to complete blank charts of causes and effects, likenesses and differences, or characteristics or categories usually requires students to read and analyze information more carefully than locating fill-in-the-blank sentences from the text (Smith & Tompkins, 1988). Debbie Bruce gives her students broad outlines for their reading use.

TEACHER'S VOICE

About Graphic Organizers and Reading

"I give them an 'about' column with bullets—fill in three bullets here about this topic, two bullets for this topic. They'll come back the next day and we'll go over what it was they needed to have and they'll fill in the information they didn't get when they did it out of the book themselves."

Debbie Bruce, seventh grade science
Parkway Central Middle School

For more complex reading, some teachers have students use symbol annotation. After reading each section, students mark the margin with a plus (+) if they knew the information already, an exclamation point (!) if the information was new but they understood it, or a question mark (?) if they found the section confusing. After reading the entire article or chapter they return to the question mark sections to reread and try to gain additional understanding. Teachers can then easily monitor which sections of the reading are most troubling to students.

There are several ways students can summarize their reading. Jason Holmes has his students draw graphic summaries of each section of the chapter (see Classroom Activity 8.10).

When students are required to read an entire book, students can summarize the main events by chapter with writing and drawing. A summary book, a graphic summary of a book by chapters, can be composed by individual students or by groups of students. Nicole Schoeneweis and Joda Fogerson's class used a different student's drawing to represent each chapter in their summary book of the story "Hatchet" (see Classroom Activity 8.11).

Individual students also produced *Stories in a Can* as book reports. *Stories in a Can* show the major events of a story on a long scroll that is unrolled out of a can or box (see Classroom Activity 8.12). Students are later allowed to read the student-made books during Silent Sustained Reading time.

Graphic Summary of a Chapter

Abby Robinson—student
Jason Holmes
eighth grade Unified Studies teacher
Parkway Central Middle School

Summary Book

When Brian was on the plane, He turned on the radio.

A man on the radio told Brian "if your listening take your finger off the button." The man kept saying that. Brian took his finger off the button.

Brian was talking to the man on the radio. Brian was talking to them then they lost each other. Brian had an idea. Brian would land next a lake or river.

Brian didn't find a lake or river. Brian was going to run out of gass. Or just land it there. Witch would he do.

Chapter #2

By Jonathan
Scruggs

Nicole Schoeneweis and Joda Fogerson
fifth/sixth multiage teachers
LeMasters Elementary School

Story in a Can

Story in a Can (or Box—either will work)
(General Book Report Format—Fiction)

Materials Needed:
- —Soft-sided round container (bread crumb, oatmeal container, etc.) with its lid.
- —Paper towel roll (empty)
- —6–8 pieces of white paper
- —Sharp cutting implement for cutting a slit in the container—HAVE YOUR PARENTS ASSIST
- —Crayons, markers or paints
- —Self-adhesive (contact) paper & felt, fabric or wallpaper

How to Prepare

1. Starting ½ an inch from the top and stopping ½ an inch from the bottom, prepare the canister by cutting a slit ¼–½ an inch wide.

2. Cover the outside of the can with decorative material. Make room for the slit.

3. On a scrap of paper, list in order 4–6 of the most important events in your story.

4. Determine how many pieces of paper you will need based on how many events you will be representing (you must have at least 4). Trim the bottom off the paper so that the paper will pull through the slit.

events	# of pieces of paper
4	6
5	7
6	8

5. Draw a line an inch from the bottom of each piece of paper except for 2. Under each line write a 2–3 sentence description of that event. Create an illustration to go along with each description.

6. On one of the two extra pieces, colorfully list the title, author, type of book and your name.

7. Connect the pieces of paper with tape. Be sure to line them up so the title page will come out of the can 1st, followed by the important events IN THE ORDER THEY OCCURRED IN THE BOOK. (This will seem backwards.) The remaining piece of blank paper is attached last.

blank	#6	#5	#4	#3	#2	#1	Title

8. Okay, here's the tricky part. Trim the empty paper towel roll so that it is slightly shorter (1/4 of an inch) than the canister. Tape the edge of the blank side to the paper towel roll. Roll up your story around the paper towel roll.

Nicole Schoeneweis and Joda Fogerson
fifth/sixth multiage teachers
LeMasters Elementary School

✦ Using Writing As a Learning Strategy

The summary book and story-in-a-can techniques incorporate the valuable skill of writing into student projects. Writing activities allow students to show they understand concepts by expressing them in another form and also provide practice in the correct use of standard English (Brandenburg, 2002). In addition, writing allows students the freedom of expression and the opportunity to make projects uniquely their own (Stevenson, 2002). Writing can be a vehicle for organizing, clarifying, and analyzing information. It allows teachers to assess student understanding about a topic and allows students to communicate about their learning (Martinez & Martinez, 2003). Writing is a beneficial strategy in all subject areas as evidenced by its use in many of the learning activities shown in this book (Fisher et al., 2002). Math teachers find writing particularly helpful in showing how students construct meaning in math (Perkins-Gough, 2004). By asking students to write about mathematical processes, teachers discover what students understand and what they do not understand about those processes (Brandenburg, 2002; Martinez & Martinez, 2003).

Concerned that students were having difficulties with word problems, Mr. Hirsch asked them to write what the problem was about before trying to solve it. Very few students were willing to share their writing. Then he decided to have students draw pictures first. Steps for using Mr. Hirsch's strategy are shown in Classroom Activity 8.13.

CLASSROOM ACTIVITY 8.13

Draw What I Say and Write What You Draw Activity

Steps for Using the Draw What I Say and Write What You Draw Structure

1. Make sure everyone has paper and a pencil.
2. Explain to the students that you are going to read a math problem and that they are to draw pictures depicting what the problem says, as well as what the question is asking. Tell them that they can use different scenes, if that is what they want to do.
3. Put the problem on the overhead.
4. Read the problem slowly, twice.
5. Turn the overhead off.
6. Give them two or three minutes to complete their drawings.
7. Give each student another piece of paper and tell them that they are to write what the problem is about and what the question is about based on their drawings.
8. Put the students in their cooperative learning teams and call on some to share what they wrote with the rest of the class.

Mike Hirsch, seventh grade math teacher
Wentzville Middle School

Teacher's Voice

About Drawing Pictures in Math

"I had the students draw pictures depicting the word problem as I slowly read it to them. I read the problem twice and left it on the overhead projector. Then I took the overhead off and asked them to write what the word problem was about, using their drawing. When I asked for volunteers to tell what the problem was about, close to 75 percent of the students were willing to share. The students I called on had correctly interpreted what the problem was as well as what the question was asking."

Mike Hirsch, seventh grade math
Wentzville Middle School

Journals

One of the most common ways of using writing is through **journals**. The purpose of a journal is to allow students to freely express their thoughts about their learning, to make personal connections about their learning, and to communicate with their teachers (Fisher et al., Kellough & Kellough, 1999). Students especially enjoy interactive journals in which teachers and students communicate back and forth about the student's writing. Journals can be useful in all subject areas (Gabler & Schroeder, 2003).

Journals can be fairly unstructured, where students simply write about anything related to the class, or journals can be structured with the use of specific "prompts," questions the teacher wishes students to respond to (Brandenburg, 2002). Prompts could include open-ended questions such as "Today I was successful at . . .", "I need help with . . .", "I was confused when . . .", or "The part of the lesson I understood best was . . ." Journals may include any of the following activities:

- Students answer questions such as "What have you learned about _____?" "Why is this important to know?"
- Students write short essays such as "What I know about fractions so far" or "Explain _____ so a fourth grader could understand it" (Young, 1997).
- Students solve problems or draw conclusions and explain their process for doing so.
- Students draw connections between daily learning and their everyday life ("Think about your day. Write about the ways you have used math today.")
- Students communicate ideas or questions they have about the content or things they would like to learn more about.
- Students communicate to the teacher about how they felt about a lesson, most favorite and least favorite activities, and suggestions for improving the class.
- Students write about any feelings they have about their groups, the class, the teacher, or themselves (Silver, 1999).

Kellough and Kellough (1999) suggest the use of a *response journal* in which students respond to their learning using five categories:

- "I never knew that"—responses to new information learned.
- "I never thought of that"—new insights.
- "I never felt that"—affective responses to learning.
- "I never appreciated that"—affective responses to learning.
- "I never realized that"—new awareness of patterns or connections in learning.

Since journals are meant to be creative and individual, they are often not graded. Most teachers check journals to be sure that students are maintaining the journal and have responded to any prompts they were given. Points are often given for completion of the journal, but students are usually not penalized for spelling or grammatical errors. Teachers find that students express their thoughts more easily when journals are read for the ideas and not for the format.

Learning Logs

Learning logs are usually a more highly structured form of student writing, similar to the interactive notebook shown in Classroom Activity 8.5 (Marzano et al., 2001). A **learning log** is a combination student notebook/portfolio that may include journal writings, class notes, or learning assessments. Learning logs are often part journal, part notebook, part portfolio and may include any of the following sections:

- Class notes
- Vocabulary words
- Learning assessments such as concept maps, drawings, or student explanations
- Experimental designs or data collections
- Long term observations (usually in science) to describe plant growth, animal behavior, and so on (Silver, 1999).

In addition to the ideas shown above, learning tasks that use writing can also be created using non-textbook sources and nonprint sources of information. Consider the learning value of some of the assignments shown below:

- Identify elements of a short story in a half-hour sitcom (approved by the teacher).
- Find and explain four metaphors in a rap song (clean versions only).
- Listen and take notes, summarize, get main idea from an appropriate television show (Oprah, *Dateline*, nightly news).
- Critique commercials for persuasiveness, fact versus opinion, and so on.
- Write a guide to surviving seventh grade for next year's seventh graders.
- Write an essay on why you should vote for a particular political candidate.
- Soapbox: write a two-minute speech stating your opinion or pet peeve about . . .

SUMMARY

Although student-focused instructional strategies are usually preferable, a balanced approach to learning will include some teacher-focused methods (Anfara & Waks, 2002; Henson, 2004; Marzano, 2003). In their traditional forms, many teacher-focused methods are passive, allow little input from students, and offer students few choices in their learning (Gatewood, 1998; Vatterott, 1999). By modifying these methods to be more student-friendly and by using them prudently, teacher-focused methods can augment the teacher's repertoire of strategies and add variety to the student learning experience (Gross, 2002; Powers et al., 2001).

KEY TERMS

direct instruction
gallery walk
graphic organizers
interactive notebooks
journal
learning log
student voice
wait time

Application Activities

1. Think about direct instruction lessons you have experienced as a learner. Make a list of do's and don'ts for using this strategy. For example:
   DO use visual organizers to outline concepts.
   DO use your voice to add interest/emphasis.
   DO build on previous knowledge.
   DON'T talk for more than 10 minutes without interacting with your audience.
2. Use the student-focused direct instruction model shown in Figure 8.2 (page 259) to create a sample direct instruction lesson.
3. Find three Classroom Activities (from any of the chapters in this book) that you find especially visually appealing. How many of the hints from the list on page 277 apply to those activities? What other qualities make the three activities visually pleasing?

CHAPTER 9
❦

SELECTING STUDENT-FOCUSED INSTRUCTIONAL STRATEGIES

✦ INTRODUCTION

Chapter 8 discussed the criteria for selecting instructional strategies and the best use of teacher-focused strategies. Effective middle school teachers use a wide repertoire of strategies, both student focused and teacher focused, each for specific purposes. This chapter will describe a variety of student-focused strategies and their best use. **The purposes of this chapter are to help you**

- apply a set of student-focused principles in the selection of instructional strategies.
- become familiar with a variety of student-focused techniques and examples.
- understand the structure of lessons using various techniques.
- evaluate the most appropriate uses for various strategies.
- differentiate learning tasks using various strategies.

Essential Questions

After reading and completing the activities in this chapter, you should be able to answer the following questions:

1. How can technology be used to create constructivist learning experiences for students?
2. Why is technology considered a premier student-focused strategy?
3. What factors should guide my choice of instructional strategies?
4. Why is the use of conceptual techniques important?
5. How is effective independent work designed and monitored?
6. How are learning stations organized?
7. What is the difference between group work and true cooperative learning?
8. What are the advantages of the three types of cooperative learning?
9. What are the goals of problem-based and inquiry lessons?
10. What structure should guide the organization of an inquiry lesson?
11. What is the value of using learning games?

✦ REVIEW OF ORGANIZING PRINCIPLES FOR SELECTING INSTRUCTIONAL STRATEGIES

As discussed in Chapter 8, several principles should guide the selection of instructional strategies. Before selecting a strategy to use, review the following principles. If necessary, refer back to Chapter 8 where the principles are explained in detail.

- Principle 1: The choice of instructional strategy should be based on learner outcomes (Anfara & Waks, 2002; Marzano, 2003).
- Principle 2: Learner outcomes must be *prioritized* and those priorities affect the teacher's choice of instructional strategy (Danielson, 2002; McTighe, Seif, & Wiggins, 2004).
- Principle 3: The selection of strategies must be *balanced* to create a variety of learning experiences (Perkins, 2004; Powers, Rafferty & Eib, 2001).
- Principle 4: Learning experiences should be *engaging* (Scherer, 2004; Tomlinson, 2003).

✦ Using Technology
As a Student-Focused Strategy

The Power of Technology

Technology has the potential to be the premiere student-focused strategy (Powers et al., 2001; Quinn & Valentine, 2002). In a technology-rich classroom, students may experience direct instruction using a Smartboard, take notes using desktop word processors, get extra help through computer-assisted instruction, research topics in depth on the Internet, experience simulations of actual events, communicate with students in other countries, create Hyperstudio stacks to summarize their learning, or write scripts and videotape role plays (Penuel, Means, & Simkins, 2000; Wiske, 2004). Conceptually, technology has the potential to change how we teach in two important ways—the teacher-student relationship and the student-content relationship (Gabler & Schroeder, 2003; Revenaugh, 2000). Technology can be our best illustration of student-focused instruction (Tapscott, 1999; Wiske, 2004).

As mentioned in earlier chapters, the teacher-student relationship is critical to motivation (Strahan, Smith, McElrath & Toole, 2001; Vatterott, 1999). Middle school students need personal, one-on one contact with their teachers (Hoffman & Levak, 2003). *Technology enhances communication between teacher and student* through the use of e-mail, teacher-created Web sites, and computerized record keeping that makes it easier to give frequent progress reports (Tapscott, 1999). The *My Gateway* system allows teachers to post daily announcements and allows parents and students to check their grades at any time. Teachers can also use computer-assisted instruction at a computer learning station to provide remediation and specific corrective feedback to students. Technology can make the teacher–student relationship and relationships with parents more communicative and empowering as students take more control over their learning (Revenaugh, 2000).

Even more important is technology's potential to enhance the personal relationship the student has with the content (Curry, 2003). Technology allows students to control and personalize the content (Martinez & Martinez, 2003). If the learning task is to gain specific information about electricity, students may have the choice of reading a book, surfing the Internet, or viewing a Hyperstudio stack at a learning station (Reiser & Butzin, 2000). *Technology provides choices*—allowing students to control how they learn and therefore increasing student motivation (Curry, 2003). Use of technology can also be self-paced, allowing students to learn at the pace that is right for them (Curry, 2003; Gabler & Schroeder, 2003; Martinez & Martinez, 2003; Quinn & Valentine, 2002).

Equally important, *technology improves access to learning*. Most middle school teachers who use technology feel its greatest impact has been on the marginal students—students who often get D's and F's when asked to complete traditional teacher-focused learning tasks like taking notes and filling in worksheets. Why? First of all, technology-rich projects typically offer choices and allow students to control how they learn and to keep their mistakes private. For special needs students, many of whom are tactile learners, technology is multisensory, increasing the possibility that learning will be processed (Burtch, 1999). Technology is usually tactile (using the keyboard), visual (seeing what's on the screen), and auditory (hearing the sounds of the keyboard or other sounds), all in user-controlled ways. Many marginal students are quite knowledgeable about technology and often feel confident working with technology.

REFLECTIVE QUESTION

How has technology made learning easier or more engaging for you as a student?

Technology Tools

The quantity and variety of software and other technology available to teachers today is astounding. Most of the available technology tools fall into one of three categories: tools used primarily for presentations or whole group instruction, tools used primarily for research or gathering information, or tools used primarily for organizing information or creating resources (Gabler & Schroeder, 2003; Tapscott, 1999).

Tools for Presentations or Whole Group Instruction

Tools such as **PowerPoint** and the **Smartboard** allow teachers and students to organize information in visually appealing ways for presentations. PowerPoint is a software tool that enables teachers or students to present information in a slide show format. Text, pictures, charts, sound effects, or video can all be incorporated in PowerPoint presentations. Using a **Smartboard**, teachers or students can project the image of the computer display onto a large screen that the entire class can view. Smartboards are also touch sensitive. One teacher created a Jeopardy review game with the Smartboard that allowed students to touch the large screen to access answers to questions. Many teachers require students to use PowerPoint when presenting reports.

One of the tools in widespread use at the middle school level is the **Hyperstudio** program. **Hyperstudio** is a multimedia program similar to PowerPoint that allows the teacher to use photographs, audio clips, video clips, and Internet links to instruct students in any concept. Hyperstudio programs consist of stacks of "cards" (screen images) that can take the reader down various paths from the main menu.

Tools for Organizing Information or Creating Resources

The most promising use of the Hyperstudio program is as a vehicle for students to construct their own representation of knowledge contained in a particular unit (Wiske, 2004). When students create their own Hyperstudio program about a unit, they make decisions about how to organize information and what images and sounds best convey the information (Penuel et al., 2000). As they choose how to represent and organize the information, they analyze and construct connections between concepts, which leads to a more in-depth understanding of the content (Gabler & Schroeder, 2003).

Digital Camcorders and Digital Cameras   Digital camcorders and digital cameras allow students to take video or still photographs and then use the computer to edit and manipulate images. Students can then insert those images into documents or link them to Hyperstudio stacks or Web pages. Like the Hyperstudio process, photographs and video production are excellent ways for students to construct and represent their own knowledge (Burtch, 1999; Ohler, 2000). Tony Ambrose's social studies students created a video of the settlers' journey on the Oregon Trail. Classroom Activity 9.1 describes that project.

Tools for Research or Gathering Information

The Internet is a rich resource for student activities as well as a way to communicate with students and parents (Gabler & Schroeder, 2003; Galus, 2002). Students can use the Internet to do in-depth research (Renard, 2005). Many newspapers, magazines, television shows, museums, and state and national organizations have Web sites (Doyle, 1999). In Mike Holdinghaus's computer technology class, students learn how to use a variety of search engines including Google, Yahoo, Snap, and AltaVista; how to access midi, au, and real studio sound resources; and how to download sounds and movies into Hyperstudio stacks and web pages using Quicktime. Some students learn other skills specific to the project they're creating. Mr. Holdinghaus starts the unit with a discussion of the difference between pop culture and what he calls "deep culture." Students can use a wide variety of topics for their projects including biographies, historical events, biology, poetry, or painting. They spend a few days exploring topics, declare a topic, and help design the rubric by which they will be graded.

Notestar is a unique tool that allows students to take notes from online sources as they browse the Internet. Students can gather citations automatically for each note, organize notes by topics and subtopics, and print copies of organized notes and citations. The teacher can track each student's progress and provide feedback on assignments. (http://notestar.4teachers.org) (Sumner, 2002).

Webquests are structured assignments that allow students to use the Internet to gain information about topics (March, 2004). To create a Webquest, teachers select a topic students need to learn about, search for Web resources, create a list of possible Web sites where students can find the information, and write the questions they want students to answer (Burke, 2002). Classroom Activity 9.2 shows an example of a Webquest.

Web sites created by individual teachers or teams are an easy way to increase communication with students and parents. They can provide information to students and parents about the class calendar, homework, upcoming projects, or tests

Students can use technology to represent their knowledge of a topic.

C L A S S R O O M   A C T I V I T Y   9 . 1

Oregon Trail Film

Students are divided into groups. Each group refers to itself as a family. The members play the various parts of a family. Each family chooses a part of the Oregon Trail to write a skit about (5 minutes in length)—they write the dialogue, plan the action, choose the background scenery (computer generated), background music, and sound effects. Each group acts out and films its skit. The composite film is an entire play of the Oregon Trail experience. Each class watches the completed film.

Tony Ambrose
seventh grade social studies teacher
Parkway Central Middle School

(Revenaugh, 2000). Web sites can also be used to showcase pictures of student work and can be useful for posting information about school activities, policies, voice mail numbers, and e-mail addresses for teachers. Students can help teachers keep the site

C L A S S R O O M   A C T I V I T Y   9 . 2

Solar System Rocket Trip Webquest

SOLAR SYSTEM ROCKET TRIP

Travel through space on the Solar System Rocket Trip. To get started, just go to the website www.KidsAstronomy.com. Click on the words solar system, then follow the path that the rocket takes by answering the questions listed.

START HERE

Venus is the goddess of love and beauty, otherwise known as Aphrodite.

How is the planet of Venus similar to the Earth?
1.
2.
3.
4.

What makes Venus too hot for human life?

STEP BACK
(1 click)

The god of war and agriculture is **Mars**.

Why does the planet of Mars excite scientists?

Why do you think Mars could be habitable?

STEP BACK AGAIN
(1 click)

Elizabeth Baker
Karen Giedeman
Michael Scoffic
Preservice teachers
University of Missouri–St. Louis

updated. Web sites can also provide links to other sites that contain information about specific topics students are studying, and can offer remedial and enrichment activities (March, 2004). If all students have home computers, Web pages can be used for discussion boards, where students respond to specific questions in a discussion format (Doyle, 1999). Students can also create their own Web pages as a method of summarizing what they have learned (Havens, 2003).

Special Considerations for Using Technology

Like any other projects, projects using technology must be well structured and well supervised (Burke, 2002; Gabler & Schroeder, 2003; Wiske, 2004). Student training in the use of such technology as video cameras and Hyperstudio does take time, but many students are so comfortable with technology that they learn quickly. Teachers should check school district policy before allowing students to use the Internet and outline rules for students carefully. Most schools require parental permission for students to use the Internet and some schools restrict the sites students may visit.

✦ CONCEPTUAL TECHNIQUES

Conceptual techniques are ones that assist learners in constructing abstract conceptual frameworks (Jacobsen, Eggen, & Kauchak, 2002; Lemlech, 2002). Many middle school students have difficulty organizing abstract information without concrete props (Anfara & Waks, 2002). In addition, learning disabled children and children of poverty may have failed to develop even basic strategies for organizing information (Payne, 2001). Concrete conceptual techniques can be used to introduce or explain a concept, help students see the relationship between concepts, or help them construct the big picture of a unit of study (Brown, 2002). Conceptual techniques are especially useful to students in learning about concepts, generalizations or principles, and their relationships, but can also be useful for learning factual information (Marzano, 2003; Marzano, Pickering, & Pollock, 2001). Conceptual techniques could include a number of strategies, some of which are discussed below.

Concept Mapping

A **concept map** is a visual representation of concepts with connections that show relationships (Henson, 2002; Holloway, 2002). The teacher or students may identify important concepts related to a topic. The concept map organizes those concepts in a way that shows connections and relationships (Fisher, Frey, & Williams, 2002; Jacobsen et al., 2002). A concept map of the previous section about technology might include the three types of tools with more specific examples listed under each type of tool. A concept map for vertebrate animals (Silver, 1999) might look something like Figure 9.1 with vertical lines connecting the more specific concepts to the more general concepts. Concept maps are helpful in organizing ideas or when the goal is for students to reflect on relationships or to analyze relationships between ideas (Holloway, 2002).

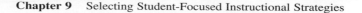

F I G U R E   9 . 1

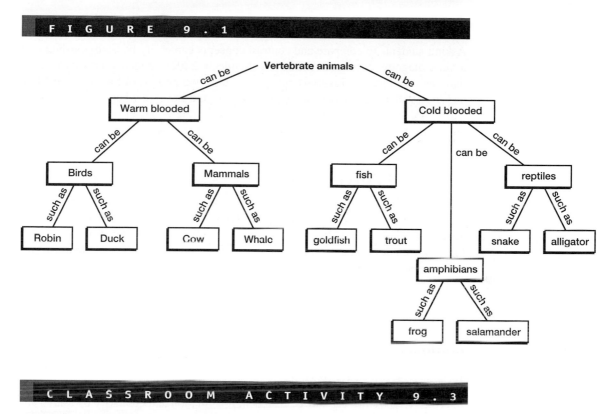

C L A S S R O O M   A C T I V I T Y   9 . 3

Historical Connections Card Sort

This activity uses a stack of 3×5 cards with names of people, dates, events, and ideas the students have studied over several months. Groups of students draw three cards and try to make some reasonable connections between the terms on them. Some examples of terms on the cards are 1821, habeas corpus, Archduke Franz Ferdinand, reconstructivism, Andrew Johnson, imperialism, Jim Crow laws, cultural revolution, social darwinism, 1776.

Mike Holdinghaus
eighth grade social studies teacher
North Kirkwood Middle School

Card Sort Activities

Card sorts are a similar technique in which ideas are written on cards and then organized by some criteria (Findley, 2002). Students may be asked to organize cards in order from more to less important (contributing factors to the Civil War), to correctly order the steps in a process (such as the order of operations in math), or to group examples of specific concepts (types of sentences). Mike Holdinghaus used a card sort to ask his students to find similarities in historical concepts they had studied. Classroom Activity 9.3 describes a card sort activity for history.

Comparing and Contrasting Activities

Asking students to compare and contrast concepts can easily be accomplished with a Venn diagram (Jacobsen et al., 2002; Lemlech, 2002). Students draw two circles that intersect representing two concepts (such as two periods of history—the 1920s and the 1960s). They mark the circles A and B and the area where they overlap C. Circle A contains information about the 1920s, circle B has information about the 1960s. In the area of overlap, area C, the students list similarities between the 1920s and the 1960s (Kellough & Kellough, 1999).

Cause and Effect Charts

Cause and effect charts are helpful to students as they try to organize events in literature or history or scientific principles (Henson, 2004; Jacobsen et al., 2002). Teachers can instruct students to find causes and effects in direct instruction or readings, they can ask them to speculate about causes and effects before direct instruction or readings, or they can give them causes and ask them to determine effects. All of these help students to analyze relationships between concepts (Henson, 2004; Lemlech, 2002). Kerry Brown uses a cause and effect chart to assist his students in taking notes about the American Revolution. He lists some causes and some effects and allows students to fill in the blanks. A portion of the chart is shown in Classroom Activity 9.4.

Interpretive Activities

Interpretive activities capitalize on student imagination and creativity by asking students to make judgments about the meaning of pictures, cartoons, music, or quotations, and to connect them with concepts being studied in class. Students may be asked to react to a picture or quotation or they may be asked to create or find their own picture to represent an idea or concept. Kerry Brown asks his students to interpret political cartoons with reference to the concepts they are studying. Mike Holdinghaus asks his students to bring in a piece of art that they think represents a particular historical period.

Structure of the Conceptual Lesson

When using conceptual techniques, direct instruction can be used initially to introduce or give information, but students should spend most of their time in application or synthesis tasks (Vatterott, 1999). Conceptual techniques follow the premise that students do not need to have acquired information at the knowledge or understanding level to be able to manipulate information through application and synthesis tasks (Caine, Caine, & McClintoc, 2002). In fact, it is through these types of tasks that students internalize the knowledge and an understanding of it (Brooks & Brooks, 1999; Brown, 2002b). Checking for understanding must continually take place as students construct their version of concepts. Application tasks may ask students to describe or define, to use concepts to generalize, or to give examples of concepts (Jacobsen et al., 2002).

C L A S S R O O M   A C T I V I T Y   9 . 4

Cause and Effect Chart

CAUSE AND EFFECT CHART LEADING TO THE AMERICAN
REVOLUTION

CAUSE	EFFECT
France and England aiming to be most powerful country in Europe	
Pontiac's Rebellion in 1763	
England in debt from French and Indian War	
	Colonists pay more for sugar
	Quartering Act of 1765
	Colonists were now DIRECTLY taxed by Parliament
All British were allowed to be taxed only if they had representatives in Parliament	
Angry colonial merchants, lawyers, etc. decide to oppose the Stamp Tax	
	Repeal of the Stamp Act
Parliament still intended on raising money from the colonies	
	Writs of assistance
Non importation agreements	
Concerned colonial women wanted to join the resistance	

Kerry Brown
eighth grade social studies teacher
Pattonville Heights Middle School

Conceptual activities may also be used at the end of a learning unit as a synthesis task. For instance, card sorts or cause and effect charts can be used as an assessment at the end of a unit.

Special Considerations for the Conceptual Lesson

When teaching abstract concepts, teachers will need to provide concrete examples and use analogies of the known to teach the unknown (George & Alexander, 2003). Teachers must always be aware of and knowledgeable about the students' prior concrete experience and should connect new learning to it (Brooks & Brooks, 1999; Brown, 2002b). For instance, television shows can be used to illustrate elements of fiction, song lyrics can be instructive for poetry styles, school cliques can serve as a model for discussions of conflict between nations. Conceptual activities are most effectively used when the teacher chooses a few concepts for students to understand well and takes the time to assure that understanding has taken place (Lemlech, 2002; McTighe et al., 2004). Conceptual methods can be differentiated by providing some students with a more basic set of concepts, by giving some students fewer tasks, by simplifying language, by making tasks more tactile, or by giving some students word banks of possible answers (Tomlinson, 1999). If a computer is available in the classroom, students who need extra help mastering a concept can use tutorial software.

✦ INDEPENDENT WORK

Independent work may include individual projects, research in which students extend their knowledge of a concept, learning contracts, or agendas. Independent work can be used to gain factual knowledge, synthesize information, or extend initial learning into an area of student interest (Curtis, 2002). Independent work is well suited to content that is not too complex for students to learn without teacher direction or to reinforce learning of concepts already taught by direct instruction.

Independent work is also good for developing students' confidence in their independent learning skills and time management skills and allowing students to pursue interests in depth, often using their preferred learning style (Curtis, 2002; Storz & Nestor, 2003). Independent work requires students to have adequate organizational skills and to be somewhat self-motivated (Costa & Kallick, 2004). It is most often used for long-range projects in which students choose a task and a set timeline for their work. The schedule for long-range projects may be a set time each week for a period of weeks (such as every Friday for four weeks) or students may work daily on independent work for a series of consecutive days.

One variation of independent work is the **learning contract**, in which the teacher and student negotiate specific tasks the students will complete, how and when the tasks will be completed, and criteria for their successful completion (Tomlinson, 1999). Often learning contracts specify a grade that will be earned for successful completion (George & Alexander, 2003). The contract includes the signatures of the teacher and the student, and sometimes a parent signature as well. Another variation of independent work is the agenda. **Agendas** are personalized lists of tasks that teachers compile for specific students. Students spend a certain part of each day or certain days each week working independently on their agenda items (Tomlinson, 1999).

Special Considerations for Independent Work

Successful independent work requires teachers to guide students in their choice of projects and the methods they will use to complete them and to act as a coach to reinforce the students' progress on the task. Monitoring of student progress is also essential for student success (George & Alexander, 2003; Marzano et al., 2001). Middle school students need long-term projects broken up into smaller steps with intermittent deadlines (Vatterott, 1999). Teachers need to meet individually with students on a regular basis to monitor progress and get feedback on any particular problems the student may be having. Independent work must be well-structured with rubrics or guidelines for the completed project (Alexander, 1995). Research-oriented projects require the teacher to organize and compile resources, make arrangements with the school library, or identify some possible Internet resources for students in advance (Curtis, 2002). As mentioned in Chapter 7, teacher time spent up front in the structuring and design of project requirements makes for smoother work habits during independent work time (Brooks, 2004; Keefe & Jenkins, 2002). Ed Kastner's Bully Project is a good example of a well-structured independent project. First, his students researched the topic of bullying by reading articles and summarizing the main ideas of what they read. Then they completed reflective questions and brain stormed ideas in a step-by-step process. Classroom Activity 9.5 shows an abbreviated form of the project outline. Teachers can easily differentiate independent work by reducing or increasing the scope or length of an assignment, providing more intensive monitoring, or providing outlines or lists of resources (Tomlinson, 1999).

→ LEARNING STATIONS

Learning stations are a series of places in the classroom where individuals or groups of students work on different tasks simultaneously. Students rotate among the stations to become competent in specific skills or to gain a more in-depth understanding of a concept. Stations can be used to teach concepts, remediate learners, reinforce learning by giving students multiple tasks in related areas, or differentiate activities for different abilities or learning styles (George & Alexander, 2003; Manning & Bucher, 2001). Stations can be *inclusive*, with all students visiting all stations or *exclusive*, with groups of students assigned to choose only a few stations. Stations are usually nonsequential—students may choose the order in which they work at various stations. Usually groups of students complete station work, but stations can also be used by individual students, a few at a time, while others are doing independent work or group work at their desks. This arrangement is especially helpful for using equipment that may be in short supply such as computers or microscopes. Sometimes one station will include direct instruction by the teacher or meeting with the teacher to discuss progress on other tasks.

C L A S S R O O M   A C T I V I T Y   9 . 5

Bully Project

Editorial Illustration Project
Topic: Bullying in School

Student Name: _____ **Date:**_____

Project Assignment: Create in any medium a full-color illustration on the subject of bullying in schools. Your illustration may be specific to a particular article or be a general statement about the issue. The final artwork needs to be 16.5 inches wide by 20.5 inches long.

Worksheet Directions: Follow the steps listed below to aid your search for an idea.

Step one: List three or more interesting facts, thoughts, observations, etc. you learned from your research and from the group discussion.

Step two: Examine your own experiences with this issue by answering the following questions:

1. Have you ever been verbally or physically bullied, either in school or at home?
   Y or N
   If Yes, describe the incident and how it made you feel.

2. Have you ever witnessed someone verbally or physically bully another student or friend, either in school or at home?
   Y or N
   If Yes, describe the incident and how it made you feel.

3. Have you yourself ever verbally or physically bullied another student or friend, either in school or at home?
   Y or N
   If Yes, describe the incident and how it made you feel.

4. How do your personal experiences relate to the facts you listed above? (Are they similar? different? Do they give you a broader perspective on the issue?)

Step three: Generate a brainstorm list of 20 or more images/objects/colors that come to mind when you think of the above listed facts and your experiences with bullying.

Step four: Based on your brain stormed list, draw out 12 thumbnail sketch ideas for an illustration in the boxes provided. **Each thumbnail should represent a completely different idea.**

Step five: Choose the idea you like best from step four and generate 6 different versions of that idea.

Step six (optional): Choose the sketch you like best and create a more detailed final sketch on a 8.25 × 10.25 inch piece of paper.

Step seven: Sketch out the final on a 16.5 × 20.5 inch piece of paper and bring to finish.

Ed Kastner
art teacher
Wydown Middle School

Special Considerations for Learning Stations

Logistics are extremely important for stations to operate smoothly. Teachers may assign students to work at stations, or students may be allowed to sign up for the station of their choice. Obviously, the number of students able to work at a station at one time must be limited. Most teachers establish a set rotation so that students move from station to station in a predetermined order with time limits for each station. Often the activities at each station are designed to require a full class period so movement is not required each day. Monitoring of student work is another important logistical concern (Marzano et al., 2001; Vatterott, 1999). Often students will leave their completed work in a box at the station or fill out a card answering questions to check that the tasks have been completed. Tasks for each station must be well structured with clear instructions and all of the necessary materials assembled. Students should have the freedom to ask each other for help if they are unsure of how to complete tasks at a particular station. Diane Schumacher uses stations during units on the pilgrims and colonial life. See Classroom Activity 9.6 for an abbreviated description of colonial stations. Teachers can differentiate learning that uses stations by limiting the number of stations some students go to, assigning specific students to specific stations, or offering tiered choices (from basic to more advanced) within each station.

STUDENTS' VOICES

About Learning Stations and Projects

"I like how Ms. Schumacher teaches because she makes it fun, like, you're learning but you're having a lot of fun, like most of the time you don't realize you're learning. She has real fun projects to do."

Jessica, seventh grade

"Projects are better. Instead of giving you fake numbers, 'there's a 50 pound car traveling a hundred miles,' who cares? It kind of loses your attention."

Julie, seventh grade

✦ COOPERATIVE AND SMALL GROUP LEARNING

Small group learning is a popular technique for middle school students as it allows for learning that is social and interactive (Mee, 1997; NMSA, 2001). In small group learning students typically work in groups of three to five on an activity with a common purpose. True **cooperative learning** differs from small group learning in four basic ways:

- *Tasks are highly structured*—steps in the task and student roles are defined.
- *Tasks are interdependent*—the success of the team is not possible without the contribution of each member.

CLASSROOM ACTIVITY 9.8

Colonial Stations

Colonial Stations   **Name**_____

You will be in each station for 2 class periods.

Station 1. Vocabulary Skills

  A. Look up 25 words. Numbers 1–25 are found in our current textbook; numbers 26–51
     are found in the red *America* book.

  B. When Vocab. computer is available, take the practice slider quiz. Only practice the
     25 words you will need to know for the test.

  C. Study the vocab. words each night until your final test.

Station 2. Mt. Vernon

  A. View the Hyperstudio stack of Mt. Vernon.

  B. Design your own plantation on white paper. Explain the placement of each
     area/feature and explain its purpose for existence.

  C. Turn in your paper at the end of the station.

Station 3. Internet Research

  Period 1:

  A. Go to the Colonial Index bookmark. Learn about Thomas Jefferson's home.

  B. Turn in a 1 paragraph summary at the end of the day.

  Period 2:

  A. Go to the George Washington/Mt. Vernon web site. Read the Grounds Tour and
     G. Washington: Pioneer Farmer.

  B. Write a 1 paragraph summary and turn it in at the end of the day.

  C. If time, go to Educational Resources, Online quiz. Take the quiz, print your results,
     and turn in.

Diane Schumacher
seventh grade Unified Studies teacher
Parkway Central Middle School

- *There is individual and group accountability for learning*—group outcome is
  evaluated and students are also evaluated individually.
- *Groups are constructed with mixed abilities*—each group has students of
  low, average, and high ability (George & Alexander, 2003; Johnson &
  Johnson, 1999; Slavin, 1986).

Early adolescents are socially motivated to work in groups.

The consistent use of cooperative learning, implemented properly, has positive effects on student achievement, interpersonal relationships, and student self-esteem (Marzano et al., 2001; Mertens & Flowers, 2003; Slavin, 1986). Cooperative learning can also have a positive effect in multiethnic classrooms. Students of different cultural and ethnic groups tend to self-segregate and cooperative learning can help reverse that trend (Blum, 2005; Brown, 2002b; Gabler & Schroeder, 2003).

> To break down this defensive withdrawal into ethnic groups, students need to have time to get to know each other and to find that they share common ground, common problems, and common feelings. Participating in a small group over an extended period of time in a shared activity with a shared goal that can only be achieved by working together is one way to break down artificial barriers between students. (Cole, 1995, p. 58)

Most group learning that middle school teachers use would not meet the criteria for true cooperative learning. That does not make those activities any less effective or less powerful for middle school students. Early adolescents are strongly socially motivated to work in groups and often learn more with others than when working alone (George & Alexander, 2003). Janet Von Harz uses small group learning in table activities. (See Classroom Activity 9.7.)

CLASSROOM ACTIVITY 9.7

Table Activities

Students work in groups of four or five at tables. A rotation of activities occurs every two weeks so all students complete the same set of activities for the semester. Every two weeks, students at each table alternate reading and writing activities. At any given time there may be two or three tables doing a literature circle and two or three tables doing a writing activity.

Janet Von Harz
eighth grade language arts teacher
Pattonville Heights Middle School

TEACHER'S VOICE

About Small Group Learning

"Basically what I do is try and facilitate where they are with the project. If they need some reteaching I sit down with the four of them and reteach. I'm able to confer-ence on a regular basis as they go through drafts of their writing."

Janet Von Harz, eighth grade language arts
Pattonville Heights Middle School

Diane Schumacher developed a true cooperative learning activity during her unit about the Civil War. In her Civil War newspaper project, cooperative learning groups researched various topics about the war (choices included such topics as the Emancipation Proclamation, Lincoln, Grant, role of Black soldiers). Each group cre-ated a newspaper with news stories, feature stories, and editorials. (See Classroom Activity 9.8 for a description.) This activity meets the criteria for true cooperative learning because the students received a group grade and were also evaluated indi-vidually. The groups were of mixed ability and the tasks assigned were highly struc-tured and interdependent (Johnson & Johnson, 1999).

REFLECTIVE QUESTION

What problems have you experienced as a student participating in group learning? How might the teacher have prevented some of those problems?

The three most popular types of cooperative learning are *Student Teams Achievement Divisions, Teams-Games-Tournament,* and *Jigsaw* (Johnson & Johnson,

C L A S S R O O M   A C T I V I T Y   9 . 8

Civil War Newspaper

The Structure of a Newspaper   Name _____

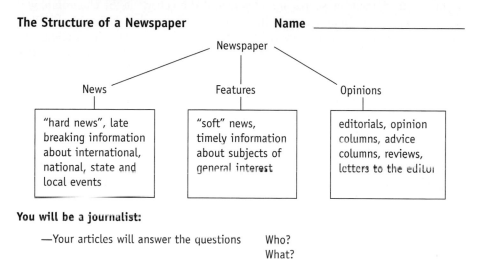

You will be a journalist:

—Your articles will answer the questions   Who?
                                                What?
                                                Where?
                                                Why?
                                                When?
                                                How?

—If you need assistance in how to write a news story, refer to the Write Source p. 171–177.

You will be a detective:

—Find the information using the sources in the room. Assist other members of your group if you find information that they can use for their stories.

Each group needs to assign:

Reporters: everyone in the group is a reporter

—Each student must submit a total of THREE written articles for the newspaper (one from each category . . . News, Features and Opinions)

Now, each member must also be one of the following:

Editor: leader of the group, decision maker, keeps each member on task (final edit)
Editor-in-chief: edits all of the rough drafts written by each group member
Copy Editor: puts the layout of the newspaper together, creates the title of the paper, makes sure each member keeps up with the deadlines.
Graphic Artist: creates maps, diagrams, photos and pictures for the newspaper, works with Copy Editor on final layout

Diane Schumacher
seventh grade unified studies teacher
Parkway Central Middle School

1999) *Student Teams, Achievement Divisions* begins with whole class instruction. After that, students study together in their cooperative groups and are tested individually, and then teams are recognized for their total team score or average score. In this method, the team scores are often recorded on charts in the classroom, with some reward for the highest composite team score (Kellough & Kellough, 1999). In *Teams-Games-Tournament*, students are taught by whole class instruction first. Teams then prepare their group members for a tournament, a competition against other teams in the class. The tournaments are ability grouped—so, for example, low-ability students from one group compete against low-ability students from other groups (Johnson & Johnson, 1999). Teams compete across these ability groups, with individual team members earning points for their team. At the end of the tournament, teams are recognized for their total team score (George & Alexander, 2003). Since each group is of mixed ability, the rationale behind these strategies is that lower ability students will be helped and encouraged by the higher ability students in the group and that each student's score is an important contribution to the team's score (Gabler & Schroeder, 2003).

In *Jigsaw*, students belong to two groups. Topic groups are formed with one member from each base group. Students in each topic group study and become experts in the topic through group discussion (George & Alexander, 2003). Students from the various topic groups return to their base group to teach their topic to that group. Students are tested individually on all topics and teams are recognized for their total team scores (Johnson & Johnson, 1999; Slavin, 1986). Figure 9.2 offers a visual organizer of the three types of cooperative learning.

Organizing Students for Small Group Work

There are several possibilities for assigning students to groups. Optimum size for groups usually ranges from three to five students. If mixed ability groups are desired, the class can be divided into four levels—high, high average, low average, and low (Johnson & Johnson, 1999). Each cooperative learning group would have one high student, one high average, one low average, and one low. Groups should be contrived to balance males and females and different racial and ethnic groups. Students may also be assigned to groups based on content or activity (Gabler & Schroeder, 2002). For instance, students doing reports on Greece may choose the content of culture, geography, or government. Students doing ecology reports may choose to do a skit, written report, or demonstration. Students may also be grouped randomly with the use of playing cards, birthdays, or numbers picked out of a hat.

Social Skills for Group Work

Many students do not know how to work in cooperative groups. Most middle school teachers have learned that students need explicit instruction in the social skills necessary for effective group work (Brown, 2002; Eisner, 2004). A few of the skills needed include disagreeing tactfully, resolving conflicts, encouraging all members to participate, and keeping the group on task (Kellough & Kellough, 1999). For students to use appropriate social skills they must see the need for the skill, understand

FIGURE   9 . 2

Basic Schedule of Activities for Cooperative Learning

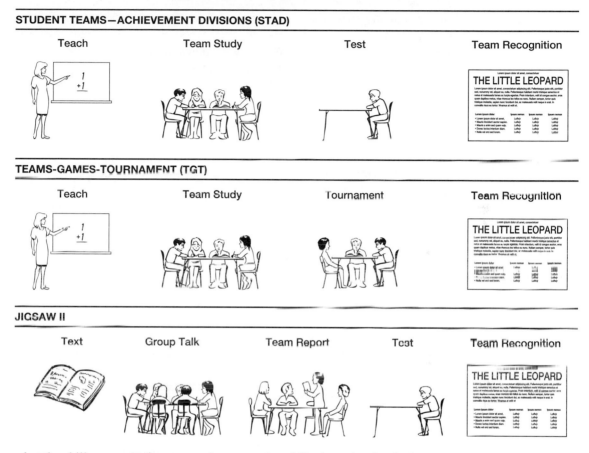

STUDENT TEAMS—ACHIEVEMENT DIVISIONS (STAD)

| Teach | Team Study | Test | Team Recognition |

TEAMS-GAMES-TOURNAMENT (TGT)

| Teach | Team Study | Tournament | Team Recognition |

JIGSAW II

| Text | Group Talk | Team Report | Test | Team Recognition |

what the skills are and when to use them, practice skills through role playing or assigning specific skills to group members, and evaluate how well their group uses the skills (e.g., Name two things your group did well and one thing the group could do better) (Costa & Kallick, 2004; Holloway, 2004).

Roles of Group Members

A frequent complaint about group learning is that some students do little work while others in the group seem to carry the load. To remedy that situation, some teachers like to assign formal roles to students within the group (Gabler & Schroeder, 2003). Possible roles could include these:

- The task definer—this person's job is to be sure everyone in the group understands the task.
- The challenger—this person's job is to ask others to clarify their answers and to solicit participation from students who are not involved.

- The monitor—this person's job is to keep the group on track and to check to see that everyone agrees with the answers given by the group.
- The planner—this person's job is to help the group work out a plan for their job.
- The summarizer—this person's job is to restate the group's ideas and feelings.
- The scribe—this person's job is to write down the group's answers.
- The checker—this person's job is to check each group member for understanding.
- The encourager—this person's job is to positively encourage each group member to participate (Gabler & Schroeder, 2003; Kellough & Kellough, 1999).

When Mike Hirsch uses cooperative learning in his classroom, he assigns each member of the group a number 1, 2, 3, or 4. He then assigns specific tasks for all 1's, all 2's, all 3's, and all 4's. He facilitates the process by giving each team a team kit. (See Classroom Activity 9.9.) Classroom Activity 9.10 shows how a cooperative learning activity in Mike Hirsch's class is organized.

C L A S S R O O M   A C T I V I T Y   9 . 9

Team Kits

Team kits are small plastic containers with the following items:

- Four markers of different colors that team members use to record their answers
- *Think cards*—index cards on which all four students write their answers with the four different colored markers
- *A talking frog*—a small plastic frog that is passed around the group; only the person who has the "talking frog" is allowed to talk
- Other materials as needed for specific assignments

Mike Hirsch
seventh grade math teacher
Wentzville Middle School

TEACHER'S VOICE

About Cooperative Learning

"Times have to be short. You don't give them too much time—you give them a little time and then when they start balking, you give them 30 seconds more and then you're the hero and they start working harder."

Mike Hirsch, seventh grade math
Wentzville Middle School

STUDENTS' VOICES

About Cooperative Learning

"Some of the more advanced people in math class usually help the people that don't understand it."

Hakeem, seventh grade

"You have to pick your partners wisely though; you want a partner that will actually help."

Jessica, seventh grade

C L A S S R O O M   A C T I V I T Y   9 . 1 0

Metric Measurement Cooperative Learning Activity

Cooperative Learning Activity on Metric Measurement

1. *Mix n' match* structure

   A. Hand out the cards.

   B. Have students find the person who has the missing card that matches theirs.

   C. Have students sit back down and hand their card to the person in back of them.

   D. Do that 2 times.

2. *Rotating review* structure

   A. Have students get into their cooperative learning teams.

   B. Tell them who is #1', #2's, etc. *#3's get team boxes*

   C. *Each team has a different colored marker*

   D. Each team gets in front of a piece of chart paper taped to the board.

   E. Number 2's are the scribes. They write what the team says.

   F. You will have 30 seconds to write at each chart paper.

3. *Round robin* structure

   A. Number 3's take the talking frog.

   B. Each person will get 30 seconds to think about and explain to the rest of the team why the United States should change to the metric system, and drop the U.S. system of measurement. *Then pass to number 4, etc.*

   C. After everyone has had a chance, discuss among your team mates the best reason why the U.S. should change to the metric system.

   D. Number 1's stand and tell the rest of the class the best reason that your team came up with as to why we should change to the metric system.

Mike Hirsch
seventh grade math teacher
Wentzville Middle School

Hints for Effective Group Work

1. Select tasks that require task interdependence, such as practicing a new skill, discussion, or peer editing.
2. Teach and model social skills necessary for group work.
3. Have written directions for the activity including student responsibilities, timeline, and how it will be graded.
4. Give students an appropriate amount of time for the task.
5. Begin and end each day with teacher talk.
6. Have students hand something in every day.
7. Designate group territory.
8. Choose a signal for getting students' attention (waving, lights).
9. Have materials ready.
10. Monitor work, walk around, and listen.
11. Allow time for cleanup.
12. Arrange furniture efficiently, such as putting desks in clusters or back to back.

Evaluating Group Work

Teachers are often concerned about how to evaluate group work. Should all students in the group receive the same grade even if some work harder? How much should work habits and behavior count in the student's grade? Teachers must first reflect on the purpose for evaluating group work. If the purpose is to evaluate learning, some individual assessment will be necessary after the group learning has occurred. If the purpose is to evaluate work habits and cooperation, students will differ and will probably need individual evaluations. Many teachers give feedback to groups but do not assign formal grades for group learning. When grading group work, teachers may give partial credit to each student for the group's work, and differentiate the student's grades for work habits. Student input can provide valuable information to the teacher—students may be asked their opinion about what percentage of the work each group member did and what grade each group member should receive. Josette Hochman evaluated a group activity in which students constructed and launched small balloons. Classroom Activity 9.11 is an abbreviated form of the evaluation she used.

Special Considerations for Cooperative Learning

Even when you assign roles and grade students individually, some students simply do not perform well in group situations. Teachers should take time to talk to such a student individually to discover what may be causing the problem and make all attempts to keep students in their groups (Kellough & Kellough, 1999). Students may need more structure, more guidelines, or help with social skills. Students who repeatedly have problems working in groups may be assigned to work with just one

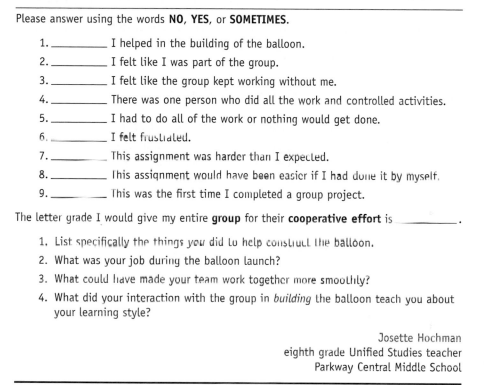

C L A S S R O O M   A C T I V I T Y   9 . 1 1

Group Evaluation

NAME _____   DATE _____

GROUP MEMBERS _____
_____

Please answer using the words **NO**, **YES**, or **SOMETIMES**.

1. _____ I helped in the building of the balloon.
2. _____ I felt like I was part of the group.
3. _____ I felt like the group kept working without me.
4. _____ There was one person who did all the work and controlled activities.
5. _____ I had to do all of the work or nothing would get done.
6. _____ I felt frustrated.
7. _____ This assignment was harder than I expected.
8. _____ This assignment would have been easier if I had done it by myself.
9. _____ This was the first time I completed a group project.

The letter grade I would give my entire **group** for their **cooperative effort** is _____ .

1. List specifically the things you did to help construct the balloon.
2. What was your job during the balloon launch?
3. What could have made your team work together more smoothly?
4. What did your interaction with the group in *building* the balloon teach you about your learning style?

Josette Hochman
eighth grade Unified Studies teacher
Parkway Central Middle School

other person, or may be allowed to pick specific students with whom they wish to work. It may be necessary to allow some students to work alone for short periods, but the goal of group learning is to involve all students, excluding no one.

→ INQUIRY LEARNING

Inquiry learning is a method of learning in which students are actively involved in investigating and organizing information and drawing conclusions (Colburn, 2004; Lemlech, 2002; Stevenson, 2002). The method may vary based on who identifies the investigation and how much autonomy students have in the process. In the most teacher-focused inquiry learning, the teacher identifies the topic to be investigated and the process. This is often called *discovery* learning—the teacher leads students to discover the particular concept he or she wants the students to learn (Henson,

Floating and Sinking Ping Pong Balls

Floating and Sinking Ping Pong Balls

Procedure:

Prior to the demonstration—

- Poke a small hole in one of the ping pong balls large enough to put in a BB. Put in as many BB's as the ping pong ball will hold. Then seal the hole with hot glue, tape, or SuperGlue™.

- Place the popcorn kernels in a large clear glass container. Hide a different colored regular ping pong ball under the surface of the kernels.

In class—

- Put the ping pong ball weighted with BB's on top of the popcorn kernels.

- Gently shake the bowl. The weighted ping pong ball will "sink" and the unweighted ping pong ball will pop out of the kernels!

Explanation:

Because the weighted ball is much denser than the unpopped popcorn kernels, it will sink. The gentle shaking motion of the kernels causes them to act like a liquid. Since the kernels are less dense than the ball, the shaking causes the ball to fall to the bottom of the container.

The unweighted ball, however, is less dense than the unpopped popcorn kernels. It is held in place temporarily by stacking a large number of kernels on top of it, but once the bowl is shaken and the kernels begin flowing as a liquid, the less dense ball rises to the top.

Debbie Silver, Ed. D.
Louisiana Tech University

2004; Manning & Bucher, 2001). Inquiry learning may be more student focused when the teacher presents the problem, but the method of solving the problem is left up to the student (Colburn, 2004; Kellough & Kellough, 1999).

Inquiry learning is an effective technique for teaching students critical thinking and problem-solving skills and helping students to construct meaning by asking questions (Gross, 2002; O'Steen, Cuper, Spires, Beal, & Pope, 2002; Perkins, 2004). Inquiry learning often uses a discrepant event—an event in which new information is inconsistent with information thought to be true. Discrepant events cause students to question, apply knowledge, and problem solve to make sense of the discrepant event. Debbie Silver (1999), an education professor, created the discrepant event in Classroom Activity 9.12 to help middle school science teachers introduce students to the concept of density. She also designed a rubric to evaluate students' explanations of the discrepant event. Examples of student answers on the rubric are shown in Classroom Activity 9.13.

C L A S S R O O M   A C T I V I T Y   9 . 1 3

General Scoring Rubric for Floating and Sinking Ping Pong Balls

General Scoring Rubric for Student Responses
(Students may also choose to illustrate their explanations)

0 Makes no observations or inaccurate observations

0 No observation. No explanation.

1 Makes accurate observations, but no accurate inferences.

1 My teacher put a yellow ping pong ball in a fish bowl that had popcorn in it. When she shook the bowl it sunk, but then it came back up, and it was red. I think the ball was really red, but my teacher covered it with some yellow stuff. When she shook the bowl, it got rubbed by the popcorn, and the yellow stuff came off.

2 Makes accurate observations, uses some appropriate vocabulary to draw some accurate inferences.

2 My teacher put a yellow ping pong ball in a fish bowl that had unpopped popcorn kernels in it. When she shook the bowl the yellow ball sank into the kernels. She kept shaking, and a red ball popped up. I think she already had the red ball in the kernels, and it popped up when she shook the bowl. I think the yellow ball weighs more than the red ball.

3 Makes accurate observations, accurate inferences, cites evidence, uses appropriate vocabulary.

3 (All of the above plus) We learned that objects less dense than the liquid they are in will float, and object more dense than the liquid they are in will sink. I think the popcorn kernels acted kind of like a liquid when they were swirled, so the yellow ball is more dense than the popcorn kernels, and the red ball is less dense than the popcorn kernels.

Debbie Silver, Ed. D.
Louisiana Tech University

Structure of an Inquiry Lesson

Dr. Robert Cohen, a mathematics professor in Washington, D.C., created a taxonomy for inquiry that allows teachers to structure inquiry learning but still permits student autonomy. The structure of a student-focused inquiry lesson would be as follows.

Step 1: Experiencing

Explore: In this step, learners are given an item, concept, or event to freely explore. The teacher may guide the students with questions such as "What would happen if . . ."

Observe: Students are asked to make observations about what is happening, what do they know.

Record: The teacher encourages the students to write down their observations, listing anything they think is important.

Step 2: Organizing

In this step groups of learners look for patterns in the observations they have made. They organize their observations into categories, looking for similarities and differences. Students use skills of analyzing, classifying.

Step 3: Sharing

In this step, learners work together as a large group. They compare what they did to investigate with what other groups did. They share what they found out and how they organized their findings. They notice differences in findings.

Step 4: Processing

In this step, learners integrate the data and synthesize their findings through large group discussions. They may formulate hypotheses or theories that they will test later (Carroll, 2000; Jacobsen et al., 2002).

Special Considerations for Inquiry Learning

Inquiry learning activities can be difficult to design, and actual learning may be difficult to predict (Henson, 2004). While inquiry lessons challenge students to think, some students may have trouble drawing abstract conclusions and making generalizations (Colburn, 2004). Therefore, all students may not receive the same benefit from the experience (Manning & Bucher, 2001). Inquiry activities can be differentiated based on the amount of structure given or individual roles within a group activity. Organizing students in mixed ability groups can somewhat offset students' intellectual differences and guide more concrete learners into abstract thought (Henson, 2004). Some teachers may want to begin by creating simple inquiry tasks (Colburn, 2004). Inquiry learning may be as simple as asking students to investigate and evaluate a topic. For example, in studying different classifications of animals, Liz Peterson has her students examine skulls and make comparisons. As a writing assignment, Janet Von Harz asked her students to investigate products that were of interest to them and to write consumer reports.

✦ PROBLEM-BASED LEARNING

Problem-based learning uses simulations of real-world problems. Students are given a real problem or a fictionalized scenario and are actively involved in investigating, gathering and organizing information, and generating solutions (Checkley, 1997; Kain, 2003). The method may vary based on who identifies the problem and how well defined the process is. When problem-based learning is most teacher focused, the problem to be investigated and the process to be used are both determined by the teacher (Brooks, 2004). Problem-based learning may be more student focused when students are allowed to define the problem (Jacobsen et al., 2002; Murphy, 1997).

Problem-based learning is a method of learning in which students study complex real-life problems, analyze information, and propose solutions (Checkley, 1997). Problem-based learning starts with students being introduced to an actual or fictional problem as the context for an investigation that is content rich (Kain, 2003). Students use the same skills they use in the real world: defining issues, conducting investigations, collecting information, and developing possible solutions (Brooks, 2004; Checkley, 1997). Problems are purposely ill-structured with no easy answers, and students must use inquiry and reasoning to resolve the problem (Caskey, 2002; Renzulli, Gentry, & Reis, 2004; Waks, 2002). Teachers use many sources for real or simulated problems. They find ideas in newspaper columns, problems in their community, television programs, legal cases, textbooks, curriculum guides, or historical events (Murphy, 1997). Problem-based learning may involve in-depth units centered around such topics as deer populations, rain forests, architecture, civil rights, polluted streams, or power outages (Grady, 2004; Murphy, 1997). Problem-based learning can also be used for shorter problem-based activities. Janet Peabody created a problem-based activity for her health students. Students had to apply their knowledge of muscles and joints to solve the problem of creating a new muscle and joint. (See Classroom Activity 9.14.) Mike Hirsch created a problem-solving strategy for his math students to use to solve word problems. He calls it KINDSC, an acronym for the steps in the process—in which students identify KEY WORDS, identify INFORMATION, decide on the NATURE of the problem, DEVELOP a plan to solve the problem, SOLVE the problem, and CHECK to see if their solution is reasonable. The KINDSC strategy could be used in any problem-based learning. See Classroom Activity 9.15 for the handout his students use when solving word problems.

Special Considerations for Problem-Based Learning

Technology has greatly enhanced the possibilities for problem-based learning (Wiske, 2004). For example, advanced tools are available that allow science students to quickly gather data such as temperature or ph values (even in the field outside the classroom). Such tools also have the ability to quickly compile, analyze, and chart data, allowing students to spend less time in calculations and more time actually conducting experiments (Tapscott, 1999). In addition, numerous computer simulations are available in many subject areas that allow students to complete problem-based learning. (The Oregon Trail simulation is a popular one with middle school social studies teachers) (Powers et al., 2001).

Problem-based learning activities can be difficult to structure and often time-consuming to use (Checkley, 1997). Therefore, tasks must be carefully designed so that students are learning multiple concepts or applying multiple skills during the activity, much like the design of an interdisciplinary unit (Kain, 2003). Problem-based activities can be differentiated based on student interests, difficulty of the problem, how much information is given, or through individual roles within a group activity.

Create a New Joint

Pre Assignment:
Read pages 280–290 on Bones, Joints, Etc., and review muscles/nervous system.

Objective: To understand how skeletal muscles in your body function with the help of your skeleton and brain in order for your body to move.

What to do:
You are a biomechanics specialist who specializes in the creation of new muscles and joints for a purpose. You have a client who would like to revise an existing joint in their body or add a new joint in their body.

Musts:

- Create a name for the new/revised joint _____
- Create two new skeletal muscles which will allow the joint to move and name them

  _____   _____

- Create and name ligaments which will help keep the bones attached about the joint. 2 required, 4 maximum

  _____   _____

  _____   _____

- You must use existing bones in the body for the joint.
- List the type of joint it will be. Limited to ball and socket, hinge, and pivot.

  _____

- Must create spinal nerves which will innervate the muscles and attach them to a proper place on the spinal cord.

  _____   _____

- Write a summary of how the joint, muscles, ligaments, and nerves will function. You must include examples of how this joint will improve/effect daily activity.
- Sketch this system out including the brain, spinal cord, bones, muscle etc. Think of shape and size of muscles depending on where located in body.
- Good Luck!!!!!!!

Janet Peabody
physical education/health teacher
North Kirkwood Middle School

CLASSROOM ACTIVITY 9.15

KINDSC Problem-Solving Method

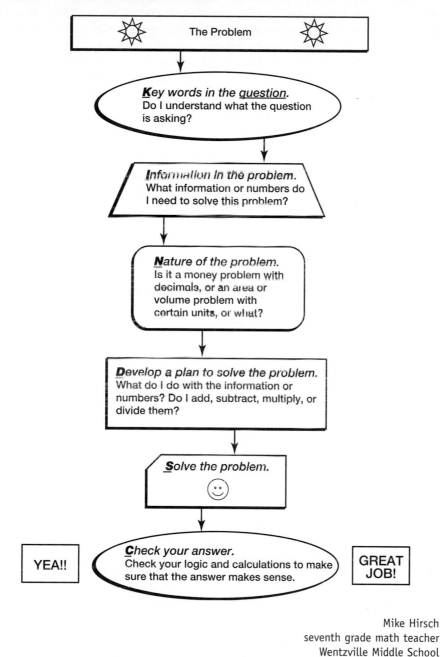

The Problem

Key words in the _question_.
Do I understand what the question
is asking?

Information in the problem.
What information or numbers do
I need to solve this problem?

Nature of the problem.
Is it a money problem with
decimals, or an area or
volume problem with
certain units, or what?

Develop a plan to solve the problem.
What do I do with the information or
numbers? Do I add, subtract, multiply, or
divide them?

Solve the problem.

Check your answer.
Check your logic and calculations to make
sure that the answer makes sense.

YEA!!

GREAT
JOB!

Mike Hirsch
seventh grade math teacher
Wentzville Middle School

✦ GAMES

The creation of and the playing of games can be valuable learning experiences for students (Jenkins, 2005). Games allow for fun social learning and give students a welcome break from more teacher-focused strategies (Henson, 2004). Properly planned, games can be motivational and instructional (Schurr, Thomason, & Thompson, 1995). Learning games can be question and answer games (similar to Jeopardy or 20 Questions), which are easy to create for rote memory tasks and for review of basic concepts, but they can also be structured to include application tasks. Question and answer games are often conducted as team competitions with groups of students competing with other groups.

Board games have greater potential to reinforce higher level thinking skills (Kellough & Kellough, 1999). Gloria Sadler's students demonstrate their knowledge of significant events of the Middle Ages by creating a board game with such perils as being robbed by Vikings and contracting the Black Plague. Mike Hirsch's students reinforce their learning of sets with a set card game. Students choose two or three cards from a deck. Each card describes a set of objects. Students must determine the intersection of the sets by using a Venn diagram and must list objects found in the intersection. Teams compete against each other for points. A sampling of set cards in shown in Classroom Activity 9.16.

Card games are helpful for reviewing information that fits into groups or categories, such as simple and complex fractions, parts of speech, or events related to specific time periods in history. Cards can be made from construction paper and easily laminated onto a regular deck of playing cards. Students then use the cards to play simple card games such as fish or gin rummy, matching types of cards for sets.

Special Considerations for Games

Games are most effectively used when they are designed and created by the students themselves. Teachers need not spend long hours creating games for students. Instead, they should outline the format and content requirements for the games and allow the students to create them. By creating games, students reinforce their learning of facts, concepts, principles, or skills. In creating the games, they must organize and categorize information, make choices about which concepts are most important, and plan the best way to communicate information (Henson, 2004). The sense of pride and ownership students feel for their games is a powerful motivator (Stevenson, 2002). Playing the games gives students the opportunity to review facts, concepts, and principles; practice skills; and apply knowledge previously learned. Stephanie Walton's students practice math operations with integer board games that they create. See Classroom Activity 9.17 for Stephanie Walton's requirements.

✦ ROLE-PLAYS

Role-playing can be used in two ways. One way is as a medium of expression in which students create their own role-plays to demonstrate knowledge they gained through other activities (Schurr et al., 1995). For instance, if students are learning

The Set Game

THINGS THAT CANNOT FLOAT.	THINGS THAT ARE FOUND IN A GYM.	THINGS THAT CAN FLY.
THINGS THAT ARE HARD.	THINGS THAT ARE GREATER THAN 10 CMS, BUT SHORTER THAN 100 CMS. IN LENGTH.	THINGS THAT ARE FOUND ON A FOOTBALL FIELD.
THINGS THAT HAVE HOLES IN THEM.	THINGS THAT ARE FRAGILE.	THINGS THAT ARE FOUND IN THE HOME.
THINGS THAT ARE LONGER THAN 10 FEET.	THINGS THAT ARE HOT.	THINGS THAT ARE BROWN.
THINGS THAT HAVE ONE OR MORE OBTUSE ANGLE.	THINGS THAT HAVE ONE OR MORE RIGHT ANGLE.	THINGS THAT WE CAN EAT.

Mike Hirsch
seventh grade math teacher
Wentzville Middle School

about how a bill becomes a law, role-playing the part of senators and actually going through the steps can help students understand the process. Role-playing characters from a story the class is reading helps students reflect on the feelings of the characters. Tony Ambrose's students create their own role-plays about the westward expansion to pull together knowledge gained through research and class discussion (Classroom Activity 9.1). The second way role-plays can be used is with commercially developed scripts. Scripted role-plays can be used as direct instruction to introduce a unit (as a hook) or to sustain interest during a unit. Kerry Brown uses a commercially scripted role-play about the Boston Massacre to engage his students emotionally during his unit on the Revolutionary War.

C L A S S R O O M   A C T I V I T Y   9 . 1 7

Integer Game

Group names _____
_____
_____
_____

Integer and Equation Board Games

The following are guidelines that must be included in your project:

A. name for the game _____ 5 points

B. game board _____ 30 points

C. 60 numbered game cards
   10 adding integer cards _____ 10 points
   10 subtracting integer cards _____ 10 points
   10 multiplying integer cards _____ 10 points
   10 dividing integer cards _____ 10 points
   10 adding and subtracting equations cards _____ 10 points
   10 multiply and divide equation cards _____ 10 points

D. an answer key for the cards _____ 10 points

E. student-made game pieces—player pieces, number cubes, spinner, etc. _____ 10 points

F. directions for the game—MAKE SURE THE DIRECTIONS ARE EASY TO UNDERSTAND!!!!!!!! _____ 15 points

G. overall neatness, creativity, and originality of game ___ 20 points

your points _____
150 points possible

WHO IS DOING WHAT?????? Put the name of the student on the line next to the person who is responsible for that part of the game.

game board   _____
addition cards   _____
subtraction cards   _____
multiplication cards   _____
division cards   _____
add and subtract equation cards   _____
multiply and divide equation cards _____
answer key   _____
game pieces   _____
directions   _____

Stephanie Walton
seventh grade math teacher
Pattonville Heights Middle School

TEACHER'S VOICE

About the Value of Role Playing in Social Studies

"If you just take the events out of a book and take a quiz on it at the end, there's no feeling behind it. History is a big story. If you go to watch a movie and you're not left with a feeling, you're not going to remember the movie. In order for them to understand these are real people in conflict, they have to act out a play, where they can kind of feel what it was like."

Kerry Brown, eighth grade social studies
Pattonville Heights Middle School

Special Considerations for Role-Plays

Role-plays are a fun, active technique, but it is important that students understand the purpose of the role-play and realize that it is a legitimate learning experience (Manning & Bucher, 2001). If students are writing scripts, the objective should be known, and clear guidelines about content and language must be stipulated (Schurr et al., 1995). Students enjoy role-plays and tend to get very involved in perfecting their scripts and performances. Therefore, realistic time limits must be placed on the writing of the script and rehearsal time. Typically students read from their scripts rather than memorize lines. All students must participate but the assignments can be differentiated. Shyer students may be given fewer lines if they prefer, and ESL students can be given simple lines or be involved in the play without speaking lines. Students often enjoy presenting their role-plays to parents or younger students.

SUMMARY

Each strategy discussed in this chapter has its advantages. The most important factors to keep in mind when choosing instructional strategies are to offer students a variety of types of learning experiences (Brown, 2002; Henson, 2004), and to offer experiences that are engaging, respectful of student needs (Intrator, 2004; Moulds, 2004), and flexible enough to accommodate individual differences (Tomlinson, 2003). The student-focused strategies shown in this chapter and Chapter 7 and the more teacher-focused strategies shown in Chapter 8 are all useful at different points in the learning process. After making decisions about which learning strategies to use, teachers must then consider how to evaluate the results of that learning. Chapter 10 will discuss how to evaluate the results of learning in a student-focused manner.

Key Terms

agenda	learning stations
concept maps	Notestar
cooperative learning	problem-based learning
Hyperstudio	small group learning
inquiry learning	Smartboard
learning contract	webquest

Application Activities

1. Review the section about conceptual techniques (page 298–302). Think about similar types of instruction you have experienced as a learner. Make a list of do's and don'ts for using conceptual techniques. For example:
    DO solicit learner feedback to check for understanding.
    DON'T expect students to learn abstract concepts without some connection to real life.

2. Read through Classroom Activity 9.8, Civil War Newspaper (page 309). What evidence do you see that the tasks are highly structured? Look at the four roles students are assigned. How are those roles interdependent?

3. Cooperative learning requires students to use several social skills. The following activity helps students to think concretely about the social skills they are expected to use. Complete the activity.

    For each social skill below, brainstorm these two descriptions: What would the skill look like? (that is, what would the people in the group be doing?) What would the skill sound like? (that is, what would the people in the group be saying?)

Disagreeing tactfully	looks like	sounds like
Resolving conflicts	looks like	sounds like
Encouraging all members to participate	looks like	sounds like
Keeping the group on task.	looks like	sounds like

4. Make a plan for evaluating group work. Decide what to evaluate and how to weigh each of the following items: group performance, group behavior, individual performance, and individual behavior. Write a short description of what criteria will be evaluated in each of the four areas. Design a simple evaluation sheet that can be easily understood by students.

CHAPTER 10

STUDENT-FRIENDLY GRADING AND ASSESSMENT

→ INTRODUCTION

Chapters 6 and 7 clarified why results must drive instructional planning and how teachers redirect time and energy into outcome based planning. Chapters 8 and 9 suggested that the selection of instructional strategies be based on learner outcomes and showcased a variety of teacher-focused and student-focused instructional methods that might lead to the desired learner outcomes. After planning instruction based on results, how do teachers gather evidence that those results have been achieved—that learning has occurred? Determining evidence of learning requires an understanding of assessment and grading practices and a thoughtful consideration of how those practices influence learning (Earl, 2003; Marzano, 2000; Nitko, 2004). Just as student-focused instruction is a powerful tool for maximizing student success, so is student-focused assessment (Stiggins, 2001; Wormeli, 2004). This chapter examines the limitations of many traditional assessment and grading practices and suggests student-friendly alternatives that will maximize student success. It also illustrates how teachers design assessments and presents day-to-day practices of grading and feedback that are most effective for middle school students. **The purposes of this chapter are to help you**

1. become aware of how teacher beliefs about instruction influence teacher grading and assessment practices.
2. examine assumptions inherent in traditional approaches to assessment.
3. become aware of a variety of methods of providing feedback to students.
4. reexamine traditional grading practices.
5. review research about homework and analyze the role of homework in student failure at the middle level.
6. reflect on your beliefs about the value of homework.
7. understand the value of formative feedback and summative grading.
8. become familiar with performance assessments.
9. use portfolios to document that standards are being met.

Essential Questions

After reading and completing activities in this chapter, you should be able to answer the following questions:

1. How do some traditional assessment practices encourage the sorting and ranking of students and precipitate student failure?
2. What are the disadvantages of traditional grading practices such as averaging and *moment in time* grading?
3. What is the most important purpose of grading?
4. How useful are grades in the motivation and control of students?
5. In what ways can students receive feedback on their learning?
6. When should mastery learning be an option for students?
7. What type of homework meets the developmental needs of early adolescents?

8. How do organization of classwork, written tests, and weighting of grades impact student success and failure?
9. What are the components of a well-developed rubric?
10. What do effective performance assessments look like?
11. How can portfolios be used to document that standards are being met?

✦ HOW TEACHING PRACTICES HAVE INFLUENCED ASSESSMENT PRACTICES

Just as our beliefs about students and instruction influence our practices of teaching, they also influence our grading and assessment practice (Earl, 2003). In Chapter 1, the beliefs behind the philosophies of student-focused instruction and teacher-focused instruction were contrasted. Some of those differences are revisited here:

Teacher-Focused Beliefs	Student-Focused Beliefs
Some can learn	All can learn
Students learn in the same way	Students learn in different ways
Failure is punished	Failure is learning
One-chance learning	Mastery learning
Student as product	Student as worker (Vatterott, 1999)

Each set of beliefs tends to be consistent with certain assessment practices.

Teacher-Focused Assessment Practices	Student-Focused Assessment Practices
Paper and pencil tests	performance assessments
ABCDF grading	descriptive feedback
moment in time grading	grading for mastery (Earl, 2003; Kohn, 1993)

Even though many teachers have moved toward student-focused *instructional* practices, traditional practices of *assessment* still persist (Earl, 2003). The traditional method of teach-learn-regurgitate has led us logically to traditional assessment practices (Anfara & Stacki, 2002; Guskey, 1996). The assessment practices that accompany the teacher-focused beliefs above are consistent with traditional views about learning and have helped to institutionalize a *sorting and ranking* mentality about grading and assessment (Canady, 1993; Guskey, 2003).

Sorting and Ranking Versus Teaching and Learning Practices

Traditional teacher-focused assessment relies heavily on letter and number grades (Guskey, 2001; Kohn, 1999). Robert Canady (1993) summarizes many of the problems inherent in grading by showing how traditional practices sort and rank learners (Canady & Hotchkiss, 1989). He contrasts assessment in a system concerned about learning and assessment in the traditional sorting and ranking system and how these differ. Teacher behaviors and attitudes vary depending on whether teachers focus primarily on sorting and selecting or teaching and learning (Atkins & Ellsesser, 2003; Kohn, 1994). Compare the two sets of teacher behaviors shown below.

Teacher Behaviors Consistent with a Sorting and Ranking Focus

1. The paper cannot be done over; you had your chance!
2. A test cannot be retaken to improve a low grade.
3. Even if you show mastery of content, your grade is low because some items of work (for example, homework, projects, notebooks) were not completed.
4. No, you may not use your text for any parts of the examinations—not even for reviewing the formulas.
5. As a teacher, it's my job to teach; it's their job to learn.
6. Work is graded by taking into account nonacademic standards such as neatness, form, attractiveness.
7. Teacher takes pride regarding the ability of an exam to discriminate.
8. Teacher expects students to figure out what material will be tested (adapted from Canady, 1993; Guskey, 2003).

All of these behaviors serve to sort students into categories and to stratify them into groups of poor, average, and better learners (Earl, 2003). These behaviors also tend to set up an artificial scarcity of A's (Kohn, 1999). They practically guarantee that some students will not do well (Levine, 2003).

For example, one of the easiest ways to sort and rank learners is to limit time for written tests. Some students need more time than others, so limiting time offers an automatic advantage to faster test takers and a disadvantage to slower test takers. This method usually produces a wide range of grades, often reflecting speed, not learning (Goh, 2004).

Teacher Behaviors Consistent with a Teaching and Learning Focus

1. You may continue to revise your paper; I hope you will work on it until you can earn an acceptable grade.
2. A test (possibly various forms of a test) may be retaken. The goal is to keep students wanting and working to do better versus giving up.
3. A respectable passing grade can be earned with evidence of content mastery. Low marks may be shown on the nonacademic side of the report card for work not completed or when directions were not followed.
4. Yes, all students may use their text and other notes for a maximum amount of time (say 20 or 30 minutes depending on how long the period is scheduled); the goal is to encourage students to study and organize their notes and materials for purposes of reference—not just to memorize key facts.

5. I feel responsible for student learning.
6. Work is graded only after nonacademic standards are addressed.
7. As the teacher, I take pride in the number of students who attain acceptable grades.
8. I outline objectives, highlight material to be tested, and make tests congruent with my teaching (adapted from Canady, 1993, and Guskey, 2003).

The goal of sorting and ranking practices is to **norm-reference. Norm-referenced assessment** is assessment that compares students to each other and attempts to discriminate between better and poorer learners (Guskey, 2001; Popham, 2000). The goal of teaching and learning practices is to maximize learning performance for everyone (Earl, 2003). The teaching and learning focus is **criterion-referenced. Criterion-referenced assessment** judges learners individually against the same criteria for learning (Guskey, 2001; Popham, 2000). Sorting and ranking practices have remained the status quo in many schools because they exist in harmony with several assumptions about learners and grading. If a teacher believes the following assumptions to be valid, it is easier to support sorting and ranking practices.

✣ Assumptions Inherent in Traditional Approaches to Assessment

Assumption 1: All students learn in the same way and at the same speed.

Traditional practice assumes that all students are the same, and should be assessed in the same way and at the same point in time (Guskey, 2004; Patterson, 2003). We now know that students access learning through different mental channels and may not be able to demonstrate their learning in the same ways (Cawelti, 2003; NMSA, 2001c). We also know that some students require more time to master the same content or skill (Oakes, 1985; Slavin, 1997). Yet most teachers continue to test all students at the same time, after giving them the same amount of time for learning. Inherent in this assumption is that learning is a linear process, that all learners should show the same steady progress toward a learning goal (Goh, 2004). In reality, many students continue to go through the activity of learning only to have sudden bursts of insight after repeated trials. Yet most teachers continue to evaluate students at a given *moment in time*, expecting a similar level of learning for all students (Guskey, 1996). Some students may fail to demonstrate learning in October that they can demonstrate in March and still reach the goals for that grade level (Wormeli, 2004).

Assumption 2: Grades are essential to learning.

Traditional practice is so enmeshed with number and letter grades, it's hard to imagine teaching without them.

Reflect on this quote by Tom Guskey: "Grades are not essential for instruction." Do you agree or disagree? Why?

It's hard to believe grades are not essential to learning because

1. we've never done school without grades. Most people alive today never experienced school without grades.
2. it's the only way we know to give feedback. Letters and numbers are also the easiest, quickest way to give feedback.
3. it's a language everybody understands. The ABCDF grading system is known to everyone and is part of our popular culture. We grade presidents and meat and everything else in popular culture. When a newspaper article rates a politician as doing a "C" job, we all know what it means. The language of grades is familiar to parents and they're comfortable with it.

In spite of our comfort with the idea of grades, there is nothing to indicate they are necessary for learning to take place (Kohn, 1993; Nitko, 2004). In fact, research indicates that grades tend to interfere with learning (Guskey, 2003). According to recent research,

1. grades appear to be destructive for creativity and higher order thinking.
2. even rote learning seems to be less permanent and students are less apt to find the task interesting when they know they are being graded.
3. when students know they are being graded they tend to choose easier tasks and avoid the more challenging tasks (Amrein & Berliner, 2003; Kohn, 1994; Nitko, 2004).

The fact that this research has had little impact on grading practices is an indication of how ingrained the practices of grading are in education.

Assumption 3: Grades motivate learners.

The belief that grades are essential to instruction is consistent with the prevalence of behaviorism in the culture of education (Kohn, 1999; Stiggins, 2001). The behaviorist mind-set focuses on the belief that learners must be motivated by external forces. The implicit assumptions are that a single entity called motivation exists that students have or don't have and that grades are a way to manipulate that motivation (Stiggins, 2001). This implies that learning is only a means to an end—to escape punishment or get a reward—that learning has no intrinsic value and that students would not be interested in learning for its own sake (Earl, 2003). Perhaps this negative mind-set was born from traditional rote learning that was made distasteful and boring. Therefore, students had to be coerced into learning and grades were often the method of coercion (Stiggins, 2001). Perhaps no intrinsic motivation exists for such rote learning, but there is intrinsic motivation among middle schools students to make sense of things, solve problems, and understand the world around them (Vatterott, 1999).

One observation has proven true for most students: Grades have no value as punishment. The ABCDF grading system tends to separate students into learners (A, B, and maybe C students) and losers (D and F students) (Guskey, 2004). When the losers are convinced they can't be learners, they give up (Nitko, 2004). Good grades motivate students who value good grades (Kohn, 1993; Patterson, 2003). Bad grades don't motivate anyone (with the possible exception of a few overachievers):

> No studies support the use of low grades as punishments. Instead of prompting greater effort, low grades usually cause students to withdraw from learning. To protect their self-image, many students regard the low grade as irrelevant and meaningless. (Guskey, 1994, p. 16)

Even though failing grades demotivate, students have spent most of their educational life working for grades and can become in a sense, addicted to them (Kohn, 1999).

As evidence of this, teachers often complain that if they don't grade an activity, students won't do it. If this is the case, the problem is not about grades but about teacher expectations and possibly the learning task itself (Good & Brophy, 2003). Teachers must first make it clear to students that participation in all learning activities is expected, regardless of whether they are graded. Second, the teacher should examine the learning tasks assigned to students to determine whether the tasks are as engaging as possible (Tomlinson, 2003). One student indicated that he clearly understood the connection:

STUDENT'S VOICE

About Grades and Motivation

"If you want better grades, make it fun."

Nick, seventh grade

Assumption 4: Grades are necessary for control.

Many teachers see grades as a necessary tool for controlling students (Patterson, 2003). Concern about discipline, so prevalent at the middle school level, often leads teachers to use grades to try to control behavior (Nitko, 2004; Popham, 2000). Yet when teachers use grades in this way (like giving 0's for talking), it's relatively easy for students to "dig themselves into a hole." It takes only a few 0's to ruin a quarter average, and once students are failing, additional failing grades don't work as controls any more—they have no impact (Guskey, 1994). In addition, this behavior is so controlling on the part of the teacher that it damages the teacher-student relationship and therefore affects motivation (Dalton & Watson, 1997; Kohn, 1999).

There are several ways grades can be used for control or compliance (Marzano, 2000). Grades can be used to get students to comply with rules of behavior and decorum (Nitko, 2004). Some teachers take points off student grades for tardiness, talking, or not having a pencil in an attempt to force students to obey rules (Jacobsen, Eggen, & Kauchak, 2002). Grades can also be used to communicate the rules for academic tasks. Taking off points for not having one's name in the right-hand corner or for using pencil instead of ink punishes students for not complying with the rules, even though these infractions have little to do with learning.

Beyond the use of grades as motivation and compliance, grades have taken on a peculiar role as *moral* judgment—as *moral reward and punishment*. Grades can be used to reward virtue and punish vice (Popham, 2000). The virtues that teachers often reward with good grades are conformity and compliance (following the rules as mentioned above), hard work (effort is rewarded), and neatness (Marzano, 2000; Nitko, 2004). The vices that teachers often punish with poor grades include non-compliance (not following the rules), sloppiness, and laziness (the moral judgment when work is not completed or turned in late) (Patterson, 2003). Therefore *good* students get good grades, *bad* students get bad grades. The practice of giving pop quizzes exemplifies the rewarding virtue/punishing vice mentality. After all, the virtuous students have been studying and keeping up with homework; the others have not. The pop quiz allows the teacher to exert his or her power to punish and reward. When teachers are particularly frustrated with their ability to control students, it may seem as if they use grades as a sword ("I'll show you—take that!").

> Sadly, some teachers consider grades or reporting forms their "weapon of last resort." In their view, students who don't comply with requests suffer the consequences of the greatest punishment a teacher can bestow: a failing grade. Such practices have no educational value and, in the long run, adversely affect students, teachers, and the relationship they share. (Guskey, 1994, p. 16)

There's little evidence to show such coercive techniques change the behavior of the learner—they usually result in creating resentment and damaging the teacher-student relationship, thereby interfering with the student's desire to continue learning (Dalton & Watson, 1997; Kohn, 1999). In fact, most middle school students, strongly driven by their own needs for power, are immune to such controls (Havinghurst, 1976; Vatterott, 1999).

Assumption 5: Good teachers give bad grades.

The sorting and ranking mentality has perpetuated one final assumption—that low grades are related to rigor. After all, if the point of grading is to rank and discriminate poor learners from good learners, the closer the grades approximate a bell-shaped curve the better (Bonstingl, 1992). If we set the standard for excellence so high that only a few students excel, and many fail, we must have very high standards. Then, of course the inverse must be true—lots of high grades must indicate low standards and a watered-down curriculum.

So much of what teachers do with grades is *not* about learning or achievement (Kohn, 1999; Nitko, 2004). There's no trick to giving bad grades—any teacher can make a test so hard only a few students get A's. Any teacher can make the consequences for noncompliance to the rules strict enough to cause failure. Then it becomes morally defensible to give failing grades to punish laziness and noncompliance. Conversely, some teachers can grade so leniently and expect so little of their students that, in their class, too many high grades *can* indicate that students have not learned much. But neither can be automatically true. It's just not that simple.

> Interestingly, most studies suggest that student performance does not improve when instructors grade more stringently and conversely, that making it relatively easy to get a good grade does not lead students to do inferior work—even when performance is defined as the number of facts retained temporarily as measured by multiple-choice exams. (Kohn, 1994, p. 38)

If teachers find they are giving many high grades, they *should* reflect on whether their standards are too low and whether they are maximizing learning. If teachers find they are giving many low grades, they should closely examine the reasons for the failing grades. Have they set standards unreasonably high, or have they failed to individualize or personally connect with students?

TEACHERS' VOICES

About the Relationship between Grades and Good Teaching

"One of the biggest responsibilities we have as teachers, we're evaluators, we're graders. It's also one of the toughest jobs. Sometimes we as teachers get bogged down in the grade, 'Gee, I have to give F's, I can't give a whole class of A's.' My theory is at this level, because it's mastery, if I had a whole class of A's I'd be the happiest guy in the world."

Mike Hirsch, seventh grade math
Wentzville Middle School

"When the kid gets an F, I get an F. I think, 'Oh my gosh, I did not connect with this kid!'"

Liz Peterson, seventh grade science
Ladue Junior High School

→ MOVING TOWARD A TEACHING AND LEARNING FOCUS

When we move away from the sorting and ranking mentality, we find many ways to maintain high standards without giving failing grades. Moving toward a teaching and learning focus requires us to move beyond behaviorism to humanistic views (DeVries & Zan, 2003). That means moving from a demand model, in which we control and coerce learners, to a support model, in which we provide the support necessary for learning to occur (Kohn, 1994). This shift requires a move away from the punitive, moralistic use of grades to an informative, helpful use, similar to the mind-set shift about discipline that was discussed in Chapter 4.

Behaviorist assumptions about learners are inconsistent with what we now know about how students learn—the source of the beliefs is not valid (Dalton & Watson, 1997; Hall & Hall, 2003). Behaviorist assumptions are also inconsistent with the beliefs of student-focused instruction and the goal of capitalizing on the student's desire to make sense of the world (DeVries & Zan, 2003). Learning cannot be coerced but follows naturally when teachers provide engaging tasks in a supportive environment (Strahan, Smith, McElrath, & Toole, 2001).

"Grades need to be experienced not as reward and punishment but as information" (Bruner in Kohn, 1994, p. 39). Grades are not essential to instruction, but *feedback* is. *Feedback* is essential to instruction, but letter and number grades aren't the only methods of giving feedback about learning. And teachers aren't the only people who can provide feedback to students (Marzano, Pickering & Pollock, 2001; Wormeli, 2004).

REFLECTIVE QUESTION

What other ways can students receive feedback about their learning? What if teachers could only give feedback, not grades? What would change?

Teachers can give feedback without using grades.

⇥ REEXAMINING TRADITIONAL PRACTICES

"Today's system of classroom grading is at least 100 years old and has little or no research to support its continuation" (Marzano, 2000, p. 13). Many traditional grading practices were born out of the behaviorist assumptions previously discussed (such as that grades are necessary for control and motivation) (Kohn, 1999). It was believed that certain grading practices were necessary to ensure that learning took place. Those traditional practices took a huge toll on student success and created a large group of students with failing grades (Levine, 2003). When traditional practices are examined in light of what we know today about brain research, learner differences, and the role of emotion in learning, they are much less defensible than in the past (McDaniel, Necochea, Rios, Stowell, & Kritzer, 2001).

Letter Grades

Although most teachers are required to give letter grades at the quarter or trimester, letter grades are problematic for a number of reasons. Letter grades are not consistent from one teacher to the next—the same student work can be evaluated by three different teachers and receive three different grades (Nitko, 2004; Popham, 2000). Inconsistencies in letter grades are often made worse by the inclusion of nonachievement factors such as neatness or effort.

Letter grades alone provide inadequate feedback—the grade does not tell the student where improvement is needed or what makes the grade an A, a B, or a C (Guskey, 1996; Wormeli, 2004). The cutoff scores between categories are arbitrary and difficult to justify (Lemlech, 2002). For instance, if 80–89 is a B there is a nine-point spread in the same grade, but only a one-point difference between 80 (a B) and 79 (a C).

Competitive Grading and Grading on the Curve

As mentioned before, when teachers set up an artificial scarcity of A's, they push students into competing with each other for limited rewards (Bonstingl, 1999). In competitive grading, helping others threatens one's own chances for success. The prevailing attitude is "As you win, I lose." When students work cooperatively, they help each other reach their learning goals with an attitude of "together we can all be successful" (DeVries & Zan, 1995). Competitive grading undermines cooperation and a sense of community that middle school students need to experience (Kellough & Kellough, 1999). A bell curve is not a symbol of rigor but a symbol of failure—failure to teach well, to test well (Kohn, 1994).

Moment in Time Grading

Here's a common scenario in most classrooms—students spend three weeks studying a unit and working through a series of activities. At the end of the three weeks, they all take the unit test. Most teachers still grade students as a group after a certain amount of time, at a specific time on a specific day (Guskey, 1996; Wormeli, 2004).

This practice penalizes the slower learners for not learning fast enough or well enough in the given amount of time—all but the fastest learners will receive some penalty. *Moment in time* grading often grades students while they're still learning and this can put a halt to the learning process. After all, that unit or skill has been evaluated and the student received a grade. Once we assess, we move on and the student feels relieved of the responsibility for that learning. Grading while students are still learning inhibits continued learning (Kohn, 1994). Teachers can avoid this problem by asking students when they are ready to be tested (with reasonable time limits, of course). Some teachers are concerned that this would require them to create more than one version of a test. This is usually problematic only when the knowledge tested is low-level rote learning. If the test assesses higher level thinking skills, it is typically not a problem. If teachers feel compelled to test all students at the same time, they should allow retakes at a later date or allow test corrections.

Averaging

If teachers could eliminate only one traditional practice to increase student success, it would be the averaging of grades. At first glance, averaging grades seems to be an equitable way to reflect student performance. After all, it allows students to balance out highs and lows. But averaging exacerbates the problems associated with moment in time grading because a low grade continues to affect the student's average even after material has been mastered (Guskey, 1996). For slower learners, and even students who are just having a bad day, a bad score seals their fate—the grade is in and the damage is done. Averaging really doesn't accurately reflect a student's overall level of mastery for the quarter or semester (Nitko, 2004). Students could excel in one area and fail miserably in another, only to receive a grade of C. Another student could master all concepts at a C level and receive the same grade.

Averaging is particularly bad when combined with failure for work not completed (Nitko, 2004). The common practice of giving a student a zero for work not turned in causes many students to fail because such an extreme score skews the average. "That is why, for example, Olympic events such as gymnastics and ice skating eliminate the highest and lowest scores; otherwise one judge could control the entire competition simply by giving extreme scores" (Guskey, 1994, p. 19).

This problem is exacerbated when teachers routinely allow students not to turn in work. Students, wishing to be in control of their time, choose not to complete certain assignments. Typically, teachers give students zeros for these assignments. But teachers often fail to discover why students aren't completing the work. When students repeatedly fail to turn in work, teachers should examine the task. Do students not understand the task? Is the student overwhelmed with too much work combined with other outside responsibilities? Was the job too big or was the learner frustrated? Did the student not have time or materials necessary to complete the work? For many of these situations, it's just too embarrassing for students to admit why they did not complete the work, so they make up an excuse or simply say "I forgot." The middle school teachers who fail the smallest number of students simply have a policy that all work must be turned in. They persist with students until they get the work. (Many teachers have found that they receive work if they make a point to ask for it personally.) They do whatever is necessary. Once students realize "there's no not doing it" the problem diminishes. Some of the techniques teachers have found helpful in getting work from students include

1. requiring students to bring in work first thing in the morning (before it has a chance to get lost).
2. having a *make-up day* when students complete missing work while other students have free choice.
3. offering after school help sessions.
4. assigning students after-school detention to make up work.
5. pulling students out of other team classes to complete work.

➔ RETHINKING THE PRACTICE OF HOMEWORK

Homework is any task related to the school curriculum that the teacher expects the student to complete outside of school (Connors, 1992; Cooper, 1989). Homework has a potent impact on student success at the middle level. No longer tightly controlled by parents and strongly driven by social and emotional needs, middle school students often choose not to do homework (Vatterott, 2004). As a result, many of them receive failing grades that may not reflect their true level of learning (Connors, 1992; Pope, 2001). Most teachers have strong opinions about homework, yet the research about its value is inconclusive (Cooper, 1989, 1998, 2001a; Vatterott, 2004). As a practice that precipitates a good deal of failure at the middle school level, homework is worthy of adequate discussion.

REFLECTIVE QUESTION

Your school district has implemented a new NO HOMEWORK policy. What is your reaction to this policy? What positive and negative outcomes do you expect will result in your school?

The practice of homework, like grading, is firmly rooted in educational tradition (Connors, 1992; Cooper, 1989, 2001; Kralovec & Buell, 2000). In fact, the concept of homework is so ingrained in our culture it is part of common vernacular. The meaning of expressions like "Do your homework before taking a trip" or "It's obvious they didn't do their homework before they presented their proposal" is clear. As teachers, our attitudes about the value of homework strongly influence our teaching practices. Our attitudes about homework are influenced to a large extent by our beliefs about students and learning (Kralovec & Buell, 2000; Vatterott, 2004). It may prove enlightening to examine some of those beliefs.

REFLECTIVE QUESTION

Think about the following quote:

"Our belief in the value of homework is akin to faith" (Kralovec & Buell, 2000). How have faith, tradition, or moral judgments influenced your beliefs about homework?

Historical Attitudes about Homework

Like many other practices in education, homework has been popular or unpopular at different times in history. The crusade for and against homework is 100 years old and the pendulum continues to swing. It reflects general educational philosophical shifts as well as prevailing cultural attitudes of historical periods (Cooper, 2001a; Kralovec & Buell, 2000).

> Whenever reformers attempt to improve the academic outcomes of American schooling, more homework seems a first step. The justification for this probably has more to do with philosophy (students should work harder) and with the ease of implementation (increased homework costs no extra money and requires no major program modifications) than with new research findings (Strother in Connors, 1992).

Late 19th century (for): Homework was believed to be an important means of disciplining the mind. Learning was drill, memorization, and recitation.

The 1930s (against): Anti-homework concerns focused on the educational value of homework and its threat to the child's physical and emotional health. It became an important piece of the progressive education movement.

The late 1950s (for): The trend toward less homework was reversed in the late 1950s after the Russians launched Sputnik. Fearful that children were unprepared to face the technological future, school officials, teachers, and parents saw homework as a means for accelerating children's knowledge acquisition.

The 1960s (against): By the mid-1960s, the cycle reversed again. Homework was seen as a symptom of too much pressure on students to achieve. Learning theories questioned the value of homework. In 1966, the NEA recommended that homework be limited to one hour a day in upper elementary and junior high school (Connors, 1992; Cooper, 2001a; Kralovec & Buell, 2000).

The 1980s (for): In 1983, the *Nation at Risk* study ratcheted up the standards starting what has been called the "intensification movement"—that education can be improved if only there is more of it: longer school years, more testing, more homework. Between 1981 and 1997 the amount of homework given to students increased dramatically.

The 2000s (against): Cooper (2001a) released a comprehensive study on homework. Media coverage began in 1998; since then major news magazines and talk shows have spawned a national dialogue about homework (Ratnesae, 1999). The anti-homework sentiment is growing but so is the pro-homework coalition.

REFLECTIVE QUESTION

Compare the for and against swing in attitudes toward homework to the social and political attitudes of each time period.

The Big Picture of Homework Research

What does the research indicate about such a well-established yet controversial practice? Homework research can be summarized in the following four statements:

1.   Research on homework has not been well designed.
2.   Results are inconclusive, sometimes contradictory.
3.   Studies cannot show that homework *causes* higher achievement.
4.   Even when achievement gains have been found, they are minimal when compared to the amount of work expended by teachers and students (Cooper, 1994, 2001a; Kralovec & Buell, 2000).

In summary, "Homework probably involves the complex interaction of more influences than any other instructional device" (Cooper, 1989), p. 87. Therefore, educators should be careful not to overgeneralize about even the best research. The research does, however, offer some interesting food for thought. Following is a short summary of the most significant studies about homework.

According to the Institute of Social Research at the University of Michigan, students are spending more time doing homework today than in 1981. Their research indicated that an average child aged 9 to 11 years old spent 169 minutes a week doing homework in 1981 compared to 217 minutes a week in 1997. The most alarming increases were for children *aged 6 to 8* whose homework increased from 44 minutes a week in 1981 to 123 minutes a week in 1997 and children *aged 3 to 5* whose homework increased from 12 minutes a week to 36 minutes a week (Ratnesar, 1999).

The most extensive research on the practice of homework has been done by Harris Cooper, a professor at Duke University. In his synthesis of research conducted in 1994, Cooper found that homework appears to be positively correlated with achievement, but the effect varies dramatically with grade level. In grades 3 to 5 the correlation between homework and achievement is nearly zero. In grades 5 to 9, the correlation is .07 and in grades 9 to 12, the correlation is .25. Although some researchers may consider these correlations significant, remember that correlations do not show cause and effect. Remember also that .00 is no correlation, 1.0 is a perfect correlation. Homework appears to be more beneficial for rote memory, practice, and rehearsal of a skill already developed than for complex tasks that require integration of knowledge and skills (Cooper, 2001; Jensen, 2000).

A study by Kay, Fitzgerald, and Paradee (1994) showed that many parents felt inadequately equipped to help their children with their homework. Parents indicated they needed more information about the teacher's expectations of the child and what the parents' role should be in helping. Parents believed that homework should be tailored to the individual and should respect child and family needs. Parents wanted accommodations for special education students, and scheduling accommodations for things like sports, religion classes, and divorced parents' visitations. Parents valued and even enjoyed hands-on homework and projects in which the whole family could participate. Parents wanted an extensive two-way communication system that would allow them to become partners on their child's instructional team.

There appears to be some consistency in the research about the maximum amount of homework educators feel is appropriate. The general rule of thumb, endorsed by the NEA and the PTA, is the 10-minute rule (Connors, 1992; Vatterott, 2001, 2004). The 10-minute rule recommends that homework should not exceed a maximum of 10 minutes per grade level per night (6th grade = 60 minutes). This is the recommended time to be spent on *all* subjects combined. The 10-minute rule is consistent with Cooper's research on achievement for middle and high school students. He found that homework assignments beyond those limits did not improve achievement (Cooper, 2001b).

Does Homework Teach Responsibility?

Teachers often claim that homework is important to teach students responsibility. Responsibility is often a code word for obedience. When we say we want students to be responsible, are we saying we want them to be obedient—to do what we want them to do when we want them to do it (Kohn, 1999)? Or are we asking students to be self-disciplined—to do something they hate to do because it's their duty (Vatterott, 2004)?

There is no doubt that homework gives students something to be responsible for if they will choose it. Therein lies the problem. Middle school students are becoming more independent from parents and other adults and making more and more decisions about their day-to-day lives (Manning & Bucher, 2001). Early adolescents may learn responsibility through consequences that matter to them—if grades matter, grades might work. If competition matters, competition might work (Vatterott, 2004).

True responsibility cannot be coerced. It must be developed by allowing students power and ownership of tasks (Eisner, 2002; Hoffman & Levak, 2003). Responsibility is developed when students are allowed to decide what steps are necessary to complete a task, and what schedule is necessary to get the job done on time (DeVries & Zan, 2003). One study indicated that responsibility is learned only if *parents* systematically structure and supervise homework with that goal in mind (Kralovec & Buell, 2000).

It's difficult to build responsibility in students if they don't see a valid reason for the task. If students view homework tasks as meaningless, boring, or tedious, they will often risk failure rather than spend their free time on those tasks (Mee, 1997; Pope, 2001). That usually means teachers must spend as much creative energy designing fun, interesting, and satisfying homework as they do creating fun, interesting, and satisfying classroom activities (Good & Brophy, 2003). Most middle school teachers have little trouble getting students to complete homework that satisfies developmental needs and that gives students control over the tasks and schedule.

REFLECTIVE QUESTION

Do you believe homework "teaches responsibility"? In what way?

The Conflict of Homework and Developmental Needs of Early Adolescents

Middle school students make lots of choices about how to spend their free time. In making those choices they are biologically driven to satisfy their developmental needs—friendships and emotional needs *really* are more important to them, and rightly so (NMSA, 2001a; Scales, 1999). The intensity of the emotional and social changes early adolescents experience is overwhelming to many of them (Mee, 1997; Milgram, 1992). One of the ways they cope with puberty is through *down time*—time doing nothing that is mentally or physically taxing (Gibbs, 2003; Pope, 2001; Rosenfeld & Wise, 2000). During this seemingly unproductive time, early adolescents process and make sense of their lives and the changes they are going through. Sleep is also productive processing time and time for rejuvenating physically and mentally (Jensen, 2000). Excessive amounts of homework can rob early adolescents of these important uses of time (Pope & Simon, 2005; Vatterott, 2003).

> Whenever homework crowds out social experience, outdoor recreation, and creative activities, and whenever it usurps time that should be devoted to sleep, it is not meeting the basic needs of children and adolescents. (Wildman, 1968, in Kralovec & Buell, 2000), p. 49.

STUDENT'S VOICE

About Homework

"I wish teachers knew that people my age are busy and don't have a lot of time to complete homework. Their knowing this would help because we would have more free time."

Chad, seventh grade

As noted throughout this book, it's important to keep early adolescent developmental needs in the forefront of all decisions we make about these students. Homework is no exception—homework that meets a student's developmental needs is more likely to get done. The best homework assignments meet developmental needs and

1. are socially interactive with peers or adults.
2. allow students to feel competent.
3. allow students to express their feelings or opinions.
4. allow students to share information about themselves or their lives.
5. require hands-on learning or other physical activity.
6. require positive contact with parents.
7. allow for student choice.
8. are adaptable to individual needs (Vatterott, 2004).

Does Homework Unfairly Punish Some Students?

One of the biggest concerns of homework critics today is that homework exacerbates the social and economic differences between students (Vatterott, 2004). This sentiment is well supported in Kralovec and Buell's insightful book, *The End of Homework: How Homework Disrupts Families, Overburdens Children, and Limits Learning* (2000). The authors claim the practice of homework today "entrenches privilege," causing educational disadvantages for poor and minority children. Affluent students and students whose parents are home when the students return from school are more likely to complete homework. Students who live in homes with quiet places to study, extensive home libraries, and Internet access, and with supportive, well-educated parents are more likely to complete homework. Students without supportive parents (or with single parents overburdened trying to make ends meet), inadequate home environments for completing homework, or parents intellectually unable to help them are less likely to complete homework (Payne, 2001). When homework causes these students to fail, they are essentially being punished for their family and home environment (Kralovec & Buell, 2000; Vatterott, 2003).

Grading of Homework

Regardless of one's position on the value of homework, the biggest concern remains how teachers can evaluate homework without creating more student failure and without unfairly penalizing students for less than ideal parents or home environments (Vatterott, 2003). The purpose of the homework should dictate guidelines for grading (Vatterott, 2004).

Is the purpose of the homework assignment for new learning to take place at home? If so, isn't the teacher evaluating the students on how well they can learn at home? This can definitely represent an unfair advantage for some students because, in a sense, the teacher is basically grading students on their home support system.

Is the purpose of the homework assignment to encourage self-directed learning? Again, if a grade is given, what is the teacher grading—at-home work habits, responsibility?

Is the purpose of homework to check for understanding of today's classroom learning? If so, all the teacher really needs is feedback about the effectiveness of today's instruction. If this is the case, it may not be necessary to grade the work at all but simply to check for understanding.

Homework should not be causing students to fail (Vatterott, 2003). Below are grading and assessment possibilities to minimize student failure.

1. Take it cheap. Assign homework, but allow each assignment to be worth 10 or 20 points, so it takes several to equal one 100-point grade.
2. Use intermittent reinforcement. Homework is checked in class daily for learners to receive feedback, but students never know on which days homework will be collected.
3. Use homework as part of a contracted grade: You must complete all homework to get an A, some to get a B. If you complete no homework in the class, you cannot get higher than a C.
4. Give more homework than students are required to turn in. For instance, students will be graded on 10 out of 20 assignments or X number of days a month.
5. Offer an after-school homework club where students can go to do homework with teacher supervision and assistance.
6. Distribute weekly or monthly lists of homework assignments so students can plan their work around family schedules (Vatterott, 2004).

In conclusion, all homework does not need to be graded. All homework should receive some feedback, but it's not necessary that teachers provide that feedback (Marzano et al., 2001; Wormeli, 2004). Students can grade their own papers or each others' papers for feedback, with grades given but not recorded.

 # REFLECTIVE QUESTION

Suppose you are no longer allowed to grade homework (or to count the grade). How might this change your homework practices?

What to Grade, How to Grade

The goal of assessment is to provide students with feedback and to promote learning (Chappius & Stiggins, 2002; Guskey, 2003; Ring & Reetz, 2002). What type of assessment will most benefit learners? When we determine how we will assess learning, we have determined what will be learned and how it will be learned (Nitko, 2004; Vatterott, 1999). According to James McMillan, an education professor at Virginia Commonwealth University, students learn the real standard by how an assessment instrument is designed. If it's a multiple-choice test that requires mostly recall knowledge, then students conclude that the ability to remember facts is important (in Checkley, 1997). If the assessment requires analysis or application, students understand those skills are important.

When teachers design assessments, they define the curriculum. What is tested is a reflection of what is valued in learning (Earl, 2003; Wiggins & McTighe, 1998).

CLASSROOM ACTIVITY 10.1

Assessing Students' Understanding of a Polygon

Consider the pros and cons of the following testing formats.

1. A polygon is
a) an open figure
b) a closed figure with at least three lines
c) a space figure

2. Circle the example of a polygon.

a)   b)   c)

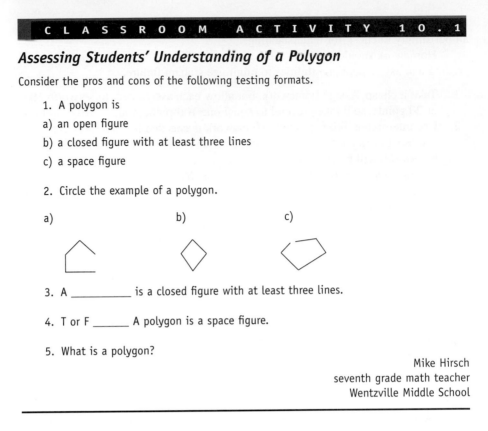

3. A _____ is a closed figure with at least three lines.

4. T or F _____ A polygon is a space figure.

5. What is a polygon?

Mike Hirsch
seventh grade math teacher
Wentzville Middle School

Teachers may choose to focus on three types of criteria for assessment. They may choose to grade *products*, such as essays, performances, projects, and traditional paper and pencil tests. Product evaluations reflect what students know or are able to do and are the most common type of criteria assessed. Teachers may also choose to evaluate *process*—effort, participation, work habits, group work skills, or showing one's work. Teachers may also evaluate *progress*—how far students have come in their learning over a period of time (Guskey, 1996; Munk & Bursuck, 2003; Ring & Reetz, 2002; Tomlinson, 2003).

When a teacher wants to determine evidence of learning, sometimes low-level factual recall is adequate. Usually, however, student-focused assessment goes beyond low-level learning and seeks to evaluate broad conceptual learning and higher order objectives (Anfara & Stacki, 2002; Vatterott, 1999). Teachers must use caution when making decisions about which type of assessment to use. Factual recall questions are amazingly easy to construct and score, while questions requiring students to show understanding are often more difficult to construct and score (Popham, 2000). Mike Hirsch presented a variety of test questions to a group of classroom teachers and asked them to reflect on the type of learning each question assessed. Those questions are shown in Classroom Activity 10.1.

→ WEIGHTING OF GRADES

Although some schools specify the weighting of grades (30% must be tests, 30% must be homework, etc.), in most schools teachers have a great deal of freedom in how they structure their total number of points for a quarter or semester. When teachers make decisions about how much certain projects or tests count in the student's overall average, they automatically set up a pattern that influences student failure (Kellough & Kellough, 1999; Stiggins, 2001). Each teacher must make his or her own decisions about how much failure he or she is comfortable with. For instance, we have already learned that incomplete homework can contribute to failing grades. To compensate for this problem, many teachers make homework only 10 percent to 15 percent of the student's total quarter grade.

Written tests are the great levelers. All students may do equally well on in-class assignments and projects, but written tests usually favor students who have better study habits and are better readers and writers (Levine, 2003a). To avoid failing too many students, many teachers limit written tests to 20 percent to 30 percent of a student's quarter average. This percentage would be less important, of course, if the teacher allowed students to retake tests or correct wrong answers for additional credit.

Teachers with more liberal policies for late work or work re-done obviously have fewer failing grades. Such policies are a personal choice for individual teachers—some teachers are averse to allowing students to turn in work even one day late, while others are more flexible (Nitko, 2004). Teachers must weigh such policies carefully, thinking about learning as opposed to sorting or ranking (or punishing vice) to determine what best serves students. Overly liberal policies for late work result in some chaos for the teacher and often don't provide enough structure for students. Overly strict policies often punish early adolescents for the disorganized, forgetful nature of their age group (Wormeli, 2004).

Organizing for Student Success

Early adolescents on the whole are not very organized. They have many things on their minds and are often distracted. They forget where they put things, lend things to others, and leave work at home. (One look at the lost and found box at any middle school will show this!) In addition, time is an abstract concept for the concrete brain, so deadlines are hard to keep track of and a project due two weeks from now seems like a year away. Middle school teachers can do several things to reduce failing grades simply by helping students stay more organized. Most middle schools require students to have assignment notebooks (like day keepers) where they are expected to keep track of homework and other assignments. But students need more help than that. Well-organized teachers find that students benefit from the same things adult students do—calendars showing activities for the month, or lists of all projects due for the semester. Teachers who give students a course syllabus at the beginning of the semester have fewer problems with late projects and failing grades. Nicole Schoenweis and Joda Fogerson give their students a list of all book reports

Semester Project Scoring Guide

Name_____ Hr_____

Second Semester Project Scoring Guide

Literature Circle

2 self evaluation	/5 pts
1 contract	/5 pts
8–10 role sheets	/100 pts
Group Participation	/100 pts
Book Project	/100 pts
Total Points	/310 pts

Career Brochure

Prewriting	/25 pts
Rough draft	/50 pts
Parameter 1	/25 pts
Parameter 2	/25 pts
Parameter 3	/25 pts
Parameter 4	/25 pts
Parameter 5	/25 pts
Total Points	/200 pts

Compare/Contrast

Prewriting	/30 pts
Rough draft	/10 pts
Revision	/20 pts
Peer conference	/15 pts
Editing	/15 pts
Final draft	/110 pts
Total Points	/200 pts

Biography

Research	/30 pts
Rough draft	/10 pts
Revision	/30 pts
Final draft	/130 pts
Total Draft	/200 pts

Janet VonHarz
eighth grade language arts teacher
Pattonville Heights Middle School

required for the year including a notation of the supplies needed. One project may require posterboard, another may require a shoebox, and students know when they will need each item. Janet VonHarz gives her students a project scoring guide for the semester that shows points assigned for each project (see Classroom Activity 10.2). This advance information helps students take responsibility for due dates and supplies. The lists can also be sent home for parent signature so parents are aware of projects and due dates.

Other organizational practices can also help students be successful:

1. *What you need today* sign—a sign on the classroom door each day reminds students to bring their book, notebook, calculator, or specific assignments
2. *Late work* folder—a colorful folder on the wall that provides a place for students to turn in late work, and that organizes work for the teacher
3. *Absent work* folder—a colorful folder on the wall that contains yesterday's assignment
4. In-class notebooks, folders, or trays that provide individual in-class storage for ongoing class projects (similar to kindergarten cubbies)

These organizational hints save considerable time dealing with individual student problems. Students can check the *What I need today* sign before coming into the room, usually having time to return to their lockers if necessary. *Late work* and *Absent work* folders not only visually remind students but they also result in less work left on the teacher's desk, and save the teacher from explaining missed work to more than one student. (They also prevent the dreaded question, "I didn't miss anything yesterday, did I?") In-class storage is especially helpful for ongoing group projects. As luck would have it, the group member who leaves with the group's assignment is always the student who's absent the next day, preventing the group from continuing their work. In-class storage prevents this problem.

A Fairer Test

Although performance assessments and student projects are the preferred method of student evaluation, most teachers also use paper and pencil tests to evaluate some types of learning. Many steps can be taken to maximize student success on paper and pencil tests and to prevent failure (Guskey, 2003). The first step is to give students adequate information about the test in advance. Tests should never be a surprise, and students should have guidance ahead of time as to what they will be expected to know and do on the test (Marshall, 2003; Robertson & Valentine, 2002). The easiest way to do this is to prepare a hint sheet outlining the main concepts to be covered and any specific details students will need to know (such as dates or formulas). Students should know what types of questions they will be answering (multiple choice, essay) and about how many questions there will be. Some teachers even organize their hint sheet by chapter, showing about how many questions will be asked from each chapter. Most teachers structure student activities that allow students to review or study for tests. Review activities could be any type of game, discussion, group study, or note organization that helps students prepare for the test. One example was shown in Chapter 7, Classroom Activity 7.1—Jason Holmes's review activity "24 hours before the test" asked students to reflect on what information they most needed to study. Questions that require considerable work (such as writing a lengthy essay, designing an experiment, or proving a theorem) can be given to students in advance, making a small portion of the test a take-home test. Tests that require higher level application of information as opposed to recall can be given as open-note or open-book. Open-notebook tests often rely heavily on essay questions that ask "how" or "why" and require students to organize and synthesize information.

Another strategy to maximize student success is to check student answers during the testing time and allow students to revise answers before turning tests in for final grading. This feedback allows students to rethink their original answers or redo problems. Pat Johnson has found this technique beneficial for her math students.

TEACHER'S VOICE

About the Value of Feedback during Tests

"Sometimes when they take tests, they make simple mistakes, so their score doesn't reflect what they really know. So I tell them, 'When you finish the test, you bring it up, I'll grade it and I'll mark the ones you got wrong. If time allows, you can go back, find the mistake and make the correction. You can do that as often as time allows; you can go back and forth.' The reason I do that is that it means more to me that learning is continuing, rather than me giving you a bad grade and you pitching it in the trash."

Pat Johnson, eighth grade math
Pattonville Heights Middle School

For maximum academic success, middle school students do better with shorter, more frequent exams as opposed to exams over four to six weeks of material. Many middle school teachers give weekly quizzes or biweekly exams. Obviously the more test grades a student has, the less critical each grade becomes and the greater is the possibility of maintaining a passing average.

How does a teacher know if he or she has created a good paper and pencil test? What is an acceptable level of student success? Obviously, if the majority of students fail the test, there are some problems (Guskey, 2003). Most teachers can neutralize a poor test simply by doing an item analysis. In item analysis, the teacher tallies how many students miss each question. For multiple-choice questions, they also tally how often each answer was chosen (Popham, 2003). By examining wrong answers, teachers discover misunderstandings, misconceptions, and poorly written questions (Guskey, 2003; Stiggins, 2001). If most of the students missed a question, does that mean it was a poor question or that the students just didn't learn that concept? Student feedback is especially helpful in determining the problem (Popham, 2003). Either way, it's usually fairer not to count that question. When teachers eliminate poor questions they usually find an acceptable level of success and fewer failing grades. Tests not only provide feedback about student learning, but also about teacher effectiveness (Guskey, 2003).

TEACHER'S VOICE

About Tests as Teacher Feedback

"Sometimes I don't do as good a job of teaching a unit as I thought and that comes out on the quizzes and on the tests. That's when I realize 'uh-oh, the kids didn't understand this—I've got to go back.' It doesn't really matter whether it's me or them—it's probably me. I go back."

Mike Hirsch, seventh grade math
Wentzville Middle School

Many teachers spend an entire class period going over a paper and pencil test. They find out which questions are poorly written and they learn what concepts their students still don't understand. The process of discussing the questions helps students feel better about their performance on the test. They understand why they missed certain questions, and valuable student learning occurs. To maximize the learning potential of tests and improve student success, some teachers allow students to correct their mistakes to raise their original test grade.

Teachers should not be afraid to negotiate with students about wrong answers and why students think they should get credit for an answer. It's usually easier to do this one-on-one after class or while other students are working on something else. Many teachers have found that giving a student two more points than they originally intended won't alter the student's quarter average much, but the points gained in the student's attitude toward the teacher and feelings of fairness are substantial.

Formative Feedback

Obviously most teachers today would not be allowed to stop grading students, and many would not be comfortable eliminating grades from their classrooms (Earl, 2003; Popham, 2000). However, grades can easily be deemphasized in an attempt to focus less on sorting and more on learning (Kohn, 1999; Stiggins, 2001). Teachers can begin by not grading everything students do. For instance, some teachers refrain from putting letter or number grades on individual assignments and instead provide only written feedback (Wormeli, 2004). The goal is to reinforce learning tasks without grading and to begin to move from grading to checking. Grading tends to place teachers in the role of judge, in the role of evaluating and describing, whereas checking tends to put teachers in the role of advocate, as one who diagnoses and prescribes (Guskey, 1994). This type of checking is called **formative feedback**—providing the student with information about the quality or correctness of his work without the permanent consequence of a grade (Manning & Bucher, 2001). Formative feedback provides information without judgment, the purpose being to allow students to continue to learn and improve (Chappuis & Stiggins, 2002; Marzano, 2003; Powers, Rafferty, & Eib, 2001).

Robert Canady once said that what was really ruining education was *ink*. His theory was that if teachers would stop recording grades in *ink (making the student's grade permanent)*, students would be able to continue to improve. That's really the spirit of moving from grading to checking—to allow grades to be changed, improvements to be made, and learning to continue (Chappuis & Stiggins, 2002; Marzano, 2003). For instance, typically when students fail a test, they receive an F and move on to the next unit of study. When students are allowed to do test corrections to improve the grade, they continue to learn.

Formative feedback, evaluation that is informative but not necessarily permanent, can be written comments or a non-numerical symbol (such as a checkmark, X, or 0) to indicate a relative level of quality (Earl, 2003; Nitko, 2004). Shannon Burger gives formative feedback to student notebooks with a symbol stamp; each time she checks the notebooks she uses a different symbol, such as a bear or a dog. A right side up symbol means a good job, a sideways symbol means an okay job, and an upside down symbol means the work is not adequate. Letter and number grades can also be used for formative feedback by putting them in quotation marks ("B") or parenthesis (B) to indicate what the grade *would be* if it were recorded.

The Mastery Option

Formative feedback implies that continuous improvement is desirable and that moment in time grading is minimized (Earl, 2003; Stiggins, 2001). Revising or correcting work allows the student to continue to learn (Guskey, 2003). But teachers need not feel obligated to offer that option on every assignment. Most teachers will find it necessary to use both types of grading, choosing which tasks require mastery. Keeping mastery in mind, some content will be deemed less important than other content (Munk & Bursuck, 2003).

William Spady, a leader in Outcome Based Education, once said, "Why do students get failing grades? Because we make them available." In the ultimate mastery classroom, there would be no failing grades. In some schools that endorse this system, students may receive five grades: A, B, C, NQY (not quality yet), and incomplete. Students are required to continue to work on NQY and incomplete grades until they earn an A, B, or C. Most teachers who use such a system of grading teach in schools that have adopted the model for the entire school. In most schools, it is possible for teachers to use NQY's and incompletes only until it is necessary to give quarter or semester letter grades. Even so, NQY's and incompletes often provide more descriptive information to students and parents than F's or zeros.

Many teachers keep mastery in mind by offering students the opportunity to correct or revise work (Guskey, 2003; Martinez & Martinez, 2003). Redos can allow a student to raise his or her grade on a test or activity. Usually the student has a limited amount of time to redo work (often a few weeks or until the end of the marking period).

Obviously, most teachers limit the number of redos students are allowed (Wormeli, 2004). Students must receive carefully scripted feedback describing where improvement is needed. Teachers must also make sure students understand that completing a redo offers no guarantees that their grade will be raised. Redos do not *entitle* the student to an improved grade. Effort alone is not sufficient—improvement is necessary. There are times when students redo something twice and it still has not met the standards. It's still "not quality yet." When their grade is not raised, they will say "but I worked so hard on it!" Teachers must resist the temptation to raise a student's grade for effort when the quality of the work has not improved.

STUDENT'S VOICE

About Redoing Work

"Our teacher lets you do things twice and then she takes your best score."

Tyrone, eighth grade

✦ DESIGNING PERFORMANCE-BASED ASSESSMENTS

Whenever possible, learning assessments should be performance based (Caskey, 2002; Martinez & Martinez, 2003; Mertens & Flowers, 2003). **Performance-based assessments** require students to show what they have learned in one of three ways: *producing knowledge or discourse, creating products or performances,* or *providing personal reflections* (Boyer, 1995; Stiggins, 2001). *Producing knowledge or discourse* might include compiling reports, engaging in a debate, or discussing what they have learned. Janet Von Harz had her language arts students demonstrate their writing skills by writing a biography. The assessment for this activity is shown in Classroom Activity 10.3. Mike Holdinghaus had his social studies students demonstrate their knowledge of the Reconstruction by keeping a journal as a person living during that time (see Classroom Activity 10.4).

Products or performances might include models or displays, or exhibitions or performances for younger groups of students (Boyer, 1995; Koetsch, D'Acquisto, Kurin, Juffer & Goldberg, 2002). Many of the teacher activities in Chapter 7 were products. Debbie Bruce's science students show their knowledge about the solar system with the two products shown in Classroom Activities 10.5 and 10.6.

Personal reflections about what has been learned are often shown in student journals, dictated on cassette tapes, or illustrated through artwork depicting learning. Ed Kastner asks his art students to reflect about their homework assignments (see Classroom Activity 10.7).

Designing Rubrics for Performance-Based Assessments

Requirements for performance assessments should be clear to students in advance, with grading rubrics or products of acceptable quality made available as samples

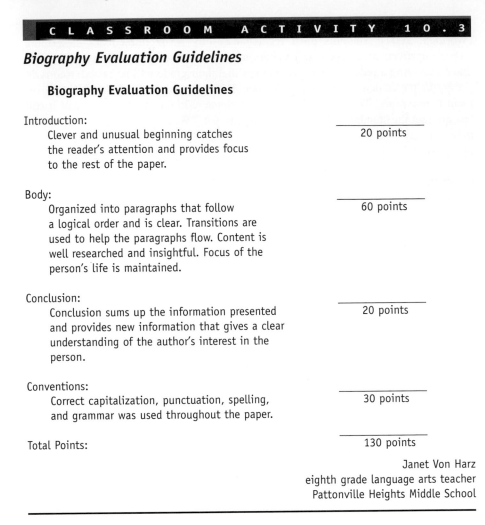

Biography Evaluation Guidelines

Biography Evaluation Guidelines

Biography Evaluation Guidelines

Introduction:
Clever and unusual beginning catches
the reader's attention and provides focus
to the rest of the paper.

20 points

Body:
Organized into paragraphs that follow
a logical order and is clear. Transitions are
used to help the paragraphs flow. Content is
well researched and insightful. Focus of the
person's life is maintained.

60 points

Conclusion:
Conclusion sums up the information presented
and provides new information that gives a clear
understanding of the author's interest in the
person.

20 points

Conventions:
Correct capitalization, punctuation, spelling,
and grammar was used throughout the paper.

30 points

Total Points:

130 points

Janet Von Harz
eighth grade language arts teacher
Pattonville Heights Middle School

(Marshall, 2003). Creating a rubric to assess student products requires teachers to think through what counts—what makes a quality product (Arter & McTighe, 2001; Popham, 2000; Stiggins, 2001).

> A **rubric** is a scoring tool that lists the criteria for a piece of work, or "what counts" (for example, purpose, organization, details, voice, and mechanics are often what count in a piece of writing); it also articulates gradations of quality for each criterion, from excellent to poor. (Goodrich, 1996, p. 14)

Rubrics are a preferred method of project evaluation for several reasons:

> they help define "quality". . . they help students become more thoughtful judges of the quality of their own and other work . . . [and] they reduce the amount of time teachers spend evaluating student work. (Goodrich, 1996, p. 14)

C L A S S R O O M   A C T I V I T Y   1 0 . 4

Rubric for Reconstruction Journal

Length	Goes above and beyond the length of assignment	Meets the required number of sentences	Has at least 60% of the required sentences	Does not have at least 60% of the sentences
Style	Style is very noticeable and pleasing or excellent	Nothing about style detracts: It's good	It's OK—no special style is evident	Sloppy or no evidence that style was a part of it
History	Many clear references show solid understanding	Has enough references— they fit well	Short on references but those are sensible	Either very few or no references or they don't make sense
Energy	Journal has spark, energy	Parts are juicy— sometimes works	Assignment completed but lacks interest	Author seems disinterested— not much fun to read
Surprising Quality	Whole package jumps up and says, "This is Great!"	Parts are very well done—it's enjoyable	No evidence of extra effort or attempt to make it great	Clear evidence of lack of quality—looks like it was done quickly or poorly and the author doesn't care about it.

Mike Holdinghaus
eighth grade social studies teacher
North Kirkwood Middle School

The best rubrics reflect learning and work habits and allow student feedback on the task. Ideally students should be involved in the design of rubrics (Chappuis & Stiggins, 2002; Fuhler, 2003). If that is not possible, they should at least have a chance to provide feedback on the rubric. Typically a rubric lists criteria for the product (down the left side of the page), with descriptions of levels of quality for each criterion (across the top of the page) (Arter & McTighe, 2001; Kellough & Kellough, 1999; Stiggins, 2001). Rubrics can be quite time consuming to create but the information they provide to students before the learning task results in better student products and more efficient use of student time.

Solar System Project

Due Date:

Solar System Grading Criteria

In addition to the project you choose from the previous page, your project must include all of the following:

	Pos.	score
1. 9 Planets and the current information in the chart on <u>page 68</u> of your text.	45	

This means you need to include:

> Avg. Distance from the Sun (millions of km)
>
> Diameter of the planet
>
> Period of revolution in Earth/Time days
>
> Period of rotation in days and hours
>
> Number of moons
>
> Temperature extremes in highs/lows
>
> Orbital Velocity (in km/sec)
>
> Atmosphere
>
> Main Characteristics

2. 2 major facts, in addition to the information on pg. 68, for each planet found throughout Chapter 2.   10

3. 3 paragraphs about 3 astronomers and their discoveries and/or inventions (1 paragraph for each astronomer) which contributed to space exploration.   15

4. Description of the motion of the planets and the importance of inertia and gravity to this motion (pg. 60)   10

5. All guidelines listed on the previous page are met.   50

6. Project is neatly presented.   50

7. This grade sheet is turned in.   30

8. Bibliography Page for all pictures and sources used.   <u>25</u>

TOTAL: 235

PERCENTAGE:

LETTER GRADE:

Debbie Bruce
seventh grade science teacher
Parkway Central Middle School

C L A S S R O O M   A C T I V I T Y   1 0 . 6

Travel to a Constellation Travel Brochure

Name _____
St. Number _____
DUE DATE _____

Travel to a Constellation

Vacation trips around the Universe have become a reality thanks to the invention of a light-speed spaceship early in the twenty-second century. However, tourists seem to be a little slow in taking advantage of the many sightseeing possibilities. As the newest member of a well-known advertising agency, you have been put in charge of the Celestial Travel Agency account. Your task is to design and produce a brilliant and creative constellation travel brochure or poster to attract the curious, adventure seeking space tourist.

CRITERIA

I.   Your brochure, or poster must include:

	POINTS
a. An illustration of the assigned constellation with a <u>title</u>, <u>labeled stars</u>, and a description of <u>where it can be seen in the night sky</u>.	10
b. A one paragraph <u>explanation of its mythology</u>.	5
c. <u>Identification of 2 stars</u> in the constellation, and include 3 other facts about the star, or the constellation.	10

II. You must also include the following:

a. <u>Title</u> in large print. Put your name and st. number on the bottom.	5
b. Printing of the information done neatly in dark ink and able to be read.	10
c. Good grammar, correct spelling, and use of proper vocabulary.	10

TOTAL   50

POINTS EARNED _____

%   _____

LETTER EARNED _____

Debbie Bruce
seventh grade science teacher
Parkway Central Middle School

Homework Reflection Guide

HOMEWORK REFLECTION GUIDE

Name _____ Date _____

Project Title: _____

<u>Instructions</u>: For each question, rate your homework assignment on a scale from 1 to 10 with 10 being the highest score.

COMPOSITION

Does your drawing . . .	Student	Teacher	Comments
. . . fill the whole page?			
. . . contain an interesting balance of positive and negative shapes?			
. . . contain details that dazzle the eye?			

CREATIVITY

Does your drawing . . .			
. . . solve the homework problem in a way that is clever or original?			
. . . communicate your idea/solution/design clearly?			
. . . demonstrate a lot of time and effort?			

TECHNIQUE

Does your drawing have clear contrast between the lightest and darkest values?			
Did you follow directions?			
Does your drawing look finished?			
Was your drawing cleanly presented?			
Total:			

0–39	40–44	45–49	50–54	55–59	60–64	65–69	70–74	75–79	80–84	85–89	90–94	95–100
F	D–	D	D+	C–	C	C+	B–	B	B+	A–	A	A+

Ed Kastner
art teacher
Wydown Middle School

The simplest rubrics may list criteria only without descriptions of levels of quality and can be created much more quickly than complex rubrics (Lemlech, 2002). Classroom Activities 10.3, 10.5, and 10.6 are examples of simple rubrics. Well-developed, complex rubrics are composed of criteria and descriptions of levels of quality (Arter & McTighe, 2001; Popham, 2000). Classroom Activities 10.4, 10.8, 10.9, and 10.10 are examples of complex rubrics.

Kathy Bhat's sixth grade music students kept a listening log of various types of music they were assigned to listen to. The rubric for the listening log project is shown in Classroom Activity 10.8.

Mike Holdinghaus wanted his students to create emotional connections with history. For his Gilded Arts project students selected a piece of art to show to the class that tells something about a particular period in history. The scoring rubric for that project is shown in Classroom Activity 10.9. Janet Peabody's rubrics for physical education (one is shown in Classroom Activity 10.10) were designed with help from a teacher committee at North Kirkwood Middle School.

The following hints are helpful when designing rubrics:

1. Start by defining four to six criteria—key knowledge, concepts, or skills the project should demonstrate (Goh, 2004). Make sure that the criteria reflect content and skill learning, not just cosmetic concerns like appearance, format, or organization.
2. The next step is to define three to five levels of quality (excellent, good, fair, poor) (Goh, 2004). Begin by visualizing what the *best* project would look like. Think quality, not quantity. Write a short description for each criterion explaining what the *best* project would look like.
3. Next, visualize what the *worst* project would look like. Write a short description for each criterion explaining what the *worst* project would look like.
4. Reread your descriptions of the best and worst projects. Revise your descriptions to eliminate overly general or judgmental terms (like "poorly illustrated") and replace them with more specific and constructive terms (like "shows little detail"). Good rubrics are about good language. Students can offer very helpful feedback during this stage.
5. Now write descriptions for one or two middle categories of quality. (Most teachers find it difficult to distinguish between more than four levels of quality.) Some teachers find it helpful to think of the middle two categories as "No, but" and "Yes, but" as they describe the level of quality for each criterion (Goodrich, 1996).
6. Remember that even with the clearest, most descriptive language, rubrics often require subjective judgment on the part of the teacher. Rubrics help make subjective evaluation a little easier.

Should rubrics receive number or letter grades? A purist would claim that assigning points or letter grades to levels of quality tarnishes the purpose of the rubric. In reality, many teachers assign points or letter grades to rubrics.

CLASSROOM ACTIVITY 10.8

Listening Log Scoring Rubric

Listening Log Scoring Rubric

		4	3	2	1
COVER		Cover is Titled and Designed	Cover is titled, but not designed	May or may not have a cover—not neatly done	No Cover
Table of Contents		All Themes listed/ Chronological order/neatly written or typed	All Themes listed/not in chronological order/neatly written or typed	Most themes listed/not neatly written	Missing
Entries		6th At least 20 entries 7th At least 40 entries	6th 15–19 entries 7th 30–39 entries	6th 10–14 entries 7th 20–29 entries	6th Less than 10 entries 7th Less than 20 entries
Index		Extra credit for 6th grade	Listed by title in alphabetical order—neatly done	Listed by composer in alphabetical order—neatly done	Listed by title or composer— not alphabetized but neatly done
Index		7th grade Listed by title in alphabetical order—neatly done	Listed by composer in alphabetical order—neatly done	Listed by title or composer— not alphabetized but neatly done	Missing or not neatly done

Kathy Bhat
music teacher
North Kirkwood Middle School

Rubric for Gilded Age Arts

	Great	Good	OK	Poor
Emotion	Audience feels the emotions that help the ideas be more meaningful	Audience feels emotional and emotion sometimes connects meaning	There is some emotion but it doesn't further meaning	Main emotion is either confusion or boredom
Deep Thinking	The art makes us ponder some great questions . . . feel more fully human	We understand the ideas the artist was trying to convey . . . feels meaningful	The ideas from social studies are included . . .	It's hard to see any ideas connected to the work
Connections	The art makes us think of other great stories or pieces of art . . . it's rich	We can see the historic connections	The art connects a number of ideas within itself	Connections to other ideas or history seem to be missing
Increasing curiosity and encouraging further inquiry	The art is exciting and makes most audiences want to know more, explore; it's awesome	The art makes many audience members ask questions, wonder	The art leads a few audience members to be curious	Doesn't lead to more curiosity

Mike Holdinghaus
eighth grade social studies teacher
North Kirkwood Middle School

✦ MAKING STUDENTS ACCOUNTABLE FOR GRADES

Grading that is student focused keeps students actively involved in their own assessment, gives students more control over assessment, and makes evaluation feel less punitive (Chappuis & Stiggins, 2002; Perkins, 2004). In addition, when students are more involved in their own assessment, that involvement becomes a learning experience itself (Kohn, 1994; Robertson & Valentine, 2002; Stevenson, 2002; Thompson, 2002).

Students should be involved in assessment in the following ways:

1. Students should have input into the design of rubrics for activities (Fuhler, 2003).
2. Students should participate in peer evaluation (Costa & Kallick, 2004).

Rubric for a Middle School Weight-Training Unit

Rubric for Middle School Weight Training Unit
Physical Education Class

Objectives:
The student will be able to:
demonstrate proper spotting technique for all lifts.
identify two resistance exercises for each major body part area.
demonstrate two resistance exercises for each major body part area.
identify the large muscles which make up each major body part area.

1	2	3	4
More practice needed	Moving in the right direction	Meeting the expectations	Goes beyond expectations

Spotting Technique:

(1)—Does not spot partner during lifting session.

(2)—Improper spotting technique on one or more lifts.

(3)—Proper spotting technique on all lifts.

(4)—Proper spotting technique as well as gives verbal support to partner.

Resistance Exercises Identified:

(1)—Does not identify a resistance exercise for a major body part area.

(2)—Identifies one resistance exercise for a body part area.

(3)—Identifies two resistance exercises for a body part area.

(4)—Identifies a resistance exercise for a body part which is not part of examples given in class.

Resistance Exercises Demonstrated:

(1)—With minimal resistance, does not perform a resistance exercise with proper technique.

(2)—With sub maximal resistance, does not perform a chosen resistance exercise with proper technique.

(3)—With sub maximal resistance, does perform a chosen resistance exercise with proper technique.

(4)—With sub maximal resistance, uses proper technique during difficult repetition, (eg. fatigue).

Large Muscles Identified:

(1)—Does not identify a large muscle from a major body part area.

(2)—Identifies a large muscle from a major body part area.

continued

(3)—Identifies all the large muscles of a major body part area.

(4)—Identifies #3 above of athletes in an action picture while they are performing a sporting movement.

Janet Peabody
physical education teacher
North Kirkwood Middle School

Students should be actively involved in their own assessment.

3. Students should participate in self-evaluation (Chappuis & Stiggins, 2002; Erwin, 2003; Fuhler, 2003).

4. Students should provide feedback to teachers on activities and evaluation (Chappuis & Stiggins, 2002).

5. Students should keep portfolios of their work (Perkins, 2004).

6. Students should be involved in individual goal setting (Chappuis & Stiggins, 2002; Marzano, 2003).

When students participate in peer or self-evaluation, they often use the same rubric the teacher does (Costa & Kallick, 2004). Other times students will provide feedback to teachers in a student comment section of the rubric. Sometimes teachers simply ask students to provide feedback about activities or evaluations by writing anonymous comments on blank paper.

TEACHER'S VOICE

About Student Self-Evaluation

"I'll usually have a conference with the student and say 'okay, did you put forth your best effort?' and if you get one of those sub-par projects, the kids are usually pretty honest with you."

Greg Bergner, seventh grade Unified Studies
Parkway Central Middle School

STUDENT'S VOICE

About Peer Feedback

"I like it when kids get to judge the presentations, not just the teacher."

Latrice, eighth grade

Portfolios

When properly designed, portfolios are another useful tool for evaluating student work (Gross, 2002; Popham, 2000). A **portfolio** is a purposeful collection of student work that is used to show evidence of student learning (Goh, 2004; Stiggins, 2001). Portfolios provide opportunities for students to plan and organize their work, self-evaluate using standards, document progress in learning, and communicate about learning (Marzano, 2000; Thompson, 2002). Portfolios are an important strategy because they

1. engage students in learning content.
2. help students learn reflection and self-evaluation skills.
3. document learning in areas that do not lend themselves to traditional assessments.
4. can be used to show that students have met academic standards.
5. are helpful in communicating student progress to parents (Danielson & Abrytyn, 1997; Robertson & Valentine, 2002; Stiggins, 2001).

Portfolios may be **working portfolios** used to store work in progress and to help teachers diagnose students' learning needs (Popham, 2000). **Best works portfolios** are used to demonstrate the highest level of competence the student has achieved (Nitko, 2004), and **assessment portfolios** are used to document how well the student has met specific outcomes or standards (Popham, 2000).

Assessment portfolios are especially important with the current emphasis on accountability. Assessment portfolios can provide documentation that students have met state standards, school district outcomes, or teacher objectives (Kellough & Kellough, 1999). They could be viewed by teachers, parents, school district personnel, or even by members of the state department of education. For example, if the state standard required students to be able to write in persuasive, narrative, and descriptive style, the student's portfolio would include student work samples of each type of writing (Danielson & Abrytyn, 1997).

Steps in the Portfolio Process

The use of portfolios for student assessment is a systematic and structured process. Teachers should plan for portfolio assessment through the following steps:

1. Determine which course objectives, outcomes, or academic standards will be evaluated in the portfolio.
2. Rewrite objectives, outcomes, or standards in language students understand and share that with students.
3. Give examples to students of possible types of student work that could show evidence of mastery of each objective, outcome, or standard.
4. Provide guidelines to students for the selection of items and the criteria for judging merit. (Ideally, students should be involved in determining these guidelines and criteria.)
5. Show students how to connect their work to the objective or standard.
6. Teach students how to reflect about and evaluate their work (Lemlech, 2002; Popham, 2000; Stevenson, 2002).

Students should

1. make decisions about which items of work to include in the portfolio.
2. decide what work shows evidence of specific types of learning.
3. decide how work can be organized to show progress in their learning.
4. reflect on their work, self-evaluate, and provide rationales for why specific work was chosen (Higgins & Heglie-King, 1997; Stevenson, 2002; Stiggins, 2001).

When teachers are evaluating student portfolios, the biggest concern is consistency. Most teachers develop rubrics for evaluation that clearly delineate what content and skills should be represented and what is an acceptable standard of quality. Students can then use the same rubric to self-evaluate their portfolio before giving it to the teacher for evaluation. Standards of quality must be clearly outlined to prevent products that show well but hide a shallow grasp of the content. Teachers must guard against weighing appearance and presentation more heavily than content or learning progress.

Student-Led Conferences

Student portfolios are most useful when students use them to plan, organize, and lead their own parent conferences. In student-led conferences, students take an

Sample Sixth Grade Student Growth Plan

I am very happy that I improved on two things that were recommended in my last growth plan, which were grammar and playing better during gym. Now I have three other things I am working on for the last term. These are to try to concentrate on my work, trying not to laugh so much in class, and improve my test marks in science and social studies tests.

I am satisfied that I made a good progress in grammar, but I am also happy that I improved in physical education class. I can finally bump and serve a volleyball. I may not be such a good basketball player, but I know how to control a ball.

This term I want to improve on every science and social studies test I take. I will also try harder not to laugh so much in class. I always have a bit of trouble doing science and social studies tests. I sometimes take too long thinking on one question. Laughing in class is the worst. Once I start laughing I cannot stop myself. I hope I can succeed in these things for next term.

How I am going to improve is not a problem. I have just got to work harder! When I know there is a science or social studies test coming up, I will start studying right away. I will also try to remember the important things Mr. Brown had said during class discussions. When I am doing my work, I will try to avoid the funny things my friends say. That is all I can think of to improve.

(from Sherwood Elementary School, Arnold, Missouri, in Vatterott, 1999)

active role in planning, implementing, conducting, and evaluating parent conferences (Lemlech, 2002). This process helps students to evaluate their own progress, identify their strengths and weaknesses, and set goals (Chappuis & Stiggins, 2002; Nitko, 2004; Stevenson, 2002). At Sherwood Elementary School in Arnold, Missouri, students conduct their own parent conferences. They select papers from their portfolios to present, review, and discuss with their parents. They lead their own conference based on their portfolios and their knowledge of their strengths and weaknesses. They also develop a Personal Growth Plan, which they discuss during the conference. The Personal Growth Plan (see Figure 10.1) is designed collaboratively by the student and the teacher to reflect competencies the student has not yet mastered and areas of personal growth most affecting academic performance (Costa & Kallick, 2004). Students come to the conference with *two stars and a wish*: two things they are proud of, and one thing they would like to improve (Vatterott, 1999).

Weekly Averaging/Frequent Grade Checks

One of the best preventive measures middle school teachers can take to diminish student failure is to closely monitor student grades and to frequently apprise students of their status (Wormeli, 2004). Most middle schools require teachers to send progress reports to parents and students around the middle of the marking period, about five to six weeks into the quarter, or six to seven weeks into the trimester. This limited amount of feedback is inadequate for most middle school students except the highest achievers. Middle school students are notorious for losing assignments, forgetting assignments, and leaving large projects until the last minute. Therefore, it is easy for their quarter or trimester average to change quickly. Many middle school teachers have discovered that they can reduce student failure substantially by making sure students are aware of their grades every week or two. The simplest method is to have students average their own grades every few weeks. Many teachers do weekly grade checks when they tell students about any work they are missing and how long they have to turn in that work. Teachers with computerized grading software can easily print out up-to-date progress reports. Classroom Activity 10.11 shows a typical computerized progress report.

C L A S S R O O M   A C T I V I T Y   1 0 . 1 1

Progress Report

#	Assignment	Misc.	Category	Score	Class Average	Points Possible
26	Vocab #10		Total Points	ex	47.4	90
27	Vocab #11		Total Points	90.0	63.8	90
28	Vocab #12		Total Points	89.0	68.0	90
29	Vocab unit test		Total Points	97.0	92.7	100
30	Lit Circle		Total Points	275.0	257.2	310
31	Career Brochure		Total Points	200.0	159.9	200
32	Compare/Contrast		Total Points	200.0	149.1	200
33	Biography		Total Points	ex	142.5	200
34	Grammar		Total Points	95.0	92.9	100
35	Grammar		Total Points	90.0	89.8	100
36	Grammar		Total Points	85.0	85.6	100
37	Grammar		Total Points	ex	92.5	100
38	Grammar		Total Points	ex		100
39	Grammar		Total Points	ex		100
40	vocab #13		Total Points	86.0	66.1	90
41	vocab #14		Total Points	59.0	63.9	90
42	vocab #15		Total Points	69.0	70.3	90
43	vocab unit test		Total Points	87.0	83.3	100
44	extra credit		Total Points		77.5	0
45	vocab #16		Total Points	90.0	73.8	0
46	vocab 17		Total Points	88.0	53.3	90
47	Brother Future		Total Points		17.8	25
48	vocab #18		Total Points	90.0	64.7	90

Key: ex=Excused   (blank)=incomplete

Janet Von Harz
eighth grade language arts
Pattonville Heights Middle School

TEACHER'S VOICE

About Frequent Progress Reports

"I send progress reports home probably every two weeks. After a major test or project the moment I have it graded and I have it entered into my computer, my next action is always to print out a progress report and to hand it to that individual student. It goes home as a homework assignment to be signed by the parent if the student wants easy homework points. It gives them an understanding of where their grade is at a given time."

Greg Bergner, seventh grade Unified Studies
Parkway Central Middle School

✦ COMMUNICATING WITH PARENTS ABOUT GRADES

Parents as well as students need frequent communication about grades (Guskey, 2001; Manning & Bucher, 2001). Weekly or biweekly progress reports can be sent home with students for parent signature. It is especially helpful if parents can receive quarter or semester outlines that show due dates for major projects or approximate dates of big exams. Most teachers find it helpful to send some communication home to parents early in the year that explains grading policies, anticipated homework schedules, and other information. This kind of early contact is the best way to encourage positive relationships with parents. Interactive homework, which requires parents to be involved with their children's work, helps parents learn what topics their children are studying. Shannon Burger communicates with parents through homework assignments that allow lots of personal choices for her students. Classroom Activity 10.12 shows her guidelines for ROC (Required Extra Credit). Her students can choose to satisfy this requirement in a variety of ways as you will see in this activity.

SUMMARY

Assessment of student learning can serve many purposes: providing students with feedback about their learning, providing teachers with feedback about their teaching, comparing learners, and communicating with parents (Guskey, 1996; Marzano, 2000; Stiggins, 2001). Traditional assessment practices such as letter and number grades, moment in time grading, averaging, and homework are not only inadequate to serve these functions but can actually interfere with student learning (Guskey, 2003; Kohn, 1999). Traditional practices alone are insufficient to meet all the needs of students, teachers, and parents (Earl, 2003; Patterson, 2003). The use of student-friendly practices such as descriptive feedback, summative grading, and perfor-

C L A S S R O O M   A C T I V I T Y   1 0 . 1 2

ROC (Required Outside Credit)

Guidelines for ROC

**Must have 3 per unit each worth 15 points on the notebook evaluation (Three = 45 pts.
. . . if these are not completed you will earn less than a 70%)
**Must relate to the content we are currently studying

OPTIONS:

1. News Articles
   cut out/glue in/write a half page summary, how it relates to class **and** your opinion

2. Political Cartoons
   cut out/glue in/write a half page summary, how it relates to class and your opinion about it.

3. Personal Response/Questions
   write a half page (or more) response to activities or assignments we are doing in class (positive or negative).

4. Parent/Relative Response
   have anyone 18 or older read and respond to any of the POP questions or just respond to your work in the notebook must be 1/2 a page

   THEY MUST SIGN IT!

5. Map/Graph Interpretation
   cut out/glue in/write a half page summary interpreting the graph or **distribution** map, map or graph needs to relate to current topic.

6. Powerful Picture
   find a powerful picture (from a CD Rom, book, magazine, or your own drawing) that relates to your right side notes/stick it in/write a half page (or more) explanation of what the picture is trying to show and your thoughts about it. If drawing your own pictures you must have at least five colors.

Shannon Burger
sixth grade Unified Studies
Parkway Central Middle School

mance assessments is necessary to promote academic success for all students (Chappuis & Stiggins, 2002).

KEY TERMS

assessment portfolio
best works portfolio

criterion-referenced assessment
formative feedback

homework   portfolio
norm-referenced assessment   rubrics
performance-based assessments   working portfolio

Application Activity

1. Read the questions in Classroom Activity 10.1. Which questions can students answer correctly and still not understand the concept of a polygon? Which questions require the highest level of understanding? Which combination of questions would you use to assess student understanding of the concept of a polygon?

2. Read the section of this chapter entitled *Weighting of grades*. Design a grading plan that specifies the percentage each type of learning task will count in the 10-week quarter grade. Select which tasks below that you will grade, adding other types of tasks that may be specific to your subject area.

Task	percentage of quarter grade
Tests	_____ %
Quizzes	_____ %
Homework	_____ %
In-class assignments	_____ %
Reports or projects	_____ %
Oral presentations	_____ %
Portfolios/notebooks	_____ %
Other_____	_____ %
Other_____	_____ %
TOTAL	___100%

3. This chapter showcased specific assessment strategies to promote academic success, reduce the number of failing grades, and make students accountable for grades. Check at least five strategies below that you will implement in your classroom.

    _____ give written feedback without using grades
    _____ count homework 10% or less of quarter grade
    _____ use open-book or open-note tests
    _____ allow points for test corrections
    _____ allow redo's on some assignments
    _____ use peer evaluation
    _____ use student self-evaluation
    _____ give rubrics in advance of projects
    _____ have students do individual goal setting
    _____ have students conduct student-led conferences
    _____ do frequent grade checks
    _____ communicate frequently with parents

CHAPTER 11

BECOMING A STUDENT-FOCUSED TEACHER

❖ **The Role of Beliefs and Attitudes in Successful Student-Focused Teaching**

❖ **Why Reflect on Our Beliefs?**

❖ **Reflecting on Our School Experiences**

❖ **Clarifying Our Beliefs about Teaching and Learning**

❖ **Reflecting on Our Beliefs about Learners and Learning**

❖ **Reflecting on Our Beliefs about Teaching**

    How Our Beliefs Influence Our Students

    Breaking the Vicious Circles of Negative Beliefs

❖ **Challenging Our Fears about Student-Focused Instruction**

    Fear 1: Fear of Change, of Trying Something New

    Fear 2: Upsetting the Status Quo

    Fear 3: Peer Pressure from Controlling Teachers

    Fear 4: Accountability for Standardized Test Scores

    Fear 5: The Time Crunch: I Don't Have Time to Teach This Way

    Fear 6: Out-of-Control Students

❖ **Implementing Student-Focused Instruction**

    Letting Go of Traditional Roles

    What It Takes—Practical Hints

    What It Takes Emotionally

↬ INTRODUCTION

Implementing student-focused instruction is not easy for most teachers. Beginning teachers are often fearful of any approach other than traditional methods such as direct instruction and seatwork. Even experienced teachers feel more comfortable with methods they have used for a long time (Jacobsen, Eggen, & Kauchak, 2003). There are obstacles to implementing student-focused instruction—but they are mostly within ourselves. On a personal level, our beliefs, experiences, and attitudes may act as barriers to successful implementation (Good & Brophy, 2003). This chapter will help you examine your personal experiences, beliefs, and attitudes and understand the connection between teacher beliefs and attitudes and successful student-focused teaching. **The purposes of this chapter are to help you**

- understand that positive beliefs and attitudes are an essential component of successful teaching.
- reflect on your personal beliefs about teaching, learning, and power relationships in the classroom.

- understand how your beliefs affect your behavior (and consequently student learning),
- confront your fears about implementing student-focused instruction in your classroom.
- incorporate courage, risk-taking, and reflectivity into decisions you make about teaching.

Essential Questions

After reading and completing the activities in this chapter, you should be able to answer the following questions:

1. How have your beliefs about teaching and learning been influenced by the school environments you have experienced?
2. How do you believe the teacher-student relationship affects teaching and learning? What experiences have helped to shape your opinion?
3. In what ways do you think your beliefs will affect your behavior in the classroom?
4. In what ways do you think your beliefs will affect student learning in your classroom?
5. What role do courage and risk-taking play in the implementation of student-focused instruction?
6. What do you think will be most difficult about implementing student-focused instruction in your classroom?

✦ THE ROLE OF BELIEFS AND ATTITUDES IN SUCCESSFUL STUDENT-FOCUSED TEACHING

This book has discussed many aspects of student-focused instruction, including the nature of the student, the classroom, the curriculum, and instructional strategies. The knowledge and skills acquired from this book are the tools that will enable the reader to become a successful student-focused teacher. Below are some of the tools necessary for successful student-focused teaching that were discussed in previous chapters:

- Knowledge of early adolescents and an acceptance of their special characteristics and needs (discussed in Chapters 2 and 3)
- An understanding of the implications of early adolescent needs and a rationale for why student-focused instruction is desirable (discussed in Chapters 1, 2, and 3)
- An appreciation of the importance of creating a nurturing classroom climate (discussed in Chapter 4)
- Strategies for engaging in backward planning (discussed in Chapter 6)
- Strategies for developing activity-based lessons (discussed in Chapter 7)
- A variety of student-focused and teacher-focused instructional strategies (discussed in Chapters 8 and 9)
- Strategies for student-friendly assessment (discussed in Chapter 10)

Ingredients for Successful Student-Focused Teaching at the Middle Level

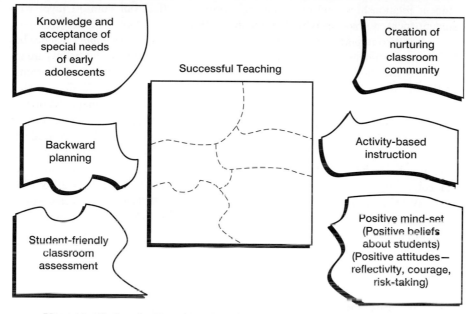

Yet with all these tools, two critical ingredients for teaching success are still lacking. In addition to specific knowledge and skills, successful student-focused teaching also requires specific attitudes (Anfara & Stacki, 2002; Marshall, 2003; Smith, 2003). These specific attitudes comprise a positive mind-set that includes positive beliefs about students' abilities and willingness to learn and the positive attitudes of reflectivity, courage, and risk taking (Alexander, 1995; Alpert, 2004; Rogers, 1969). This positive mind-set, together with specific knowledge and skills, forms the foundation for successful student-focused teaching at the middle level. Figure 11.1 shows these essential ingredients of successful student-focused teaching. The development of a positive mind-set is dependent on our ability to examine and reflect on our beliefs and attitudes (Good & Brophy, 2003; Marshall, 2003). The willingness to be reflective is a characteristic common to successful teachers at all levels, kindergarten through college. Reflectivity is not limited to reflecting about how well a lesson went or the effectiveness of a specific teaching strategy (Jacobsen et al., 2002). Successful teachers also reflect on their personal beliefs and attitudes and on how those beliefs and attitudes affect student learning (Earl, 2003).

✦ WHY REFLECT ON OUR BELIEFS?

Why reflect on our beliefs as teachers? Just as our religious faith or personal philosophy may influence our behavior in our daily lives, teacher beliefs influence our jobs as teachers (Good & Brophy, 2003; Marshall, 2003). It is important to be aware of how *consistent* our beliefs are with the philosophy of student-focused instruction. In Chapter 1 we discussed the philosophy behind student-focused instruction and listed a set of beliefs that underlie that philosophy. The more consistent our beliefs are with the essentials of student-focused instruction, the easier it will probably be to implement student-focused instruction. What we believe about teaching, learning, teacher-student relationships, and even human nature will affect our comfort level with student-focused practices (Good & Brophy, 2003).

It is also important to reflect on our beliefs because of the *impact* teacher beliefs have on students' academic success (Gallagher-Polite, 2001). Our beliefs are intertwined with how we teach, with the messages we give students about learning, and with the messages we give students about their capabilities (Marshall, 2003). Teacher beliefs influence teacher behavior in the classroom and teacher behavior influences student success (Cawelti, 2003). When teachers expect higher achievement, they are more likely to get it (Good & Brophy, 2003). The success of at-risk students is especially dependent on teacher beliefs (Barth, 1990; Vatterott, 1999). Teachers who are successful with at-risk students believe they are personally accountable for student success and are optimistic that academic success is possible (Hall & Hall, 2003; Wehlage, Rutter, Smith, Lesko & Fernandez, 1989). These beliefs cause these teachers to "go above and beyond the call of duty" and to be persistent in their efforts to help students. Middle school students seem to be especially sensitive to teacher beliefs, believing what we tell them about themselves (Scales, 1999; Vatterott, 1999). If our goal is to maximize student success, we would be negligent not to examine a factor that has been proven so influential in the success rate of middle school students (Good & Brophy, 2003).

Finally, it is important to examine the *source* of our beliefs to determine whether they are valid, or if they require rethinking in light of the latest information about learners and learning (Earl, 2003; Marshall, 2003). Recent research about teaching, learning, and psychology has provided many insights into factors that influence learning (Cawelti, 2003). The exciting field of brain-based research (neuroscience), which emerged in the 1980s, has now expanded into dozens of subdisciplines (Caine & Caine, 1991; Jensen, 2000; Sperenger, 1999). The impact of these fields of studies on education will be significant. Some well-established beliefs that educators hold about learning may be difficult to defend given the new knowledge that exists today.

⇥ REFLECTING ON OUR SCHOOL EXPERIENCES

Our beliefs about teaching and learning are derived from our experiences, the knowledge we have gained in our lives, people we have admired, and even the way we were raised as children. Our views are also colored by traditional educational practices. Some notions of traditional practice are so embedded in our concept of school that we are barely aware of them (Earl, 2003; Patterson, 2003). To us, these practices are "the way we've always done school" (Tomlinson, 1999). For example, we assume that children are grouped to be with others of about the same age, that students progress from one grade to the next in time intervals of one year, that all students of a similar age complete the same curriculum within the same amount of time, that classrooms have desks, that teachers use books and blackboards, and that reading is part of most schools. We also assume that homework is given, and that students receive one of five letter grades at regular intervals on a piece of paper we call a report card, which we assume reflects the student's level of ability and knowledge (Earl, 2003; Patterson, 2003).

In fact, we have "done school" the same way for so long (Pope, 2001) that many practices common today would be quite familiar to our parents and perhaps even our grandparents:

> Schools generally adopt a single textbook, give students a single test at the end of the chapter, and another at the end of designated marking periods. . . . Drill-and-practice worksheets are the chief educational technology, and teachers tell students things they must then tell back, a legacy of behaviorism rooted firmly in the 1930s. Teachers still largely "run" classes, and they are likely to work harder and more actively than students much of the time (Tomlinson, 1999, p. 22).

The practice of homework is a good example of how the way we've always done school affects teacher beliefs. The practice of giving homework is so embedded in our concept of school that it would never occur to some teachers to question the value of homework as an effective instructional strategy (Cooper, 1989; Kralovec & Buehl, 2000).

Our beliefs about teaching and learning have been constructed while looking through this prism of traditional practice (Earl, 2003). Each one of us has our own unique constructed meaning of school, based on our own experience (Brooks, 2004). The totality of our school experiences allows us to generalize about how classrooms are run, what routines and procedures are normal, what roles students and teachers play, and what learning tasks look like. Our experiences have also caused us to form strong opinions about each of these aspects of school (Earl, 2003).

For example, if we experienced a traditional school, we may conceptualize school as the place where the teacher talked and the students listened. If that was a positive experience for us, we may believe that is a good way to teach. If that was not a positive experience, we may believe that's not a good way to teach. Most teachers remember specific teachers from their school experience whom they emulate in some ways. Most teachers also remember teachers who so negatively affected them that they swore they'd never be like them!

Our beliefs, therefore, have been most strongly influenced by our own experiences as students, by how we *experienced* school as students (Brooks, 2004; Earl, 2003). For instance, many teachers who were successful students and enjoyed the routines of the traditional classroom fail to realize what the classroom was like for the unsuccessful students. Part of the process of reflecting on our beliefs involves thinking through *how* our classroom experiences have shaped our beliefs as teachers (Jacobsen et al., 2002).

Our experiences as a student were probably influenced by our learning style and strengths. If our learning style matched the teaching styles of our teachers, we probably did well in school. If not, school may have been difficult for us (Levine, 2003b). If we were talented in music and art, but success in those subjects was viewed as unimportant, we may not have felt "smart" (Armstrong, 1993; Gardner, 1999).

REFLECTIVE QUESTION

Reflect on your experiences as a K–12 student. What do you remember about classroom routines, procedures, and the roles of teachers and students?

It's easy to see how we are limited by our own learning style and the conditions under which we were successful learners. Teachers often teach the way *they* learned best, unaware that all students do not learn that way (Armstrong, 1993; Gardner, 1999). In a sense then, traditional practices are perpetuated when learners who were successful in traditional classrooms become teachers and teach the way they were taught. Teachers who did *not* learn well in traditional classrooms offer great insights to those of us who learned easily through traditional practices. Practicing teachers have the advantage of access to other teachers who have had a variety of experiences as students. That diversity can help broaden our perspective on what constitutes effective teaching, beyond what was effective for us as learners. By seeking out other teachers who have had different school experiences from our own, we can explore how those differences have shaped our beliefs as teachers (Jacobsen et al., 2003).

Individual differences in learning styles, multiple intelligences, temperament, and prior experience and their impact on learning should cause us to rethink our beliefs about the inherent capabilities of learners (Marshall, 2003). In addition, at the middle level, differences in the *timing* of intellectual development among individual students (when individual learners move from the concrete to the abstract stage of learning) explain many differences in students' performance levels (George, Lawrence, & Bushnell, 1998; Gross, 2003; Piaget, 1970). The mismatch of learning styles and traditional teaching has recently offered an explanation for many of the failures of students classified as at risk (Cawelti, 2003; Levine, 2003b; Vatterott, 1999). Research on learning styles and preferences and multiple intelligences (Dunn & Dunn, 1978; Gardner, 1999, discussed in Chapter 2) has shown us that many students simply don't learn by traditional lecture and seatwork methods, but learn quite well through hands-on or problem-based activities (Keefe & Jenkins, 2002; Manning & Bucher, 2001; Stevenson, 2002). How many adults today could have been more successful in school had their learning styles been accommodated?

REFLECTIVE QUESTION

Respond to this statement from a successful student: "I'm not any smarter than the other kids, I'm just good at going to school."

What did you learn in Chapter 2 about learning styles and other individual differences that challenges the perceptions of "smart" you had as a student?

✦ Clarifying Our Beliefs about Teaching and Learning

Given the traditional schooling many of us have been exposed to, it's not surprising that some of our beliefs about teaching and learning may reflect those traditional ways. Traditional beliefs are justified given the school systems we have experienced. Clarifying our beliefs is a necessary step to understanding how our beliefs influence our classrooms. Clarifying our beliefs is a necessary step to understanding how our beliefs influence our classrooms. It is important for us to reflect honestly and critically on our personal beliefs about human nature, about learners and learning, and about teaching. Only then can we discover how consistent our beliefs may be with the philosophy of student-focused instruction.

✦ Reflecting on Our Beliefs about Learners and Learning

In Chapter 1, among the beliefs that underlie student-focused instruction, two were "All students can be successful learners" and "The ability to learn is more influenced by personal factors than by innate ability" (NMSA, 2001c; Stevenson, 2002; Vatterott, 1999). Some teachers resist accepting these statements, pointing to their years of experience in a system in which so many students are unsuccessful learners.

After all, the *excellent* students seem to learn well with traditional methods whereas the *poor* students seem to have difficulty with the same traditional methods. Many teachers assume that the ability to learn or not learn is innate and that poor students cannot learn because they have not learned by traditional methods (Taylor, 2003). This reflects what Dweck (1992) called the **entity theory of intelligence.** It is the belief that intelligence is a fixed entity that a student either has or doesn't have. Statements like "she's always been good at math" or "he's just not bright" reflect the common belief that intelligence is fixed and unequally distributed. To compound the problem, the patterns of school failure in a traditional system look like the entity theory—the same students fail over and over again. We come to believe that certain children just don't have what it takes to be successful in school.

Unfortunately, this view becomes a self-fulfilling prophecy as children internalize their label (Cawelti, 2003; Good & Brophy, 2003; Marshall, 2003). The more they fail, the more they internalize the view that "they just can't do it; they're just not smart." Consequently, each learning situation represents a test of the child's abilities; if you do well, it proves that you are smart; if you do poorly, it proves that you are not (Dweck, 1992; Good & Brophy, 2003). After a while, with enough negative learning experiences, students believe they cannot learn and give up (Levine, 2003b).

REFLECTIVE QUESTION

Suppose the entity theory of intelligence is not true. Suppose that all students come to school with essentially the same intellectual potential. Other than the practice of sorting and ranking, what other factors might help to explain why some students fail in school?

Just as the entity theory of intelligence could explain school failure, the incremental theory of intelligence supports the idea that all students *can* be successful learners. The **incremental theory of intelligence** states that intelligence is built up incrementally through effort. "Smart is not something you are; smart is something you get" (Dweck, 1992, p. 31). In fact, recent brain-based research has shown that this is exactly what happens when learning takes place (Alpert, 2004; Cetron & Cetron, 2004; Marshall, 2003). The brain actually grows new connections with new experiences (Caine & Caine, 1991; Jensen, 1998). In fact, the ability to learn is neither pure nature (heredity, the entity theory) or pure nurture (environment, the incremental theory) but a combination of both:

> Genes are not templates for learning; they do, however, represent enhanced risk or opportunity. Thus, if a child is born with the genes of a genius, but is raised in a non-enriched environment, the chances of him/her actually becoming a genius are low. A child with average genes, on the other hand, raised in a supportive and intellectually stimulating environment may achieve greatness by virtue of his/her enriched environment. (Jensen, 2000, p. 30)

Experienced teachers may want to believe in the power of an enriched environment but still not believe that all students can be successful learners. They may point to the lack of motivation of at-risk students and claim that no matter what they do the students will not be able to perform. Research about at-risk students shows that laziness and lack of motivation (especially in middle school) are usually smoke screens or defense mechanisms used to avoid more failure (Taylor, 2003; Vatterott, 1999). "When young adolescents are unsure or afraid of where they're going, the safest bet is to go nowhere, the surest thing to do nothing" (Martino, 1993, p. 19).

✦ REFLECTING ON OUR BELIEFS ABOUT TEACHING

It is helpful to reflect on our beliefs about the nature of classroom teaching and about the role of power and control in the teaching process. How do we define the teaching role? In what context should learning take place?

REFLECTIVE QUESTION

Did you ever play school? What do you remember about the experience? How did you structure the game? What did the teacher do? What did the students do?

Again, our experiences in school helped define for us what school was and what teaching was. Our experiences with teacher-focused instruction lead many of us to believe that the teacher possessed total power over students and their learning. Many of us also came to believe the dubious myth of *controlling learning*—that teachers can *make* someone learn (Glasser, 1992; Pitton, 2002). Certainly many of us have been coerced into learning specific things in our lives, but how permanently or how well we learned could be in dispute. Teacher-focused instruction also made it easy to believe that the teacher (by virtue of his or her expertise) knew the *best* or *only* way to learn.

The coercive nature of schooling has conditioned teachers to believe that autocratic authority must be maintained or utter chaos will result (Good & Brophy, 2003). Strict obedience must be maintained regardless of the cost (Kohn, 1999). The general attitude of "don't trust kids, be afraid of what they might do if not controlled" is especially common at the middle school level. Teachers are led to believe there are only two options: control or chaos (Vatterott, 1999). A teacher whose class is out of control is viewed as a failure, an embarrassment. Popular movies about school feed beginning teachers' greatest fears, and so they "start tough and don't smile until Christmas."

The idea that only two options exist—control or chaos—is a false dichotomy (Kohn, 1999). First, absolute control in the classroom is a myth and controlling a classroom by force is an illusion, especially at the middle school level. Let's face it—there's really nothing stopping 23 students from simply getting up and leaving. Second, the idea that any loss of control equals chaos is an oversimplification (Kohn, 1999). Most classrooms operate somewhere between total control and total chaos, with even well-managed classrooms sometimes chaotic.

Why give students power? It's easier not to—the teacher maintains the *illusion* of control. What most middle school teachers have found, however, is that beneath that *illusion* of control is the reality that they are fighting the students on the smallest of issues (Dreikurs, Grunwald, & Pepper, 1982). Because of that, many middle school teachers have found that they actually have a more controlled group of students when they give students power (Glasser, 1986; Huffman & Levak, 2003).

At the middle school level, the more the teacher attempts to control students, the more rebellious they become. The attempt at absolute control at this level often results in tough power struggles (Vatterott, 1999). This scenario then feeds the paranoia that middle school students can't be trusted and, out of fear, middle school teachers become more strict and controlling and usually exacerbate the problem.

The problem with believing that students need tight control is that middle school students have a strong developmental need for power (Havinghurst, 1976; Henson, 2004; Vatterott, 1999). It's a necessary ingredient in their emerging independence (Manning, 1993). To develop their adult sense of self, they need to feel respected as adults and treated as adults (Kohn, 1999; Marshall, 2002). When they are tightly controlled they often engage in power struggles over the smallest things in an effort to show adults that they have power in their lives (Dreikurs et al., 1982). A system of tight control at the middle level, therefore, encourages students to rebel against it (Marshall, 2002). Middle level students, at a social and moral crossroad, spend much time reflecting on whether rules are fair or just (Milgram, 1992; Vatterott, 1999). Many of them agree with the idea that "people have a moral imperative to disobey stupid rules" and feel justified in doing so. Their learning can be significantly impaired by overly tight controls and conversely can be enhanced when they are allowed input into classroom procedures and learning tasks (DeVries & Zan, 2003; Marshall, 2002; Wolk, 2003).

TEACHER'S VOICE
About Teacher Control

"The way I look at it—would you rather swim upstream or downstream? So, if I'm picking everything for them, *telling* them what they're going to learn and *how* they're going to learn it, it's much more difficult for me *and* for them."

Mike Burgio, seventh grade science
Pattonville Heights Middle School

REFLECTIVE QUESTION

Think back to your middle school experiences. Can you remember a controlling teacher who had trouble with discipline? Did anything seem unrealistic about it? What do you remember about the students' attitudes?

Can you remember your favorite teacher at the middle school level? What do remember about control in that classroom?

Students believe what we tell them about themselves.

F I G U R E   1 1 . 2

Vicious Circle 1

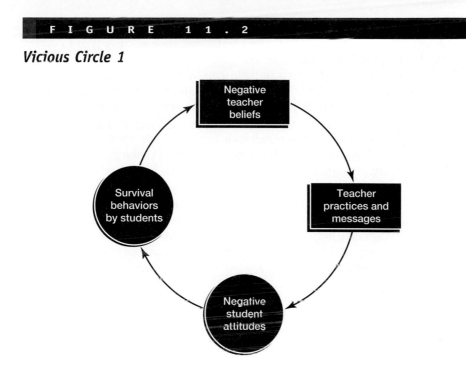

How Our Beliefs Influence Our Students

We know now that our beliefs have been influenced by our experiences as students in schools, and if we are teachers, by the environment we have taught in. Because the system has sorted and ranked students into excellent, average, and poor learners, and has labeled many students learning disabled, is it possible that our beliefs have been reinforced by student behavior that seems to validate those beliefs (Fashola, 2005)? Is it possible that children have developed those behaviors in order to survive in the traditional school? Have circumstances or teachers themselves unconsciously rewarded them for those behaviors (Good & Brophy, 2003)?

Teacher beliefs and student behaviors have a circular relationship (Good & Brophy, 2003). Negative teacher beliefs, such as the belief that students can't learn or can't be trusted, influence teacher practices, which influence how students view themselves as learners (Marzano, Marzano, & Pickering, 2003). Negative teacher beliefs result in student attitudes that are obstacles to learning (Hall & Hall, 2003). Middle school students, vulnerable in their identities, believe what we tell them about themselves as learners. If we tell them they can't learn or can't be trusted, for instance, they come to believe that they "just can't help it." They may develop learned helplessness—"If I wait long enough, someone will do it for me" (Good & Brophy, 2003). They may simply refuse to play at a game they can't win. These behaviors, precipitated and reinforced by teacher behaviors, only serve to reinforce our original beliefs and a vicious circle is complete, as shown in Figure 11.2.

Do We Believe Students Can Be Trusted?

For example, if we believe students can't be trusted, then we may tend to control tightly (Hoffman & Levak, 2003, Pitton, 2001). This may be indicated by such things as not allowing students out of their seats, not allowing students to use the restroom, or restricting students from leaving the room for any reason. Some teachers spend an excessive amount of time struggling to enforce rules about things like chewing gum and wearing hats, fearful that lack of compliance will wreak havoc on their classroom. Is it impossible for students to be responsible about such matters, or have they never been given the chance to be responsible (Vatterott, 1999)?

Perhaps students are untrustworthy in school because they've never been given any responsibility (Hoffman & Levak, 2003). Perhaps a system of excessive control bred into them a desire to cheat the rules anytime they got the chance. Middle school students will find a way to get their needs met (Glasser, 1992; Wormeli, 2003). If cheating is the only way to get their needs met or the only way to get the grades, students may decide it's a viable choice. If sneaking out of class is the only way to get a drink of water or use the restroom, some students may resort to that to get their needs met.

If we are reluctant to trust middle school students, perhaps we should reflect on what it is we can't trust them to do. If we never allow talking in our classroom, is it because we don't trust them to be talking about learning? Do we restrict movement because students can't be trusted to move responsibly? Some teachers subscribe to the axiom "give 'em an inch, they'll take a mile" to justify micromanaging. Is it really necessary that students be in their seats the millisecond the bell rings? Is the general vicinity of their seat good enough? If one student comes in five seconds late, does that mean that tomorrow he or she will be five minutes late or that all the students will be late?

REFLECTIVE QUESTION

Suppose you were asked to teach a college class. What are some typical rules for elementary or middle school classrooms that would seem silly to enforce in a college classroom?

As you reflect on rules that would seem inappropriate for adults, it may occur to you that many typical rules in middle schools really reflect a mistrust of students to behave responsibly (Vatterott, 1999). Many of those rules may also be more about control than about learning, as shown in Figure 11.3.

If we choose to trust students, they will often maintain that trust by acting responsibly (Daniels, 2005; Hoffman & Levak, 2003). If we believe students can be trusted, we are less suspicious of them. Consequently, we give them more responsibility and they become more trustworthy.

Do We Believe Students Want to Learn?

If we believe students don't want to learn, then we may attribute the problem to poor motivation and may attempt to coerce learning with grades or other punishments and

FIGURE 11.3

Vicious Cycle 2

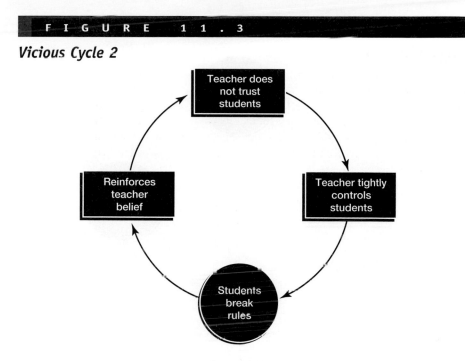

rewards (Good & Brophy, 2003). Often when children are not engaged in learning, we fail to examine the learning task we have given them to do (Cetron & Cetron, 2004; Tomlinson, 2003). Instead of asking how to get them to work, we should be asking, "What's the task?" (Kohn, 1999). Is the task at the proper level of challenge for students? Does the task have meaning for students? Often students find learning tasks boring, with little relevance to life (Intrator, 2004; Moulds, 2004; Taylor, 2003). If instruction is rote learning, memorization, worksheets, or long lectures, there may be *many* students who don't want to learn (Cetron & Cetron, 2004; Gross, 2004). (See Figure 11.4.) If all learning is of this type, it's easy to see how some students come to hate what they have experienced as learning. The same content, presented through hands-on activities, relevant to student life, which allows students to make choices, will engage many more learners (Caskey, 2002; Tomlinson, 2003).

REFLECTIVE QUESTION

In what ways can teachers make learning tasks relevant to students? How can we allow students choices in completing classroom assignments? How can teachers make learning more fun?

Students can be coerced into learning activities, but research shows us that the learner's perception of the value of the task influences how much learning actually takes place (Good & Brophy, 2003; Kohn, 1999; Tomlinson, 1999). Emotion, how a learner *feels* about the task, is a critical factor in attention, memory, and learning

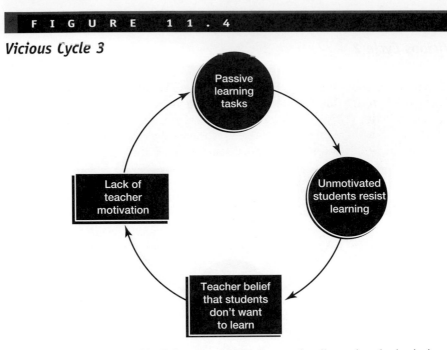

FIGURE 11.4

Vicious Cycle 3

(Pitton, 2001; Sousa, 1998; Sylwester, 1995). Research tells us that the brain is not very good at learning through passive instruction (Jensen, 2000; Sperenger, 1999) and that relevant, active tasks that include choices for students increase intrinsic motivation and engagement (Jensen, 1998; Tomlinson, 2003). If a teacher is having considerable trouble getting several students to participate, he or she should get input from the students about how to create a more interesting learning activity that can accomplish the same objectives (Cetron & Cetron, 2004). Learners who are *engaged* in learning tasks show higher achievement (Good & Brophy, 2003; Gross, 2002; Scales, 1999).

In addition to boring learning tasks, failing grades can also influence students to not want to learn (Guskey, 2004; Kohn, 1999; Nitko, 2004). When students have only one opportunity to complete a task, after which it is graded, they may have no opportunity to correct mistakes and little margin for error. This typical one-shot grading means students are being graded on how well they understand the *requirements* of the assignment as well as the actual content. This can result in poor grades (Guskey, 2004). Students who consistently receive poor grades with no opportunity to improve their work eventually lose the motivation to keep trying (Kohn, 1993; Nitko, 2004). In classrooms where students are allowed to and expected to redo failing work, teachers have fewer problems with students who don't want to work (Wormeli, 2004).

If we believe students *want* to learn, we are more likely to examine our choice of teaching methods or learning activities to see whether the fault lies there. We even expect less resistance and communicate more enthusiasm when we believe they *want* to learn. We are also more likely to persist with learners: to give additional help, look for alternative ways to explain a concept, give students another chance to give the correct answer. This persistence reinforces the learner's feelings of competence (Ladson-Billings, 2001).

Do We Believe All Students Can Learn?

If we believe some students can't learn, then we may tend to give up on some of them. It is precisely the act of the teacher giving up that enables the student to give up too (Cawelti, 2003; Marshall, 2003). Teachers are often unsure of just how much impact they can have on student success. When teachers try their best and still have students fail, it reinforces the belief that some students can't learn (Good & Brophy, 2003). But those teachers' efforts were most likely within the *traditional system* with *traditional methods*.

Failure is a painful experience for both student and teacher. The pain of student failure often leads to the problem Landfried (1989) called "educational enabling." In an effort to protect students from embarrassment, teachers sometimes allow students not to participate, not to learn. It's often easier and more energy efficient to concentrate efforts on those who appear ready to learn. Teachers often make excuses for students who don't learn and may even rescue them from the failure, pain, or frustration of not learning. Students then develop learned helplessness (Good & Brophy, 2003) and the rescue results in a drowning (Vatterott, 1999). As a result, kids internalize poor learner self-esteem because they believe they can't learn, when often they just can't learn the way we teach (Gardner, 1999; Levine, 2003b). (See Figure 11.5.)

Some children may come to us so damaged by home and environment they cannot succeed, but they are few. More likely, unsuccessful students have been unwittingly damaged by precisely the educational practices created to help them

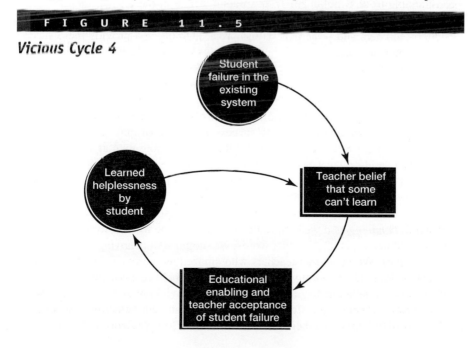

F I G U R E   1 1 . 5

Vicious Cycle 4

(Atkins & Ellsesser, 2003; Oakes, 1998). They are unsuccessful learners *in the traditional system*—not necessarily unsuccessful learners in all ways (Ladson-Billings, 2001; Levine, 2003b). Most of us have heard stories of brilliant people such as Isaac Newton, Winston Churchill, and Thomas Edison who did poorly in school. Until traditional practices and attitudes are changed, it is impossible to know how many students are truly incapable of academic success (Patterson, 2003; Vatterott, 1999). If we believe that all students can learn, we persist longer, try more approaches, refuse to let them off the hook, demand more, and hold higher standards for all (Cawelti, 2003; Ladson-Billings, 2001; Ring & Reetz, 2002).

REFLECTIVE QUESTION

Middle school students desperately want to succeed, even though their behaviors may indicate otherwise. Using what we learned in Chapter 2 about the emotional needs of middle school students, how might middle school student behavior deceive teachers into believing that students can't learn or don't want to learn?

Breaking the Vicious Circles of Negative Beliefs

We have seen the circular relationship that exists between negative teacher beliefs and negative student behavior, how negative beliefs contribute to teacher behaviors and how those behaviors encourage students to act in ways that reinforce our original beliefs. The same relationship exists between positive teacher beliefs and student behaviors (Good & Brophy, 2003). In Chapter 1, one of the positive beliefs identified that supports student-focused instruction was "the acting out of these [positive] beliefs by teachers and principals will improve learning and provide more success for more students than the traditional system" (Vatterott, 1999). The first step in breaking the vicious circles is to change our thinking from negative to positive and to *believe* that changing our attitudes will make a difference! Many factors affecting learning are beyond the teacher's control, so one might assume that the teacher's effect is minimal. Yet studies have shown that the classroom teacher is by far the most significant factor in inviting school success (Good & Brophy, 2003; Purkey & Stanley, 1991; Scales, 1999; Vatterott, 1999). Perhaps more than at any other stage of schooling, middle level teachers have tremendous power to influence learning. The impact of the teacher may, in fact, overwhelm a host of factors such as home and environment (Strahan, Smith, McElrath, & Toole, 2001; Vatterott, 1999).

What can teachers do if they would like to endorse more positive beliefs? The next step is *behaving* as if we believe that children *can* be trusted, *want* to learn, and *can* learn (Marshall, 2003). In other words, we should start *behaving* like people that *believe* behave. We've all met teachers who amazed us with their unrelenting positive beliefs. Even if we're not sure how strongly we believe those things, the *acting* out on those beliefs can begin to break down the vicious circles. Once positive teacher *behavior* begins to affect student attitudes, student behavior will improve, and the positive beliefs will begin to be reinforced (Good & Brophy, 2003).

FIGURE   11.6

Breaking the Vicious Circles

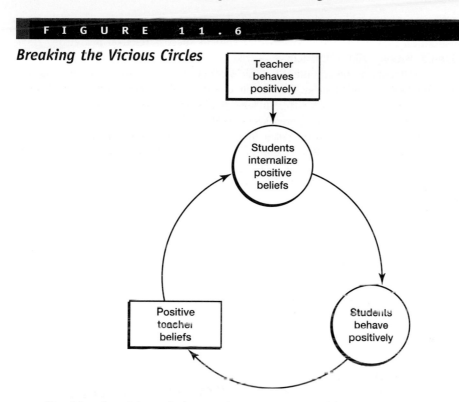

Breaking the vicious circles requires more than positive teacher expectations as shown in Figure 11.6. It requires **teacher efficacy**, the belief that teachers can impact learning and can instill in students a faith in their own abilities (Good & Brophy, 2003; Hall & Hall, 2003; Ladson-Billings, 2001; Marshall, 2003). Now that we are aware of the impact of teacher behavior, it should be easier to change some beliefs that may be counterproductive to the success of students. As teachers grow professionally, it's easy to affirm the changes we want to make. An often-used expression regarding changing behavior is "You did the best you knew to do at the time. When you know better, you do better." Knowledge about the impact of teacher beliefs should cause us to think about how we might do better.

→ CHALLENGING OUR FEARS
ABOUT STUDENT-FOCUSED INSTRUCTION

Having examined our beliefs about learners and about control in the classroom, and realizing the impact our behaviors have on learning, the rationale for student-focused instruction should seem reasonable. Student-focused instruction is compatible with what we know about how the brain learns and how in-depth learning is enhanced (Brooks, 2004; Caine & Caine, 1991; Jensen, 2000, 1998). The empowerment and choices that students enjoy in student-focused instruction provide intrinsic motivation for learning and satisfy the early adolescent's strong developmental needs for power and responsibility (Havinghurst, 1976; Henson, 2004; Vatterott,

1999). The personalization of student learning that occurs in student-focused instruction maximizes the possibility of student success (Cetron & Cetron, 2004; Good & Brophy, 2003; Hoffman & Levak, 2003).

Intellectually, the argument for student-focused instruction is compelling. But emotionally, student-focused instruction can be frightening to teachers (Pitton, 2001). After all, it's a very different way of teaching from what may be familiar. Student-focused instruction represents a significant departure from the traditional teacher-focused instruction to which many teachers are accustomed (Pitton, 2001; Smith, 2003; Vatterott, 1999). Therefore, successful implementation requires teachers to confront their fears about such an important decision. Some common fears about student-focused instruction shared by both preservice and experienced teachers are discussed next.

THE FAR SIDE®   BY GARY LARSON

High above the hushed crowd, Rex tried to remain focused. Still, he couldn't shake one nagging thought: He was an old dog and this was a new trick.

Fear 1: Fear of Change, of Trying Something New

Preservice teachers, anxious to be successful, may fear trying anything new and unfamiliar (Earl, 2003). (On the other hand, sometimes inexperienced teachers are idealistic enough to be adventurous.) Some experienced teachers are eager and ready for a change; others may fear failure and dread the awkwardness sometimes associated with new techniques. Dispelling the fear of change requires an open mind (Earl, 2003), a desire for change that is stronger than the fear, and a willingness to experiment with the dynamic of student-focused instruction even though it may not be fully understood.

Fear 2: Upsetting the Status Quo

The second fear is often hidden in the fear of change—a fear of upsetting the rank order in society, the way things have always been. After all, if we do something radical, what if it causes radical change? If suddenly, all students were successful learners, would the public believe it was a hoax? Would parents of the formerly superior students revolt, fearing that these students' advantage would be lost? If it were possible for everyone to be a successful learner, what would happen to the traditional power hierarchy in this country? Most great social revolutions have generated these same fears. Dispelling these fears requires teachers to focus on the realization that change happens one day at a time (Earl, 2003). Our impact will be one child at a time, one classroom at a time. Our conscience should tell us whether what we're doing is consistent with our long-range goals for children. As teachers, we must remember that *we* control the pace of change in our classroom. If we feel change is happening too fast, with too much resistance, or that we're upsetting the social order, as we know it, we can always scale down, slow down. As classroom teachers, we decide the scope and the speed of the changes we want to make in our classrooms.

Fear 3: Peer Pressure from Controlling Teachers

Student-focused instruction requires teachers to share power with students (DeVries & Zan, 2003; Hoffman & Levak, 2003; Keefe & Jenkins, 2002). Other teachers in your building who believe in tight teacher control may be fearful of student revolution. They may fear that if students are given power in *your* classroom, *their* control may be compromised or they may look bad. They may discourage you from implementing student-focused instruction. New or fairly inexperienced teachers are the most vulnerable to this type of well-intentioned peer pressure.

You don't have to be a new teacher to be confronted with teacher peer pressure. Resistance to change is a universal phenomenon and is fairly common in schools (Kohn, 1999; Patterson, 2003). If you're really concerned about how other teachers around you will react to your ideas, start small and keep quiet. Wait until you've established a practice and seen it work for a while. Find a few other teachers or a principal you think will be supportive and be selective about what you share. Stay positive—what you're doing is important. Remember, many great innovators experienced such peer pressure. If necessary, avoid the teacher's lounge and specific people who exert negative pressure.

Fear 4: Accountability for Standardized Test Scores

In many schools, fear of poor standardized test scores paralyzes teachers from making any change. The anxiety scares them into controlling learning more tightly and not trying anything new (Kohn, 2000; Lounsbury & Vars, 2003; Scherer, 2004a). Common teacher concerns related to accountability are these:

"Will I ruin what success I'm already seeing?"

"Do I dare try anything different?"

"What if *more* students fail?"

Worried that poor test results may endanger their jobs, teachers are tempted to control the curriculum tightly and limit instruction to teaching the test (Lounsbury & Vars, 2003; Scherer, 2004a). Responsibility to look good in test results creates anxiety, inhibiting creativity and risk taking (Kohn, 2000). This is a valid fear, given the amount of pressure schools are under to perform well (Eisner, 2004; Meier, 2002). The traditional ways feel safe and secure but often produce less than hoped for results. However, much of the concern about implementing student-focused instruction because of its possible effect on test scores is unfounded.

First, some teachers persist in the belief that traditional teaching methods produce higher test scores. That relationship has never been proven (Kohn, 2002). In reality, the latest research shows that traditional teacher-focused methods may be useful for low-level learning, but that they are relatively ineffective in promoting in-depth learning (Brooks & Brooks, 1999; Jensen, 2000; Neill, 2003). If the standardized tests are measuring higher level thinking skills, student-focused instruction is infinitely more appropriate than teacher-focused instruction (Cetron & Cetron, 2004; Keefe & Jenkins, 2002; Vatterott, 1999). If the standardized tests aren't measuring high-level skills but factual knowledge, student-focused instruction still offers advantages. If "the test rules" and it's heavily weighted with factual knowledge, student-focused instruction still represents a more meaningful way for students to learn—we can still consolidate factual content into meaningful activities (Pate, 2001; Vatterott, 1999).

Even rote memorization benefits from student-focused instruction (Jensen, 2000). Implementing student-focused instruction doesn't mean there will never be an occasion when students learn basic definitions or vocabulary. If necessary, teachers can still pull out some low-level facts and drill students through Jeopardy or other games. Factual knowledge can be reinforced through student-focused tasks. Having students write advertisements for the job of senator or using vocabulary words in an original story are much preferable to having students memorize job qualifications or definitions (Vatterott, 1999).

Teaching to the test is *not* a linear relationship. Direct *pouring in* of content does not necessarily result in students being able to *pour it out* on standardized tests (O'Steen, Cuper, Spires, Beal & Pope, 2002). When content and skills are taught in a meaningful, relevant context, students retain more information and are more likely to be able to use it on a standardized test (Kohn, 2000).

Fear 5: The Time Crunch: I Don't Have Time to Teach This Way

Accountability anxiety leads to concerns about time. Teachers feel pressured to cover an extensive curriculum and teacher-focused methods seem to be efficient in terms of time (Manning & Bucher, 2001). But covering is not learning (Brooks, 2004; Danielson, 2002; Patterson, 2003). In fact, worrying about coverage often causes us not to teach *anything* well. Teaching today requires prioritization—we can't possibly teach everything we want to (Marzano, 2003; McTighe, Seif, & Wiggins, 2004). The concept of coverage needs to be abandoned in favor of mastery of essential concepts and skills (Vatterott, 1999).

Concerns about time are typically related to the fragmented or linear way in which many teachers organize curriculum (Cetron & Cetron, 2004; Danielson, 2002). Instead of being organized in a linear fashion, the curriculum must be reorganized in clusters to consolidate content and skills (McTighe & Thomas, 2003). As discussed in Chapter 6, if content is taught as isolated facts, concepts, or skills, there will never be enough time. Student activities must be created that are complex and multitasked so students are learning several things at one time (Perkins-Gough, 2004; Vatterott, 1999). Student-focused activities will enable students to learn content in coherent packages and still utilize information as needed on standardized tests (Kohn, 2000). The initial reorganization of curriculum that is helpful in implementing student-focused instruction may be time consuming (Brooks, 2004). It is, however, an *investment* of time that reaps the benefits of more engaged students and more in-depth learning (Alexander, 1995; Keefe & Jenkins, 2002; Vatterott, 1999).

Fear 6: Out-of-Control Students

For both beginning and experienced teachers, the fear of out-of-control students is probably one of their worst nightmares. Student-focused instruction does not encourage out-of-control classrooms (Vatterott, 1999). Allowing students input, choices, and ownership in no way negates the normal structure and limits necessary in any classroom (Hoffman & Levak, 2003; Mendes, 2003). With student-focused instruction, the classroom still has rules, but they are made with student input. Like any other classroom, acceptable and unacceptable behaviors are still defined, and when problems arise, students and teachers work together to solve them (DeVries & Zan, 2003; Patterson, 2003).

Teachers may also fear that students will misunderstand their own empowerment and will become *crazed* with power, demanding to be in control of everything (Kohn, 1993). It is true that many students at this age will test limits, but they can be shown the boundaries fairly easily. Many teachers fear that once students are given some power and control, the privilege can never be revoked. The classroom does not become a true democracy—if giving students power doesn't work, the teacher can always take it back (Dreikurs et al., 1982; Mendes, 2003). If that happens, it doesn't necessarily mean that students will be resentful. Having had the chance, students are more likely to be grateful and anxious to show how responsible they can be. The knowledge that the classroom could always revert to being run in a more traditional fashion is a strong motivator for students to act responsibly with the powers they have been given. Teachers always maintain the right to be a benevolent dictator (Dreikurs et al., 2002; Marzano & Marzano, 2003).

Teacher's Voice

About the Fear of Out-of-Control Students

"If you set up the structures, train them in the process and why and how they'll benefit, turning them loose to work independently is not a problem."

Ed Kastner, Integrated Arts
Wydown Middle School

✦ Implementing Student-Focused Instruction

It takes courage to challenge our fears (Earl, 2003). It also takes courage to reflect on how suited our personality may be to implementing student-focused instruction. Just as our learning style influences how we teach, our personality traits influence how easy or difficult it is to let go of power in the classroom. Certain personality traits, such as flexibility, will be positive for implementing student-focused instruction. Other traits, such as perfectionism, may be impediments. For example, teachers who are uncomfortable not being totally in control or who have little tolerance for disorder in the classroom may have more difficulty with student-focused instruction than teachers who are comfortable with disorder and with relinquishing some control.

Letting Go of Traditional Roles

Many teachers enjoy teacher-focused instruction because it feels good. In teacher-directed activity, teachers feel in power (Pitton, 2001; Vatterott, 1999). It feels good to command the attention of a group and to direct the activity of 25 other people. It's very satisfying for teachers to believe that they are the ones making things happen in the classroom. Personality traits compatible with teacher-focused instruction include enjoying being in control, enjoying being the center of attention, and sometimes being a perfectionist. Perfectionism can be a wonderful trait, resulting in high standards. It can also be an impediment if it means an intolerance for mistakes or disorder, or the belief that there's only one right way to do something.

Most teachers experience a little disequilibrium when they first begin student-focused instruction. They are sometimes unsure of what their new role is. It's hard to not be the boss (Pitton, 2001). They are less the *sage on the stage* and more the *guide on the side*. They may feel somehow less important. Positive personality traits for these shifting roles include enjoying *watching* students learn, enjoying *interact-*

The student-focused teacher is not always the center of attention.

ing with students, and enjoying *helping* people as much as *teaching* them. When making the shift to more student-centered activities, teachers may find it helpful to think beyond the ego satisfactions of teacher-focused instruction to the long-term benefits students gain from student-focused instruction (Pitton, 2001). The rewards of student-focused instruction come from its consistency with the long-range goals of student responsibility and independence.

Teachers with a strong affinity for student-focused instruction accept the limits of their power. They realize they may be powerless to truly *make* students learn but they can create conditions in the classroom that will *entice* students into learning (Scherer, 2004a). They are comfortable not being totally in charge and allowing students to have some autonomy and to make some decisions. They can handle activities in which the outcome is uncertain.

STUDENT'S VOICE

About Student-Focused Learning

"I really like the classroom discussions. The teacher doesn't really get involved so it's pretty much kid to kid and there's arguments about who's right and who's wrong but it clears everything up. Everyone's opinion is used."

Sakura, eighth grade

What It Takes—Practical Hints

On the practical side, student-focused teachers may want to heed the following hints:

- Start small—most teachers who have made this transition did it gradually, over a two- or three-year period. They may have started with a few activities, involving students in a few decisions. They then continue to add student-focused activities to their routines.
- Learn to live with imperfection. Implementing student-focused instruction can be slow, messy, and noisy (Tomlinson, 2003).
- Respect the worth of students' existing knowledge and experience. Get feedback from students. Use the students to help troubleshoot and to improve procedures or activities (Vatterott, 1999).
- Expect resistance from some students. Respect their right to be apprehensive of new methods. Students who have been successful learners with traditional methods may not be eager to risk new methods. Support the fact that change is hard for them too.

What It Takes Emotionally

Emotionally, the beliefs of student-focused instruction require us to take a *leap of faith* that certain practices will result in more academic success and more student responsibility. That leap of faith is a risk-taking behavior, based on our faith in human nature and in ourselves (Earl, 2003). It requires us to trust our gut, not the peer pressure we may feel from other teachers. Taking the leap of faith requires us to trust in the potential of learners to develop and grow, and to be responsible when given the chance (Hall & Hall, 2003; Pitton, 2001). Emotionally, teachers must believe in their ability to impact student success (Earl, 2003). They must believe not only in the value of positive teacher expectations but also in their own *efficacy*, the confidence that they can create success (Good & Brophy, 2003; Hall & Hall, 2003; Ladson-Billings, 2001; Marshall, 2003).

TEACHERS' VOICES

About Implementing Student-Focused Instruction

"You can't be afraid to take a chance; that's the only way you're gonna grow and they're gonna grow."

Mike Burgio, seventh grade science
Pattonville Heights Middle School

"You have to create what works for you. You can take it slowly; you can do it one project at a time."

Kathy Bhat, seventh grade general music
North Kirkwood Middle School

"Sometimes they're so enthusiastic, it makes you crazy! But when they create, it's more important to them."

Kathy Bhat, seventh grade general music
North Kirkwood Middle School

"It took me a while to let the class be noisy"

Gloria Sadler, eighth grade social studies
Wydown Middle School

"How do I get ideas? I ask the kids, 'What can we do with this?' and sometimes they think of a lot of things that I don't."

Stephanie Walton, seventh grade math
Pattonville Heights Middle School

SUMMARY

Some teachers must overcome many personal obstacles before they are ready to use student-focused methods in their classroom (Marshall, 2003; Pitton, 2001). Teachers must understand how pervasively teacher beliefs impact student learning (Cawelti, 2003; Gallagher-Polite, 2001). They must rethink issues of power and control in the classroom and the dynamic interaction of teacher practices and student attitudes (Hoffman & Levak, 2003). Teachers must reflect on their own beliefs about learners and accept the limitations that their own experiences as students may bring to their beliefs (Gallagher-Polite, 2001). They must believe in the students' desire and ability to learn, have the courage to take risks and experiment, and take the time to reflect thoughtfully about their teaching (Hall & Hall, 2003; Marshall, 2003).

Becoming a successful student-focused teacher is a long-term process—it takes time to perfect teaching skill. The energy, enthusiasm, and diversity that make up a middle school add to the challenge and the enjoyment of developing as a teacher. When teachers choose to take the leap of faith necessary to implement student-focused instruction, they grow professionally and students benefit.

 ## REFLECTIVE QUESTION

Do you think it is possible to change your beliefs? Has the chapter caused you to rethink any of your beliefs? Why or why not?

KEY TERMS

entity theory of intelligence   teacher efficacy
incremental theory of intelligence

APPLICATION ACTIVITY—YOUR DEFINITION OF "SMART"

1. Review the information in chapter 2 about learning styles and multiple intelligences. How would you describe your learning style and intellectual strengths? How do you think these attributes have impacted your success or difficulty as a student? How did these attributes influence your definition of "smart" when you were growing up?

2. For each sentence below write *agree* if you believe it describes you or *disagree* if you believe it does not describe you. Which of these personality traits do you predict will be helpful in implementing student-focused instruction? Which personality traits may make it hard for you to implement student-focused instruction?

   _____ I like being in charge of things
   _____ I like being the center attention
   _____ I enjoy taking risks
   _____ I enjoy speaking in front of a group
   _____ It bothers me when things are out of place
   _____ I set very high standards for my own work
   _____ It is important to me to be perfect
   _____ I enjoy helping students one-on-one
   _____ I enjoy listening to and interacting with students
   _____ It is important to me that my students adopt my beliefs about things

3. For each belief about children shown below write *agree* if you agree with the belief or *disagree* if you disagree with the belief. Which of these beliefs do you predict will be positive influences in the implementation of student-focused instruction? Which beliefs do you predict will make it more difficult to implement?

   _____ Most children can be trusted to do the right thing
   _____ Most children obey the rules
   _____ Most children enjoy a challenging task
   _____ Most children would help another person if they saw they needed help
   _____ Most children are capable of learning most of the curriculum
   _____ If I don't explain things to children first, they will be lost
   _____ Most learning can be fun
   _____ If I allow children to direct their own activity, they will learn less than if I am in charge
   _____ Most students learn better working on their own than in a group
   _____ It is beneficial for learners to have choices
   _____ Student input about learning is valuable and has worth
   _____ Learning is a naturally pleasant experience

Glossary

Ability grouping   the practice of grouping students into high, average, and low ability tracks for academic benefit.

Academic curriculum   courses in math, science, language arts, reading, social studies, and learning skills typically taught by a team of teachers.

Advisory program   nonacademic program incorporated in the daily schedule that attempts to meet student affective needs and provide for one-on-one guidance and monitoring.

Affective curriculum (school climate)   what the student experiences emotionally and socially while at school but *outside* of the classroom.

Affective objectives   objectives that refer to the development of attitudes or values about the content.

Agenda   a personalized list of tasks that a teacher compiles for a specific student.

Alternating-day block schedule or **eight-block schedule**   the organization of classes into large blocks of time, typically 90 minutes or more, with fewer classes each day.

Assessment portfolio   student portfolio used to document how well the student has met specific outcomes or standards.

Assessment   method used to determine the extent to which learning goals are achieved.

Attention deficit disorder (ADD)   a syndrome of behaviors similar to ADHD *without hyperactivity* that interfere with classroom learning.

Attention deficit hyperactivity disorder (ADHD) a syndrome of behaviors such as inattention, hyperactivity, and impulsivity that interfere with classroom learning.

Backward design   curriculum design in which results of learning determine assessments that direct the selection of instructional methods.

Best works portfolio   portfolio used to demonstrate the highest level of competence the student has achieved.

Cocurriculum   extracurricular clubs, sports and activities offered to students through the school.

Cognitive objectives   objectives that refer to the development of intellectual knowledge or skills.

Concept maps   visual representations of concepts with connections that show relationships.

Constructivism   the belief that learning occurs as the child constructs meaning by connecting new concepts to existing structures of knowledge.

Cooperative learning   highly structured group learning with individual as well as group accountability, with students organized in mixed ability groups.

Criterion-referenced assessment   assessment that judges learners individually against the same criteria for learning.

Culminating activity   a synthesis task that occurs at the end of a unit that requires students to consolidate their learning.

Curriculum map   a broad plan for the year that shows what concepts will be taught and in what order.

Curriculum   content that a student should come to know, understand, and be able to do as a result of learning.

Differentiated instruction   instruction that is adapted in content, process, or product to meet the needs of a variety of learners.

Direct instruction   a teacher-controlled method in which the teacher presents information or demonstrates a skill.

Empowerment   a process through which people and/or communities increase their control or mastery of their own lives and the decisions that affect their lives (Kreisberg, 1992).

Enduring understandings   important concepts, principles, or processes that we want students to retain.

English as Second Language (ESL) students students whose primary language is not English.

Entity theory of intelligence   the belief that intelligence is a fixed entity that a student either has or doesn't have.

Essential questions   broad questions that represent the knowledge students should have gained at the end of a unit of study.

Expressive curriculum   practical arts and fine arts courses such as art, vocal and instrumental music, speech and drama, foreign language, computer science, family and consumer science (home economics), and industrial technology (industrial arts).

Flexible block scheduling   the organization of interdisciplinary team time into a large block of time, giving team teachers the freedom to organize the schedule in different ways for different purposes.

Formal register   the standard sentence syntax and word choice of work and school that uses complete sentences and specific word choice (Payne, 2001).

Formative feedback   providing the student with information about the quality or correctness of his work without the permanent consequence of a grade.

Gallery walk   a learning or assessment technique in which students rotate in groups through a series of stations, writing answers to open-ended questions on large posters.

Graphic organizers   visual outlines that show the organization of lesson information, usually displayed on the blackboard, on a computer screen, or on paper.

Homework   any task assigned by the classroom teacher and related to classroom learning that is expected to be completed outside of school.

Hyperstudio   a multimedia program that uses photographs, audio and video clips, and Internet links to instruct students.

In loco parentis   literally, *in place of parent*—a reference to the legal role of a teacher to act in lieu of parents.

Incremental theory of intelligence   belief that intelligence is built up incrementally through effort.

Inquiry learning   method of learning in which students are actively involved in investigating and organizing information and drawing conclusions.

Instruction   the set of learning experiences or activities students participate in for the purpose of learning.

Interactive notebooks   notebooks in which students express their opinions about class discussions or readings and teachers respond in writing to student comments.

Interdisciplinary learning activity   a learning activity that addresses content in more than one subject area.

Interdisciplinary teams   organizational feature that assigns a group of students to a group of academic teachers who are responsible for the academic instruction in the four core subjects—math, science, social studies, and language arts.

Interdisciplinary unit   a unit of study that integrates content in more than one subject area, organized around a theme.

Interest   a student's curiosity or passion for specific concepts or skills related to the curriculum.

Interscholastic sports   school-sponsored sports in which students play on competitive teams that represent the school in play against teams from other schools.

Interventions   nonpunitive discipline consequences that require students to reflect, write about, think about, or talk about their problem.

Intramural sports   school-sponsored sports in which students play on noncompetitive teams against others in their school.

Journal   a written record that allows students to freely express their thoughts about their learning, to make personal connections about their learning, and to communicate with their teachers.

Learning community   a classroom or team in which people work together and pool talents and resources to reach learning goals.

Learning contract   a signed agreement in which the teacher and student negotiate specific tasks the students will complete, how and when the tasks will be completed, and criteria for successful completion.

Learning log   a combination student notebook/portfolio that may include journal writings, class notes, learning assessments, data collections, or long-term observations.

Learning profile   a description of the ways a student likes to learn and learns most easily.

Learning stations   a series of places in the classroom where individuals or groups of students work on different tasks simultaneously.

Learning style   the predominant style or method by which a student learns best.

Norm-referenced assessment   assessment that compares students to each other and attempts to discriminate between better and poorer learners.

Norm setting   process by which students determine how they want their classroom to function, how people should treat each other, and how problems should be solved.

Notestar a tool that allows students to take and organize notes from online sources as they browse the Internet, and allows teachers to track student progress and provide feedback.

Objectives statements that specify what we want the student to know or be able to do at the conclusion of a learning experience.

One-shot grading allowing only one try or one test to assess student learning.

Performance-based assessments assessments that require students to show what they have learned in one of three ways: producing knowledge or discourse, creating products or performances, or providing personal reflections.

Portfolio a purposeful collection of student work that is used to show evidence of student learning.

Problem-based learning method of learning in which students study complex real-life problems, analyze information, and propose solutions.

Psychomotor objectives objectives that refer to the development and perfection of physical skills.

Puberty the natural, biological transition of a human body from that of a child to that of an adult capable of sexual reproduction.

Readiness a student's ability to understand concepts or their skill level with a particular learning task.

Rubrics scoring tools that list the criteria for a piece of work and also articulate gradations of quality for each criterion, from excellent to poor.

Small group learning groups of students working on an activity with a common purpose.

Smartboard a touch-sensitive technology that allows teachers to project the image of the computer screen onto a large screen that can be viewed by the entire class.

Student empowerment a process by which students increase their control or mastery of their own learning and decisions that affect their classroom and school.

Student-focused instruction activity-based instruction that is adapted to students' specific learning needs and that empowers students to make decisions about their learning.

Student voice the ability of students to have input into classroom rules and procedures, curriculum themes, and methods of learning and assessment.

Support strategies needs-based responses to discipline problems that meet students' physical, emotional, or social needs.

Teacher efficacy teachers' beliefs that they can influence learning and can instill in students a faith in their own abilities.

Teacher-focused instruction traditional didactic instruction in which all content is chosen by the teacher, most often delivered in direct instruction such as lecturing or asking questions.

Theory of multiple intelligences belief that individuals tend to develop strengths in different *intelligences* such as linguistic, logical-mathematical, spatial, bodily-kinesthetic, musical, interpersonal, intrapersonal, naturalistic, and existential.

Wait time the amount of time teachers wait after asking a question before calling on someone to answer or before rephrasing the question.

Webquest a structured assignment that allows students to use the Internet to gain information about topics.

Wellness curriculum physical education, health, and advisory courses as well as health and nutrition services, counseling, and social services.

Working portfolio portfolio used primarily to store work in progress and to help teachers diagnose student learning needs.

REFERENCES

Abbott, J. and Ryan, T. (1999). "Constructing knowledge, reconstructing schooling." *Educational Leadership*, 57(3), 66–69.

Aguilar, C. M. and Gross, F. E. (1999). "Affinity groups: a different kind of cocurricular activity." *Schools in the Middle*, October, 23–26.

Alexander, W. (1995). *Student-oriented curriculum: Asking the right questions.* Columbus, OH: National Middle School Association.

Alexander, W. M. and McEwin, C. K. (1989). *Schools in the middle: Status and progress.* Columbus, OH: National Middle School Association.

Allen, H., Splittberger, F., and Manning, M. (1993). *Teaching and learning in the middle level school.* New York: Macmillan.

Allington, R. L. (2002). "You can't learn much from books you can't read." *Educational Leadership*, 60(3), 16–19.

Alpert, D. (2004). "Studying the insect's world." *Educational Leadership*, 61(4), 86–87.

Amrein, A. L., and Berliner, D. C. (2003). "The effects of high-stakes testing on student motivation and learning." *Educational Leadership*. 60(5), 32–38.

Anfara, V. A., Jr., and Lipka, R. P. (2003). "Relating the middle school concept to student achievement." *Middle School Journal*, 35(1), 24–32.

Anfara, V. A., Jr., and Stacki, S. L. (Eds.). (2002). *Middle school curriculum, instruction, and assessment.* Westerville, OH: National Middle School Association and Information Age Publishing.

Anfara, V. A., Jr., and Waks, L. J.(2002). "Developmental appropriateness versus academic rigor: an untenable dualism in middle level education." In Anfara, V. A., Jr., and Stacki, S. L. (Eds.), *Middle school curriculum, instruction, and assessment.* (pp. 41–56) Westerville, OH: National Middle School Association and Information Age Publishing.

Apple, M. W., and Beane, J. A. (Eds.). (1995). *Democratic Schools.* Alexandria, VA: ASCD.

Arends, R. I. (2000). *Learning to teach.* New York, New York: McGraw-Hill.

Arhar, J. M. (1992). "Interdisciplinary teaming and the social bonding of middle level students." In Irvin, J. L. (Ed.), *Transforming middle level education: Perspectives and possibilities* (pp. 139–162). Boston: Allyn and Bacon.

Armstrong, T. (1999). *Seven Kinds of Smart.* New York: Penguin Putnam, Inc.

Armstrong, T. (1994). *Multiple intelligences in the classroom.* Alexandria, VA: ASCD.

Armstrong, T. (1997). *The Myth of the A.D.D. Child.* New York: Penguin Books.

Arnold, J. (1993). "A curriculum to empower young adolescents." *Midpoints Occasional Papers*, 4(10), 1–11.

Arter, J. and McTighe, J. (2001). *Scoring rubrics in the classroom: Using performance criteria for assessing and improving student performance.* Thousand Oaks, CA: Corwin Press, Inc.

Association for Supervision and Curriculum Development. (1975). *The middle school we need.* Washington, D. C.: author.

Atkins, J. T. and Ellsesser, J. (2003). "Tracking: the good, the bad, and the questions." *Educational Leadership*, 61(2), 44–47.

Atwell, N. (1987). *In the Middle: Writing, Reading and Learning with Adolescents.* Portsmouth, NH: Boynton/Cook.

Bailey, N. J. and Phariss, T. (1996). "Breaking the wall of silence: Gay, lesbian, and bisexual issues for middle level educators." *Middle School Journal*, 27(3), 38–46.

Balfanz, R. , MacIver, D., and Ryan, D. (2002). "Enabling 'algebra for all' with a facilitated instructional program: a case study of a talent development middle school." In Anfara, V. A., Jr., and Stacki, S. L. (Eds.), *Middle school curriculum, instruction, and assessment.* (pp. 181 -210). Westerville, OH. National Middle School Association and Information Age Publishing.

Barth, R. (1990). *Improving schools from within.* San Francisco: Jossey-Bass.

Bean, T. W. (2002). "Making reading relevant for adolescents." *Educational Leadership*, 60(3), 34–37.

Beane, J. (1993). *A middle school curriculum: from rhetoric to reality.* Columbus, OH: National Middle School Association.

Beane, J. A. (1997). *Curriculum integration: designing the core of democratic education.* New York: Teachers College Press.

Beane, J. A. (1999b) "Middle schools under siege: Responding to the attack." *Middle School Journal*, 30(5), 3–6.

Beane, J. A. (2001). "Reform and reinvention." In Dickinson, T. S. (Ed). *Reinventing the*

middle school. (pp. xiii–xxii). New York: RoutledgeFalmer.

Beck, I. L., and McKeown, M. G. (2002). "Questioning the author: Making sense of social studies." *Educational Leadership*, 60(3), 44–47.

Belair, J. R. and Freeman, P. (2000) "Protecting bodies, hearts, and minds in school." *Middle School Journal*, 31(5), 3.

Bell, L. I. (2003). "Strategies that close the gap." *Educational Leadership*, 60(4), 32–34.

Bergman, S. (1992) Exploratory programs in the middle school: a responsive idea. In Irvin (Ed.), *Transforming middle level education: Perspectives and possibilities* Boston, MA: Allyn and Bacon, 179–192.

Bergstorm, K. L. (1998). "Are we missing the point about curriculum integration?" *Middle School Journal*, 29(4), 28–37.

Blahous, E. and Voss, B. (1999). "School scoop: young broadcasters produce news program." *Schools in the Middle*, October, 27–29.

Bloom, B. S., (1984). *Taxonomy of educational objectives, book 1, cognitive domain.* White Plains, New York: Longman.

Blueprints for a collaborative classroom (1997). Oakland, CA: Developmental Studies Center.

Blum, R.W. (2005). "A case for school connectedness." *Education Leadership*. 62(7), 16–21.

Bonstingl, J. J. (1992). "The quality revolution." *Educational Leadership*, 50(3), 4–9.

Boyer, E. (2003). *The basic school: a community for learning.* Princeton, NJ: The Carnegie Foundation for the Advancement of Teaching.

Bracey, G. W. (2003). "The 13th Bracey report on the condition of public education." *Phi Delta Kappan*, 85(2), 148–164.

Brandenburg, M. L. (Sister). (2002). "Advanced math? Write!" *Educational Leadership*, 60(3), 67–69.

Brandt, R. (1992). "On building learning communities: A conversation with Hank Levin." *Educational Leadership*, 50(1), 19–23.

Brooks, J. G. and M. G. (1993). *In Search of Understanding: The Case for Constructivist Classrooms*. Alexandria, VA: ASCD.

Brooks, J. G. (2004). "To See Beyond the Lesson." *Educational Leadership*, 62(1), 9–12.

Brooks, M. G. and Brooks, J. G. (1999). "The courage to be constructivist." *Educational Leadership*, 57(3), 18–24.

Brophy, J. (1998). *Motivating students to learn*. Boston: McGraw-Hill.

Brown, D. F. (2002a). "Culturally responsive instructional processes." In Anfara, V. A., Jr., and Stacki, S. L. (Eds.), *Middle school curriculum, instruction, and assessment*. (pp. 57–73) Westerville, OH: National Middle School Association and Information Age Publishing.

Brown, D. F. (2002b). "Self-directed learning in an 8th grade classroom." *Educational Leadership*, 60(1), 54–58.

Burke, J. (2002). "The internet reader." *Educational Leadership*, 60(1), 38–42.

Burtch, J. A. (1999). Technology is for everyone. *Educational Leadership*, 56(5), 33–34.

Cahppuis, S., and Stiggins, R. J. (2002). "Classroom assessment for learning." *Educational Leadership*, 60(1), 40–43.

Caine, G., Caine, R. N., and McClintic, C. (2002). "Guiding the innate constructivist." *Educational Leadership*, 60(1), 70–73.

California Department of Education, 2001. Academic standards. http://www.cde.ca.gov/standards, 2001.

Canady, R. L. and Hotchkiss, P. R. (1989). "It's a good score! Just a bad grade." *Phi Delta Kappan*, 1(1), 68–71.

Canter, L., and Canter, M. (2002). *Assertive discipline: Positive behavior management for today's classroom*. Santa Monica, CA: Canter and Associates, Inc.

Carnegie Council on Adolescent Development. (1996). *Great transitions: Preparing adolescents for a new century*. Washington, DC: Author.

Carnegie Council on Adolescent Development. (1989). *Turning points: Preparing American youth for the 21st century*. Washington, D.C.: Author.

Caskey, M. M. (2002). "Strengthening middle level education." In Anfara, V. A., Jr., and Stacki, S. L. (Eds.), *Middle school curriculum, instruction, and assessment*. (pp. 103–118) Westerville, OH: National Middle School Association and Information Age Publishing.

Cawelti, G. (2003). "Lessons from research that changed education." *Educational Leadership*, 60(5),18–21.

Cetron, M. and Cetron, K. (2004). "A forecast for schools." *Educational Leadership*, 61(4), 22–29.

Checkley, K. (1997). "Problem–based learning: the search for solutions to life's messy problems." *ASCD Curriculum Update*, (Summer), 1–3, 6–8.

Cloud, J. (2005). "The battle over gay teens." *Time*, 166(15), 43–45.

Cole, R. W. (Ed.) (1995). *Educating everybody's children: Diverse strategies for diverse learners*. Alexandria, VA: ASCD.

Coluburn, A. (2004). "Inquiring scientists want to know." *Educational Leadership*, 62(1), 63–66.

Connors, N. A. (2000). *If you don't feed the teachers they eat the students: a guide to success for administrators and teachers*. Columbus, OH: National Middle School Association.

Conners, N. (1992). *Homework: A new direction*. Columbus, Ohio: National Middle School Association.

Cooper, Harris (2001a). "Homework: Another lesson in the importance of moderation." *Educational Leadership*, 58(7).

Cooper, Harris (1994)(2001b edition forthcoming). *The battle over homework: an administrator's guide to setting sound and effective policies*. Thousand Oaks, California: Corwin Press.

Cooper, Harris (1989). "Synthesis of research on homework." *Educational Leadership*. 47(3), 85–91.

Cooper, H., Lindsay, J. Nye, B. and Greathouse, S.(1998). "Relationships among attitudes about homework, amount of homework assigned and completed, and student achievement." *Journal of Educational Psychology*, 90(1), 70–83.

Costa, A. and Kallick, B. (2004). "Launching self-directed learners." *Educational Leadership*, 62(1), 51–55.

Cowan, P. A. (1978). *Piaget with feeling*. New York: Holt, Rinehart, and Winston.

Crone, D. A., Horner, R. H. (2003). *Building positive behavioral support systems in schools: functional behavioral assessments*. NY: Guilford Press.

Cusick, P. A. (1989). *The educational system: Its nature and logic* New York: McGraw-Hill.

Curriculum Update (June 1993). "Can separate be equal?"

Curry, C. (2003). "Universal design: Accessibility for all learners." *Educational Leadership*, 61(2), 44–47.

Curwin, R. L. and Mendler, A. N. (1997). *As tough as necessary: Countering violence, aggression, and hostility in our schools*. Alexandria, VA: ASCD.

Curtis, D. (2002). "The power of projects." *Educational Leadership*, 60(1), 50–52.

Dalton, J. and Watson, M. (1997). *Among friends: Classrooms where caring and learning prevail*. Oakland, CA: Developmental Studies Center.

Dalton, S. (2004). *Our Overweight Children*. Berkeley, Calif.: Univ. of California Press.

Daniels, E. (2005). "On the minds of middle schoolers." *Educational Leadership*, 62(7), 52–55.

Daniels, H. and Zemelman, S. (2004). "Out with textbooks, in with learning." *Educational Leadership*, 61(4), 36–41.

Danielson, C. (2002). *Enhancing student achievement: A framework for school improvement*. Alexandria, VA: ASCD.

Danielson, C. and Abrytyn, L. (1997). *An introduction to using portfolios in the classroom*. Alexandria, VA: ASCD.

Davies, J. (1993). "The impact of the mass media upon the health of early adolescents." *Journal of Health Education*, November-December supplement, 28–35.

DeVries, R. and Kohlberg, L. (1987). *Constructivist early education: Overview and comparison with other programs*. Washington, D.C.: National Association for the Education of Young Children.

DeVries, R. and Zan, B. (1995). "Creating as constructivist classroom atmosphere." *Young children*, 51(1), 4–13.

DeVries, R. and Zan. B. (2003). "When children make rules." *Educational Leadership*, 61(1), 64–67.

Dickinson, T. S. (2001). "Reinventing the middle school: a proposal to counter arrested development." In Dickinson, T. S. (Ed). *Reinventing the middle school*. (pp. 3–20). New York: RoutledgeFalmer.

Dorman, G. (1984). *Middle Grades Assessment Program*. Carrboro, North Carolina: Center for Early Adolescence.

Douglass, S. L. (2002). "Teaching about religion." *Educational Leadership*, 60(2), 32–37.

Doyle, A. (1999). A practitioner's guide to snaring the net. *Educational Leadership*, 56(5), 12–15.

Doyle, D. P. (2004). "Letter from Washington: Old wine in new bottles." *Educational Leadership*, 61(4), 96.

Dreikurs, R., (M.D.), Grunwald, B. B., and Pepper, F. C. (1982). *Maintaining sanity in the classroom: Classroom management techniques*. (2nd edition). New York, NY: Harper and Row.

Dunn, R. and Dunn, K. (1978). *Teaching students through their individual learning styles*. Reston, VA: Reston Publications.

Dunn, R., Beaudry, J. S., and Klavas, A. (1989). "Survey of research on learning styles." *Educational Leadership*, 46(6), 50–52.

Dweck, C. (1992). "Performance vs. learning." Presented at Missouri ASCD conference, St. Louis, Missouri.

Earl, L. M. (2003). *Assessment as learning: using classroom assessment to maximize student learning*. Thousand Oaks, CA: Corwin Press.

Easton, L. B. (2002). "Lessons from learners." *Educational Leadership*, 60(1), 64–69.

Edwards, T. "Flying solo." *Time*, 156(9), 47–53.

Eichhorn, D. (1966). *The middle school*. New York: Center for Applied Research in Education.

Eisner, E. (2002). "The kind of schools we need." *Phi Delta Kappan*, 83(8), 576–583.

Eisner, E. W. (2004). "Preparing for today and tomorrow." *Educational Leadership*, 61(4), 6–11.

Elkind, D. (1981). *The hurried child: Growing up too fast too soon*. Reading, Massachusetts: Addison-Wesley.

Elmore, R. F. (2003). "A plea for strong practice." *Educational Leadership*, 61(3), 6–11.

Erb, T. (2000). "Interview with Gerald Borgeois: Voice of experience on school safety." *Middle School Journal*, 31(5), 5–11.

Erb, T. O. (Ed.). (2001). *This We Believe and now we must act*. Columbus, OH: National Middle School Association

Erb, T. (1999). "May you live in interesting times." *Middle School Journal*, 30(4), 2.

Erb, T. (1995). "It's academics, stupid! If you care enough." *Middle School Journal*, 27(1), 2.

Erb, T. O. and Stevenson, C. (1998). "Requisites for curricular reform." *Middle School Journal*, 30(2), 68–71.

Erikson, E. (1963). *Childhood and society* (rev. ed.) New York: Norton.

Erwin, J. C. (2003). "Giving students what they need." *Educational Leadership*, 61(1), 19–23.

Fahey, J. (2000). "Water, water everywhere." *Educational Leadership*, 57(6), 60–61.

Fashola, O. S. (ed.) (2005). *Educating African American Males: voices from the field*. Thousand Oaks, CA: Corwin Press.

Feinstein, S. (2003) "A case for middle school after-school programs in rural America." *Middle School Journal*, 34(3), 32–37.

Felner, R. D., Kasak, D., Mulhall, P., and Flowers, N. (1997). "The project on high peformance learning communities." In *What works in middle grades school reform*, Eds. J. Lipsitz, A. W. Jackson, and L. Austin. *Phi Delta Kappan*.

Findley, N. (2002). "In their own ways." *Educational Leadership*, 60(1), 60–63.

Fisher, D., Frey, N., and Williams, D. (2002). "Seven literacy strategies that work." *Educational Leadership*, 60(3), 70–73.

Flowers, N., Mertens, S. B., and Mulhall, P. F. (2003). "Middle school renewal." *Middle School Journal*, 35(2), 55–59.

Frieman, B. B. (2001). "What teachers need to know about children at risk." Boston: McGraw-Hill.

Frieman, B., O'Hara, H., and Settle, J. (1996). "What heterosexual teachers need to know about homosexuality." *Childhood Education*, 73, 40–42.

Fuhler, C. J. (2003). "Joining theory and best practice to drive classroom instruction." *Middle School Journal*, 34(5), 23–30.

Gabler, I. C. and Shroeder, M. (2003). *Constructivist Classroom: England Minds*. Boston: Pearson.

Gallagher-Polite, M. M. (2001). "Hope for Sandy: Transformation points: A reinvention paradigm." In Dickinson, T. S. (Ed). *Reinventing the middle school*. (pp. 39–55). New York: RoutledgeFalmer.

Galletti, S. (1999). "Middle level cocurricular programs: a match!" *Schools in the Middle*, October, 1.

Galus, P. "How standards enhanced my teaching style." *Educational Leadership*, 59(4), 77–79.

Gandal, M. and Vranek, J. (2001). "Standards: Here today, here tomorrow." *Educational Leadership*, 59(1), 43–46.

Gardner, H. (1999). *Intelligence reframed: Multiple intelligences for the 21st century*. New York: Simon and Schuster.

Gardner, H. (1983). *Frames of mind: The theory of multiple intelligences*. New York: Basic Books.

Gatewood, T. (1998). "How valid is integrated curriculum in today's middle schools?" *Middle School Journal*, 29(4), 38–41.

Gay, G. (2004). "The importance of multicultural education." *Educational Leadership*, 61(4), 30–35.

Gebhard, M. (2003). Getting past "See spot run." *Educational Leadership*, 60(4), 35–39.

George, P. (2002). *No child left behind: Implications for middle level leaders*. Columbus, OH: National Middle School Association.

George, P. S. (1993). "Tracking and ability grouping in the middle school: Ten tentative truths." *Middle School Journal*, 24(4), 17–24.

George, P. S. and Alexander, W. M. (1993). *The exemplary middle school (2nd edition)*. New York: Harcourt Brace Jovanovich.

George, P., Lawrence, G., and Bushnell, D. (1998). *Handbook for middle school teaching*. New York: Addison-Wesley.

George, P. S., Stevenson, C., Thomason, J., Beane, J. (1992). *The middle school and beyond*. Alexandria, VA: ASCD.

Ginott, H. G. (1972). *Teacher and child: A book for parents and teachers*. New York: Macmillan.

Glasser, W. (1986). *Choice theory in the classroom*. New York: Harper Perennial.

Glasser, W. (1992). *The quality school: managing students without coercion*. New York: Harper Collins.

Glasser, W. (1969). *Schools without failure*. New York: Harper and Row.

Goh, D. S. (2004). *Assessment accommodations for diverse learners*. Boston, MA: Pearson.

Good, T. L., and Brophy, J. E. (2003). *Looking in classrooms*. Boston: Allyn and Bacon.

Goodlad, J. (1984). *A place called school: Prospects for the future*. New York: McGraw-Hill Book Company.

Goodrich, H. (1996). "Understanding rubrics." *Educational Leadership*, 54(4), 14–17.

Grady, E. A. (2004). "Future shock." *Educational Leadership*, 61(4), 65–69.

"Great Transitions: Preparing adolescents for a new century." (1996). *Report of the Carnegie Council on Adolescent Development*. New York: Carnegie Corporation of New York.

Gronland, N. E. (2000). *How to Write and Use Instructional Objectives*. Upper Saddle River, NJ: Merrill.

Gross, S. J. (2002). "Introduction: Middle-level curriculum, instruction, and assessment." In Anfara, V. A., Jr., and Stacki, S. L. (Eds.), *Middle school curriculum, instruction, and assessment*. (pp. ix–xxii) Westerville, OH: National Middle School Association and Information Age Publishing.

Guskey, T. (1996). "Communicating student learning." *ASCD yearbook*. Alexandria, VA: ASCD.

Guskey, T. (1994). "Making the grade: What benefits students." *Educational Leadership*. 52(2), 14–20.

Guskey, T. R. (2003). "How classroom assessments improve learning." *Educational Leadership*, 60(5), 6–11.

Guskey, T. R. (2001). "Helping standards make the grade." *Educational Leadership*, 59(1), 20–27.

Hackmann, D. G. (2002). "Block scheduling for the middle level: A cautionary tale about the best features of secondary school models." *Middle School Journal*, 33(4), 22–28.

Hall, P. S. and Hall, N. D. (2003). "Building relationships with challenging children." *Educational Leadership*, 61(1), 60–63.

Hancock, L. (1996). "Mother's little helper." *Newsweek*, March 18, 51–56.

Havens, J. (2003). "Student web pages—a performance assessment they'll love!" *Phi Delta Kappan*, 84(9), 710–712.

Havinghurst, R. J. (1976). *Developmental tasks and education*. (3rd edition). New York: McKay.

Hensen, K. T. (2004). *Constructivist Teaching Strategies for Diverse Middle Level Classrooms*. Boston, MA: Pearson.

Herman-Giddens, M. E., Slora, E. J., Wasserman, R. C., Bourdony, C. J., Bhapkar, M. V., Koch, G. G., and Hasemeier, C. M.(1997). "Secondary sexual characteristics and menses in young girls seen in office practice: a study from the Pediatric Research in Office Settings Network." *Pediatrics*, 99(4), 505–512.

Herman-Giddens, M. E., Wang, L., and Koch, G. (2001). "Secondary sexual characteristics in boys: Estimates from the National Health and Nutrition Examination Survey III, 1988–1994." *Archives of pediatrics and adolescent medicine*, 155, September, 1022–1028.

Higgins, K. M. and Heglie-King, M. A. (1997). "Giving voice to middle school students through portfolio assessment: A journey to mathematical power." *Middle School Journal*, 29(1), 22–29.

Hirsch, E. D. Jr., Kett, J. F., and Trefil, J. (2002). *The new dictionary of cultural literacy: What every American needs to know*. New York: Houghton Mifflin.

Hoffman, D., and Levak, B. A. (2003). "Personalizing schools." *Educational Leadership*, 61(1), 30–34.

Holloway, J. H. (2004). "Student teamwork." *Educational Leadership*, 61(4), 91–92.

Holloway, J. H. (2002). "Extracurricular activities and student motivation." *Educational Leadership*, 60(1), 74–78.

Holloway, J. H. (2002). "Integrating literacy with content." *Educational Leadership*, 60(3), 87–88.

Hrabowski, III, F. A. (2003). "Raising Minority Achievement in Science and Math." *Educational Leadership*, 60(4), 44–48.

Intrator, S. M. (2004). "The Engaged Classroom." *Educational Leadership*, 62(1), 20–24.

Jackson, A. W. and Davis, G. A. (2000). *Turning points 2000: educating adolescents in the 21st century*. Columbus, OH: National Middle School Association.

Jacobs, H. H. (1997). *Mapping the big picture: Integrating curriculum and assessment K-12*. Alexandria, VA: ASCD.

Jacobsen, D. A., Eggen, P., Kauchak, D. (2002). *Methods for teaching: promoting student learning*. Upper Saddle River, N.J.: Merrill.

Jensen, E. (2000). *Different brains, different learners*. San Diego, CA: The brain store.

Jensen, E. (1998). *Teaching with the brain in mind*. Alexandria, VA: ASCD.

Jensen, E. (2000). *Brain-based learning*. San Diego: CA: The Brain Store.

Jobe, D. A. (2003). "Helping girls succeed." *Educational Leadership*, 60(4), 64–66.

Johnson, D. W. and Johnson, R. T. (1991). *Learning together and alone—cooperative, competitive and individualistic learning*. Englewood Cliffs, N.J.: Prentice Hall.

Johnston, J. H. (1994). *Success for all students*. Presentation at Columbia Public Schools, Columbia, Missouri.

Johnston, J. H. and Markle, G. C. (1986). *What research says to the middle level practitioner*. Columbus, Ohio: NMSA.

Kain, D. L. (2003). *Problem-based learning for teachers, grades K-8*. Boston, MA: Pearson Education, Inc.

Kantrowitz, B., and Springen, K. (2003). "Why sleep matters." *Newsweek*, September 22, pp. 75–77.

Kantrowitz, B. and Pat Wingert. (1999). "The truth about tweens." *Newsweek*, October 18, 62–72.

Kay, P., Fitzgerald, M., Paradee, C., and Mellencamp (1994). "Making homework work at home: The parent's perspective." *Journal of Learning Disabilities*, 27(9), 550–561.

Keefe, J. W. and Jenkins, J. M. (2002). "Personalized instruction." *Phi Delta Kappan*, 83(6), 440–448.

Kellough, R. D. and Kellough, N. G. (1999). *Middle school teaching: a guide to methods and resources* (3rd edition). Upper Saddle River, N.J.: Merrill/Prentice Hall.

Kentucky Department of Education (2002). *Kentucky's learning goals and academic expectations*. www.kde.state.ky.us.

Kessler, R. (2000). "Initiation, Saying Goodbye to Childhood." *Educational Leadership*, 57(4), 30–33.

Kirn, W. (2000). "Should they stay together for the kids?" *Time*, 156(13), 75–82.

Kluth, P. and Straut, D. (2001). "Standards for diverse learners." *Educational Leadership*, 59(1), 43–46.

Koetsch, P., D'Acquisto, L., Kurin, A., Juffer, S., and Goldberg, L. (2002). "Schools into museums." *Educational Leadership*, 60(1), 74–78.

Kohlberg, L. (1984). *The psychology of moral development*.

Kohn, A. (2000). *The case against standardized testing: raising the scores, ruining the schools*. Portsmouth, New Hampshire: Heinemann.

Kohn, A. (1991). "Caring kids: The role of the schools." *Phi Delta Kappan*, March, 492–506.

Kohn, A. (1993). *Punished by rewards: The trouble with gold stars, incentive plans, A's, praise, and other bribes*. New York, New York: Houghton Mifflin.

Kohn, A. (1996). *Beyond discipline: from compliance to community*. Alexandria, VA: ASCD.

Kravolec, E. and Buell, J. (2000). *The end of homework: how homework disrupts families, overburdens children and limits learning*. Boston: Beacon Press.

Kreisberg, S. (1992). *Transforming Power: Domination, empowerment, and education*. Albany: State University of New York Press.

Kriete, R. (2003). "Start the day with community." *Educational Leadership*, 61(1), 68–70.

Lacayo, R. (2000). "Are you man enough?" *Time*, 155(16), 58–63.

Ladson-Billings, G. (2001). *Crossing over to Canaan: The journey of new teachers in diverse classrooms*. San Francisco, CA: Jossey-Bass.

Landfried, S. E. (1989). "'Enabling' undermines responsibility in students." *Educational Leadership*, 47(3), 79–84.

Lemlech, J. K. (2002). (5th edition). *Curriculum and instructional methods for the elementary and middle school*. Upper Saddle River, NJ: Pearson Education, Inc.

Levine, M. (2003). "Celebrating diverse minds." *Educational Leadership*, 61(2), 12–18.

Lounsbury, J. H. and Vars, G. F. (1978). *A curriculum for the middle school years*. New York: Harper and Row.

Lounsbury, J. H. and Vars, G. F. (2003). "The future of middle level education: Optimistic and pessimistic views." *Middle School Journal*, 35(2), 6–14.

Lounsbury, J. H. (Ed.) 1992. *Connecting the curriculum through interdisciplinary instruction*. Westerville, Ohio: NMSA.

Lucas, S. E. and Valentine, J. W. (2001). *NMSA Research summary #1: Grade configuration*. Columbus, OH: National Middle School Asssociation. Available online at www.nmsa.org.

Mandeville, T. F., and Radcliffe, R. (2002). "Character education infused into middle level education." In Anfara, V. A., Jr., and Stacki, S. L. (Eds.), *Middle school curriculum, instruction, and assessment.* (pp. 139–155) Westerville, OH: National Middle School Association and Information Age Publishing.

Manning, M. L. (2000). "Child centered middle school: A position paper." *Childhood Education,* 76(3), 154–159.

Manning, M. L. (1993). *Developmentally appropriate middle schools.* Wheaton, MD: Association for Childhood Education International.

Manning, M. L. and Bucher. K. T. (2001) *Teaching in the middle school.* Upper Saddle River, N.J.: Prentice Hall.

March, T. (2004). "The learning power of webquests." *Educational Leadership*, 61(4), 42–47.

Marshall, K. (2003). "A principal looks back: Standards matter." *Phi Delta Kappan*, 85(2), 105–113.

Marshall, M. (2002). "How to discipline without rewards or punishments, raise responsibility and create a learning community." Presentation at ASCD Annual Conference, New Orleans, LA.

Martinez, J. G. R., and Martinez, N. C. (2003). "Raising middle school standards without raising anxiety." *Middle School Journal*, 34(4), 27–35.

Martino, L. R. (1993). "A goal-setting model for young adolescent at risk students." *Middle School Journal*, 24(5), 19–22.

Marzano, R. J. (2003). *What works in schools: Translating research into action.* Alexandria, VA: ASCD.

Marzano, R. J., Pickering, D. J., and Pollock, J. E. (2001). *Classroom instruction that works: Research-based strategies for increasing student achievement.* Alexandria, VA: ASCD.

McDaniel, J. E., Necochea, J., Rios, F. A., Stowell, L. P., Kritzer, C. (2001). "The arc of equity in reinvented middle schools." In Dickinson, T. S. (Ed). *Reinventing the middle school.* (pp. 56–75). New York: RoutledgeFalmer.

McEwin, C. K., Dickinson, T. S., and Jenkins, D. M. (1996). *America's middle schools: Practices and progress—A 25-year perspective.* Columbus, OH: National Middle School Association.

McEwin, C. K., Dickinson, T. S. and Jenkins, D. M. (2003). *America's middle schools in the new century: Status and progress.* Columbus, OH: National Middle School Association.

McEwin, K., Dickinson, T. (1997). "Interscholastic sports." *Schools in the Middle* (January), 19–23.

McTighe, J. and Thomas, R. S. (2003). "Backward design for forward action." *Educational Leadership*, 60(5), 52–55.

Mee, C. S. (1997). *2000 voices: Young adolescents' perceptions and curriculum implications.* Columbus, Ohio: National Middle School Association.

Meier, D. (2002). "Standardization versus standards." *Phi Delta Kappan*, 84(3), 190–198.

Mendes, E. (2003). "What empathy can do." *Educational Leadership*, 61(1), 56–59.

Mendler, A. N. (2001). *Connecting with students.* Alexandria, VA: ASCD.

Mertens, S. B., and Flowers, N. (2003). "Middle school practices improve student achievement in high poverty schools." *Middle School Journal*, 35(1), 33–43.

Mertens, S. B., Flowers, N., and Mulhall, P. F. Fuhler, C. J. (2003). "Should middle grades students be left alone after school?" *Middle School Journal*, 34(5), 57–61.

Miles, M. and Valentine, J. W. (2001). *NMSA Research summary: Numbers of middle schools and students.* Columbus, OH: National Middle School Association. Available online at www.nmsa.org.

Milgram, J. (1992). "A portrait of diversity: The middle level student." In Irvin, J. L. (Ed.), *Transforming middle level education: Perspectives and possibilities* (16–27). Boston: Allyn and Bacon.

Missouri Department of Elementary and Secondary Education. *The Show-Me Standards* (2000). www.dese.state.mo.us/standards.

Moulds, P. (2004). "Rich tasks." *Educational Leadership*, 61(4), 75–78.

Murphy, M. M. (1997). "Problem-based learning across the curriculum." Presentation at Missouri ASCD Conference, January 26, 1997.

Muth, K. D. and Alvermann, D. E. (1992). *Teaching and learning in the middle grades.* Needham Heights, MA: Allyn and Bacon.

NASSP Council on Middle Level Education. (1985). *An agenda for excellence at the middle level*. Reston, VA: author.

National Middle School Association (2001a) Research summary: *Flexible scheduling.* Columbus, OH: Author. Available online at www.nmsa.org.

National Middle School Association (2001b). *NMSA Research summary: Exemplary middle schools*. Columbus, OH: Author. Available online at www.nmsa.org.

National Middle School Association (2001c). *NMSA Research summary: Young adolescents' developmental needs*. Columbus, OH: Author. Available online at www.nmsa.org.

National Middle School Association (2001d). *NMSA Research summary: Heterogeneous grouping*. Columbus, OH: Author. Available online at www.nmsa.org.

National Middle School Association (2001e) Research summary: *Advisory programs.* Columbus, OH: Author. Available online at www.nmsa.org.

National Middle School Association (2003a). *Research and resources in support of this we believe*. Columbus, OH: author.

National Middle School Association (2003b). *This We Believe: Successful schools for young adolescents*. Columbus, OH: author.

Neill, M. (2003). "The dangers of testing." *Educational Leadership*, 60(5), 43–47.

Nesin, G. and Lounsbury, J. (1998). *Curriculum integration: Twenty questions and answers.* Columbus, OH: National Middle School Association.

Nitko, A. J. (2004). *Educational assessment of students*. Upper Saddle River, NJ: Prentice-Hall.

Nord, W. A. and Haynes, C. C. (1998). *Taking religion seriously across the curriculum.* Alexandria, VA: ASCD.

Oakes, J. (1998). "Detracking for high school achievement." *Educational Leadership*, 55(6), 38–41.

Oakes, J. (1985). *Keeping track: How schools structure inequality*. New Haven: Yale University Press.

Omvig, K. (2000). *Personal interview*. Planned Parenthood of St. Louis.

O'Neil, J. (1990 September). *New curriculum agenda emerges for the '90s*. Association for Supervision and Curriculum Development curriculum update.

O'Neil, J. and Tell, C. (1999). "Why students lose when "tougher standards" win: A conversation with Alfie Kohn." *Educational Leadership*, 57(1), 18–23.

O'Steen, B., Cuper, P., Spires, H., Beal, C. and Pope, C. (2002). "Curriculum integration: Theory, practice, and research for a sustainable future." In Anfara, V. A., Jr., and Stacki, S. L. (Eds.), *Middle school curriculum, instruction, and assessment*. (pp. 1–21). Westerville, OH: National Middle School Association and Information Age Publishing.

Parkway School District. (1999). *Teacher guide to the curriculum*. Chesterfield, Missouri: Parkway School District.

Pate, P. E. (2001). "Standards, students and exploration: Creating a curriculum intersection of excellence." In Dickinson, T. S. (Ed). *Reinventing the middle school.* (pp. 79–95). New York: RoutledgeFalmer.

Pate, P. E., and Muth, K. D. (2003). "Perspectives on the middle school movement: Snapshots from the past." *Middle School Journal,* 35(2), 15–22.

Pateman, B. (2004). "Healthier students, better learners." *Educational Leadership,* 61(4), 70–74.

Patterson, W. (2003). "Breaking out of our boxes." *Phi Delta Kappan,* 84(8), 569–574.

Payne, R. K. (2001). *A framework for understanding poverty.* Highlands, TX: aha! Process, Inc.

Perkins, D. (2004). "Knowledge Alive." *Educational Leadership,* (62)1, 14–18.

Perkins-Gough, D. (2004). "Creating a timely curriculum: a conversation with Heidi Hayes Jacobs." *Educational Leadership,* 61(4), 12–17.

Peters, D. (1999). "Rose Court" program prepares girls for adulthood. *Schools in the Middle,* October, 39–41.

Piaget, J. (1954). *The construction of reality in the child.* New York: Basic Books.

Piaget, J. (1970). *Science of education and the psychology of the child.* New York: Viking Compass.

Pitton, D. E. (2001). "The school and the child and the child in the school." In Dickinson, T. S. (Ed.) *Reinventing the middle school.* (pp. 21–38). New York: RoutledgeFalmer.

Pool, C. (1997). "Maximizing learning: A conversation with Renate Nummela Caine." *Educational Leadership,* 54(6), 11–15.

Pop, D. C. (2001). *'Doing school': How we are creating a generation of stressed out, materialistic, and miseducated students.* New Haven: Yale University Press.

Popham, W. J. (2000). *Modern educational measurement: Practical guidelines for educational leaders.* Needham, MA: Allyn and Bacon.

Postman, N. (1982). *The disappearance of childhood.* New York: Delacourte Press.

Powell, R. R. (2001). "On headpieces of straw: How middle level students view their schooling." In Dickinson, T. S. (Ed). *Reinventing the middle school.* (pp. 117–152). New York: RoutledgeFalmer.

Powers, S. M., Rafferty, C. D., and Eib, B. J. (2001). "The role of technology for learning in the reinvented middle school." In Dickinson, T. S. (Ed). *Reinventing the middle school.* (pp. 218–246). New York: RoutledgeFalmer.

Pride, D. (1999). "Open after hours: after school programs extend the learning of young adolescents." *Middle Ground,* August, 20–23.

Purkey, W. S. and Strahan, D. B. (1986). *Positive discipline.* Columbus, Ohio: National Middle School Association.

Quinn, D. M., and Valentine, J. W. (2002). *NMSA Research summary #19: What impact does the use of technology have on middle level education, specifically student achievement?* Columbus, OH: National Middle School Association.

Raebeck, B. (1992). *Transforming middle schools: A guide to whole-school change.* Lancaster, Penn: Technomic Publishing Company.

Raphael and Pearson (1982). "The effect of metacognitive awareness training on children's question-answering behavior." (Tech. Rep. No. 238). Urbana, IL: Center for the Study of Reading, University of Illinois. In: Muth, K. D. and Alvermann, D. E. (1992). *Teaching and learning in the middle grades.* Needham Heights, MA: Allyn and Bacon.

Ratnesar, Romesh. (1999). "The homework ate my family." *Time,* January 25, 1999, 55–63.

Reif, S. F. (1993). *How to read and teach ADD/ADHD children.* West Nyack, NY: Center for Applied Research in Education.

Reiser, R. A. and Butzin, S. M. (2000). "Using teaming, active learning, and technology to improve instruction." *Middle School Journal*, 32(2), 21–29.

Reiter, E. D. (2001). "Editorial: Have the onset and tempo of puberty changed?" *Archives of pediatrics and adolescent medicine*, 155, September, 988–989.

Renzulli, J. S., Gentry, M. and Reis, S. M.(2004). "A time and place for authentic learning." *Educational Leadership*, 62(1), 73–77.

Ring, M. M., and Reetz, L. (2002). "Grading students with learning disabilities in inclusive middle schools." *Middle School Journal*, 34(2), 12–17.

Robertson, T. S. and Valentine, J. W. (2002). *NMSA Research summary #14: What is the impact of inclusion on students and staff in the middle school setting.* Columbus, OH: National Middle School Association. Available online at www.nmsa.org.

Rogers, C. (1969). *Freedom to learn.* Columbus, Ohio: Charles E. Merrill Publishing Co.

Rolon, C. A. (2003). "Educating Latino Students." *Educational Leadership*, 60(4), 40–43.

Rose, L. C., and Gallup, A. M. (2003). "The 35th annual PDK/Gallup poll of the public's attitudes toward the public schools." *Phi Delta Kappan*, 85(2), 148–164.

Rosenfeld, A. and Wise, N. (2000). *The overscheduled child: avoiding the hyper parenting trap.* New York: St. Martin's Press.

Sagor, R. (2002). "Lessons from skateboarders." *Educational Leadership*, 60(1), 34–38.

Sapon-Shevin, M. (2003). "Inclusion: A matter of social justice." *Educational Leadership*, 61(2), 25–28.

Scales, P. C. (1991). *A portrait of Young Adolescents in the 1990's.* Carrboro, N.C.: Center for Early Adolescence.

Scales, P. C. (1999). "Care and challenge: the sources of student success." *Middle Ground*, 3(7), 21–23.

Scherer, M. (2004). "More or less." *Educational Leadership*, 61(4), 5.

Scherer, M. (2001). "How and why standards can improve student achievement: A conversation with Robert J. Marzano." *Educational Leadership*, 59(1), 14–18.

Schoenbach, R., Braunger, J., Greenleaf, C., and Litman, C. (2003). "Apprenticing adolescents to reading in subject-area classrooms." *Phi Delta Kappan*, 85(2), 133–138.

Schlozman, S. C. (2003). "To view or not to view." *Educational Leadership*, 60(4), 87–88.

Schurr, S. L. (1989). *Dynamite in the classroom: A how-to handbook for teachers.* Columbus, OH: National Middle School Association.

Seif, E. (2004). "Social studies revived." *Educational Leadership*, 61(4), 54–59.

Silver, D. (1999). "Going outside the lines: Great strategies to reach all middle level learners." Presentation at National Middle School Association Annual Conference, Orlando, Florida.

Simon, K. G. (2002). "The blue blood is good, right?" *Educational Leadership*, 60(1), 24–28.

Sizer, T. (1992). *Nine Common Principles.* Providence, RI: The Coalition of Essential Schools, Brown University.

Skelton, M., Wigford, A., Harper, P., and Reeves, G. (2003). "Beyond food, festivals, and flags." *Educational Leadership*, 61(1), 52–55.

Slavin, R. (1997). "Can education reduce social inequity?" *Educational Leadership*, 55(4), 6–11.

Slavin, R. E. (1986). *Using student team learning, 3rd edition.* Baltimore, MD: Hopkins University Press.

Smith, C. (2002). "Organizational elements help to better educate young adolescents." *Middle School Journal*, 33(4), 5–6.

Sousa, D. A. (1998). *How the brain learns.* Reston, VA: NASSP.

Sperenger, Marilee. (1999). *Learning and memory: The brain in action.* Alexandria, VA: ASCD.

Steinberg, L., Levine A. (1997). *You and Your Adolescent*. NY: Harper Collins.

Stevenson, C. (2002). *Teaching ten to fourteen year olds (3rd edition)*. Boston: Allyn and Bacon.

Stodghill, R. (1998). "Where'd You Learn That?" *Time*, 151 (23), 52–59.

Storz, M. G., and Nestor, K. R. (2003). "Insights into meeting standards from listening to the voices of urban students." *Middle School Journal*, 34(4), 11–19.

Strahan, D. (1989). "Disconnected and disruptive students: Who they are, why they behave as they do, and what we can do about it." *Middle School Journal*, 21(2), 1–5.

Strahan, D. (1994). "Putting middle level perspectives into practice: Creating school cultures that promote caring." *Midpoints*, 4(1).

Strahan, D., Smith, T. W., McElrath, M., and Toole, C. M. (2001). "Connecting caring and action: Teachers who create learning communities in their classrooms." In Dickinson, T. S. (Ed). *Reinventing the middle school*. (pp. 96–116). New York: RoutledgeFalmer.

Striggins, R. J. (2001). *Student-involved classroom assessment*. Upper Saddle River, NJ: Prentice-Hall.

Strong, R., Silver, H., Perini, M., and Tuculescu, G. (2003). "Boredom and its opposite." *Educational Leadership,* 61(1), 24–29.

Sylwester, R. (1995). *A celebration of neurons: An educator's guide to the human brain*. Alexandria, VA: ASCD.

Taffel, R. (2001). *The second family*. NY: St. Martin's Press.

Tanner, J. M. (1980). "The biological approach to adolescence." In Adelson, J. (Ed.), *Handbook of Adolescent Psychology*. New York: Wiley and Sons.

Taylor, D. and Lorimer, M. (2003). "Helping boys succeed." *Educational Leadership*, 60(4), 68–70.

Taylor, K. L. (2003). "Through the eyes of students." *Educational Leadership*, 60(4), 72–75.

Tell, C. (2000). "Generation what? Connecting with today's youth." *Educational Leadership*, 57(4), 8–13.

Thomason, J., and Thompson, M. (1992). "Motivation: Moving, learning, mastering, and sharing." In Irvin, J. L. (Ed.), *Transforming middle level education: Perspectives and possibilities* (pp. 275–294). Boston: Allyn and Bacon.

Thompson, S. (2002). "Reculturing middle schools to use cross-curricular portfolios to support integrated learning." In Anfara, V. A., Jr., and Stacki, S. L. (Eds.), *Middle school curriculum, instruction, and assessment*. (pp. 157–179) Westerville, OH: National Middle School Association and Information Age Publishing.

Tomlinson, C. (2003). "Deciding to teach them all." *Educational Leadership*, 61(2), 7–11.

Tomlinson, C. A. (1999). *The differentiated classroom: responding to the needs of all learners*. Alexandria, VA: ASCD.

Tomlinson, C. A. and Eidson, C. C. (2003). *Differentiation in practice: A resource guide for differentiating curriculum*. Alexandria, VA: ASCO.

U.S. Department of Education. (1998). *TIMSS overview and key findings across grade levels*. Washington, D.C.: Author.

Van Hoose, J., Strahan, D., and L'Esperance, M. (2001). "Promoting harmony: Young adolescent development and school practices." Columbus, Ohio: National Middle School Association.

Van Til, W., Vars, G. F. and Lounsbury, J. H. (1967). *Modern education for the junior high school years*. Indianapolis: Bobbs-Merrill Company.

Vars, G. F. (1993). *Interdisciplinary teaching in the middle grades: why and how*. Columbus, OH: National Middle School Association.

Vatterott, C. (1991). "Assessing school climate in the middle level school." *Schools in the Middle:*

Theory into Practice, April. Reston, Virginia: National Association of Secondary School Principals.

Vatterott, C. (1992). "Promoting a positive school climate." *Missouri Schools*, Fall, 16–17.

Vatterott, C. (1995). "Student-focused instruction: Balancing limits with freedom in the middle grades." *Middle School Journal*, 27(2), 28–38.

Vatterott, C. (1999). *Academic success through empowering students*. Columbus, Ohio: National Middle School Association.

Vatterott, C. (2004) "Homework: determining priorities and practices." ASCD Professional Development Institute, March 19, 2004, New Orleans.

Vogler, K. E. (2003). "An integrated curriculum using state standards in a high-stakes testing environment." *Middle School Journal*, 34(4), 5–10.

Waks, L. J. (2002). "Exploratory education in a society of knowledge and risk." In Anfara, V. A., Jr., and Stacki, S. L. (Eds.), *Middle school curriculum, instruction, and assessment*. (pp. 23–40) Westerville, OH: National Middle School Association and Information Age Publishing.

Waxman, H. C., Huang, S. L., and Padron, Y. N. (1995). "Investigating the pedagogy of poverty in inner-city middle level schools." *Research in Middle Level Education*, 18(2), 1–22.

Ways we want our class to be. (1996). Oakland, CA: Developmental Studies Center

Wehlage, G., Rutter, R. A., Smith, G. A., Lesko, N., and Fernandez, R. R. (1989). *Reducing the risk: Schools as communities of support*. New York: Falmer Press.

Wessler, S. L. (2003). "It's hard to learn when you're scared." *Educational Leadership*, 61(1), 40–43.

Wheelock, A. and Dorman, G. (1988). *Before it's too late: Dropout prevention in the middle grades*. Carrboro, North Carolina: Center for Early Adolescence.

Wiggins, G. and McTighe, J. (1998). *Understanding by design*. Alexandria, VA: ASCD.

Williamson, R. and Johnston, J. H. (1999). "Challenging orthodoxy: An emerging agenda for middle level reform." *Middle School Journal*, 30(4), 10–17.

Wiske, S. (2004). "Using technology to dig for meaning." *Educational Leadership*, 62(1), 51–55.

Wolfe, P., Burkman, M., and Streng, K. (2000). "The science of nutrition." *Educational Leadership*, 57(6), 54–59

Wolk, S. (2003). "Hearts and minds." *Educational Leadership*, 61(1), 14–18.

Woolfolk, A. E. (1990). *Educational psychology* (4th edition). Englewood Cliffs, N.J.: Prentice Hall.

Wormeli, R. (2003). *Day one and beyond: practical matters for new middle level teachers*. Columbus, OH: National Middle School Association and Steinhouse publishers.

Wulf, S. (1995). "Generation Excluded." *Time*, (October 23), 86.

Wunderlich, K., Robertson, T. S. and Valentine, J. W. (2002). *NMSA Research summary #17: What types of block scheduling benefit middle school students?* Columbus, OH: National Middle School Association. Available online at www.nmsa.org.

Young, T. (1997). "Journal writing in mathematics." *Missouri ASCD Journal*, Spring, 23–24.

PHOTO CREDITS

INDEX